THE MAGICAL CODE OF REGULATIONS

CHRISTOPHER FRIGO

ISBN 979-8-234-07124-8 (hardcover edition)

ISBN 979-8-234-06711-1 (paperback edition)

Printed in the United States of America.

Cover design by Mahmoud Hassan.

§ 101.0 Definition of Bureaucrat.

(a) For purposes of this Code, the term "bureaucrat" means any person charged with the maintenance of forms, procedures, records, approvals, denials, certifications, reviews, or other such mechanisms without which civilization would immediately begin eating itself.

Table of Contents

Part I: General Provisions

§ 101.1 Definitions of Key Terms

(a) **General Definitions.**
For the purposes of this Code, unless otherwise specified or clearly indicated by the context in which a term is used, the following terms, phrases, and designations shall have the meanings ascribed to them below:
(1) Magic.
The term "magic" shall mean the alteration, manipulation, augmentation, or diminution of physical, metaphysical, or conceptual reality through recognized practices, whether such practices are authorized under this Code or arise from undocumented phenomena. For the purposes of this definition:
(A) The phrase "alteration of reality" shall include, but not be limited to:
(i) Elemental conjuration, which includes the summoning, expulsion, or control of fire, water, air, earth, and other recognized elemental substances;
(ii) Transmutation of matter or energy, as specified in § 2001.1, encompassing the transformation of one material state or form into another, whether physical, energetic, or magical in nature; and
(iii) Manipulation of time or causality, including practices authorized under § 2201.2, or prohibited acts involving unauthorized temporal displacement.
(B) The term "recognized practices" shall encompass incantations, rituals, symbolic gestures, and other methodologies formally acknowledged by the Council of Councils.
(C) Exclusions. The following are explicitly excluded from the definition of "magic":
(i) Phenomena arising solely from non-magical scientific principles, unless such phenomena are provoked by magical acts;
(ii) Residual effects of pre-regulated spells created prior to [C.C.D. 9824]; and
(iii) Spontaneous occurrences classified under § 101.8(c)(3) as "Unintended Magical Phenomena."
(2) Spellcaster.

The term "spellcaster" shall refer to any individual possessing an active license issued under § 202.1 and authorized to perform spells in accordance with § 401.1. For the purposes of this definition:
(A) Classification. A spellcaster shall be classified according to licensure tier, consistent with the risk classifications established under § 401.2(c), as follows:
(i) Apprentice Spellcaster. An individual authorized to perform spells only within the lowest risk classification and subject to supervision as required by this Code.
(ii) Journeyman Spellcaster. An individual authorized to perform spells within the intermediate risk classification independently, subject to the scope and limitations of licensure.
(iii) Master Spellcaster. An individual authorized to perform spells within the highest risk classification, including advanced spellcasting and original spell creation as otherwise permitted under this Code.
(B) Requirements. A licensed spellcaster must:
(i) Maintain compliance with all logging requirements under § 401.5;
(ii) Submit biennial renewal applications (Form 6589); and
(iii) Pass proficiency audits, as further defined in § 201.4.
(C) Penalties for Non-Compliance. Unauthorized spellcasting, including violations of § 401.1, shall constitute a violation subject to § 102.2.
(3) Practitioner.
The term "practitioner" shall mean any individual engaged in the study, research, or informal application of magic without holding a spellcasting license under § 201.1. For the purposes of this definition:
(A) Categories of practitioners include, but are not limited to:
(i) Alchemists, who engage in potion-making, transmutation, and chemical spell components;
(ii) Ritualists, who perform cultural or ceremonial magic; and
(iii) Theorists and researchers, whose work is governed by § 301.3 when conducted within institutional settings.
(B) Practitioners may apply for limited-use licenses (Form 4938) under § 201.9 for specific research or experimental purposes.
(4) Qualified Creatures.
The term "qualified creatures" shall mean any non-human entity, whether magical, semi-magical, or non-magical, that interacts with or is affected by magic in a regulated capacity.
(A) Rights and Protections. Qualified creatures shall be afforded the rights and protections specified under § 101.6, including ethical safeguards against misuse in experiments, rituals, or other magical activities.

(5) Council of Councils.
The term "Council of Councils" means the supreme regulatory oversight body established under § 102.1(a)(2), vested with final administrative review authority pursuant to § 102.1(e), and responsible for issuance of supplemental rulings, amendments, and clarifications under § 3101.2.

The Council of Councils shall exercise general supervisory oversight over subordinate councils and specialized bodies established under this Code, including but not limited to:
(A) The Elemental Council (relating to elemental magic as defined in § 101.1);
(B) The Necromantic Advisory Board (§ 1301.1); and
(C) The Temporal Oversight Bureau (§ 2201.3).
Jurisdiction, procedural authority, and standards of review shall be governed exclusively by § 102.1.
(6) Council of Counsel.
The term "Council of Counsel" means the adjudicative and interpretive body established under § 102.1(a)(4), exercising intermediate appellate jurisdiction and interpretive authority as provided in § 102.1(e) and (f).
The Council of Counsel shall have authority to:
(A) Hear administrative appeals from determinations of the Department of Magical Affairs;
(B) Adjudicate disputes arising under this Code, including contractual disputes involving magic (§ 1101.1);
(C) Review ethical violation determinations reported under § 701.5; and
(D) Recommend enforcement actions and penalties subject to final administrative review.
Decisions rendered by the Council of Counsel shall be binding unless modified or overturned pursuant to § 102.1(e)(3).
(7) School of Magic.
The term "School of Magic" means a recognized classification of magical practice based on the primary mechanism by which a magical effect is produced, including but not limited to elemental manipulation, transfiguration of matter or form, temporal alteration, cognitive influence, ritual invocation, or manipulation of life force, spiritual essence, or ancestral power.
(A) Recognized Schools of Magic.
For purposes of this Code, the following Schools of Magic are recognized:
(i) Elemental Magic. Magic involving the manipulation, generation, expulsion, control, or redirection of elemental forces or substances,

including fire, water, air, earth, lightning, ice, and related natural or quasi-natural phenomena.
(ii) Necromancy. Magic involving the manipulation of death, life force, souls, spirits, corpses, post-mortem energies, or other necrotic or funerary forces.
(iii) Transfiguration. Magic involving the alteration of physical form, composition, structure, material state, or biological configuration of objects, creatures, or persons.
(iv) Divination. Magic involving the acquisition, revelation, interpretation, or projection of knowledge concerning future events, hidden truths, unseen conditions, omitted facts, or otherwise inaccessible information.
(v) Alchemy. Magic involving transformation or manipulation of material substances through arcane reagents, catalysts, formulae, potions, or other structured material processes.
(vi) Blood Magic. Magic derived from, dependent upon, or materially enhanced by blood, lineage, inherited biological essence, sacrifice, or other corporeal life-signifying material.
(vii) Herbology (Magical Agriculture). Magic involving the cultivation, harvesting, breeding, propagation, manipulation, or regulated use of magical plants, fungi, botanical organisms, or magically responsive agricultural systems.
(viii) Arcane or Ancestral Magic. Magic derived from inherited power, ancestral lineage, ancient magical traditions, legacy bonds, inherited pacts, or longstanding arcane transmissions not otherwise classified under another recognized School of Magic.
(ix) Ritualistic Magic. Magic performed through ceremonial, liturgical, procedural, or coordinated acts requiring prescribed sequences, symbolic gestures, invocations, collective participation, or formalized rites.
(x) Time Manipulation Magic. Magic involving alteration of time, chronology, temporal sequence, causality, duration, acceleration, suspension, displacement, or related temporal effects.
(xi) Mind Control Magic. Magic involving alteration, suppression, manipulation, compulsion, domination, influence, intrusion upon, or reconfiguration of cognition, memory, volition, perception, judgment, or free will.
(xii) Illusory Magic. Magic involving the creation, modification, distortion, concealment, or projection of sensory phenomena, apparent realities, or false perceptions without necessarily producing corresponding physical alteration.
(B) Multi-School Classification.

A spell, magical act, ritual, artifact, procedure, or regulated practice may be classified under more than one School of Magic where its mechanism, operational effect, or foreseeable consequence materially implicates multiple recognized schools. In such cases, all applicable provisions of this Code shall apply, and where two or more provisions conflict, the more restrictive provision shall govern unless otherwise expressly provided.
(C) Catch-All Classification of Magical Disciplines.
Any spell, practice, technique, phenomenon, or magical effect not expressly enumerated under paragraph (7) shall nevertheless be deemed to fall within a School of Magic where, based on its underlying mechanism, observable effects, or intended outcome, it is reasonably analogous to or shares material characteristics with a recognized School of Magic.

Where such classification cannot be reasonably determined, the practice shall be treated as an emergent or unclassified form of magic and shall be subject to the most restrictive applicable provisions of this Code pending formal classification by the Department of Magical Affairs.

(b) **Exceptions.**
Exceptions to the definitions provided herein may be granted under the following circumstances:
(1) Emergency Writs of Magic, issued under § 602.4, may redefine specific practices or terminologies for temporary purposes;
(2) Necromantic use for legal and security use (§ 1301.5) shall be considered outside the ordinary definitions provided in this section.

(c) **Cross-References.**
For scope and applicability of defined terms, see § 101.2. For authorized spellcasters, refer to § 101.5. For general licensing requirements, consult § 401.1.

(d) **Historical Annotations.**
This section was originally established under C.C.D. 9824, 82 MR 2234, Mon. 12, 1923, and subsequently amended under C.C.D. 9942, 84 MR 3012, Sun. 8, 2019, to include expanded classifications for spellcasters, practitioners, and qualified creatures.

§ 101.2 Scope of Regulations

(a) **General Applicability.**
The provisions of this Code shall apply to all magical practices, practitioners, spellcasters, qualified creatures, and institutions, including but not limited to:
(1) All acts of spellcasting or magical manipulation conducted within the jurisdiction of recognized magical councils, educational institutions, or sovereign magical zones (see § 2501.2).
(2) The governance of all licensed individuals, entities, and councils subject to the oversight of the Council of Councils.
(3) Qualified creatures as defined under § 101.6, whose interactions with magic require compliance with applicable rights and protections.

(b) **Excluded Practices and Phenomena.**
The following shall be excluded from the mandatory application of this Code, unless otherwise provided:
(1) Pre-Code Artifacts. Magical objects or artifacts created prior to the enactment of this Code, unless such artifacts have been subsequently altered under § 801.1 (Classification of Magical Objects and Artifacts).
(2) Unintentional Magical Phenomena. Events classified as spontaneous or accidental magic under § 402.3 and § 1501.3 shall be excluded from liability under this Code only if the individual or entity responsible for the phenomenon can demonstrate that reasonable care, as defined under § 101.7, was exercised.
(A) If reasonable care or due diligence was not exercised, such phenomena shall constitute a violation subject to § 102.2.
(B) Practitioners who cause unintentional magical phenomena while failing to exercise reasonable care must report the incident within 48 hours using Form 7543-N (Unregistered Phenomenon Report). Failure to report shall constitute a separate violation subject to § 102.2.

(c) **Specific Limitations.**
This Code shall not supersede the jurisdiction of international magical treaties ratified by the Council of Councils, including but not limited to:
(1) The Universal Magical Ethics Charter, governing prohibited practices under § 701.2.
(2) The Interdimensional Travel Accords (see § 2301.8 for licensing and registration of interdimensional spellcasters).

(d) **Reporting Obligations.**
All institutions, councils, or individuals operating under the jurisdiction of this Code must submit quarterly compliance reports (Form 4921) to the Council of Councils. Non-compliance shall constitute a violation subject to § 102.2.

(e) **Cross-References.**
For additional exclusions related to self-defense, see § 601.1. For limitations on specific types of spellcasting, refer to § 401.2. For further provisions on compliance reporting, see § 201.3. For reasonable care standards applicable to unintentional phenomena, see § 101.7. For penalties, see § 102.2.

(f) **Historical Annotations.**
Originally established under C.C.D. 9824, 82 MR 2234, Tue. 12, 1923. Amended under C.C.D. 9967, 84 MR 4123, Mon. 5, 2019, to include reporting obligations for institutions and to clarify liability for unintentional magical phenomena.

§ 101.3 Definitions of Active Participation in Magical Educational Institutions

(a) **General Definition of Active Participation.**
For the purposes of this Code, active participation in a recognized Magical Educational Institution is defined as the consistent and verifiable engagement in educational, research, or practical spellcasting activities, as determined by the criteria set forth below:
(1) Educational Engagement.
Enrollment in and completion of coursework approved by a recognized Magical Educational Institution under § 301.1, which includes but is not limited to:
(A) Spellcasting seminars, laboratory-based magical studies, and theoretical lectures in recognized schools of magic (as defined in § 101.1).
(B) Participation in practical examinations and standardized testing approved by the Council of Councils, as documented through Form 4321-T (Standardized Testing Record).
(2) Research Contributions.
Documented contributions to magical research, including:
(A) Publication of scholarly articles in peer-reviewed journals recognized by accredited institutions (§ 301.3).

(B) Collaboration on institution-led magical research projects or field studies, with contributions logged and certified via Form 8872-R (Research Participation Log).
(3) Practical Spellcasting Activities.
Direct participation in supervised spellcasting activities, which must adhere to licensing and risk guidelines under § 401.1 and § 401.2. All practical spellcasting must be logged using Form 8342-L (Practical Spellcasting Record).
(4) Material Participation Standard.
Notwithstanding paragraphs (a)(1) through (a)(3), an individual shall be treated as actively participating in a Magical Educational Institution only if the individual's participation is regular, continuous, and substantial in relation to the institution's instructional activities.
In determining whether participation is regular, continuous, and substantial, the institution shall consider all relevant facts and circumstances, including but not limited to:
(A) the frequency and duration of participation during the applicable reporting period;
(B) the extent of direct involvement in instructional, research, or supervised spellcasting activities as opposed to preparatory, administrative, or observational activities;
(C) whether the individual's participation constitutes a principal component of the individual's magical practice during such period; and
(D) the degree to which participation is subject to institutional supervision and evaluation.
No single factor shall be determinative, and satisfaction of documentation requirements alone shall not, by itself, establish active participation.

(b) **Eligibility Requirements for Active Participation.**
To qualify as an active participant, a practitioner must:
(1) Be formally enrolled or employed by a recognized Magical Educational Institution (§ 301.1) or hold a provisional license as provided in § 201.2.
(2) Submit quarterly logs detailing educational and practical spellcasting activities, classified by risk level (§ 401.2). Logs must be filed via Form 8321-Q (Quarterly Participation Log).
(3) Maintain compliance with institutional codes of conduct, including adherence to ethical guidelines under § 701.1 (Ethical Use of Magic and Spellcasting).

(c) **Benefits of Active Participation.**

Practitioners designated as active participants shall be entitled to the following privileges:
(1) Exemptions from Spellcasting Limitations.
Active participants may receive exemptions from daily spellcasting limitations (§ 602.5), provided such exemptions are approved by the Council of Councils through Form 9431-E (Exemption Request).
(2) Access to Advanced Magical Resources.
Eligibility for the use of restricted ley lines (§ 901.1), high-risk magical artifacts (§ 801.1), and advanced libraries of magical knowledge maintained by accredited institutions.
(3) Institutional Legal Representation.
Protection and representation in legal matters arising from magical disputes (see Part XI), as provided under the institution's legal framework.

(d) **Penalties for Failure to Maintain Active Status.**
Practitioners who fail to comply with the requirements of this section shall be subject to the following penalties:
(1) Suspension of Privileges.
Suspension of privileges under § 401.6, including access to restricted spells and resources.
(2) Disqualification from Institutional Legal Protections.
Removal from research or spellcasting projects.

(e) **Exceptions to Active Participation Requirements.**
Certain practitioners may be granted temporary or permanent exemptions from active participation requirements, subject to the following conditions:
(1) Health or Emergency Leave.
Practitioners experiencing medical, personal, or institutional emergencies may file Form 9324-X (Exemption Request) within 30 days of the disruption. Such exemptions shall not exceed six (6) months without further review.
(2) Provisional Licenses for Gifted Students.
Under § 201.2, students under the age of sixteen (16) who demonstrate extraordinary aptitude may be granted provisional licenses allowing limited magical practice. These licenses are subject to annual review and audit.

(f) **Cross-References.**

For licensing requirements, see § 201.1 to § 201.3. For spellcasting risk classifications, refer to § 401.2. For exemptions and emergency writs, see § 602.4. For penalties, see § 102.2.

(g) **Historical Annotations.**
Originally established under C.C.D. 9784, 81 MR 1823, Mon. 15, 1920, to regulate participation in magical institutions. Amended under C.C.D. 9921, 83 MR 3041, Tue. 11, 2018, to include specific provisions for gifted students and exemptions for health-related absences.

§ 101.4 Prohibition on the Use of the Name "David"

(a) **General Prohibition.**
The use of the name "David" is strictly prohibited in all forms of magical registration, institutional naming, spell creation, and other formal magical contexts governed by this Code. This prohibition extends to all individuals, entities, magical artifacts, spells, and rituals officially documented or registered under the jurisdiction of any recognized Council or Magical Educational Institution. The name "David," including all derivatives, translations, or phonetic equivalents, is deemed inappropriate for use due to historical, legal, and ethical considerations.

(b) **Prohibited Uses in Personal Names.**
(1) Practitioner and Spellcaster Names.
No spellcaster or practitioner may register under the name "David." Applications for licenses (§ 201.1), certifications (§ 201.5), or institutional enrollment (§ 301.1) bearing the name "David" shall be automatically rejected.
(A) Individuals currently registered under the name "David" must submit Form 7765-A (Name Change Application) within thirty (30) days of the enactment of this section.
(B) Failure to comply will result in suspension of all active licenses under § 401.1 and revocation of institutional privileges under § 301.2.
(2) Familiars and Summoned Entities.
Familiars, spirits, or other summoned entities registered under the name "David" must undergo renaming via Form 6594-F (Familiar Renaming Request). Entities bound through blood magic contracts (§ 1101.2) or other irreversible spells must petition for exemption under § 602.4.

(c) **Prohibited Uses in Institutional Names.**
(1) Magical Institutions and Councils.
No Magical Educational Institution (§ 301.1), research facility, or magical council may bear the name "David." Institutions with pre-existing names must submit Form 8437-I (Institutional Renaming Proposal) within sixty (60) days of this section's effective date.
(A) Non-compliance will result in immediate withdrawal of institutional accreditation under § 301.3 and revocation of institutional licensing under § 201.7.
(B) Exceptions for historical institutions may be considered under § Part VI, provided sufficient documentation of historical significance is submitted for review.

(d) **Prohibited Uses in Spell and Artifact Naming.**
(1) Spells and Incantations.
The name "David" is prohibited in the naming or classification of all spells, curses, enchantments, or magical rituals.
(A) Existing spells bearing the name "David" must be renamed within ninety (90) days using Form 1098-D (Spell Renaming Request).
(B) Spells not renamed within the specified time frame will be classified as prohibited magic under § 701.2 and subject to penalties under § 102.2.
(2) Magical Artifacts and Constructs.
Artifacts, talismans, or constructs registered under the name "David" must be reclassified and renamed through Form 8451-A (Artifact Reclassification Request). Non-compliance may result in confiscation or destruction of the artifact under Part VIII.

(e) **Penalties for Non-Compliance.**
(1) License Suspension.
Spellcasters or practitioners found in violation of this section shall face immediate suspension of all active licenses under § 401.1, with reinstatement contingent upon compliance.
(2) Institutional Sanctions.
Institutions failing to comply with renaming directives will lose accreditation (§ 301.3) and be barred from participation in Council-funded research projects or grants.

(f) **Exceptions and Special Circumstances.**
(1) Pending Name Changes.

Individuals or entities undergoing an approved name change process may file for a temporary extension via Form 9001-E (Name Change Extension Request). Extensions shall not exceed ninety (90) days.
(2) Magical Influence.
Cases where an individual or entity has been subjected to magical compulsion resulting in the assignment of the name "David" may file Form 8872-C (Compelled Name Alteration Appeal). Evidence of magical influence must accompany the appeal, which shall be reviewed by the Council of Councils.

(g) **Cross-References.**
For magical contracts, see § 1101.1. For spell creation, refer to § 1501.1. For regulations governing magical artifacts, consult § 801.1.

(h) **Historical Annotations.**
Originally enacted under C.C.D. 5123, 72 MR 1041, Mon. 13, 1756, following the dissolution of the Davidic Conclave. Amended under C.C.D. 9756, 82 MR 3342, Wed. 25, 2014, to extend the prohibition to familiars and summoned entities.

§ 101.5 Authorized Spellcasters: Definition and Requirements

(a) **Definition of Authorized Spellcaster.**
An authorized spellcaster is an individual who meets all criteria established under this section, including educational attainment, licensure, and practical competence in magical practices. Authorization is contingent upon adherence to the requirements and standards set forth in this Code and is regulated by the Council of Councils.

(b) **Criteria for Authorization.**
(1) Completion of Educational Requirements.
To qualify as an authorized spellcaster, an individual must have successfully completed at least two (2) years of study at a recognized Magical Educational Institution as defined under § 301.1.
(A) Educational programs must include foundational instruction in magical ethics under § 701.1, theoretical principles in at least one recognized School of Magic as defined in § 101.1, and supervised practical spellcasting activities pursuant to § 401.6. At least 20% of coursework

must consist of applied spellcasting under the direct supervision of a licensed instructor or institution.
(B) Institutions providing educational qualifications must be accredited under § 301.3. Individuals attending non-accredited institutions must submit Form 8123-T (Validation of Educational Credentials) for approval by the Council of Councils.
(C) Gifted students demonstrating exceptional proficiency may be exempt from the two-year educational requirement under § 201.2. Such exemptions must be requested using Form 9431-E (Exceptional Proficiency Waiver) and approved by the Commissioner of Magical Affairs on a case-by-case basis.
(2) Possession of a Valid Spellcasting License.
All spellcasters must possess a valid license issued under § 401.1 to perform magical activities within the jurisdiction of this Code.
(A) Licenses are granted upon successful completion of a licensing examination administered by an accredited testing body. The license must specify the School(s) of Magic in which the individual is proficient.
(B) Licenses must be renewed every two (2) years through the submission of Form 8129-R (License Renewal Application). Renewal applications must include proof of continued education under § 201.3 and quarterly spellcasting logs as required by § 401.5.
(C) Individuals under the age of sixteen (16) may be issued provisional licenses pursuant to § 201.2. Such licenses impose additional restrictions on high-risk magic under § 401.2 and are subject to periodic review.
(3) Demonstration of Practical Competence.
All authorized spellcasters must complete a minimum of one hundred (100) hours of supervised practical spellcasting experience.
(A) Practical experience must demonstrate a spellcaster's ability to apply magical knowledge in professional or real-world contexts under appropriate supervision.
Activities must involve direct engagement with spellcasting processes and advance the spellcaster's practical understanding of magic. Supervision must be provided by a licensed spellcaster meeting the qualifications set forth in § 401.1 or by an accredited institution recognized under § 301.1. Practical experience is subject to the following conditions:
(i) All activities must be formally documented, verified, and logged, ensuring compliance with institutional and legal standards.
(ii) Practical experience must emphasize the safe and effective application of magic, as outlined under § 401.6, and must not involve prohibited magical practices under § 701.2.

(iii) Environments in which practical experience is conducted must comply with safety protocols appropriate to the spellcasting risk level, as classified in § 401.2.
(B) The following activities do not qualify as practical experience:
(i) Casual or recreational use of magic, including minor unsupervised household spells.
(ii) Spellcasting performed without proper documentation or oversight.
(iii) Experimental, new, or unrecognized spells not approved under § 1501.1 (Creation of New Spells).
(iv) Activities violating ethical standards set forth in § 701.1.
(C) Qualifying activities include but are not limited to:
(i) Apprenticeships conducted under approved programs with licensed spellcasters.
(ii) Field assignments requiring the application of magic in controlled or real-world environments, such as potion crafting for regulated distribution or warding installations.
(iii) Institutional research projects approved by an accredited magical council or department.
(iv) Remote or specialized activities granted special exemptions under § 201.8.

(c) **Continuing Education Requirements.**
All authorized spellcasters must complete a minimum of ten (10) hours of continuing magical education annually.
(1) Eligible Courses.
Courses must be pre-approved by the Council of Councils or an accredited institution and must relate to the spellcaster's licensed School(s) of Magic or address advanced spellcasting safety, ethics, or applied methodologies.
(2) Documentation Requirements.
Completion of continuing education courses must be reported using Form 7894-E (Continuing Education Certification). Failure to meet this requirement results in automatic suspension of the spellcasting license, with reinstatement contingent upon compliance as outlined in § 201.3.

(d) **Reporting Obligations.**
All authorized spellcasters must comply with reporting obligations under § 401.5.
(1) Spellcasting Logs.
Quarterly submission of Form 9321-L (Quarterly Spellcasting Activity Log) documenting all spells cast is mandatory.

(2) Unauthorized or Experimental Spells.
Any use of unauthorized or experimental spells must be reported immediately using Form 9230-U (Unregistered Spell Notification).

(e) **Temporal Manipulation and Duration of Study.**
(1) For purposes of subsection (b)(1), the requirement of "two (2) years of study" shall be measured by reference to the officially recognized academic calendar of the Magical Educational Institution described in § 301.1 and shall not be satisfied solely by subjective, accelerated, dilated, suspended, or otherwise altered temporal experience.
(2) Time experienced under conditions of chronomancy, temporal dilation, dimensional acceleration, or comparable manipulation governed under Part XXII shall be presumed not to satisfy the duration requirement of subsection (b)(1).
(3) The presumption described in paragraph (2) may be rebutted only if the recognized Magical Educational Institution certifies in writing that such chronomantically altered period:
(A) was conducted under its formal supervision and curricular authority;
(B) was substantially equivalent in rigor, scope, instructional hours, and supervised practical engagement to two academic years under its standard program; and
(C) was contemporaneously documented in institutional records maintained in accordance with §§ 301.1 and 301.2.
(4) The burden of establishing equivalency under paragraph (3) shall rest with the practitioner seeking qualification as an Authorized Spellcaster under this section.
(5) No period of unauthorized temporal displacement, suspended chronology, or extra-institutional acceleration shall be credited toward the duration requirement of subsection (b)(1), regardless of subjective passage of time.

(f) **Penalties for Non-Compliance.**
Violations of this section will result in penalties, including but not limited to:
(1) License Suspension.
Licenses will be suspended immediately, with reinstatement contingent upon compliance with the reporting or continuing education requirements.
(2) Institutional Sanctions.

Repeated violations may result in disqualification from institutional roles or positions of authority within accredited magical institutions under § 301.3.

(g) **Cross-References.**
For licensing procedures, see § 201.1. For reporting unauthorized spells, see § 401.5.

(h) **Historical Annotations.**
This section was enacted under C.C.D. 4761, 80 MR 2389, Tue. 20, 1987, to establish foundational licensing standards. Amendments to this section were made under C.C.D. 5123, 89 MR 6702, Mon. 20, 2022, to clarify continuing education requirements and expand the practical experience criteria. It was further amended under C.C.D. 9938, 84 MR 1127, Tue. 11, 2026, to address chronomantically altered educational periods and to prevent circumvention of statutory duration requirements through accelerated temporal environments.

§ 101.6 Qualified Creatures: Definition and Classification

(a) **Definition of Qualified Creatures.**
Qualified creatures are defined as any non-human entities, whether magical, semi-magical, or non-magical, that are subject to or capable of engaging with regulated magical practices under this Code. Qualified creatures include, but are not limited to, familiars, summoned entities, magically-enhanced beings, and creatures possessing intrinsic magical properties. A creature may only be considered "qualified" if registered and classified according to the criteria set forth in this section.

(b) **Classification of Qualified Creatures.**
Qualified creatures are classified into three primary categories based on their interaction with magical phenomena and their intrinsic magical attributes.
(1) Class I: Fully Magical Creatures.
Creatures whose existence and abilities are entirely dependent on magical forces. Examples include elemental constructs, phoenixes, and spectral entities. These creatures are subject to the highest level of regulation due to their reliance on magical ecosystems and potential to disrupt ley line stability.

(2) Class II: Semi-Magical Creatures.
Creatures with natural abilities that are augmented or influenced by magical forces. Examples include enchanted wolves and hybrid griffons. Regulation for Class II creatures focuses on ensuring their use adheres to ethical standards under § 701.7 and does not pose a risk to ecosystems or magical integrity.
(3) Class III: Non-Magical Creatures with Magical Susceptibility.
Non-magical creatures that interact with magic due to proximity to magical practices or intentional use in spellcasting processes. This class includes mundane animals such as non-magical cats bonded as familiars or mundane wolves susceptible to magical curses. Regulations under this classification ensure their treatment complies with the protections outlined in § 701.7.

(c) **Rights and Protections.**
Qualified creatures are entitled to specific protections and rights as outlined below.
(1) Ethical Treatment Standards.
All qualified creatures must be treated humanely, with particular attention to their magical needs and vulnerabilities. This includes proper housing, feeding, and care for familiars, as well as the safe management of creatures used in educational or research contexts.
(2) Restrictions on Use in High-Risk Magic.
Qualified creatures may not be used in high-risk spells classified under § 401.2 without prior approval from an accredited institution. Use in experimental or unstable magic is strictly prohibited unless a waiver is granted under this Code.
(3) Reporting Requirements for Abuse or Misuse.
Any abuse or misuse of qualified creatures, including but not limited to improper handling during magical rituals, must be reported within 24 hours using Form 4567-A (Qualified Creature Abuse Report).

(d) **Exceptions and Special Circumstances.**
Certain exceptions to the standard classifications and protections may be granted in the following circumstances:
(1) Emergency Use for Magical Defense.
Class I or Class II creatures may be used in defensive magic during emergencies, provided the spellcaster submits Form 9834-E (Emergency Creature Utilization Request) within 72 hours of the event. The Council of Councils must validate the emergency circumstances.

(2) Non-Compliant Creatures.
Creatures that do not meet the exact criteria for Class I, II, or III but are nonetheless involved in magical practices may be granted "provisional qualified status." Provisional status requires additional oversight and may be revoked upon review by the Council of Councils.

(e) **Cross-References.**
For ethical treatment guidelines and familiar-specific provisions, see § 701.7. For reporting high-risk magic involving qualified creatures, see § 401.2.

(f) **Historical Annotations.**
This section was enacted under C.C.D. 3124, 72 MR 4852, Thu. 14, 1934, to establish protections and classifications for familiars and other magical beings. It was amended under C.C.D. 4853, 78 MR 1029, Mon. 12, 1978, to extend the classification system to semi-magical and non-magical creatures and further revised under C.C.D. 5234, 89 MR 7621, Tue 2, 2023, to clarify emergency use provisions.

§ 101.7 Reasonable Care in Spellcasting

(a) **Duty of Care.**
All spellcasters must exercise reasonable care when performing any act of magic, ensuring their practices align with the safety, ethical, and procedural standards established in this Code. Reasonable care is defined as the standard of diligence, caution, attention, and supervision that a licensed spellcaster of comparable qualifications and experience would exercise under similar circumstances. Failure to uphold this duty constitutes negligence and is subject to penalties under § 102.2. This duty applies universally, regardless of the risk classification of the spell (§ 401.2) or the environment in which the spell is cast.

(b) **Attribution of Responsibility.**
Any institution, academy, guild, council, or other organized body that authorizes, directs, supervises, sponsors, or materially facilitates the performance of magic shall be responsible for compliance with this section to the same extent as the licensed spellcaster directly performing the act.

(c) **General Standards of Care.**

The following standards apply to all spellcasters engaged in magical practices:
(1) Proper Use of Casting Implements.
Spellcasters must use appropriate casting implements, such as wands, staffs, or sigils, which are maintained, calibrated, and inspected annually under the provisions of this Code. Improper or defective implements must be reported immediately using Form 9003-I (Defective Implement Notice). Failure to comply results in liability for any harm caused by the implement's malfunction.
(2) Safety Protocols.
All spellcasters must adhere to the safety protocols outlined in § 401.6, including the use of containment wards, protective enchantments, and other precautions appropriate to the spell's risk level. These precautions must be documented in the spellcaster's log under § 401.5.
(3) Environmental Considerations.
When casting spells in natural, populated, or high-risk environments, spellcasters must take reasonable steps to ensure their magic does not cause unintended harm to persons, property, or ecosystems (see Part IX). Examples of required precautions include establishing protective barriers, obtaining permits for high-risk spells, and minimizing magical disruptions in ley line-rich areas.

(d) **Specific Applications of Reasonable Care.**
The following applications and limitations govern specific areas of magical practice:
(1) Spell Preparation.
Reasonable care in preparing spells includes verifying spell components, reciting incantations precisely, and following approved techniques for spell activation. Substitutions for spell components are strictly prohibited without explicit approval from the relevant Council.
(2) Spell Duration and Termination.
Spellcasters are responsible for monitoring and terminating spells in accordance with § 501.2. Spells that exceed their intended duration must be immediately dispelled or modified to avoid harm. Failure to properly terminate a spell constitutes negligence.
(3) Interaction with Magical Creatures.
When casting spells involving qualified creatures (§ 101.6), spellcasters must ensure the creature's welfare is protected and comply with all applicable ethical standards (§ 701.7). This includes avoiding excessive strain on familiars or semi-magical creatures used in spellcasting.

(e) **Reporting Obligations.**
All incidents of negligent spellcasting must be reported within 24 hours to the relevant governing Council.
(1) Incident Reporting.
Spellcasters must file Form 9134-N (Negligence Incident Report) detailing the circumstances, spell type, and affected parties.
(2) Investigation Cooperation.
Spellcasters are required to cooperate fully with investigations conducted by the Council of Councils, including providing access to logs, implements, and spell components related to the incident. Failure to cooperate results in immediate suspension of all licenses under § 401.1.

(f) **Penalties for Breach of Reasonable Care.**
Spellcasters found in breach of this section may face temporary suspension or permanent revocation of their spellcasting licenses (§ 401.1). Reinstatement requires filing Form 9832-R (License Reinstatement Petition) and completing remedial education under § 201.3.

(g) **Exceptions and Exemptions.**
Certain situations may provide limited exemptions from the duty of reasonable care:
(1) Emergency Situations.
Spells cast in emergencies, such as immediate threats to life or natural disasters, are exempt from this section provided the spellcaster files Form 9123-E (Emergency Spellcasting Exemption) within 72 hours.
(2) Recognized Ritual Practices.
Spellcasters engaging in culturally significant rituals or religious practices may apply for a waiver of certain safety protocols by submitting Form 9034-RP (Ritual Practice Exemption) under § 701.1. Such exemptions are granted only upon demonstration of adequate safeguards.

(h) **Cross-References.**
For spell risk levels and safety protocols, refer to § 401.2 and § 401.6. For ethical standards governing qualified creatures, consult § 701.7. For termination and revocation of spells, see § 501.2.

(i) **Historical Annotations.**
Originally enacted under C.C.D. 1345, 53 MR 1245, Thu. 12, 1923, this section established the foundational principles for safe and ethical

spellcasting. Amended under C.C.D. 2754, 72 MR 4102, Mon. 14, 1967, to include reporting obligations and penalties. Further revisions under C.C.D. 5123, 88 MR 7854, Thu. 2, 2022, expanded exemptions for emergency situations and cultural practices.

§ 101.8 Spells and Situations Not Covcrcd by This Code

(a) **General Rule.**
Any spell, magical act, or phenomenon not explicitly addressed within the provisions of this Code is subject to oversight, review, and regulation by the Council of Councils. Spells or magical activities falling outside the recognized categories outlined in § 101.1 or other relevant sections are not permitted for use until formally reviewed and approved under the procedures established in § 1501.1. This general rule applies regardless of intent, context, or the classification of the spellcaster involved.

(b) **Reporting Obligations for Unregulated Spells.**
Spellcasters encountering or utilizing unregulated spells or magical phenomena must adhere to the following reporting requirements:
(1) Identification and Documentation.
Spellcasters must identify the nature, scope, and effects of the unregulated spell and document any known or observed impacts. This includes providing a detailed account of the spell's incantation, components, and intended purpose. Documentation must be submitted using Form 8451-U (Unregulated Spell Report).
(2) Notification Timeline.
Reports must be filed with the Council of Councils within 48 hours of discovery or use. Failure to report unregulated magic within the prescribed time frame constitutes gross misconduct under Part VII.
(3) Cooperation with Review.
Spellcasters are required to cooperate fully with investigations and reviews conducted by the Council of Councils. This includes submitting all related spellcasting logs (§ 401.5), casting implements, and materials for inspcction.

(c) **Examples of Unregulated Magical Activities.**
The following are examples of spells or situations not covered under this Code:
(1) Cross-School Spells.

Magical acts that combine elements of two or more schools of magic (e.g., necromantic illusions or elemental transformations) are considered unregulated unless explicitly approved under § 1501.1.
(2) New or Experimental Spells.
Spells not recognized within the categories defined in § 401.2 or lacking approval through the process established in § 1501.1 are prohibited.
(3) Spontaneous Magical Phenomena.
Unintended magical phenomena, such as ley line disruptions, uncontrolled planar rifts, or accidental time distortions, must be reported immediately. Spellcasters involved in such incidents may be held liable if negligence is demonstrated.

(d) **Limitations and Restrictions.**
The following limitations apply to unregulated spells and magical activities:
(1) Prohibition of Use Pending Approval.
No unregulated spell or magical activity may be performed until it has undergone review and received explicit approval from the Council of Councils. Violators are subject to penalties outlined in § 102.2.
(2) Liability for Harm or Damage.
Spellcasters who use unregulated spells are fully liable for any harm, damage, or disruption caused, even in cases where the spell was cast unintentionally or without malice. Liability may be mitigated if reasonable care (§ 101.7) can be demonstrated.
(3) Exemptions for Emergencies.
Unregulated spells cast in emergencies, where no regulated alternatives are available, may qualify for limited exemptions if the spellcaster submits Form 9382-E (Emergency Spellcasting Exemption Request) within 72 hours of the incident.

(e) **Penalties for Non-Compliance.**
Persistent or egregious violations will result in the revocation of all licenses under § 401.1. Reinstatement is contingent upon the successful completion of remedial training and filing Form 8423-R (License Reinstatement Application).

(f) **Exceptions and Exemptions.**
Certain unregulated spells and situations may qualify for exceptions under the following conditions:
(1) Historical Spells.

Spells originating before the establishment of this Code are exempt from reporting requirements if they are documented as part of recognized magical traditions. Such spells must still comply with ethical standards under § 701.1 and safety protocols under § 401.6.
(2) Minor Cantrips and Low-Risk Spells.
Cantrips or spells classified as low-risk under § 401.2 are exempt from immediate reporting but may be subject to later review if their effects extend beyond the scope of their classification.

(g) **Cross-References.**
For definitions and processes related to spell creation, see § 1501.1. For spell risk levels and classifications, consult § 401.2. For reporting obligations involving ley line disruptions or other ecological impacts, see § 901.1.

(h) **Historical Annotations.**
Enacted under C.C.D. 7823, 67 MR 4104, Mon. 18, 1956, to address rising instances of unregulated magical phenomena. Amended under C.C.D. 13421, 89 MR 6120, Wed. 4, 1988, to include cross-school spells and emergency exemptions. Further revised under C.C.D. 2024, 88 MR 7834, Tue. 9, 2024, to expand reporting obligations and clarify penalties.

§ 101.9 Magical Personhood and Identity Continuity

(a) **General Rule of Magical Legal Personhood.**
For purposes of this Code, a "Magical Legal Person" means a natural person, qualified creature, or lawfully recognized entity whose identity is determined by the persistence of a continuous arcane identity signature, as measured by dominant will, soul integrity, and registered thaumic resonance.
Except as otherwise provided in this section, licensure, accreditation, privileges, obligations, liabilities, sanctions, prophetic designations, and regulatory limitations attach to the Magical Legal Person and not merely to the body, vessel, memory, or knowledge set temporarily housing such identity.

(b) **Non-Transferability of License.**
(1) A license issued under this Code is personal and non-transferable.

(2) No license, accreditation, continuing education credit, active participation hour, or regulatory standing shall transfer automatically by reason of:
(A) Memory duplication;
(B) Knowledge transference;
(C) Soul bifurcation or fragmentation;
(D) Consciousness transfer into a clone, vessel, construct, or possessed host;
(E) Chronomantic acceleration; or
(F) Simultaneous multi-body operation.
(3) Any entity practicing under a duplicated, transferred, or replicated knowledge set without continuity recognition under subsection (c) shall be treated as an unlicensed practitioner.

(c) **Continuity Recognition.**
(1) A transformed, transferred, or displaced entity shall be recognized as the same Magical Legal Person only if:
(A) The arcane identity signature remains substantially continuous;
(B) No independent will has arisen within the receiving vessel;
(C) The transfer is registered with the Department of Magical Affairs within 30 days; and
(D) The Commissioner of Magical Affairs affirms continuity upon review.
(2) Temporary possession not exceeding 72 continuous hours shall not, by itself, disrupt continuity unless the host's will becomes dominant.
(3) Where continuity is not affirmed, the resulting entity shall be treated as a distinct Magical Legal Person for all purposes of this Code.

(d) **Anti-Duplication and Experience Accrual Limitations.**
(1) Experience hours, continuing education credits, spellcasting limits, and regulatory thresholds shall accrue only once per continuous Magical Legal Person.
(2) No Magical Legal Person may multiply qualifying experience by:
(A) Operating in parallel bodies;
(B) Utilizing chronomantic compression or dilation environments;
(C) Dividing consciousness across vessels; or
(D) Delegating will to autonomous constructs while claiming personal participation.
(3) The Commissioner may disregard artificial temporal acceleration when determining minimum-duration requirements under this Code.

(e) **Liability and Sanction Continuity.**
(1) Where a Magical Legal Person divides, duplicates, or transfers identity, all resulting entities shall be jointly and severally liable for obligations arising prior to the division unless continuity is formally severed under subsection (c).
(2) A disciplinary sanction imposed upon a Magical Legal Person shall attach to any vessel, body, or host through which that person continues to operate.
(3) No Magical Legal Person may evade revocation, suspension, or prophetic designation through bodily substitution.

(f) **Prophetic and Designation Continuity.**
(1) A prophetic designation, including but not limited to Chosen One, Dark One, Breacher, or analogous status, shall attach to the Magical Legal Person and persist through lawful or unlawful bodily transfer.
(2) If consciousness is transferred into a non-humanoid vessel, the designation remains unless formally revoked pursuant to this Code.

(g) **Presumption.**
In the absence of affirmative proof of continuity, any clone, vessel, construct, or possessed entity shall be presumed a distinct Magical Legal Person.
The burden of proof rests upon the entity asserting continuity.

(h) **Cross-References.**
For licensing, renewal, and revocation procedures, refer to Part II. For regulations governing mind control, see § 2101.1. For necromantic practices, consult § 1301.1 and § 1301.4. For regulation of chosen or destiny-bound individuals, see § 702.3.

(i) **Historical Annotations.**
This section was enacted under C.C.D. 5321, 94 MR 2044, Wed. 3, 2026, to address identity duplication, vessel transfer, and soul-fragmentation loopholes identified following multiple enforcement actions involving parallel-body licensure abuse and prophetic evasion. Amendments were made under C.C.D. 5348, 95 MR 1189, Tue. 12, 2027, to clarify joint and several liability in cases of split-consciousness operation and chronomantic experience inflation.

§ 102.1 Structure of Magical Governance and Administrative Procedure

(a) **Establishment of Governing Authorities.**
For purposes of administration, enforcement, interpretation, and adjudication under this Code, the following governing bodies are recognized and vested with authority as specified herein:
(1) The Crown.
The Crown retains limited emergency authority to ensure execution of this Code where all subordinate enforcement bodies have failed or refused to act. Such authority shall not extend to routine interpretation, adjudication, or modification of statutory provisions except as expressly authorized under this Code.
(2) The Council of Councils.
The Council of Councils shall serve as the supreme regulatory oversight body responsible for policy coordination, inter-agency review, and final administrative determinations as provided under subsection (e).
(3) The Department of Magical Affairs (DMA).
The DMA shall serve as the primary administrative and enforcement agency responsible for licensure, inspection, investigation, and initial determinations under this Code.
(4) The Council of Counsel.
The Council of Counsel shall exercise interpretive authority, prosecutorial discretion in administrative proceedings, and intermediate appellate jurisdiction as provided under subsection (e).
(5) Specialized Agencies and Commissions.
Any specialized body established pursuant to this Code, including but not limited to boards, registries, and oversight commissions, shall operate within the jurisdiction delegated to them and remain subject to review under subsection (e).
(6) Administrative, Interpretive, and Publication Authority.
The Council of Councils, the Council of Counsel, the DMA, and any subordinate council, bureau, or authorized body acting pursuant to this Code, shall possess authority to administer, interpret, implement, enforce, and give effect to the provisions of this Code. Such authority shall include, but not be limited to—
(A) issuance of interpretive guidance, advisory opinions, and clarifying rulings concerning the meaning, scope, or application of any provision;

(B) publication of supplementary materials, explanatory notices, procedural guidance, and administrative interpretations necessary for consistent application of this Code, including materials issued pursuant to Part XXXI;
(C) development and enforcement of procedures governing review, approval, authorization, monitoring, and compliance under this Code;
(D) resolution of ambiguities, conflicts, or gaps in application, including resolution that—
(i) harmonizes provisions across Parts; or
(ii) prevents circumvention of regulatory intent; and
(E) exercise of any ancillary or incidental authority reasonably necessary to carry out the purposes of this Code, including authority not expressly enumerated but inherently required for administration.

(b) **Jurisdiction and Delegation.**
(1) Except as otherwise provided, initial determinations regarding licensure, compliance, penalties, registration, and enforcement shall be made by the DMA.
(2) The DMA may delegate investigative or technical functions to accredited auditors, inspectors, or certified magical examiners, provided that final agency action remains subject to review under subsection (e).
(3) No subordinate body may promulgate rules inconsistent with this Code.

(c) **Administrative Proceedings.**
(1) Any person or entity subject to an adverse determination under this Code shall be entitled to notice and an opportunity to respond prior to final agency action, except in cases of immediate threat to public safety.
(2) Proceedings shall include:
(A) Written notice of the alleged violation or deficiency;
(B) Citation to applicable provisions of this Code;
(C) A reasonable period for corrective action or formal response.
(3) Emergency suspension of privileges may occur without prior hearing where delay would result in substantial harm, provided that expedited review is made available.

(d) **Burden and Standard of Review.**
(1) In administrative enforcement actions, the DMA bears the burden of demonstrating noncompliance by a preponderance of the arcane evidence.

(2) On appeal to the Council of Counsel, findings of fact shall be reviewed for clear error; conclusions of law shall be reviewed de novo, except that—
(A) where a provision of this Code is ambiguous or silent with respect to a specific issue, reasonable interpretations issued by the Council of Counsel pursuant to subsection (f) shall be afforded controlling weight unless such interpretation—
(i) is arbitrary, capricious, or manifestly contrary to the text, structure, or purpose of this Code; or
(ii) exceeds the scope of authority delegated under subsection (a); and
(B) no reviewing body shall substitute its own interpretation for that of the Council of Counsel where the interpretation satisfies the standard set forth in subparagraph (A).
(3) On final review by the Council of Councils, agency determinations shall be upheld unless arbitrary, capricious, contrary to this Code, or unsupported by substantial evidence.
(4) In reviewing interpretive determinations under subsection (f), the Council of Councils shall apply the standard set forth in paragraph (2)(A), and shall not overturn a reasonable interpretation solely because an alternative interpretation is preferred.

(e) **Appeals and Review.**
(1) Initial Determination.
Adverse determinations issued by the DMA shall constitute preliminary agency action.
(2) Intermediate Appeal.
Any affected party may appeal such determination to the Council of Counsel within thirty (30) days of issuance, unless a different deadline is specified in the relevant section.
(3) Final Administrative Review.
Decisions of the Council of Counsel may be appealed to the Council of Councils within thirty (30) days. Determinations of the Council of Councils shall constitute final administrative action under this Code.
(4) Exhaustion Requirement.
No appeal to a higher body shall be permitted unless all intermediate remedies provided under this subsection have been exhausted.

(f) **Interpretive Authority.**
(1) Pursuant to the authority established under subsection (a), the Council of Counsel may issue advisory opinions, interpretive memoranda, and binding administrative rulings clarifying provisions of this Code.

(2) Such interpretations shall—
(A) be consistent with the structure, definitions, and intent of this Code; and
(B) not create new substantive obligations except through formal amendment under Part XXXI.
(3) Interpretations issued pursuant to this subsection shall be binding on the DMA unless overturned by the Council of Councils in accordance with subsection (d).
(4) Publication of interpretive guidance shall occur in accordance with § 3101.3.

(g) **Relationship to Substantive Provisions.**
(1) Any section of this Code referencing appeals, review, revocation, or enforcement shall be construed as operating subject to the procedures set forth in this section unless expressly stated otherwise.
(2) In the event of conflict between a procedural requirement in another section and this section, the more specific provision shall control.
(3) General Conflict and Construction Rule. In the event of conflict, ambiguity, omission, or inconsistency between two or more provisions of this Code, the provisions shall be construed to give effect to the apparent intent of the Code as a whole. The more specific provision shall control, and where provisions are equally specific, the more restrictive provision shall govern unless otherwise expressly provided.

(h) **Preservation of Structural Integrity.**
Nothing in this section shall be construed to permit unilateral suspension, disregard, or selective enforcement of this Code except as expressly authorized herein.

(i) **Interpretive Treatment of Cross-References.**
(1) A cross-reference in this Code shall not be disregarded solely because the referenced provision does not exist, has been repealed, superseded, or renumbered, or does not correspond precisely to the subject matter described.
(2) Any such reference shall be construed to refer to the provision that most closely aligns with the apparent intent of the referencing text, as determined by the Department based on context, structure, related provisions, and any applicable guidance.

(3) The burden of locating the appropriate provision shall rest with the reader, practitioner, or regulated entity, who shall exercise reasonable diligence in identifying the intended authority.
(4) Except as provided in paragraph (5), failure to comply with a provision due to an incorrect or indeterminate cross-reference shall not, by itself, constitute a defense where the applicable requirement could have been identified through reasonable diligence.
(5) No penalty shall be imposed for failure to comply with a provision that cannot be reasonably located after good-faith efforts to identify the intended authority.
(6) The Department may issue interpretive guidance, technical corrections, or supplemental references to address persistent or recurring discrepancies, including those arising from prior corrections, whether or not such corrections resolve the underlying discrepancy.

(j) **Apologies.**
The Department acknowledges that editing, organizing, and maintaining approximately five hundred pages of dense, bureaucratic nonsense is a nontrivial undertaking and that certain inconsistencies, omissions, or structural irregularities may persist despite reasonable efforts to the contrary. Any reader inclined to object is encouraged to attempt the same without error, preferably under comparable time constraints.

At this point, everything is in here somewhere. Yes, even that thing you are looking for. No, it is not where you think it should be. Cross-reference it. Then cross-reference that. Then go back because you missed something. Everyone misses something. That is normal. That is fine. That is how this works. Just keep reading until it makes sense or until you convince yourself it does, which is honestly close enough! I quit.

All questions, comments, requests for clarification, or notices of perceived error shall be deemed received upon submission and immediately directed to the Department's Arcane Refuse Archive for Unresolved Inquiries, where they shall be processed in due course or otherwise.

For the avoidance of doubt, the foregoing shall not be construed to limit, delay, or excuse compliance with any provision of this Code.

(k) **Cross-References.**

For definitions, see § 101.1. For publication of supplementary materials, see § 3101.3. For procedural updates and amendments, see Part XXXI.

(l) **Historical Annotations.**
This section was enacted under C.C.D. 2981, 33 MR 118, Mon. 14, 1792 to establish a centralized framework for magical governance and adjudication. Amended under C.C.D. 5712, 44 MR 166, Thu. 9, 1937 to formalize administrative proceedings and appellate structure. Revised under C.C.D. 10044, 70 MR 201, Tue. 3, 2009 to incorporate modern standards of review, interpretive authority, and inter-agency coordination.

§ 102.2 Civil, Administrative, and Criminal Penalties

(a) **Scope and Applicability.**
(1) This section establishes uniform civil, administrative, and criminal penalty standards applicable to violations of this Code.
(2) Substantive provisions of this Code define prohibited conduct, required conduct, and conditions of compliance. Any violation of such provisions shall give rise to liability under this section.
(3) Any provision of this Code that prescribes, describes, or otherwise provides for suspension, revocation, disqualification, restriction, removal, reassignment, or other administrative or regulatory consequence shall be construed as operating in addition to, and not in lieu of, the penalties imposed under this section.
(4) The presence of such consequences in any provision shall not be interpreted to—
(A) limit, reduce, or otherwise affect the applicability of this section;
(B) substitute for penalties authorized under this section; or
(C) create an exclusive or self-contained enforcement regime.
(5) All violations of this Code shall remain subject to the penalties set forth in this section regardless of whether additional consequences are specified elsewhere.
(6) Penalties imposed under this section and administrative or regulatory consequences imposed under any other provision of this Code may be applied concurrently, cumulatively, or sequentially, as determined appropriate by the enforcing authority. Such administrative or regulatory consequences may include, without limitation, suspension, restriction, or revocation of spellcasting licenses, loss of access to specified schools of

magic, removal from authorized registries, or prohibition on participation in regulated magical activity.
(7) Remedies under this section are cumulative unless otherwise stated.

(b) **Classification of Violations.**
(1) General Rule.
Violations of this Code shall be classified based on the nature of the conduct, the degree of culpability, the level of risk created, and the extent of actual or potential harm. The classifications set forth in this subsection are intended to be illustrative and operative, and shall apply to all violations whether or not specifically enumerated.
(2) Minor Violations.
Minor violations include technical or administrative noncompliance not resulting in material harm, including isolated failures to comply with procedural, reporting, or record-keeping requirements.
(3) Major Violations.
Major violations include unauthorized practice, negligent high-risk magic, registry violations, material reporting failures, repeated minor violations, or any conduct demonstrating a substantial deviation from required standards of care.
(4) Egregious Violations.
Egregious violations include willful misconduct, fraud, reckless endangerment, exploitation of qualified creatures, deliberate concealment, systemic corruption, or conduct resulting in material harm or presenting a substantial likelihood of widespread or irreversible harm.
(5) Catch-All Classification.
Any violation not expressly described in this subsection shall be classified by the enforcing authority in accordance with the criteria set forth in paragraph (1), taking into account the totality of the circumstances, including intent, scale, duration, and systemic impact.
(6) Repeat Offender Enhancement.
Three (3) or more major violations within five years shall be treated as egregious.

(c) **Civil and Administrative Liability.**
(1) Every violation of this Code shall give rise to civil or administrative liability under this section.
(2) Civil and administrative liability shall be determined in accordance with subsections (b) through (h), and shall apply regardless of whether the same conduct also gives rise to criminal liability.

(3) The classification of a violation as minor, major, or egregious governs the baseline severity of civil and administrative penalties.
(4) Civil penalties under this section shall be imposed based on economic capacity, risk, and harm, and shall not be limited by the presence or absence of criminal liability.

(d) **Criminal Liability.**
(1) A violation shall constitute a criminal offense only where the conduct satisfies the elements set forth in subsection (o), including the required mental state.
(2) Criminal liability shall arise in addition to, and not in place of, civil or administrative liability.
(3) A violation classified as egregious under subsection (b)(4) shall not be deemed criminal unless it satisfies subsection (o).
(4) No person shall be subject to criminal penalties absent proof of the mental state specified in subsection (o).

(e) **Economic Measurement.**
(1) Annual Gross Receipts (AGR) means total economic value received during the preceding twelve months, without deduction.
(2) Total Asset Value (TAV) means the fair market value of all assets, magical and non-magical, directly or indirectly owned or controlled.
(3) The penalty shall be calculated using whichever produces the greater result: AGR-based or TAV-based calculation.

(f) **Defined Economic Tiers.**
Tier I: up to 25,000 Magical Credit Units (MCUs)
Tier II: 25,001 – 250,000 MCUs
Tier III: 250,001 – 1,000,000 MCUs
Tier IV: 1,000,001 – 5,000,000 MCUs
Tier V: 5,000,001 – 25,000,000 MCUs
Tier VI: in excess of 25,000,000 MCUs

(g) **Minor Violations – Progressive Rates.**
2% of Tier I
4% of Tier II
6% of Tier III
10% of Tier IV
12% of Tier V
15% of Tier VI

Minimum penalty: 500 MCUs.

(h) **Major Violations – Progressive Rates.**
5% of Tier I
12% of Tier II
25% of Tier III
45% of Tier IV
70% of Tier V
85% of Tier VI
Minimum penalty: 10,000 MCUs.

(i) **Egregious Violations – Progressive Rates.**
10% of Tier I
30% of Tier II
55% of Tier III
75% of Tier IV
90% of Tier V
100% of Tier VI
Minimum penalty: 100,000 MCUs.
Where Tier VI wealth exceeds 100,000,000 MCUs, forfeiture may extend beyond assets directly connected to the violation and may include additional unconnected assets sufficient to eliminate controlling economic dominance.
Minimum penalties shall not be waived solely on the basis of economic hardship where the violation involves willful misconduct or systemic risk.

(j) **Ultra-High-Wealth Individuals.**
An Ultra-High-Wealth (UHW) Individual is any person or entity whose TAV exceeds 25,000,000 MCUs.
(1) Major Violations by UHW Individuals.
Penalty shall not be less than 60% of total TAV.
Where aggravating factors exist, penalty shall not be less than 80% of total TAV.
Mandatory review for divestiture of controlling interests in enterprises connected to the violation.
(2) Egregious Violations by UHW Individuals.
Penalty shall not be less than 85% of total TAV.
Where fraud, systemic harm, creature exploitation, or catastrophic destabilization occurs, penalty shall not be less than 95% of total TAV.

Where mass harm or systemic collapse occurs, forfeiture may extend to 100% of total TAV.
(3) Enterprise Dissolution Authority.
For egregious violations by UHW individuals, the reviewing authority may order dissolution of enterprises involved, impose permanent prohibition on ownership of regulated magical assets, or transfer controlling interests into public trust or regulatory receivership.
(4) Anti-Evasion Presumption.
Asset transfers occurring within five years preceding investigation are presumed evasive unless proven otherwise.
Beneficial ownership, shell entities, trusts, dimensional holdings, or indirect control shall be included in TAV.
The burden shifts to the violator to demonstrate lack of control.
(5) No Monetary Cap for Catastrophic Harm.
Where conduct results in multiple fatalities, dimensional rupture, large-scale magical collapse, or systemic exploitation of qualified creatures, there shall be no statutory cap on monetary penalties.

(k) **Magical Capacity and Power-Based Enforcement.**
(1) Assessment of Magical Capacity.
For purposes of this section, the enforcing authority shall evaluate the relative magical capacity, capability, and influence of the violator, including—
(A) demonstrated spellcasting power;
(B) access to high-risk or restricted magic;
(C) control over magical systems, constructs, or networks; and
(D) ability to produce widespread, systemic, or cross-dimensional effects.
(2) Enhanced Penalties for High-Capacity Individuals.
Where a violator possesses substantial magical capacity, penalties under this section shall be increased to reflect the elevated risk posed by such capacity, including increases that—
(A) elevate the classification of the violation; or
(B) increase the applicable percentage ranges within subsections (g), (h), or (i).
(3) Magical Restriction Measures.
In addition to monetary penalties, the enforcing authority may impose restrictions on magical capability, including—
(A) temporary or permanent limitation of spellcasting ability;
(B) prohibition on access to specified schools of magic;
(C) restriction to low-risk spell classifications under Part IV; or

(D) mandatory supervision or containment during any authorized spellcasting activity.
(4) Severance of Magical Access.
For egregious violations involving high-capacity individuals, the enforcing authority may order partial or complete severance of access to magical energy, channels, or conduits, including severance that—
(A) prevents the casting of high-risk or complex spells; or
(B) limits the individual to non-operational or inert magical interaction.
(5) Binding and Containment.
Where necessary to prevent continued risk, the enforcing authority may require binding, dampening, or containment measures designed to reduce or neutralize magical capability, including measures that—
(A) suppress amplification or resonance effects; or
(B) prevent unauthorized interaction with magical systems or entities.
(6) Presumption of Elevated Risk.
Individuals possessing access to high-risk spell classifications, large-scale magical infrastructure, or cross-dimensional capabilities shall be presumed to present elevated systemic risk, and penalties shall be adjusted accordingly unless rebutted.

(l) **Continuing Violations.**
Each day of continuing noncompliance constitutes a separate violation.

(m) **Aggravating and Mitigating Factors.**
Penalty severity shall consider intent, harm, obstruction, repeat conduct, abuse of economic dominance, and voluntary disclosure.

(n) **Reasonable Cause.**
No civil monetary penalty shall be imposed where reasonable cause and absence of willful misconduct are demonstrated.
Ignorance of this Code does not constitute reasonable cause.

(o) **Criminal Conduct.**
A person commits a criminal offense where the person knowingly or willfully—
(1) engages in unauthorized high-risk magic;
(2) engages in or continues regulated or restricted magical activity without required authorization, including conduct occurring prior to, during, or after suspension, restriction, or revocation;

(3) falsifies, alters, conceals, or destroys registry, compliance, or reporting records;
(4) commits fraud, deception, or misrepresentation in connection with any regulated magical activity;
(5) conducts unlawful catastrophic experimentation or knowingly creates conditions likely to result in large-scale harm;
(6) engages in trafficking of magical artifacts, creatures, or restricted materials in violation of this Code;
(7) corruptly obstructs, impedes, or interferes with enforcement, investigation, or oversight;
(8) retaliates against witnesses, informants, or reporting parties; or
(9) causes or attempts to cause reckless magical catastrophe.
Attempt and conspiracy are punishable equally.

(p) **Criminal Classification and Sentencing.**
(1) Classification of Offenses.
(A) Class A Magical Felony shall include conduct resulting in death, widespread harm, dimensional instability, or systemic disruption, or involving deliberate, large-scale misuse of high-risk magic.
(B) Class B Magical Felony shall include conduct resulting in significant harm or risk of harm, or involving knowing or repeated violations of high-risk or restricted magical practices.
(C) Class C Magical Felony shall include conduct involving willful or knowing violations resulting in moderate harm or risk, or other criminal misconduct lacking large-scale or catastrophic impact.
(D) Magical Misdemeanor shall include criminal conduct involving limited harm, isolated impact, or low systemic risk.
(2) Sentencing.
Class A Magical Felony: fine up to 100% of TAV and imprisonment up to 30 years.
Class B Magical Felony: fine up to 60% of AGR or TAV; imprisonment up to 15 years.
Class C Magical Felony: fine up to 40% of AGR or TAV; imprisonment up to 7 years.
Magical Misdemeanor: fine up to 20% of AGR; imprisonment up to 2 years.

(q) **Criminal Enhancements for UHW Individuals.**
For UHW individuals convicted of Class A offenses, minimum fine shall be 90% of total TAV; imprisonment shall not be suspended; no early

parole before seventy percent of sentence served; mandatory forfeiture review shall apply.

(r) **Forfeiture.**
Upon conviction, courts may order forfeiture of magical instruments used in the offense, proceeds derived from unlawful conduct, restricted artifacts, illegally bound creatures, and controlling ownership interests.

(s) **Standard of Proof.**
Civil penalties require proof by a preponderance of evidence.
Criminal liability requires proof beyond a reasonable doubt.

(t) **Statute of Limitations.**
Civil actions must be initiated within five years of discovery.
Class A criminal offenses have no limitation period.
Class B criminal offenses must be initiated within ten years.
Class C criminal offenses and misdemeanors must be initiated within five years.
Fraudulent concealment tolls the limitations period.

§ 102.3 Binding Blood Oaths of Administrative Fidelity

(a) **General Requirement.**
Any individual who administers, interprets, enforces, or otherwise exercises authority under this Code shall, prior to exercising such authority, swear a Binding Blood Oath of Administrative Fidelity. No person shall exercise authority under this Code unless such oath has been administered and recorded in accordance with this section.

(b) **Nature of the Oath.**
The oath required under this section shall constitute a magically binding covenant between the sworn official and the lawful operation of this Code. The oath shall bind the blood and life-force of the official and shall operate as a self-executing enforcement mechanism designed to prevent the knowing and intentional subversion of the Code.

(c) **Form of Oath.**
(1) Standard Oath.

Unless otherwise provided by law, the oath shall state substantially as follows:
"I swear by blood and life that I will faithfully administer the Magical Code of Regulations; that I will exercise reasonable diligence and good faith in the execution of my duties; and that I will not knowingly disregard, undermine, or subvert the lawful operation of this Code."
(2) Equivalent Forms.
Minor variations in wording shall not invalidate the oath provided the substance of the commitments described in paragraph (1) is preserved.

(d) **Administration and Registration.**
(1) The oath shall be administered through a recognized blood-binding ritual conducted by an authorized official or cleric.
(2) The oath shall be recorded in the Magical Register and linked to the office, appointment, license, or authority under which the individual exercises power.

(e) **Scope of the Oath.**
(1) The oath binds the official's conduct when exercising authority under this Code, including regulatory determinations, enforcement decisions, interpretive rulings, certifications, and other official acts performed under color of authority.
(2) The oath does not compel any particular interpretation of ambiguous provisions but prohibits the intentional misuse of such ambiguity for the purpose of evading or defeating the lawful operation of the Code.

(f) **Standard for Violation.**
A violation of the oath occurs where an official knowingly and intentionally—
(1) refuses to enforce a mandatory provision of this Code without lawful justification;
(2) issues an official determination materially contradicting the plain meaning of a provision of this Code;
(3) uses authority granted under this Code for purposes inconsistent with its lawful operation; or
(4) engages in conduct designed to disable, suspend, or nullify the operation of the Code outside procedures authorized by law.

(g) **Automatic Enforcement.**

Where a violation described in subsection (f) occurs, the oath shall trigger automatic magical enforcement. Such enforcement shall occur without the need for judicial or administrative action and shall not depend upon the willingness of any official to administer penalties.

(h) **Escalating Sanctions.**
Sanctions imposed under this section shall escalate according to the severity and intent of the violation.
(1) Corrective Sanctions. Where the violation involves an initial or limited attempt to evade or undermine the Code, the oath may impose immediate physical distress, involuntary interruption of the unlawful act, or temporary incapacitation sufficient to prevent continuation of the violation.
(2) Compulsive Sanctions. Where the violation involves continued intentional misconduct or abuse of regulatory authority, the oath may impose immobilization, unconsciousness, or other bodily restraint sufficient to halt the unlawful conduct.
(3) Terminal Sanctions. Where the violation involves atrocities, systemic abuse of authority, or intentional efforts to dismantle or nullify the operation of the Code, the oath may impose permanent magical binding, petrification, or death.

(i) **Protection for Good-Faith Administration.**
The oath shall not be deemed violated where an official acts in good faith under a reasonable interpretation of ambiguous provisions of this Code or exercises lawful discretion granted by its terms.

(j) **Historical Annotations.**
Originally established under C.C.D. 5617, 68 MR 1142, Tue. 12, 1811, following the Collapse of the First Enforcement Council, in which multiple officials refused to enforce mandatory provisions of magical law. Amended under C.C.D. 8119, 79 MR 2216, Sun. 3, 1936, to incorporate automatic blood-binding enforcement mechanisms. Revised under C.C.D. 9924, 83 MR 2987, Mon. 19, 2017, to clarify escalating sanctions and standards for good-faith administrative judgment.

Part II: Licensing, Certifications, and Audits

§ 201.1 General Licensing Requirements

(a) **Purpose and Scope.**
This section establishes the requirements for obtaining a general license for magical practice. Licenses are required for individuals wishing to perform spells under § 401.1 or engage in regulated magical activities within the jurisdiction of the Magical Code of Regulations (MCOR). This section applies to all individuals defined as "spellcasters" under § 101.1(a)(2). Practitioners under § 101.1(a)(3) may only apply for limited licenses under § 201.9.

(b) **Eligibility Requirements.**
To apply for a general license, an individual must meet the following criteria:
(1) Educational Qualifications.
(A) Completion of at least two (2) years of study at a recognized Magical Educational Institution (MEI) accredited under § 301.3.
(B) Educational programs must include coursework in at least one recognized school of magic as defined in § 101.1 and practical spellcasting activities meeting the standards of § 301.2.
(C) Practitioners not enrolled in MEIs must submit proof of equivalent study, supported by independent assessments from the Council of Councils.
(2) Demonstrated Competence.
(A) Applicants must successfully complete a proficiency examination administered by the Department of Licensing and Authorization (DLA), demonstrating theoretical knowledge and practical application of magic.
(B) Applicants for Journeyman or Master Spellcaster levels (§ 101.1(a)(2)(A)) must also present logs of supervised spellcasting activities (§ 401.5) and endorsements from licensed instructors.
(3) Background Verification.
(A) All applicants must pass a background check confirming adherence to the ethical standards outlined in § 701.1.

(B) Individuals with prior ethical violations under this Code may be subject to additional review and potential denial of licensure.

(c) **Application Process.**
(1) Submission Requirements.
(A) Applicants must complete and submit Form 9342-A (Application for General Magical License) along with supporting documentation, including:
(i) Proof of educational qualifications (§ 201.1(b)(1));
(ii) Proficiency examination scores;
(iii) Endorsements and spellcasting logs for Journeyman or Master-level applicants.
(2) Fee Payment.
(A) A non-refundable application fee of 500 MCUs must be submitted at the time of application.
(B) Applicants seeking expedited processing may pay an additional 200 MCUs, subject to availability.
(3) Review Timeline.
(A) The Department of Licensing and Authorization must issue a decision within 60 days of receiving a completed application.
(B) Incomplete applications will result in delays and potential rejection, with reapplication requiring a new fee.

(d) **License Issuance and Validity.**
(1) License Term.
(A) General licenses are valid for two (2) years from the date of issuance, unless suspended or revoked under § 201.3.
(B) Renewal applications must be submitted no later than 30 days before expiration.
(2) Licensing Levels.
(A) Licenses will specify the spellcaster's proficiency level as Apprentice, Journeyman, or Master, in accordance with § 101.1(a)(2).
(B) Licenses are non-transferable and may only be used by the individual named on the license.

(e) **Penalties for Non-Compliance.**
(1) Unlicensed Practice.
(A) Performing spells without a valid license constitutes a violation under § 401.1 and is subject to temporary suspension of eligibility for licensure for up to two (2) years;

(2) Fraudulent Applications.
(A) Submission of false or misleading information during the application process will result in immediate rejection of the application, and prohibition from reapplying for up to five (5) years.

(f) **Cross-References.**
For limited licenses applicable to practitioners, see § 201.9. For requirements related to the classification and supervision of spells, refer to § 401.1 and § 401.2. For ethical requirements and remedial measures, consult § 701.1 and § 701.6.

(g) **Historical Annotations.**
This section was enacted under C.C.D. 4671, 84 MR 2345, Wed. 10, 1983, to establish standardized licensing requirements. Amended under C.C.D. 5123, 89 MR 5672, Mon. 15, 2004, to include additional provisions for background checks and proficiency endorsements. Further revisions under C.C.D. 6217, 93 MR 7842, Fri. 20, 2021, clarified licensing levels and penalties for non-compliance.

§ 201.2 Provisional Licensing for Gifted Students

(a) **Purpose and Scope.**
This section establishes the criteria, process, and limitations for issuing provisional licenses to individuals under the age of sixteen (16) who demonstrate extraordinary aptitude in magical practice. Provisional licenses provide a structured opportunity for young practitioners to develop their skills under strict supervision, while maintaining compliance with § 401.1 and ethical standards outlined in § 701.1.

(b) **Eligibility Requirements.**
(1) Age Limitation
(A) Provisional licenses are available only to individuals who are at least fourteen (14) years of age but not older than sixteen (16) at the time of recommendation.
(B) Upon reaching the age of sixteen (16), licensees must transition to a standard spellcasting license under § 201.1 or cease spellcasting activities until such a license is granted.
(2) Recommendation by Recognized Authority
(A) Applicants may not directly apply for a provisional license. Eligibility requires a formal written recommendation by one of the following:

(i) A licensed Master Spellcaster with at least five (5) years of experience;
(ii) The head of a Magical Educational Institution accredited under § 301.3;
(iii) The Council of Councils, based on extraordinary circumstances or contributions to magical study.
(B) Recommendations must include detailed evidence of the student's exceptional aptitude, such as:
(i) High scores in standardized magical proficiency exams recognized by the Department of Magical Affairs (DMA);
(ii) Documented advanced coursework in a recognized school of magic as defined in § 101.1;
(iii) Demonstrated mastery of practical spellcasting under institutional supervision.
(3) Commissioner Approval
(A) The Commissioner of Magical Affairs (CMA) is the sole approving authority for provisional licenses.
(B) The Commissioner must personally review each recommendation and issue final approval within sixty (60) days of submission.

(c) **Conditions of Licensure.**
(1) Authorized Activities
(A) Provisional licensees are authorized to perform low-risk spells as classified under § 401.2, provided such spells are pre-approved by an overseeing institution or instructor.
(B) Intermediate-level spells may only be performed under the direct supervision of a licensed Journeyman or Master Spellcaster.
(C) High-risk spells are strictly prohibited unless explicitly authorized by the CMA and supervised by an accredited institution.
(2) Supervision and Oversight
(A) All spellcasting activities must occur under the oversight of a designated supervisor meeting the qualifications outlined in § 401.2.
(B) Supervisors must submit quarterly reports detailing the licensee's progress and compliance, using Form 9324-S (Supervised Spellcasting Report).
(3) Reporting and Logging
(A) Licensees must maintain detailed logs of all spellcasting activities, in accordance with § 401.5, and submit these logs monthly to the DMA.
(B) Logs must include the spell type, date, location, intended outcome, and supervising authority. Failure to maintain accurate logs will result in license suspension.

(d) **Duration and Renewal.**
(1) Validity
(A) Provisional licenses are valid for one (1) year and may be renewed annually until the licensee reaches the age of sixteen (16), provided compliance with all conditions is maintained.
(2) Transition to Standard License
(A) Upon reaching sixteen (16), licensees must apply for a standard spellcasting license under § 201.1.
(B) Transition applications must demonstrate proficiency in accordance with § 101.5 and include a recommendation from their supervising authority.

(e) **Penalties for Non-Compliance.**
(1) Unauthorized Spellcasting
Engaging in unsupervised or unauthorized spellcasting constitutes a violation and will result in immediate suspension of the provisional license and potential disqualification from future licensure.
(2) Failure to Report
(A) Failure to log or report spellcasting activities as required under § 401.5 may result in license suspension or revocation.
(3) Ethical Violations
(A) Engagement in unethical practices, as defined in § 701.1, will result in penalties under § 102.2 and § 701.6.

(f) **Cross-References.**
For logging requirements, see § 401.5. For spell risk classifications and supervision protocols, see § 401.2. For ethical standards, see § 701.1.

(g) **Historical Annotations.**
Established under C.C.D. 5123, 87 MR 3456, Sun. 14, 1998, to provide pathways for young practitioners of exceptional talent. Amended under C.C.D. 6412, 91 MR 8934, Mon. 23, 2015, to require DMA oversight. Revised under C.C.D. 7124, 94 MR 2345, Thu. 18, 2023, to strengthen supervision and reporting requirements.

§ 201.3 Renewal and Revocation of Licenses

(a) **General Renewal Requirements.**
All magical practitioners and spellcasters holding licenses issued pursuant to § 201.1 must renew their licenses biennially to retain active status.

Renewal requires submission of Form 6589 (License Renewal Application) along with supporting documentation, as specified in subsection (b), no later than 30 days prior to the license expiration date. Practitioners or spellcasters failing to submit the required documentation by the deadline shall have their licenses automatically suspended pending review under subsection (e).

(b) **Documentation for Renewal.**
Applicants for license renewal must include the following materials with Form 6589:
(1) Spellcasting Logs. A complete and accurate record of all spellcasting activities conducted during the preceding two years, categorized by:
(A) Spell risk level, as defined under § 401.2;
(B) Purpose, such as academic, professional, or personal use; and
(C) Location, including proximity to ley lines or protected zones (§ 2501.4).
Failure to provide detailed logs, or submission of vague or incomplete entries, shall be grounds for rejection of the renewal application.
(2) Continuing Education Certification. Proof of compliance with the continuing education requirements outlined in § 101.5(b)(2), demonstrating completion of no fewer than ten (10) hours of accredited coursework annually.
(3) Proficiency Audit Report. Results of the most recent proficiency audit conducted pursuant to § 201.4, including evaluations of spell accuracy, ethical compliance, and adherence to safety protocols.
(4) Affirmation of Compliance. A signed declaration affirming that the licensee has adhered to all applicable regulations under this Code, including but not limited to ethical standards, spellcasting limitations, and reporting obligations.

(c) **License Renewal Fees.**
The renewal fee shall be determined based on the licensee's proficiency level:
(1) Apprentice Spellcaster: 500 MCUs;
(2) Journeyman Spellcaster: 1,000 MCUs;
(3) Master Spellcaster: 2,500 MCUs.
Fees must be paid in full at the time of application submission. A late fee of 10% of the base renewal fee will apply to applications submitted after the 30-day deadline but before the expiration date.

(d) **Provisional Extensions.**
Practitioners or spellcasters unable to meet the renewal deadline due to extraordinary circumstances, such as medical emergencies or natural disasters, may apply for a provisional extension by submitting Form 9324-P (Provisional License Extension Request) no later than ten (10) days after the original renewal deadline. Provisional licenses, if granted, shall remain valid for up to 90 days, during which the licensee must complete the renewal process.

(e) **Automatic Suspension and Revocation.**
(1) Grounds for Suspension. A license shall be suspended immediately upon the occurrence of any of the following:
(A) Failure to submit a renewal application by the expiration date;
(B) Non-compliance with continuing education requirements (§ 101.5(b)(2));
(C) Evidence of fraudulent or incomplete documentation.
(2) Notice of Suspension. The Department of Magical Affairs (DMA) shall notify the licensee of the suspension via enchanted correspondence no later than five (5) days after the suspension's effective date.
(3) Revocation Proceedings. If a suspended licensee fails to rectify the issues leading to suspension within 90 days, the license shall be subject to permanent revocation following a hearing before the Council of Counsel. Revoked licenses may only be reinstated through the process outlined in subsection (f).

(f) **Reinstatement of Revoked Licenses.**
Practitioners or spellcasters seeking reinstatement of a revoked license must submit Form 9832-R (License Reinstatement Petition) along with evidence of remediation, including:
(1) Completion of a remedial education program approved by the DMA;
(2) Payment of all outstanding fees and penalties;
(3) A written appeal demonstrating a clear understanding of the violations leading to revocation and steps taken to prevent recurrence.
The Council of Counsel shall review reinstatement petitions within 60 days of submission and issue a binding decision.

(g) **Expedited Processing for Institutional Affiliates.**
Practitioners or spellcasters employed by accredited Magical Educational Institutions (§ 301.1) or licensed magical entities (§ 201.7) may qualify for expedited renewal processing through institutional sponsorship.

Sponsoring institutions must submit Form 8841-S (Institutional License Renewal Sponsorship) and certify that the licensee is in compliance with all institutional policies and Code provisions.

(h) **Cross-References.**
For spell risk classifications and logging requirements, see § 401.2 and § 401.5. For continuing education standards, refer to § 101.5. For auditing procedures, see § 201.4. For ethical compliance requirements, consult § 701.1.

(i) **Historical Annotations.**
Originally established under C.C.D. 1974, 72 MR 2345, Wed. 15, 1923, to standardize the biennial renewal of magical licenses. Amended under C.C.D. 3452, 82 MR 8764, Fri. 21, 1982, to include continuing education requirements. Further revised under C.C.D. 9841, 93 MR 1456, Wed. 10, 2023, to streamline the reinstatement process and introduce expedited processing for institutional affiliates.

§ 201.4 Auditing Procedures and Penalties for Non-Compliance

(a) **General Auditing Requirements.**
All licensed practitioners and spellcasters, as defined under § 101.1(a)(2) and § 101.1(a)(3), are subject to periodic audits conducted by the Department of Magical Affairs (DMA) to ensure strict adherence to the provisions of the MCOR. Audits serve to confirm compliance with licensing standards, spellcasting regulations, ethical guidelines, and institutional requirements. All individuals holding active licenses under § 201.1 or provisional licenses under § 201.2 must participate fully in audits as required by law. Non-compliance with audit requirements shall result in penalties as outlined in subsection (g).

(b) **Audit Initiation and Scope.**
(1) Mandatory Biennial Audits.
(A) Standard licenses are subject to biennial audits, ensuring continuous compliance with § 201.1 and § 401.1.
(B) High-risk licenses, including provisional licenses issued under § 201.2, are audited annually due to the elevated risk associated with high-complexity spells and experimental magic.
(2) Risk-Based and Special Audits.

(A) Audits may be triggered based on risk assessments derived from patterns of spellcasting activity, proximity to magical disasters, or institutional referrals under § 301.1.
(B) Special audits may be initiated upon the filing of a credible complaint, significant deviation from logging standards (§ 401.5), or evidence of unethical behavior (§ 701.1).
(3) Random Audits.
Random audits may be conducted at the discretion of the DMA to assess compliance across a representative sample of licensees.
(4) Scope of Audits.
Audits encompass, but are not limited to:
(A) Verification of spellcasting logs (§ 401.5);
(B) Inspection of magical implements and storage facilities;
(C) Review of educational and proficiency records (§ 201.3);
(D) Examination of ethical compliance, particularly regarding interactions with qualified creatures (§ 701.7);
(E) Financial transactions involving magical assets, in accordance with Part X.

(c) **Audit Notification and Preparation.**
(1) Advance Notice.
Audited individuals shall receive a Notification of Audit (Form 9721-N) no fewer than 30 days prior to the commencement of the audit. The notice shall specify the scope, duration, and required documentation.
(2) Immediate Audits.
In cases of suspected fraud, gross negligence, or emergency circumstances, the DMA may initiate an immediate audit with no prior notice.
(3) Documentation Requirements.
Licensees must compile and submit the following records:
(A) Comprehensive spellcasting logs for the preceding audit period, categorized by risk level (§ 401.2) and including detailed spell outcomes, intended purposes, and affected entities;
(B) Maintenance records for magical implements, including inspection dates and calibration details;
(C) Proof of continuing education credits (§ 201.3);
(D) Documentation of incident reports and corresponding resolutions.

(d) **On-Site Inspections.**

Auditors may conduct site visits to the licensee's registered workspace, spellcasting area, or research facility.
(1) Inspection Areas.
Audits may include:
(A) Verification of potion storage facilities;
(B) Examination of proximity to ley lines and restricted magical zones;
(C) Evaluation of containment protocols for high-risk spells.
(2) Auditor Powers.
Auditors are authorized to:
(A) Seize non-compliant implements, spells, or materials;
(B) Conduct interviews with licensees and institutional supervisors;
(C) Require live demonstrations of spell proficiency under controlled conditions.

(e) **Audit Review Process.**
(1) Preliminary Findings.
Within 30 days of audit completion, auditors shall issue a preliminary report summarizing findings, including identified violations, areas of concern, and recommended corrective actions.
(2) Final Report.
The final audit report, issued within 60 days of audit closure, shall include:
(A) Detailed findings and evidence;
(B) Any penalties assessed;
(C) Instructions for remediation or appeals.

(f) **Appeal Procedures.**
Audited individuals may appeal findings within 30 days of receiving the final report by submitting Form 7621-A (Audit Finding Appeal) to the Council of Counsel. Appeals must detail specific grievances and include supporting documentation.

(g) **Corrective Actions and Penalties.**
(1) Mandatory Corrective Actions.
Licensees must implement all corrective actions specified in the audit report, including remedial education, re-inspection of storage facilities, or recalibration of magical implements.
(2) Penalties for Non-Compliance.
Immediate license suspension for refusal to comply with audit requirements, pending corrective action.

(h) **Cross-References.**
For spellcasting log requirements, see § 401.5. For potion storage and implement maintenance standards, refer to § 1201.3. For ethical compliance in magical practices, consult § 701.1.

(i) **Historical Annotations.**
Enacted under C.C.D. 2765, 72 MR 2876, Thu. 18, 1924, to establish audit protocols for licensed practitioners and spellcasters. Amended under C.C.D. 4853, 82 MR 8765, Fri. 22, 1983, to incorporate risk-based auditing procedures. Revised under C.C.D. 9854, 93 MR 1457, Tue. 15, 2023, to align with expanded ethical and financial regulations under § 1001.1 and § 701.1. Further amendments enacted under C.C.D. 9874, 94 MR 5688, Sat. 10, 2024, to enhance reporting protocols and penalty structures.

§ 201.5 Certification for Restricted Practices

(a) **General Certification Requirements.**
Certification for restricted practices is mandatory for all practitioners and spellcasters seeking to engage in high-risk, specialized, or ethically sensitive magical activities. Certification ensures that only qualified individuals may perform these practices, protecting public safety, ethical standards, and the integrity of magical ecosystems.

(b) **Definition of Restricted Practices.**
Restricted practices include, but are not limited to:
(1) Necromancy involving reanimation of sentient beings (§ 1301.2);
(2) Blood magic for contractual purposes (§ 1101.2);
(3) Ritualistic magic invoking planar entities (§ 101.1);
(4) Time manipulation magic involving causality (§ 2201.1);
(5) Enchantments or spells affecting large populations or geographic areas (§ 401.3);
(6) Any other practices deemed high-risk or restricted by the Council of Councils or the Department of Magical Affairs (DMA).

(c) **Eligibility for Certification.**
To qualify for certification, applicants must meet the following requirements:

(1) Possess an active license under § 201.1 or a limited license under § 201.9, with no prior suspension or revocation within the preceding five years;
(2) Demonstrate completion of advanced coursework and practical training in the relevant field of magic, as outlined in subsection (d);
(3) Submit Form 9873-C (Application for Certification) along with all supporting documentation and a non-refundable application fee of 500 MCUs.

(d) **Training and Education Standards.**
(1) Advanced Coursework.
Applicants must complete a minimum of 30 hours of advanced study in the relevant magical discipline, including theoretical and practical components.
(2) Practical Experience.
Applicants must demonstrate a minimum of 100 hours of supervised practical experience in the specific restricted practice. Supervision must be conducted by a certified practitioner in good standing or an accredited institution (§ 301.3).
(3) Ethical Training.
All applicants must complete an additional 10 hours of ethical training specific to the restricted practice, addressing potential risks, safeguards, and compliance with § 701.1.

(e) **Examination Process.**
(1) Written Examination.
Applicants must pass a standardized written examination testing knowledge of the legal, theoretical, and practical aspects of the restricted practice.
(2) Practical Examination.
Applicants must successfully perform a series of practical demonstrations under the observation of a certified examiner. Demonstrations will be graded based on precision, safety, and ethical compliance.

(f) **Certification Issuance.**
(1) Certifications are issued by the DMA upon successful completion of the application and examination process.
(2) Certifications are valid for three years and must be renewed under § 201.3.

(3) Certified practitioners are listed in the DMA Registry of Restricted Practices (RRPR), accessible to the public.

(g) **Penalties for Unauthorized Restricted Practices.**
Individuals performing restricted practices without proper certification are subject to license suspension or revocation under § 201.4;

(h) **Special Provisions for Emergencies.**
In emergency situations, uncertified practitioners may temporarily perform restricted practices provided:
(1) The act is necessary to prevent imminent harm;
(2) The practitioner files Form 7642-E (Emergency Action Report) within 72 hours;
(3) The Council of Councils retroactively approves the action.

(i) **Cross-References.**
For general licensing requirements, see § 201.1. For penalties, see § 102.2.

(j) **Historical Annotations.**
Enacted under C.C.D. 3124, 73 MR 2176, Mon. 15, 1935, to address emerging high-risk magical practices. Amended under C.C.D. 5852, 85 MR 4473, Tue. 12, 1991, to establish ethical training requirements. Revised under C.C.D. 9873, 93 MR 9834, Tue. 20, 2023, to streamline the certification process and include emergency provisions. Further revisions made under C.C.D. 9917, 94 MR 6721, Mon. 7, 2024, to align with international standards on restricted magical practices.

§ 201.6 Special Licensing for Foreign Practitioners

(a) **Definition and Purpose.**
The term "foreign practitioner" refers to any individual who is not a citizen or permanent resident of a jurisdiction governed by this Code but who seeks authorization to practice magic within such jurisdiction. The purpose of this section is to establish the requirements, procedures, and limitations applicable to the issuance of special licenses for foreign practitioners, ensuring compliance with local laws while respecting international magical agreements.

(b) **Eligibility Requirements.**
(1) General Eligibility.

Foreign practitioners must meet the following minimum requirements to apply for a special license:
(A) Proof of citizenship or residency in a foreign jurisdiction recognized by the Council of Councils.
(B) Documentation of licensure or equivalent authorization to practice magic in the foreign jurisdiction.
(C) Demonstration of proficiency in applicable Schools of Magic as defined in § 101.1.
(2) Reciprocal Agreements.
Practitioners from jurisdictions with reciprocal licensing agreements shall be eligible for expedited licensing, subject to verification of their credentials by the Department of Licensing and Accreditation (DLA).
(3) Temporary Visitors.
Practitioners seeking short-term licensure for specific purposes, such as conferences, research, or temporary employment, may apply for a provisional special license under subsection (f).

(c) **Application Procedures.**
(1) Required Documentation.
Applicants must submit the following to the DLA:
(A) Form 4017-F (Foreign Practitioner Licensing Application).
(B) Certified copies of all relevant credentials, licenses, or certifications.
(C) A detailed description of intended magical activities, including Schools of Magic involved and potential risk classifications.
(D) A completed background check from their home jurisdiction, translated into the local magical language if necessary.
(2) Submission Timeline.
Applications must be submitted no later than ninety (90) days prior to the intended start of magical activities. Expedited applications for emergency purposes are governed under subsection (g).
(3) Fees.
A non-refundable application fee of 1,000 MCUs is required for processing. Additional fees may apply for expedited applications or high-risk classifications.

(d) **Evaluation Criteria.**
(1) Review of Foreign Credentials.
The DLA shall review the applicant's credentials to verify:
(A) Equivalency to local licensing standards under § 201.1.
(B) Proficiency in ethical spellcasting practices as outlined in § 701.1.

(C) Compliance with applicable international magical treaties.
(2) Risk Assessment.
Applications involving high-risk magic, as defined under § 401.2, shall undergo additional scrutiny, including mandatory interviews and evaluations by the Council of Counsel.
(3) Cultural and Ethical Considerations.
Practices deemed culturally insensitive, ethically questionable, or otherwise incompatible with local magical standards shall be grounds for denial of the license.

(e) **Conditions of Special Licenses.**
(1) Duration and Renewal.
Special licenses shall be valid for one (1) year from the date of issuance and may be renewed annually upon submission of Form 4017-R (Foreign Practitioner License Renewal) and updated documentation.
(2) Scope of Activities.
Special licenses shall specify the approved Schools of Magic, geographic areas, and magical activities permitted. License holders may not engage in unauthorized practices under any circumstances.
(3) Mandatory Reporting.
Licensed foreign practitioners must:
(A) Log all magical activities in compliance with § 401.5.
(B) Report any incidents or irregularities immediately using Form 3019-I (Incident Report for Foreign Practitioners).
(4) Supervision Requirements.
Practitioners engaged in high-risk or experimental magic must operate under the supervision of a licensed local practitioner or institution, as mandated by § 401.2.

(f) **Provisional Licenses.**
(1) Eligibility for Temporary Licenses.
Foreign practitioners requiring short-term authorization for conferences, workshops, or other temporary engagements may apply for a provisional license, valid for a period not exceeding ninety (90) days.
(2) Expedited Processing.
Applications for provisional licenses submitted within thirty (30) days of the intended start date may be expedited for an additional fee of 500 MCUs.
(3) Limitations.

Provisional licenses shall not permit high-risk magical activities unless specifically approved by the DLA.

(g) **Emergency Licenses.**
(1) Definition.
Emergency licenses may be granted to foreign practitioners in cases of imminent danger, natural disasters, or other exigent circumstances requiring their immediate magical expertise.
(2) Approval Process.
Applicants must submit Form 5013-E (Emergency Licensing Application) and provide evidence of the emergency situation. The Commissioner of Magical Affairs has sole discretion to approve or deny such applications.

(h) **Penalties for Non-Compliance.**
Practitioners found in violation of the terms of their special license shall face immediate suspension or revocation of their license, with reinstatement contingent upon filing Form 9821-R (Reinstatement Application for Special Licenses) and undergoing additional scrutiny.

(i) **Cross-References.**
For general licensing requirements, see § 201.1. For risk classifications and reporting, consult § 401.2 and § 401.5. For institutional licensing, see § 201.7.

(j) **Historical Annotations.**
This section was established under C.C.D. 9382, 77 MR 4123, Sat. 12, 1853, to address the influx of foreign practitioners following the Necromantic Purge. Amended under C.C.D. 10342, 89 MR 2114, Fri. 23, 2020, to include provisions for emergency licenses and provisional licenses.

§ 201.7 Institutional Licensing for Magical Entities

(a) **Scope and Applicability.**
This section establishes requirements, procedures, and obligations for the issuance, renewal, and revocation of institutional licenses for magical entities engaged in regulated magical practices. Institutional licenses are required for all organizations, including but not limited to magical academies, guilds, research facilities, and corporate entities, that conduct spellcasting, magical research, or educational activities involving magic.

(b) **Definitions.**
For the purposes of this section:
(1) Institution. An "institution" refers to any organized body, including but not limited to:
(A) Magical Academies: Entities providing formal magical education (§ 301.1).
(B) Research Facilities: Entities engaging in magical experimentation or theoretical study.
(C) Guilds and Corporations: Organizations offering professional or commercial magical services.
(D) Specialized Institutions: Entities formed for unique purposes, such as cultural preservation of endangered magical traditions (§ 201.9).
(2) Institutional License. An "institutional license" is a formal authorization issued under this section permitting institutions to perform regulated magical practices within the boundaries established by this Code.

(c) **Application Requirements.**
An institution seeking a license must submit a completed Form 8001-I (Institutional Licensing Application) to the Department of Magical Affairs (DMA). Applications must include the following:
(1) Entity Information. The legal name, location, and contact details of the institution.
(2) Declaration of Purpose. A detailed statement outlining the institution's intended use of magic, including:
(A) Specific schools of magic to be practiced (§ 101.1);
(B) Anticipated risks, including environmental impacts (§ 901.3);
(C) Any proposed use of qualified creatures (§ 101.6).
(3) Compliance Documentation. Evidence of compliance with applicable sections of this Code, including:
(A) Safety protocols for high-risk spells (§ 401.6);
(B) Accreditation under § 301.3, if applicable;
(C) Ethical guidelines for the use of magic (§ 701.1).
(4) Auditor Approval. A certification signed by an accredited magical auditor (§ 201.4) affirming that the institution has met all baseline requirements for operational safety and compliance.

(d) **Issuance of Licenses.**

The DMA Commissioner, or a designated representative, shall review the application and either approve or deny the request within ninety (90) days of receipt.
(1) Approval. Licenses are issued to institutions meeting all criteria. Approved institutions shall be listed in the public register maintained by the DMA.
(2) Denial. Applications may be denied for reasons including, but not limited to:
(A) Failure to demonstrate compliance with Code standards;
(B) Incomplete or falsified application materials;
(C) Past violations of magical ethics (§ 701.6).

(e) **Terms and Conditions.**
Institutional licenses are subject to the following terms:
(1) Duration. Licenses shall be valid for a period of five (5) years and may be renewed pursuant to subsection (g).
(2) Activity Restrictions. License holders may only perform magical activities explicitly authorized by their license.
(3) Compliance Reporting. Institutions must submit annual reports (Form 8002-C) detailing all magical activities conducted, including:
(A) Spells cast and categorized by risk level (§ 401.2);
(B) Any accidents, incidents, or compliance violations;
(C) Research outcomes or publications involving magic.

(f) **Special Provisions for High-Risk Entities.**
Entities conducting high-risk magical practices must adhere to additional requirements, including:
(1) Risk Mitigation Plans. Submission of a detailed plan to prevent environmental damage (§ 901.4) and protect public safety.
(2) Insurance Requirements. Proof of magical liability insurance with a minimum coverage of 10,000,000 MCUs for accidental or negligent damage.
(3) Enhanced Audits. Mandatory annual audits conducted by a certified magical auditor (§ 201.4).

(g) **Renewal of Licenses.**
To renew an institutional license, the institution must submit Form 8003-R (License Renewal Application) no later than ninety (90) days before the expiration of the current license. Renewal applications must include:
(1) Updated compliance documentation;

(2) A summary of activities performed under the current license;
(3) Evidence of successful completion of audits during the licensing period.

(h) **Revocation and Suspension of Licenses.**
Licenses may be revoked or suspended by the DMA for violations of this section, including:
(1) Failure to comply with reporting requirements;
(2) Use of unauthorized magic or negligent practices;
(3) Violation of ethical standards.

(i) **Appeals Process.**
Institutions whose licenses are revoked or denied may file an appeal with the Council of Councils.

(j) **Exemptions and Special Cases.**
Certain institutions may be exempt from full licensure requirements, including:
(1) Temporary Institutions. Organizations established for a limited duration, such as for magical disaster relief (§ 901.5).
(2) Cultural and Religious Entities. Institutions conducting ceremonial magic may be granted partial exemptions pursuant to this Code.

(k) **Cross-References.**
For licensing of individual practitioners, see § 201.1. For ethical standards, consult § 701.1. For environmental regulations, refer to § 901.4.

(l) **Historical Annotations.**
Enacted under C.C.D. 4324, 73 MR 2121, Thu. 15, 1934, to address unregulated magical academies. Amended under C.C.D. 8723, 89 MR 5012, Fri. 12, 2018, to include reporting requirements and enhanced audit protocols. Revised under C.C.D. 9834, 92 MR 6703, Wed. 2, 2024, to streamline the application process and clarify exemptions.

§ 201.8 Does Anybody Actually Read These Things

(a) **Purpose and Scope.**
In keeping with the relentless and unyielding demand for completeness within the Magical Code of Regulations, this section (though wholly unnecessary) has been included to fulfill the arbitrary mandate that no

part of the licensing framework shall appear incomplete or wanting. It exists solely because someone, somewhere, decided that gaps in numbering are an affront to logic and decency, even in times of crisis.

(b) **Acknowledgment of Futility.**
It must be acknowledged, in the plainest of terms, that the inclusion of § 201.8 is an act of pure administrative compulsion, devoid of practical necessity. It is a regulation without substance, a line item destined to be ignored, misfiled, or skimmed over by even the most diligent of auditors. Should any individual claim to have studied this section in its entirety, they are to be regarded with suspicion and pity.

(c) **Observations on Regulatory Excess.**
This section exists, not because it serves a purpose, but because the machinery of bureaucracy demands it. Its writer, worn down by the Great Quill Shortage of 1843, found themselves in the unenviable position of having to produce regulations at a time when ink was scarce, quills were rationed, and every moment spent writing was a moment spent questioning the point of it all. This regulation, then, is both a product and a casualty of its time – a testament to the absurd lengths to which governance will go to appear orderly amidst chaos.

(d) **Clarification of Intent.**
There is no intent here. There is no guidance, no actionable instruction, no clarification of policy. This section is a placeholder masquerading as a regulation, written not with conviction but with exhaustion. The only possible justification for its inclusion is that someone may someday point to its existence as evidence of the thoroughness of the Magical Code.

(e) **Advice to Readers.**
To any reader who has ventured this far: take a moment to reflect. Consider whether the time spent reading this section was well spent, or if it might have been better used elsewhere (perhaps in the pursuit of real knowledge, or in the study of regulations with actual relevance to magical practice). Let this be a cautionary tale about the perils of overregulation and the dangers of a quill left unchecked.

(f) **Conclusion.**
In conclusion, § 201.8 is a regulation in form only, devoid of content, purpose, or utility. It stands as a monument to the trials of the Great Quill Shortage, a time when ink was precious and patience was in short supply.

May it serve as a reminder that even in the most trying of times, bureaucracy will find a way to persevere, however pointless that perseverance may seem.

(g) **Cross-References.**
None, because this section serves no practical purpose and cannot be meaningfully related to any other regulation.

(h) **Historical Annotations.**
Added during the Great Quill Shortage of 1843, when the Council of Councils demanded uniform numbering despite the dire scarcity of resources. Amended slightly in 2024 to ensure it still conformed to modern formatting requirements, because even a pointless section must maintain appearances.

§ 201.9 Special Permits for Endangered Magical Traditions

(a) **Purpose and Scope.**
This section establishes the criteria, application procedures, and oversight requirements for the issuance of special permits authorizing the continued lawful practice of endangered magical traditions. For purposes of this section, the term endangered magical tradition means any historically recognized school, methodology, or lineage of magic that has been determined by the Council of Councils to be at risk of extinction due to:
(1) Diminished numbers of qualified practitioners;
(2) Loss of essential ritual knowledge;
(3) Depletion of necessary magical resources; or
(4) Legal prohibitions in other jurisdictions.

(b) **Eligibility Requirements.**
(1) Practitioner Qualifications. An applicant must:
(A) Demonstrate verifiable lineage or documented training within the endangered tradition;
(B) Possess a valid general license under § 201.1 or a limited license under § 202.1; and
(C) Have no record of license revocation or ethical violations under § 701.6 within the preceding ten (10) years.

(2) Tradition Certification. The magical tradition for which a permit is sought must:
(A) Be formally listed on the Registry of Endangered Magical Traditions maintained under this Code; or
(B) Be provisionally certified as endangered by the Commissioner of Magical Affairs upon recommendation from an accredited cultural preservation council, provided that:
(i) The recommending body is recognized under § 301.3; and
(ii) The recommendation includes historical, cultural, and safety justifications for preservation.

(c) **Application Procedures.**
(1) Submission Requirements. Applications shall be submitted on Form E-2719 (Special Permit Application for Endangered Magical Traditions) to the Department of Magical Affairs (DMA).
(2) Required Documentation. Each application must include:
(A) A complete historical account of the tradition, including origins, cultural significance, and known surviving practitioners;
(B) A description of all spells, rituals, and practices to be performed under the permit;
(C) Evidence of compliance with ethical and safety provisions under § 701.1 and § 401.6; and
(D) Proposed measures to ensure continuity, such as:
(i) Training apprentices in accordance with § 301.2; and
(ii) Recording ritual procedures in a form acceptable to the Council of Councils.
(3) Application Fee. A non-refundable application fee of 750 MCUs shall accompany all submissions.

(d) **Terms and Conditions of Permit.**
(1) Scope of Authorization. Each permit shall specify:
(A) Authorized spells, rituals, and practices;
(B) Geographic areas in which the tradition may be lawfully practiced; and
(C) Any limitations on the use of restricted materials or qualified creatures under § 101.6.
(2) Recordkeeping. All permitted activities must be logged in accordance with § 401.5, with copies submitted annually to the DMA for archival preservation.

(3) Compliance. Any deviation from the approved scope of practice constitutes a violation subject to penalties under § 102.2.

(e) **Renewal and Review.**
(1) Permits are valid for five (5) years and may be renewed by submitting Form E-2720 (Renewal Application for Endangered Tradition Permit) no later than ninety (90) days prior to expiration.
(2) Renewal requires:
(A) Demonstration of active preservation efforts;
(B) Continued compliance with all applicable provisions of this Code; and
(C) Submission of updated historical and instructional records.

(f) **Revocation.**
(1) Grounds for revocation include:
(A) Ethical violations under § 701.1;
(B) Unauthorized alteration of the tradition's practices in a manner that endangers public safety;
(C) Fraudulent misrepresentation in the permit application; or
(D) Cessation of practice for more than two (2) consecutive years without approved exemption under § 602.4.

(g) **Cross-References.**
For licensing requirements applicable to practitioners, see § 201.1. For cultural preservation protections, see § 2601.3. For ethical and safety standards, refer to § 701.1 and § 401.6. For regulations governing the use of restricted creatures and materials, see § 101.6.

(h) **Historical Annotations.**
Enacted under C.C.D. 7321, 85 MR 5624, Sun. 19, 1995, to safeguard declining magical traditions of cultural and historical significance. Amended under C.C.D. 9012, 90 MR 1183, Thu. 14, 2022, to expand eligibility criteria and strengthen preservation reporting requirements.

§ 202.1 Limited Licenses for Practitioners

(a) **Purpose and Scope.**
This section establishes the requirements, restrictions, and administrative procedures for the issuance of limited licenses to practitioners as defined in § 101.1(a)(3). A limited license authorizes the holder to perform specific, enumerated magical acts under regulated conditions, without

conferring full spellcasting privileges available to licensed spellcasters under § 201.1.

(b) **Eligibility Requirements.**
(1) General Qualifications. An applicant must:
(A) Be at least eighteen (18) years of age;
(B) Demonstrate basic competency in the proposed magical activity through documented training, apprenticeship, or examination; and
(C) Maintain a clean disciplinary record with no prior suspension or revocation of any magical authorization within the preceding five (5) years.
(2) Scope Limitation. The applicant must specify:
(A) The exact magical activities for which the license is sought; and
(B) The intended purpose of such activities, which must be consistent with lawful and ethical use under § 701.1.

(c) **Application Procedures.**
(1) Applications shall be submitted on Form 4938-L (Application for Limited Magical License) to the Department of Magical Affairs (DMA).
(2) Applications must include:
(A) Proof of training or competency under subsection (b)(1)(B);
(B) A detailed description of each magical act or practice to be authorized; and
(C) Any safety protocols, containment procedures, or ethical safeguards to be employed.
(3) A non-refundable application fee of 300 MCUs shall accompany all submissions.

(d) **Authorized Activities.**
(1) A limited license shall specify:
(A) Each authorized magical act;
(B) Any associated Schools of Magic as defined in § 101.1; and
(C) The geographic area or premises within which such acts may be performed.
(2) Activities not explicitly listed on the license are prohibited unless separately authorized by amendment under subsection (g).

(e) **Restrictions.**
(1) Holders of a limited license may not:
(A) Engage in high-risk spellcasting as defined in § 401.2(c);

(B) Perform original spell creation under § 1501.1; or
(C) Serve as a supervising authority for apprentice spellcasters under § 301.2.
(2) All licensed activities must be logged in accordance with § 401.5, with records maintained for a minimum of three (3) years.

(f) **Term and Renewal.**
(1) Limited licenses are valid for two (2) years from the date of issuance.
(2) Renewal requires submission of Form 4938-R (Limited License Renewal Application) no later than sixty (60) days before expiration, along with:
(A) Updated activity logs;
(B) Proof of continued competency; and
(C) Payment of a renewal fee of 300 MCUs.

(g) **Amendments.**
(1) License holders may request amendment to add or remove authorized activities by filing Form 4938-A (Amendment to Limited License).
(2) Amendments are subject to the same review process and eligibility requirements as the original application.

(h) **Revocation and Suspension.**
(1) A limited license may be suspended or revoked for:
(A) Violations of this Code, including ethical breaches under § 701.1;
(B) Repeated failure to maintain accurate logs under § 401.5; or
(C) Unauthorized performance of activities outside the scope of the license.

(i) **Cross-References.**
For definitions of practitioner, see § 101.1. For logging requirements, see § 401.5. For restrictions on high-risk magic, see § 401.2. For ethical standards, see § 701.1.

(j) **Historical Annotations.**
Originally enacted under C.C.D. 6214, 85 MR 4312, Thu. 8, 1997, to regulate limited magical practice for non-spellcasters. Amended under C.C.D. 8123, 90 MR 6732, Fri. 15, 2020, to expand eligibility and clarify application procedures.

Part III: Participation in Magical Educational Institutions

§ 301.1 Magical Educational Institutions: Definitions and Requirements

(a) **Definition of Magical Educational Institution.**
For purposes of this Code, a Magical Educational Institution is any organized entity, whether public or private, that provides structured instruction, supervised practice, research, assessment, or credentialing in one or more Schools of Magic enumerated in § 101.1. An entity shall be treated as a Magical Educational Institution upon engaging in recurring or scheduled magical instruction, irrespective of its name, legal form, governance structure, physical location, or asserted exemption. Instruction shall be considered structured where it is planned, supervised, evaluated, or documented in any manner suggesting continuity or institutional control.

(b) **Applicability and Institutional Status.**
This section shall apply to all Magical Educational Institutions upon the commencement of instructional activity involving regulated magical practices. Institutional status shall attach regardless of whether instruction is characterized as formal or informal, academic or traditional, theoretical or practical, experimental or foundational. An entity shall not avoid classification under this Part by limiting enrollment, restricting participation to a closed group, or asserting that instruction is incidental to another purpose.

(c) **Relationship to Active Participation.**
Active Participation, as defined in § 101.3, exists only where an individual is formally enrolled, appointed, apprenticed, or otherwise recorded by a Magical Educational Institution as participating in instruction or supervised magical activity.
(1) Active Participation shall be institution-specific and program-specific and shall exist only for the period reflected in institutional records.
(2) Active Participation shall terminate immediately upon graduation, withdrawal, suspension, dismissal, or expiration of institutional

authorization, regardless of whether instruction is incomplete or institutional materials remain outstanding.
(3) Each institution shall maintain contemporaneous records sufficient to establish the commencement, scope, and termination of Active Participation for each individual and shall make such records available for inspection upon request.

(d) **Institutional Requirements.**
A Magical Educational Institution shall satisfy the following requirements as a condition of lawful operation:
(1) Curriculum and Instructional Scope. The institution shall maintain a written curriculum identifying the Schools of Magic instructed and the general scope of instruction provided. Such curriculum shall distinguish between theoretical instruction, supervised practical instruction, and supervised spellcasting activities and shall identify the highest spell risk classification implicated by the instructional program under § 401.2.
(2) Instructional Personnel and Supervision. Instruction shall be conducted only by individuals who are authorized spellcasters under § 101.5 and properly licensed pursuant to Part II. The institution shall assign supervisory responsibility for each instructional activity and shall ensure that instructional personnel act within the scope of their licensure and institutional authorization.
(3) Licensing, Policies, and Recordkeeping. The institution shall obtain and maintain an institutional license under § 201.7 and shall remain subject to audit and review under § 201.4. The institution shall adopt written policies governing instructional standards, ethical conduct, reporting obligations, and disciplinary procedures consistent with Part VII and shall maintain records sufficient to demonstrate compliance with licensing, safety, and oversight requirements.
(4) Facilities, Safety, and Containment. Facilities, wards, safeguards, containment measures, and emergency procedures shall be appropriate to the highest level of spell risk instructed and shall be maintained in operational condition. Such measures shall be documented, periodically reviewed, and made available for inspection upon request.

(e) **Scope and Limitations of Instruction.**
A Magical Educational Institution may provide theoretical instruction, demonstrations, supervised spellcasting, and research activities only within the scope of its licensing and accreditation. Instruction involving restricted or high-risk magical practices shall require certification under §

201.5 and shall be subject to enhanced reporting, inspection, and oversight. No institution may confer authority upon students or participants to engage in independent spellcasting beyond that permitted by the individual's licensure, provisional status, or applicable exemptions under Part VI, and no institutional designation shall substitute for such authorization.

(f) **Institutional Resources and Access.**
Magical Educational Institutions may maintain libraries, laboratories, ritual spaces, instructional artifacts, and other resources necessary to support authorized instruction. Access to institutional resources shall be limited to Active Participants and authorized personnel and shall be conditioned upon continued compliance with institutional rules and this Code. Institutions shall ensure that institutional resources are not used to circumvent licensing, logging, reporting, or ethical requirements imposed elsewhere in this Code. Loss of Active Participation status shall immediately terminate access to institutional resources, notwithstanding any pending instructional activity.

(g) **Oversight and Compliance.**
Magical Educational Institutions shall be subject to inspection, audit, and enforcement pursuant to Part II and Part VII. Institutions shall cooperate fully with oversight authorities, including the timely production of curricula, records, policies, safety documentation, and compliance materials. Failure to comply with this section may result in suspension or revocation of accreditation under § 301.3, institutional licensing penalties under § 201.7, or both.

(h) **Cross-References.**
For definitions of Active Participation, see § 101.3. For authorized spellcasters, see § 101.5. For institutional licensing and audit requirements, see Part II. For accreditation standards, see § 301.3. For spell risk classifications applicable to instructional environments, see § 401.2. For ethical standards and oversight obligations, see Part VII.

(i) **Historical Annotations.**
This section was originally established under C.C.D. 9784, 81 MR 1823, and subsequently amended under C.C.D. 9921, 83 MR 3041, to clarify institutional responsibilities and the relationship between Magical Educational Institutions and Active Participation under § 101.3.

§ 301.2 Participation Requirements by Institution

(a) **General rule.**
Participation in a Magical Educational Institution shall be permitted only in accordance with the requirements of this section, § 301.1, and § 101.3. No individual may engage in instructional activities, supervised practice, or institutionally sanctioned spellcasting unless the individual has been granted participation status by the institution and such status is consistent with this Code.

(b) **Eligibility standards.**
Each Magical Educational Institution shall establish written eligibility standards governing participation in its instructional programs. Such standards shall address, at a minimum, prerequisites related to prior instruction or demonstrated competency, applicable licensing or provisional status under Part II, and any limitations inherent to the Schools of Magic instructed. Eligibility determinations shall be applied uniformly and documented in institutional records.

(c) **Enrollment and authorization.**
Participation shall commence only upon formal enrollment, appointment, apprenticeship, or other documented authorization issued by the institution. Authorization shall specify the scope of permitted participation, including whether participation is limited to observation, theoretical instruction, supervised practical work, or supervised spellcasting. Any expansion, reduction, or modification of authorized activities shall require updated documentation reflecting the revised scope.

(d) **Conditions of participation.**
Participation shall be conditioned upon compliance with institutional rules and policies, including safety protocols, instructional limitations, and ethical standards under Part VII. Institutions shall provide participants with written notice of such conditions and shall maintain records evidencing acknowledgment and acceptance. Conditions of participation may include limitations on locations, times, materials, or categories of magic in which the participant may engage.

(e) **Supervision requirements.**

Where participation involves practical instruction or spellcasting, the institution shall ensure that such activities occur under appropriate supervision by authorized instructional personnel. The level and immediacy of supervision shall correspond to the participant's licensure or provisional status and the risk classification of the activity under § 401.2. Institutions shall assign supervisory responsibility in advance and maintain records sufficient to demonstrate ongoing compliance.

(f) **Monitoring and ongoing compliance.**
Institutions shall monitor participant activity to ensure continued compliance with this Code and institutional policies. Where deficiencies, violations, or safety concerns are identified, the institution shall take corrective action, which may include additional supervision, restriction of activities, or remedial instruction. Monitoring activities and corrective actions shall be documented.

(g) **Suspension, restriction, and termination.**
An institution may suspend, restrict, or terminate participation for violations of institutional rules, this Code, or applicable licensing requirements. Such action may be taken immediately upon determination by the institution and shall not be delayed by pending instructional activities. Institutions shall document the basis for any suspension, restriction, or termination and shall update participation records accordingly.

(h) **Effect of loss of participation status.**
Loss of participation status shall immediately revoke any institutional authorization to access instructional resources, participate in supervised activities, or represent affiliation with the institution for purposes of this Code. Termination of participation shall not relieve the individual or the institution of reporting, recordkeeping, or compliance obligations arising from prior participation.

(i) **Cross-references.**
For definitions of Active Participation, see § 101.3. For institutional requirements, see § 301.1. For licensing and provisional participation requirements, see Part II. For spellcasting limitations and supervision standards, see Parts IV and VI. For ethical standards applicable to participants, see Part VII.

(j) **Historical annotations.**
This section was originally established under C.C.D. 9784, 81 MR 1823, and subsequently amended under C.C.D. 9915, 83 MR 2987, to clarify eligibility, authorization, supervision, and termination standards for participation in Magical Educational Institutions.

§ 301.3 Accreditation of Magical Educational Institutions

(a) **General requirement.**
No Magical Educational Institution may hold itself out as accredited, confer credentials, certify completion of instruction, or serve as the basis for Active Participation under § 101.3 unless such institution has been granted accreditation in accordance with this section.

(b) **Purpose and effect of accreditation.**
Accreditation under this section establishes that a Magical Educational Institution satisfies minimum standards of instructional integrity, safety, oversight, and administrative capacity sufficient to support regulated magical instruction. Accreditation shall be a condition precedent to institutional licensing under § 201.7 and to the recognition of participation, instruction, or credentials for purposes of this Code.

(c) **Accrediting authority.**
Accreditation shall be granted, denied, suspended, or revoked by the appropriate accrediting body designated by the Commissioner of Magical Affairs. Accrediting bodies shall operate pursuant to published standards and procedures and shall act independently of the institutions subject to accreditation.

(d) **Standards for accreditation.**
In determining whether to grant or maintain accreditation, the accrediting body shall evaluate, at a minimum, whether the institution demonstrates:
(1) administrative capacity sufficient to manage instructional programs, maintain records, and ensure compliance with this Code;
(2) instructional integrity, including the coherence, completeness, and consistency of curricula across the Schools of Magic instructed;
(3) qualifications and licensure of instructional personnel in accordance with § 101.5 and Part II;

(4) facilities, wards, safeguards, containment measures, and emergency procedures appropriate to the highest level of spell risk instructed under § 401.2; and
(5) policies and practices sufficient to enforce ethical standards under Part VII and to prevent circumvention of licensing, supervision, or reporting requirements.

(e) **Application and review process.**
An institution seeking accreditation shall submit an application in the form and manner prescribed by the accrediting body, together with such documentation as is necessary to demonstrate compliance with the standards of this section. The accrediting body may conduct inspections, request supplemental materials, require corrective actions, or impose conditions as part of its review. Accreditation determinations shall be made in writing and shall state the basis for approval, denial, or conditional approval.

(f) **Duration and continuing obligations.**
Accreditation shall remain in effect for the period specified by the accrediting body, subject to periodic review. An accredited institution shall remain in continuous compliance with the standards of this section and shall promptly report material changes affecting instructional scope, facilities, personnel, or governance. Failure to do so may constitute grounds for adverse action.

(g) **Suspension and revocation.**
An accrediting body may suspend or revoke accreditation upon a finding that the institution no longer satisfies the standards of this section, has materially misrepresented its operations, or has failed to correct identified deficiencies. Suspension or revocation shall take effect upon notice, notwithstanding any pending instructional activity, unless otherwise specified by the accrediting body.

(h) **Effect of loss of accreditation.**
Upon suspension or revocation of accreditation, an institution shall immediately cease representing itself as accredited and shall not confer credentials or support Active Participation under § 101.3. Loss of accreditation may result in institutional licensing consequences under § 201.7 and shall not relieve the institution of recordkeeping, reporting, or compliance obligations arising prior to such loss.

(i) **Cross-references.**
For institutional definitions and requirements, see § 301.1. For participation classifications affected by accreditation status, see § 301.2 and § 101.3. For institutional licensing and audit procedures, see Part II. For spell risk classifications relevant to accreditation standards, see § 401.2. For ethical oversight, see Part VII.

(j) **Historical annotations.**
This section was originally established under C.C.D. 9784, 81 MR 1823, and subsequently amended under C.C.D. 9946, 84 MR 3120, to formalize accreditation standards and to align institutional recognition with licensing and participation requirements under this Code.

§ 301.4 Dual Enrollment in Magical Educational Institutions

(a) **General rule.**
An individual may participate in instructional activities at more than one Magical Educational Institution during the same reporting period only in accordance with this section. Dual enrollment shall not be presumed permissible and shall be recognized solely to the extent documented, approved, and administered in compliance with this Code.

(b) **Definition of dual enrollment.**
For purposes of this section, dual enrollment means the simultaneous enrollment, appointment, apprenticeship, or other authorized participation of an individual in instructional programs at two or more Magical Educational Institutions, whether such participation is concurrent or overlapping in time.

(c) **Institutional authorization.**
Dual enrollment shall require express authorization by each participating Magical Educational Institution.
(1) Authorization shall be granted in writing and shall specify the scope of permitted instruction at each institution.
(2) Authorization shall identify the Schools of Magic involved, the nature of instruction provided, and any limitations imposed on participation.
(3) Absent such authorization, participation at a secondary institution shall be treated as unauthorized for purposes of this Code.

(d) **Coordination and supervision.**
Institutions authorizing dual enrollment shall coordinate supervision to ensure compliance with this Code.
(1) Each institution shall designate supervisory personnel responsible for monitoring the individual's activities within its instructional scope.
(2) Supervision shall be structured to prevent duplication of credit, supervision gaps, or circumvention of spellcasting limitations.
(3) Where instructional activities involve practical spellcasting, institutions shall ensure that supervision is proportionate to the highest spell risk classification implicated under § 401.2.

(e) **Participation classification.**
Dual enrollment shall not, by itself, establish Active Participation at either institution.
(1) Participation status shall be determined separately for each institution pursuant to § 301.2 and § 101.3.
(2) Activities conducted at one institution shall not be aggregated with activities at another institution for purposes of establishing Active Participation unless expressly permitted by this Code.
(3) An individual may be treated as an active participant at one institution and a non-active participant at another during the same reporting period.

(f) **Recordkeeping and reporting.**
Each institution participating in a dual enrollment arrangement shall maintain records sufficient to document authorization, instructional scope, supervision, and participation.
(1) Records shall identify the other participating institution and the period of authorized dual enrollment.
(2) Institutions shall make such records available for inspection or audit upon request.
(3) Failure to maintain or produce required records may result in adverse participation determinations.

(g) **Restrictions and limitations.**
Dual enrollment shall not be used to circumvent licensing requirements, spellcasting limitations, ethical obligations, or reporting requirements under this Code.
(1) No individual may engage in instructional or spellcasting activities at one institution on the basis of authorization granted by another.

(2) Dual enrollment shall not permit access to restricted resources, ley lines, or artifacts except as expressly authorized by each institution.

(h) **Suspension or termination of dual enrollment.**
An institution may suspend or terminate its authorization of dual enrollment upon a determination that continued participation would result in noncompliance with this Code or institutional policy.
(1) Suspension or termination shall take effect upon notice.
(2) Termination by one institution shall not obligate another institution to continue authorization.

(i) **Effect of unauthorized dual enrollment.**
Participation conducted without proper authorization under this section shall be treated as unauthorized instructional activity.
(1) Such activity shall not be recognized for purposes of participation classification, credentialing, or licensing.
(2) Unauthorized dual enrollment may give rise to institutional and individual penalties under applicable provisions of this Code.

(j) **Cross-References.**
For institutional requirements, see § 301.1. For participation classification, see § 301.2 and § 101.3. For accreditation requirements, see § 301.3. For licensing and provisional participation, see Part II. For spell risk classifications and supervision standards, see § 401.2.

(k) **Historical Annotations.**
This section was originally established under C.C.D. 9961, 84 MR 3287, to regulate simultaneous participation in multiple Magical Educational Institutions and to prevent circumvention of participation, supervision, and licensing requirements.

§ 301.5 Grouping of Activities

(a) **General rule.**
For purposes of determining participation status, supervision obligations, eligibility for institutionally sanctioned activities, and the application of requirements under § 101.3 and § 301.2, a Magical Educational Institution may require that instructional, research, and supervised practical activities be grouped and treated as a single aggregated activity, or as multiple separate activities, in accordance with this section.

(b) **Purpose and effect.**
Grouping under this section is intended to ensure that participation determinations reflect the substantive nature of an individual's involvement in institutional activity and to prevent fragmentation, duplication, or recharacterization of activities for purposes of obtaining favorable participation status, access to restricted resources, or other regulatory effects.
(1) Grouping affects the classification of participation under § 301.2 and the application of the Active Participation standard under § 101.3.
(2) Grouping under this section shall not modify any licensing requirement under Part II or any spell risk classification under § 401.2.

(c) **Definitions.**
For purposes of this section:
(1) Activity. An activity means a discrete set of institutionally sanctioned functions, including instruction, supervised practice, research, assessment, laboratory work, field study, or supervised spellcasting, that is carried on within an instructional program or administrative unit of a Magical Educational Institution.
(2) Grouping. Grouping means the treatment of two or more activities as a single activity for purposes of participation determination, logging, supervision assignment, and compliance evaluation.
(3) Appropriate economic and instructional unit. An appropriate economic and instructional unit is the grouping configuration that most clearly reflects the manner in which the institution organizes, manages, supervises, evaluates, and records the activity of participants.

(d) **Permissible grouping standards.**
An institution may group activities only to the extent the grouping constitutes an appropriate economic and instructional unit based on all facts and circumstances. In determining whether activities form an appropriate unit, the institution shall consider, among other factors:
(1) Common control and supervision. Whether the activities are subject to common supervisory personnel, common evaluation standards, or common oversight mechanisms.
(2) Common curriculum or program. Whether the activities are conducted pursuant to a unified curriculum, credential track, or instructional program.

(3) Common location and facilities. Whether the activities are conducted within shared facilities, wards, laboratories, instructional spaces, or containment environments.
(4) Interdependence of functions. Whether the activities are interdependent, including whether completion or performance in one activity is prerequisite to, integrated with, or functionally necessary for the performance of another.
(5) Common recordkeeping. Whether participation, supervision, and compliance are recorded and maintained in a common institutional record system pursuant to § 301.1 and § 301.2.
(6) Spell risk alignment. Whether the activities are reasonably similar with respect to spell risk classification under § 401.2 and the supervisory and containment requirements associated with such classification.
(7) Consistency with institutional operations. Whether the grouping is consistent with the institution's ordinary administrative and instructional operations and is not adopted primarily to achieve a participation classification outcome.

(e) **Required grouping in certain cases.**
An institution shall group activities where separation would materially distort participation classification or permit circumvention of this Code. Required grouping includes the following:
(1) Integrated program requirement. Activities forming a single credential track or instructional program that is designed and administered as an integrated unit shall be grouped unless the institution demonstrates that separate treatment is necessary to preserve accurate supervision or risk management.
(2) Shared supervision requirement. Activities conducted under the same designated supervisor, or supervisory chain, and evaluated under a unified standard shall be grouped unless separation is necessary due to materially different spell risk classifications.
(3) Anti-fragmentation rule. Activities shall be grouped where separation would have the principal effect of converting Non-Active Participation into Active Participation under § 101.3, or of creating duplicative participation credit across activities that are, in substance, a single instructional undertaking.

(f) **Prohibited grouping.**

An institution shall not group activities where grouping would undermine supervision, conceal risk, or obscure compliance responsibility. Prohibited grouping includes:
(1) grouping of activities across materially different spell risk classifications where such grouping would reduce or confuse required safeguards, containment, or supervision;
(2) grouping of instructional activity with non-instructional administrative activity where such grouping would improperly inflate participation time or scope;
(3) grouping adopted or modified retroactively for the principal purpose of avoiding an adverse participation determination, audit finding, disciplinary action, or licensing consequence; and
(4) grouping that combines activities conducted within an accredited scope under § 301.3 with activities outside the accredited scope.

(g) **Elections and consistency requirements.**
An institution that adopts a grouping configuration for an instructional program shall apply such grouping consistently for all similarly situated participants and for all relevant reporting periods, unless a material change occurs.
(1) A material change includes a substantial change in curriculum, governance, facilities, supervision structure, accreditation scope under § 301.3, or spell risk classification under § 401.2.
(2) A change in grouping shall not be effective unless documented contemporaneously in institutional records and applied prospectively beginning with the next reporting period, except where immediate modification is required to address safety, containment, or supervision failures.
(3) An institution shall maintain documentation sufficient to substantiate the basis for grouping determinations and changes thereto.

(h) **Election to Group Activities.**
(1) In General. A practitioner may elect to treat one or more activities as a single activity for purposes of this Code. An election under this subsection shall apply only if made in accordance with this paragraph.
(2) Manner of Making Election. An election under this subsection shall be made by the practitioner by clearly identifying the activities to be grouped and by making a declaration containing the statement set forth in paragraph (h)(3). Such declaration shall be made in such form and manner as the Department of Magical Affairs may prescribe and shall be

included with or attached to any filing, record, or other documentation required under this Code for the period to which the election relates.
(3) Required Statement. A declaration under this subsection shall include the following statement, without material modification:
"I hereby elect, pursuant to §301.5 of the Magical Code of Regulations, to treat the identified activities as a single activity, and I represent that such activities constitute an appropriate grouping under this section."
(4) Time for Making Election. An election under this subsection shall be made contemporaneously with, or not later than, the time prescribed for the filing of the return, report, or other documentation for the period to which the election relates.
(5) Failure to Make Election. If a practitioner does not make an election in accordance with this subsection, each activity shall be treated as a separate activity for all purposes of this Code.
(6) Binding Nature of Election. An election made under this subsection shall be binding for the period to which it applies and for all subsequent periods in which the grouped activities are carried on, unless the practitioner establishes that a material change in facts and circumstances has occurred or the Department permits a change in grouping.

(i) **Interaction with dual enrollment.**
Grouping under this section applies only within a single Magical Educational Institution and shall not aggregate activities across institutions. For dual enrollment rules, see § 301.4.
(1) Activities conducted at separate institutions shall be treated as separate activities for participation purposes, regardless of similarity, coordination, or joint programming, unless another provision of this Code expressly provides otherwise.
(2) An institution shall not rely upon activities at another institution to substantiate participation, supervision, or compliance within its own records.

(j) **Recordkeeping and disclosure.**
Each institution applying grouping shall maintain records describing the grouping configuration, the activities included, the supervisory assignments, and the basis for the grouping determination.
(1) Such records shall be retained in accordance with institutional recordkeeping obligations under § 301.1 and shall be made available upon request in connection with audits under § 201.4 or oversight under Part VII.

(2) Where grouping affects participation status under § 301.2 or the availability of benefits under § 101.3, the institution shall reflect the grouping in the participant's participation records for the applicable reporting period.

(k) **Authority to recharacterize.**
The Commissioner of Magical Affairs, or an authorized accrediting or auditing authority acting pursuant to Part II or Part VII, may recharacterize, disregard, or require modification of any grouping arrangement that is inconsistent with this section.
(1) A recharacterization may be applied for purposes of participation classification, audit findings, eligibility determinations, and enforcement actions.
(2) The existence of institutional documentation shall not preclude recharacterization where the grouping does not reflect the institution's actual operations or is inconsistent with the facts and circumstances.

(l) **Cross-References.**
For definitions and general requirements applicable to Magical Educational Institutions, see § 301.1. For participation requirements and institutional participation records, see § 301.2. For accreditation scope limitations, see § 301.3. For dual enrollment limitations, see § 301.4. For Active Participation standards, see § 101.3. For spell risk classifications relevant to grouping and supervision, see § 401.2. For audits and inspections, see § 201.4. For ethical oversight, see Part VII.

(m) **Historical Annotations.**
This section was originally established under C.C.D. 9968, 84 MR 3379, and subsequently amended under C.C.D. 9973, 84 MR 3512, to standardize grouping methodology, impose anti-fragmentation rules, and authorize recharacterization of grouping arrangements inconsistent with institutional operations and participation requirements under this Code.

Part IV: Spellcasting Regulations

§ 401.1 Spellcasting Licenses and Classification of Spells

(a) **General Rule.**
Except as otherwise provided in this Code, no Magical Legal Person shall cast, attempt to cast, assist in casting, or materially facilitate the casting of any regulated spell within the jurisdiction of the MCOR unless such person holds a valid and active spellcasting license issued pursuant to Part II.
For purposes of this section, a "regulated spell" means any intentional manipulation of arcane, elemental, spiritual, cognitive, transfigurative, temporal, or analogous forces designed to produce a material, perceptible, or legally cognizable effect beyond naturally occurring phenomena.

(b) **Scope of License.**
(1) A spellcasting license authorizes only those spells within the scope and proficiency level expressly granted under Part II.
(2) A license does not authorize the casting of any spell assigned a risk level under § 401.2 that exceeds the holder's approved classification.
(3) Nothing in this section shall be construed to supersede other restrictions imposed by this Part.

(c) **Classification of Spells.**
All regulated spells shall be classified according to both school of magic and assigned level of risk.
(1) School of Magic.
Each spell shall be categorized according to its primary school of magic as recognized under the applicable Part governing Schools of Magic. Where a spell implicates multiple schools, classification shall be determined by the dominant operational effect.
(2) Risk Level.
Each spell shall be assigned a level of risk pursuant to § 401.2. The assigned risk level governs eligibility for performance under a given license.

(d) **Misclassification.**

(1) Knowingly misrepresenting a spell's school or assigned risk level for purposes of avoiding licensure requirements constitutes a violation of this section.
(2) Where a spell is cast under an asserted risk level lower than that properly assigned under § 401.2, the casting shall be treated as unauthorized to the extent the license does not permit the higher risk level.

(e) **Declared Invocation and Citation Requirement for Designated Spells.**
(1) General Rule. No practitioner shall cast or attempt to cast any spell designated under this subsection unless such practitioner expressly declares the spell and the legal authority under which such spell is cast.
(2) Manner of Declaration. The declaration required under paragraph (1) shall—
(A) identify the spell being cast;
(B) identify the specific provision of this Code authorizing such casting; and
(C) be made contemporaneously with the initiation of the spell using formal statutory language, including but not limited to "pursuant to," "in accordance with," or "as authorized under."
(3) Fireball Codification. The spell commonly known as "Fireball," including any substantially similar explosive or area-of-effect combustion spell, shall be subject to the requirements of this subsection.
(4) Sufficiency of Citation. A declaration under this subsection shall be sufficient only if a reasonable person would be able to identify the legal basis for the casting from the statement made.
(5) Failure to Properly Invoke Authority. Failure to comply with the requirements of this subsection shall constitute a violation of this Code, regardless of whether the practitioner would otherwise be authorized to cast the spell.
(6) Illustrative Example. A compliant declaration under this subsection may include a statement substantially similar to:
"In accordance with §601.1 of the Magical Code of Regulations, I cast Fireball."

(f) **Unauthorized Spellcasting.**
(1) Casting a regulated spell without a valid and active license constitutes unlicensed spellcasting.
(2) Each separate casting event constitutes a separate violation.

(3) Casting a spell assigned a high-risk designation under § 401.2 without appropriate licensure constitutes an aggravated violation.

(g) **Penalties for Non-Compliance.**
A person who violates this section shall be subject to one or more of the following:
(1) Immediate suspension of spellcasting privileges;
(2) Revocation of spellcasting licensure;
(3) Mandatory retraining and re-examination prior to reinstatement of licensure;
(4) Temporary or permanent prohibition on casting spells above a specified risk level.

(h) **Cross-References.**
For assignment of spell risk levels, see § 401.2. For issuance, scope, suspension, and revocation of spellcasting licenses, see Part II.

(i) **Historical Annotations.**
Enacted under C.C.D. 6892, 94 MR 3107, Tue. 9, 1884, to establish unified licensure requirements for regulated spellcasting and to formalize dual classification by school of magic and assigned risk level pursuant to § 401.2.

§ 401.2 Levels of Spell Risk and Complexity

(a) **Requirement of Risk Classification.**
All spellcasting, enchanted activities, ritual operations, magical conveyance, artifact activation, environmental manipulation, or other conduct constituting "magic" within the meaning of § 101.1 shall be properly classified by risk level prior to initiation, authorization, supervision, or facilitation.

No magical activity shall commence unless and until a risk classification has been affirmatively assigned and documented in accordance with this section.

Failure to classify an activity as required under this subsection shall constitute a violation of § 101.7.

(b) **Standard of Determination.**

Risk level shall be determined based upon the totality of the circumstances, including but not limited to:
(1) The foreseeability of bodily injury, property damage, ecological disruption, or thaumic instability.
(2) The magnitude of potential harm in the event of malfunction, instability, or loss of control.
(3) The degree of operational control reasonably expected during ordinary use.
(4) The involvement of unlicensed, provisional, supervised, or otherwise vulnerable practitioners.
(5) The use of enchanted objects subject to Part VIII.
(6) The environmental context in which the activity occurs, including the presence or absence of containment measures.
(7) Any prior documented incidents, instability reports, enforcement findings, or corrective actions involving substantially similar activities.

No single factor shall be determinative. Classification shall not depend upon the subjective confidence, intent, or reputation of the spellcaster.

(c) **Risk Categories.**
(1) Level I. Minimal Risk.
A spell shall be classified as low-risk where, under ordinary execution and reasonably foreseeable variance, it presents no material probability of bodily injury, property damage, ecological disruption, metaphysical instability, cascading thaumic interference, or irreversible consequence.
(A) In determining whether a spell qualifies as low-risk, relevant considerations include:
(i) Whether the operative mechanism remains fully within the immediate and continuous control of the spellcaster;
(ii) Whether the effect terminates upon cessation of will, incantation, or channeling;
(iii) Whether the spell produces no autonomous, semi-autonomous, or self-sustaining manifestation;
(iv) Whether the spell does not materially alter identity, personhood, temporality, probability, causation, biological integrity, or metaphysical continuity;
(v) Whether the spell does not propagate beyond its intended subject, object, or locus of effect;
(vi) Whether the spell does not materially interact with ambient magical fields in a manner capable of amplification or destabilization.

(B) A spell shall not be classified as low-risk solely by virtue of familiarity, frequency of use, instructional context, cultural tradition, or absence of prior enforcement.
(C) Where a spell classified as low-risk produces instability or collateral consequence under reasonably foreseeable conditions, reclassification under paragraph (2) or (3) shall be required.
(2) Level II. Intermediate Risk.
A spell shall be classified as intermediate-level where, absent baseline safeguards consistent with § 401.6, it presents a foreseeable risk of instability, unintended propagation, collateral consequence, localized harm, or material interference with persons, property, environment, or existing enchantments.
(A) Classification under this subsection is appropriate where one or more of the following factors are present:
(i) The spell alters physical form, elemental balance, biological condition, environmental state, arcane structure, or constructed enchantment in a non-trivial manner;
(ii) The spell produces effects that persist beyond the moment of casting;
(iii) The spell interacts with existing wards, enchantments, constructs, ley lines, or ambient magical infrastructure;
(iv) The spell requires sustained concentration, phased execution, delayed triggering, or conditional activation;
(v) The spell produces effects capable of influencing non-consenting persons within its operative sphere;
(vi) The spell involves bounded probability manipulation, limited temporal alteration, or contingent causal modification.
(B) Multiple low-risk spells executed in coordinated sequence, unified design, or cumulative ritual shall be classified as intermediate where their combined effect materially increases foreseeable instability or consequence.
(C) In any enforcement, civil, or administrative proceeding, the burden of demonstrating that a spell meeting the criteria of this subsection qualifies as low-risk rests with the responsible spellcaster and must be supported by contemporaneous documentation.
(3) Level III. High Risk.
A spell shall be classified as high-risk where, absent enhanced safeguards, it presents a foreseeable risk of serious bodily injury, structural destabilization, large-scale ecological imbalance, metaphysical fragmentation, systemic interference, irreversible alteration, or cascading consequence beyond localized containment.

(A) Classification under this subsection is appropriate where:
(i) The spell materially alters identity, memory, consciousness, soul-binding status, metaphysical continuity, or personhood;
(ii) The spell manipulates temporality beyond isolated, reversible, or narrowly confined bounds;
(iii) The spell alters probability, causation, or fate in a manner capable of cascading systemic effect;
(iv) The spell materially disrupts life-force thresholds, resurrection parameters, or existential stability;
(v) The spell produces autonomous, semi-autonomous, or self-propagating manifestations;
(vi) The spell has a documented history of catastrophic misuse, structural instability, or enforcement intervention.
(B) Any spell whose effects cannot be reasonably reversed, terminated, or mitigated through ordinary restorative or containment magic shall be presumed high-risk.
(C) The burden of rebutting high-risk classification rests with the responsible spellcaster and must be supported by technical analysis, precedent, and documented compliance history.

(d) **Documentation and Presumption.**
Risk classification required under subsection (a) shall be documented in accordance with § 401.5. Failure to document classification creates a rebuttable presumption that the spell was at least intermediate-level. In civil or administrative proceedings, absence of documentation shall be admissible as evidence of non-compliance.

(e) **Aggregation.**
Magical activities substantially connected by operational purpose, shared enchanted devices, supervisory authority, or temporal proximity shall be aggregated for classification purposes. Artificial segmentation to reduce risk level shall constitute circumvention under § 702.2.

(f) **Cross-References.**
For logging requirements, see § 401.5. For reasonable care, see § 101.7. For restricted or prohibited practices, see § 201.5.

(g) **Historical Annotations.**
Established under C.C.D. 4102, 86 MR 1197, Wed. 9, 1996, following widespread noncompliance arising from inconsistent institutional

classification practices and the routine mischaracterization of hazardous spells as "ordinary" or "traditional." Amended under C.C.D. 4776, 89 MR 2330, Tue. 18, 2004, to clarify burden allocation and aggregation principles. Amended under C.C.D. 5320, 94 MR 2011, Fri. 3, 2026, to address compounded-risk casting, ambient field amplification, and classification disputes involving hybridized schools of magic.

§ 401.3 Spellcasting in Public Areas

(a) **General Rule.**
No person shall cast, attempt to cast, or materially facilitate the casting of a regulated spell in a Public Area unless such casting is (1) authorized under § 401.1, and (2) permissible under the assigned risk level pursuant to § 401.2.
For purposes of this section, a "Public Area" means any location open to, accessible by, or reasonably foreseeable to be entered by members of the public, including streets, marketplaces, plazas, transportation corridors, publicly accessible buildings, and privately owned premises held open to public use.

(b) **Risk-Based Limitations.**
(1) Spells assigned a low-risk designation under § 401.2 may be cast in a Public Area provided that the casting does not create unreasonable risk of bodily harm, property damage, magical contamination, or public disruption.
(2) Spells assigned an intermediate-risk designation may be cast in a Public Area only where reasonable containment, stabilization, and safety precautions are implemented prior to casting.
(3) Spells assigned a high-risk designation shall not be cast in a Public Area unless:
(A) The area has been temporarily restricted or secured; or
(B) The casting is necessary to prevent imminent harm and no reasonable alternative exists.

(c) **Foreseeability and Precaution.**
(1) A person casting a regulated spell in a Public Area shall assess foreseeable secondary effects, including ricochet discharge, residual enchantment, structural instability, sensory distortion, panic response, or unintended summoning.

(2) The failure to take reasonable precautions proportional to the spell's assigned risk level constitutes a violation of this section independent of actual harm.

(d) **Prohibited Conduct.**
(1) No person shall knowingly cast a spell in a Public Area in a manner likely to incite panic, mass confusion, stampede conditions, or uncontrolled magical amplification.
(2) No person shall cast a spell in a Public Area while impaired, distracted, experiencing recent heartbreak, emotionally destabilized, or otherwise incapable of exercising reasonable magical control.
(3) No person shall conduct experimental, untested, or materially modified spellcasting in a Public Area.

(e) **Permits and Temporary Authorizations.**
(1) A person may obtain written authorization to conduct otherwise restricted spellcasting in a Public Area where:
(A) The spell is assigned an intermediate or high-risk classification; and
(B) Adequate safeguards, barriers, or evacuation protocols are documented in advance.
(2) Temporary authorization does not exempt the holder from compliance with § 401.1 or § 401.2.

(f) **Strict Liability for Collateral Effects.**
Where a regulated spell cast in a Public Area produces collateral magical discharge affecting third parties, the casting party shall be presumed responsible for such discharge unless it is demonstrated that the effect resulted solely from external interference beyond reasonable control.

(g) **Penalties for Non-Compliance.**
A person who violates this section shall be subject to one or more of the following:
(1) Immediate suspension of authorization to cast spells in Public Areas;
(2) Restriction to lower-risk classifications;
(3) Revocation of spellcasting licensure in cases of repeated or aggravated violations.

(h) **Cross-References.**
For general licensure requirements, see § 401.1. For risk level assignments, see § 401.2.

(i) **Historical Annotations.**
Enacted under C.C.D. 7021, 94 MR 3321, Sat. 3, 1886, to regulate spellcasting in publicly accessible spaces and to impose risk-proportional safeguards consistent with § 401.2.

§ 401.4 Use of Magical Objects and Artifacts in Spellcasting

(a) **General Rule.**
No person shall employ, activate, deploy, channel through, or materially rely upon any magical object, artifact, conduit, focus, amplification device, enchanted implement, pre-loaded construct, or stored enchantment in connection with the casting of a regulated spell unless such use is authorized under § 401.1 and consistent with the assigned risk level under § 401.2.
For purposes of this section, an "artifact" includes any object that:
(1) Stores magical energy;
(2) Amplifies spell output;
(3) Automates execution of a spell;
(4) Conditions activation upon a trigger; or
(5) Replicates a spell effect without contemporaneous incantation.

(b) **Effective Risk Reclassification.**
(1) Where the use of an artifact increases the magnitude, duration, propagation radius, persistence, volatility, or secondary interaction potential of a spell, the spell shall be evaluated according to its effective risk level after amplification.
(2) A spell otherwise classified as low or intermediate risk shall be treated as reclassified if the artifact materially increases:
(A) destructive capacity;
(B) likelihood of uncontrolled discharge;
(C) cross-planar or cross-domain interaction;
(D) duration beyond originally authorized parameters; or
(E) replication or autonomous activation capacity.
(3) In determining effective risk level, the totality of circumstances shall be considered, including foreseeable cascading effects and environmental context.
(4) The burden of demonstrating that artifact use does not elevate the effective risk classification rests with the license holder.

(c) **Automation and Conditional Execution.**
(1) A spell cast through automated, delayed, conditional, reactive, or pre-programmed artifact mechanisms shall be treated as occurring at the time of activation.
(2) Pre-loading, encoding, or programming a spell into an artifact constitutes regulated spellcasting activity under § 401.1.
(3) Repeated automated activations shall not be treated as a single event where each activation produces a discrete magical effect.
(4) Delegation of activation authority does not relieve the license holder of responsibility unless expressly authorized under the scope of licensure.

(d) **Modification and Safety Controls.**
(1) Any material modification to an artifact that alters its output, containment integrity, activation parameters, or safety thresholds shall require reevaluation of risk classification prior to use.
(2) Use of a modified artifact without reassessment constitutes a violation independent of the underlying spellcasting event.
(3) Removal, bypassing, or disabling of built-in containment or stabilization mechanisms shall create a rebuttable presumption of reckless conduct.
(4) Failure to inspect an artifact where degradation, instability, or magical drift would be reasonably foreseeable constitutes non-compliance under this section.

(e) **Distribution and Transfer.**
(1) Transfer of an artifact containing a stored intermediate or high-risk spell to an unlicensed individual constitutes a separate violation under this Part.
(2) Commercial manufacture, sale, lease, barter, export, or other transfer for value of enchanted objects capable of performing regulated spells shall be treated as ongoing spellcasting activity for purposes of this Part.
(3) In addition to liability under this section, distribution of such artifacts may constitute a regulated trade in magical assets and shall be subject to applicable provisions of Part X governing magical commerce, valuation, disclosure, and lawful transfer.
(4) A person may not fragment, componentize, mislabel, or otherwise structure artifact transactions for the primary purpose of avoiding risk classification or trade compliance requirements.

(f) **Anti-Circumvention Rule.**

No person shall structure, divide, automate, stagger, or otherwise manipulate artifact-assisted spellcasting for the primary purpose of avoiding reassignment of risk level under § 401.2 or compliance obligations under this Part.

(g) **Penalties for Non-Compliance.**
A person who violates this section shall be subject to one or more of the following:
(1) Confiscation of the artifact used in violation;
(2) Suspension of authorization to use amplification devices;
(3) Restriction to non-artifact spellcasting;
(4) Revocation of spellcasting licensure in cases involving reckless, commercial-scale, or repeated misuse.

(h) **Cross-References.**
For general licensure requirements, refer to § 401.1. For risk level assignments, consult § 401.2. For recordkeeping, see § 401.5. For trade regulation of magical assets, refer to Part X.

(i) **Historical Annotations.**
Enacted under C.C.D. 7154, 94 MR 4012, Thu. 21, 1887, to regulate amplified and automated spellcasting. Revised under C.C.D. 7391, 95 MR 621, Thu. 4, 1891, to incorporate risk reclassification and anti-circumvention standards. Further amended under C.C.D. 8022, 96 MR 1448, Wed. 17, 1899, to address commercial distribution of enchanted artifacts and integration with trade regulations under Part IX.

§ 401.5 Spell Logging Requirements by Risk Level

(a) **General Requirement.**
Any person casting a regulated spell assigned an intermediate or high-risk designation under § 401.2 shall create and maintain contemporaneous records sufficient to demonstrate compliance with this Part and with the scope of licensure under § 401.1.
For purposes of this section, "contemporaneous" means created at or near the time of casting and prior to the occurrence of any inquiry, investigation, enforcement action, or dispute relating to the spell.

(b) **Timing of Record Creation.**

(1) A required log entry shall be initiated prior to commencement of casting where practicable.
(2) In all cases, the log entry shall be completed no later than the close of the same calendar day on which the spell was cast.
(3) For high-risk spells, failure to initiate documentation prior to casting shall create a rebuttable presumption of non-compliance.
(4) Post hoc reconstruction of records after notice of inquiry shall not satisfy the contemporaneous requirement.

(c) **Minimum Required Content.**
Each contemporaneous log entry shall include:
(1) Date and precise time of casting;
(2) Location of casting;
(3) Assigned school of magic;
(4) Risk level under § 401.2;
(5) Description of intended effect;
(6) Identification of artifacts or amplification devices used under § 401.4;
(7) Description of containment, stabilization, or mitigation measures;
(8) Description of observed secondary or collateral effects within twenty-four hours;
(9) Duration of spell persistence, where applicable.

(d) **Aggregation and Anti-Fragmentation Rule.**
(1) Multiple low-risk spells cast in coordinated sequence that collectively produce an intermediate or high-risk outcome shall be treated as a single higher-risk activity for logging purposes.
(2) Fragmentation, staggering, or structuring of spell components for the primary purpose of avoiding contemporaneous logging requirements constitutes an independent violation.
(3) Aggregation determinations shall consider timing, intent, cumulative effect, and shared objective.

(e) **De Minimis Exception.**
(1) Isolated intermediate-risk spells producing no material collateral effect and lasting less than one hour may qualify for abbreviated contemporaneous logging.
(2) Abbreviated entries must still be created contemporaneously and include date, risk level, and general description of effect.
(3) The de minimis exception shall not apply to spells cast in Public Areas under § 401.3 or artifact-assisted spells under § 401.4.

(f) **Safe Harbor for Technical Defects.**
(1) A contemporaneous record shall not be treated as non-compliant solely by reason of minor technical omissions if the record, taken as a whole, substantially satisfies subsection (c).
(2) The safe harbor shall not apply where omissions conceal material risk reassignment, artifact amplification, or collateral effects.
(3) Correction of minor defects within thirty days of discovery shall not defeat contemporaneous status if the original record was timely created.

(g) **Substantial Compliance Doctrine.**
(1) Substantial compliance may satisfy this section only where contemporaneous documentation exists and reasonably reflects the spellcasting activity.
(2) Substantial compliance shall not apply where records were created after inquiry, fabricated, materially altered, or intentionally delayed.

(h) **Retention and Availability.**
(1) Required logs shall be retained for not less than seven years from the date of casting.
(2) Logs shall be maintained in a durable and reproducible format.
(3) Failure to produce contemporaneous records upon lawful request creates a rebuttable presumption of non-compliance.

(i) **Reasonable Cause Exception.**
No penalty shall be imposed under subsection (k) if the license holder demonstrates that failure to create contemporaneous records was due to reasonable cause and not willful neglect. Administrative oversight, emotional distraction, or routine workload shall not constitute reasonable cause.

(j) **Falsification and Retroactive Creation.**
(1) Knowingly altering, destroying, fabricating, or retroactively creating records to simulate contemporaneous compliance constitutes an aggravated violation.
(2) Aggravated violations preclude reliance on safe harbor, de minimis, or substantial compliance provisions.

(k) **Penalties for Non-Compliance.**
A person who violates this section shall be subject to one or more of the following:

(1) Mandatory compliance review or audit under Part II;
(2) Temporary suspension of authorization to cast intermediate or high-risk spells;
(3) Restriction to supervised spellcasting;
(4) Revocation of spellcasting licensure in cases of willful or repeated non-compliance.

(l) **Cross-References.**
For general licensure requirements governing spellcasting authority, refer to § 401.1. For assignment and interpretation of risk levels, consult § 401.2. For restrictions applicable to spellcasting in Public Areas, see § 401.3. For compliance obligations relating to artifact-assisted spellcasting, refer to § 401.4. For audit authority and compliance review procedures, consult § 201.4. For ethical compliance standards and professional conduct requirements, see § 701.1.

(m) **Historical Annotations.**
Enacted under C.C.D. 7302, 94 MR 5128, Thu. 14, 1889, to establish contemporaneous recordkeeping requirements for intermediate and high-risk spellcasting. Revised under C.C.D. 7544, 95 MR 1132, Fri. 6, 1894, to incorporate aggregation rules and safe harbor provisions. Further revised under C.C.D. 8112, 97 MR 2044, Thu. 18, 1902, to codify substantial compliance and reasonable cause standards.

§ 401.6 Safeguards and Proportional Compliance Obligations

(a) **General Duty of Proportional Safeguards.**
All magical activity classified under § 401.2 shall be conducted with safeguards proportionate to its assigned risk level. The scope, intensity, redundancy, and documentation of safeguards shall increase commensurately with classification level.

Failure to implement safeguards proportionate to risk constitutes a breach of reasonable care under § 101.7, irrespective of whether actual harm results.

(b) **Baseline Safeguards Applicable to All Magical Activity.**
For all spells, regardless of classification, the responsible spellcaster shall:

(1) Possess licensure, qualification, or authorization appropriate to the school of magic involved;
(2) Verify operative stability prior to initiation;
(3) Maintain the ability to terminate, withdraw, or counteract the spell where reasonably possible;
(4) Assess environmental conditions reasonably likely to affect spell performance;
(5) Refrain from execution where material instability is apparent.
Failure to satisfy this subsection shall constitute noncompliance independent of classification level.

(c) **Additional Safeguards for Level II Activity.**
For activity classified as Level II under § 401.2(c)(2), the responsible spellcaster shall, in addition to subsection (b):
(1) Implement protective measures sufficient to mitigate foreseeable instability or collateral consequence;
(2) Ensure active supervision where unlicensed or provisional practitioners are involved;
(3) Evaluate interaction with ambient magical fields, existing enchantments, or environmental variables;
(4) Establish intervention capability proportionate to the nature of the anticipated instability;
(5) Document safeguard measures contemporaneously.
Absence of documented Level II safeguards creates a rebuttable presumption of noncompliance.

(d) **Additional Safeguards for Level III Activity.**
For activity classified as Level III under § 401.2(c)(3), the responsible spellcaster shall, in addition to subsections (b) and (c):
(1) Implement redundant stabilization mechanisms where a single point of failure could result in serious consequence;
(2) Establish containment measures sufficient to prevent foreseeable propagation beyond the intended locus of effect;
(3) Stage restorative, countervailing, or mitigation resources prior to initiation;
(4) Conduct a documented pre-execution risk review;
(5) Limit participation to individuals possessing demonstrable competence in the relevant school or schools of magic.

Failure to implement enhanced safeguards required under this subsection shall create a presumption that the activity was conducted in reckless disregard of § 101.7.

(e) **Escalation and Reclassification During Execution.**
Where material conditions change during execution such that the activity satisfies criteria of a higher risk level under § 401.2, the responsible spellcaster shall immediately:
(1) Suspend or stabilize the activity;
(2) Implement safeguards consistent with the higher classification; or
(3) Terminate the activity where proportional safeguards cannot be established.
Continuation of activity without escalation of safeguards shall constitute a violation of this section.

(f) **Supervisory and Institutional Responsibility.**
The individual or entity exercising operational authority over a magical environment shall bear responsibility for compliance with this section, regardless of delegation or distribution of technical execution among participants.

(g) **Good-Faith Compliance and Presumption of Reasonable Care.**
(1) Presumption of Compliance.
Where a spellcaster or responsible institution has, prior to initiation of a magical activity:
(A) properly classified the activity in accordance with § 401.2;
(B) implemented safeguards proportionate to that classification under this section;
(C) documented such classification and safeguards in accordance with § 401.5; and
(D) acted in objective good faith reliance upon the information reasonably available at the time,
there shall arise a rebuttable presumption that the spellcaster exercised reasonable care under § 101.7 with respect to the matters governed by those provisions.

(2) Objective Standard.
Good faith under this subsection shall be determined according to an objective standard. Subjective belief, professional reputation, institutional

tradition, instructional context, or absence of prior enforcement shall not, standing alone, establish good faith.

(3) Limitations.
The presumption created by paragraph (1) shall not apply where:
(A) material facts were knowingly misrepresented, concealed, or omitted in the classification process;
(B) safeguards were nominal, illusory, or implemented solely for documentation purposes;
(C) known instability, prior incident history, or enforcement findings materially affecting risk were disregarded;
(D) the activity materially exceeded the scope of the original classification; or
(E) the harm resulted from conduct unrelated to the classification or safeguard requirements of this Part.

(4) Effect in Proceedings.
In any civil, administrative, or disciplinary proceeding, the presumption established by this subsection may be rebutted by a showing that a reasonably prudent spellcaster of comparable qualifications would have undertaken additional or alternative precautions under similar circumstances.

(5) No Absolute Immunity.
Nothing in this subsection shall be construed to create absolute immunity from liability. Compliance with classification and safeguard requirements shall constitute evidence of reasonable care but shall not preclude a finding of negligence where the totality of the circumstances demonstrates unreasonable conduct.

(6) Burden of Production.
The party asserting the benefit of this subsection bears the initial burden of producing contemporaneous documentation sufficient to demonstrate substantial compliance with §§ 401.2, 401.5, and 401.6.

(h) **Anti-Recharacterization Rule.**
Safeguard obligations shall be determined by operational effect and foreseeable consequence, not by nomenclature, tradition, instructional framing, ceremonial characterization, or asserted intent.

Artificial reclassification or mischaracterization to reduce safeguard burden constitutes circumvention under § 702.2.

(i) **Documentation and Evidentiary Presumptions.**
Where required safeguards are not documented in accordance with § 401.5:
(1) The activity shall be presumed to have been conducted without adequate safeguards;
(2) The burden of rebuttal rests with the responsible spellcaster or institution;
(3) Absence of documentation shall be admissible as evidence of negligence or regulatory noncompliance in any civil or administrative proceeding.

(j) **Cross-References.**
For risk classification, see § 401.2. For logging and recordkeeping, see § 401.5. For reasonable care, see § 101.7. For penalties, see § 102.2.

(k) **Historical Annotations.**
Established under C.C.D. 4102, 86 MR 1203, Wed. 9, 1996, to implement proportional safeguard requirements corresponding to risk classifications adopted under § 401.2. Amended under C.C.D. 4891, 90 MR 3118, Wed. 2, 2008, to clarify supervisory liability and escalation obligations. Amended under C.C.D. 5320, 94 MR 2016, Sun. 18, 2024, to address compounded-risk execution, safeguard documentation failures, and burden allocation in civil enforcement proceedings.

§ 401.7 Secrecy of Magic Act Compliance for Public Spellcasting

(a) **General Rule.**
No person shall cast, activate, channel, release, discharge, or otherwise employ a spell in any location where such activity is visible, audible, detectable, or otherwise perceptible to non-magical populations unless such activity is adequately concealed or otherwise authorized under § 401.8.

(b) **Public Spellcasting.**
(1) Prohibition.

Spellcasting conducted in streets, marketplaces, festivals, transportation corridors, public gatherings, or other locations where non-magical persons may reasonably be present is prohibited unless concealment measures described in subsection (c) are implemented.

(2) Locations Deemed Public.

For purposes of this section, public locations include any area in which a practitioner reasonably knows or should know that non-magical persons may be present. Such locations include—

(A) roads, pathways, and thoroughfares;

(B) markets, taverns, shops, and other commercial establishments;

(C) public festivals, gatherings, or civic events;

(D) transportation hubs or transit corridors; and

(E) other locations open to or commonly used by non-magical persons.

(c) **Concealment Requirements.**

(1) General Requirement.

A practitioner engaging in spellcasting in proximity to non-magical populations must implement concealment measures sufficient to prevent the observation or detection of magical activity.

(2) Factors Considered.

Adequacy of concealment shall be determined with reference to—

(A) visibility of the spell or magical effect;

(B) audible manifestations associated with the spell;

(C) magical residue or lingering arcane signatures;

(D) duration of the magical effect; and

(E) environmental disruption caused by the spell.

(3) Approved Methods.

Concealment measures may include—

(A) illusion or perceptual masking;

(B) environmental wards;

(C) containment fields or localized shielding;

(D) dimensional or spatial isolation; or

(E) other concealment methods appropriate to the level of risk associated with the spell.

(d) **Accidental Exposure.**

(1) Immediate Remediation Required.

If magical activity is observed or reasonably believed to have been observed by a non-magical person, the responsible practitioner shall immediately take corrective measures to eliminate or minimize exposure.

(2) Corrective Measures.
Corrective measures may include—
(A) stabilization or termination of the spell;
(B) reversal or dissipation of visible magical effects;
(C) repair of damage to structures, terrain, or surrounding property; and
(D) removal, alteration, or neutralization of observable magical evidence.

(e) **Associated Magical Phenomena.**
(1) Creatures and Constructs.
Magical creatures, constructs, animated objects, summoned entities, or similar manifestations created or revealed during spellcasting must be concealed or contained in accordance with applicable provisions of this Code.
(2) Applicable Requirements.
Compliance with this subsection shall include adherence to creature concealment and containment requirements described in this Code.

(f) **Institutional Responsibility.**
(1) Supervision.
Magical institutions, guilds, academies, and licensed practitioners supervising apprentices shall implement procedures designed to prevent unauthorized public spellcasting.
(2) Compliance Programs.
Such procedures may include—
(A) training and instruction on secrecy obligations;
(B) supervision standards for apprentices;
(C) incident response procedures; and
(D) internal disciplinary measures for violations.

(g) **Violations.**
A practitioner who knowingly or negligently exposes magical activity to non-magical populations in violation of this section may be subject to administrative sanctions, disciplinary proceedings, suspension or revocation of licensure, restitution for damages resulting from the exposure, or other enforcement actions authorized under the Code.

(h) **Cross-References.**
Emergency spellcasting and temporary exposure exceptions are governed by § 401.8. Financial reporting obligations relating to magical trade are addressed in § 701.9 and related provisions under the Magic Secrecy Act

(§ 701.9). Classification and protection of restricted magical operations are governed by the Magical Acts of Secrecy (§ 2901.1–7).

(i) **Historical Annotations.**
Originally established under C.C.D. 4417, 62 MR 913, Wed. 3, 1786, to regulate public spellcasting and prevent exposure of magical activity to non-magical populations. Amended under C.C.D. 5192, 68 MR 1441, Fri. 18, 1854, to include concealment requirements for summoned creatures and magical constructs. Further amended under C.C.D. 7448, 77 MR 2982, Tue. 11, 1927, to clarify remediation obligations following accidental magical exposure. Revised under C.C.D. 9914, 83 MR 2716, Mon. 22, 2016, to expand compliance requirements for practitioners operating in mixed-population settlements.

§ 401.8 Emergency Measures for Public Magical Exposure

(a) **General Rule.**
Notwithstanding § 401.7, a practitioner may engage in spellcasting in a location where magical activity may become perceptible to non-magical populations when such spellcasting is reasonably necessary to prevent imminent harm to persons, property, or the stability of the surrounding environment.

(b) **Definition of Emergency.**
(1) In General.
For purposes of this section, an emergency exists where immediate magical action is required to prevent—
(A) serious bodily injury or loss of life;
(B) substantial destruction of property;
(C) uncontrolled magical phenomena posing immediate risk to the surrounding area; or
(D) the escape or manifestation of a magical creature, entity, or construct presenting a danger to nearby persons.
(2) Limitations.
An emergency shall not include circumstances created by the practitioner's own negligent or reckless conduct unless immediate spellcasting is necessary to prevent further harm.

(c) **Scope of Authorized Spellcasting.**

(1) Minimum Necessary Action.
Spellcasting conducted under this section must be limited to the minimum magical activity reasonably necessary to resolve the emergency.
(2) Prohibited Conduct.
A practitioner may not use the existence of an emergency to justify—
(A) unnecessary displays of magic;
(B) spellcasting unrelated to the emergency condition; or
(C) conduct that increases the likelihood of magical exposure beyond what is reasonably required to resolve the emergency.

(d) **Post-Exposure Remediation.**
(1) Corrective Measures Required.
Where emergency spellcasting results in the observation or detection of magical activity by non-magical persons, the practitioner shall take reasonable measures to remediate such exposure.
(2) Examples of Remediation.
Remediation measures may include—
(A) termination or stabilization of visible magical effects;
(B) repair of damage to structures, terrain, or surrounding property;
(C) removal or concealment of magical residue or artifacts; and
(D) other measures reasonably necessary to restore secrecy consistent with § 401.7.

(e) **Institutional Response Authority.**
Magical law enforcement agencies, regulatory authorities, or other authorized entities may take control of emergency situations involving magical exposure and may direct practitioners to cease, modify, or assist in spellcasting activities necessary to contain the incident.

(f) **Incident Reporting.**
(1) Reporting Requirement.
A practitioner who engages in spellcasting under this section must report the incident to the Department of Magical Affairs within a reasonable period following resolution of the emergency.
(2) Contents of Report.
Such report shall include—
(A) a description of the emergency circumstances;
(B) the nature of the spell or spells used;
(C) the extent of any magical exposure; and
(D) the corrective measures taken to restore compliance with § 401.7.

(g) **Interaction With Other Provisions.**
Nothing in this section relieves a practitioner from compliance with applicable provisions of this Code governing the handling of magical creatures, artifacts, or high-risk magical activities, including requirements set forth elsewhere in related provisions.

(h) **Historical Annotations.**
Originally established under C.C.D. 4439, 62 MR 1004, Wed. 3, 1786, to permit limited emergency spellcasting in populated areas where immediate action was required to prevent harm. Amended under C.C.D. 6128, 71 MR 2093, Thu. 14, 1889, to clarify post-incident remediation obligations. Further amended under C.C.D. 9842, 83 MR 2487, Thu. 7, 2014, to include incident reporting requirements and coordination with magical authorities.

§ 401.9 Warding Protocols for High-Risk Spellcasting Environments

(a) **General Rule.**
Any practitioner conducting high-risk spellcasting shall establish and maintain appropriate warding measures designed to contain magical effects, prevent unintended spread of magical energy, and protect persons, property, and surrounding environments from harm.

(b) **High-Risk Spellcasting Defined.**
(1) In General.
For purposes of this section, high-risk spellcasting includes any spellcasting activity that—
(A) involves destructive, volatile, or unstable magical forces;
(B) has the potential to affect a wide physical area or large number of persons;
(C) may generate uncontrolled magical residue or environmental disruption; or
(D) presents a material risk of cascading magical reactions.
(2) Illustrative Activities.
High-risk spellcasting may include, but is not limited to—
(A) large-scale elemental manipulation;
(B) dimensional or planar openings;
(C) summoning of entities not fully bound to the caster's control;
(D) large-area transfiguration or transformation magic; and

(E) experimental or untested spellcasting procedures.

(c) **Required Warding Measures.**
(1) Containment Wards.
A practitioner must establish wards sufficient to prevent magical effects from extending beyond the intended spellcasting area.
(2) Protective Barriers.
Appropriate barriers shall be implemented to shield nearby persons, structures, and terrain from harmful magical effects.
(3) Environmental Stabilization.
Where spellcasting may alter weather patterns, terrain stability, magical currents, or dimensional boundaries, additional stabilizing wards must be employed to prevent unintended environmental disruption.

(d) **Location Requirements.**
(1) Approved Environments.
High-risk spellcasting shall be conducted only in locations reasonably suited for such activity, including laboratories, warded training grounds, licensed magical facilities, or other controlled environments.
(2) Prohibited Locations.
High-risk spellcasting may not be conducted in populated areas or locations accessible to non-magical persons unless authorized under § 401.8 or otherwise approved by the Department of Magical Affairs.

(e) **Monitoring and Supervision.**
(1) Supervision Requirement.
Where high-risk spellcasting is conducted by apprentices, students, or unlicensed practitioners, supervision by a licensed practitioner is required.
(2) Environmental Monitoring.
Practitioners must monitor the spellcasting environment for signs of instability, including magical fluctuations, containment breaches, or unexpected spell interactions.

(f) **Failure of Warding Measures.**
(1) Immediate Response.
If warding measures fail or become compromised, the practitioner shall immediately cease spellcasting activity and take corrective measures necessary to restore containment.
(2) Containment Measures.

Corrective measures may include reinforcement of wards, termination of the spell, evacuation of affected persons, or other actions necessary to prevent escalation of the incident.

(g) **Penalties.**
(1) In General.
Any person who knowingly or negligently conducts spellcasting in a designated High-Risk Spellcasting Environment without maintaining the warding, containment, or supervision measures required by this section shall be subject to enforcement actions consistent with § 102.2.
(2) Aggravating Factors.
In determining the appropriate penalty under § 102.2, the Department may consider—
(A) whether the violation resulted in environmental instability, containment failure, or uncontrolled magical phenomena;
(B) the extent of damage to persons, property, or surrounding magical infrastructure;
(C) whether the practitioner ignored or disabled required warding or monitoring systems; and
(D) whether the practitioner had prior violations involving high-risk spellcasting environments.

(h) **Cross-References.**
For secrecy requirements governing public spellcasting, see § 401.7. For emergency spellcasting provisions, see § 401.8.

(i) **Historical Annotations.**
Originally established under C.C.D. 4439, 62 MR 1006, Thu. 6, 1786, to regulate containment measures for volatile magical practices. Amended under C.C.D. 6182, 71 MR 2147, Wed. 9, 1892, to include supervision requirements for apprentices. Revised under C.C.D. 9918, 83 MR 2734, Wed. 11, 2016, to expand environmental containment protocols for large-scale spellcasting activities.

§ 402.1 Real-Time Spell Surveillance and Reporting for High-Risk Magic

(a) **General Rule.**
Spellcasting activities classified as Level III under § 401.2 shall be subject to real-time surveillance and reporting requirements designed to detect

unstable magical activity, containment failures, or uncontrolled magical manifestations.

(b) **Applicability.**
(1) Level III Spellcasting.
The requirements of this section apply to any spellcasting activity classified as Level III under § 401.2.
(2) Designated Environments.
The Department may require compliance with this section for spellcasting conducted within environments designated under § 401.9 where the Department determines that real-time monitoring is necessary due to environmental instability, magical amplification effects, or the presence of volatile magical infrastructure.
(3) Experimental Spellcasting.
The Department may designate experimental or untested spellcasting procedures as subject to surveillance requirements where such activity presents a material risk of uncontrolled magical effects.

(c) **Monitoring Requirement.**
(1) Real-Time Observation.
Spellcasting activities subject to this section must be monitored in real time through Department-approved magical surveillance systems or equivalent monitoring mechanisms capable of detecting the activation and progression of the spell.
(2) Monitoring Capabilities.
Monitoring systems must be capable of identifying—
(A) activation of Level III spells;
(B) abnormal fluctuations in magical energy;
(C) containment breaches or ward failures; and
(D) interactions between concurrent magical effects that may result in cascade events or environmental destabilization.

(d) **Incident Reporting.**
(1) Reportable Events.
Any practitioner or facility conducting spellcasting subject to this section shall report the following events to the Department as soon as reasonably practicable after detection—
(A) containment failures or environmental instability;
(B) uncontrolled magical manifestations or cascade events;

(C) structural or environmental damage caused by spellcasting activity; and
(D) any spellcasting event producing effects materially different from those reasonably anticipated by a licensed practitioner.
(2) Method of Reporting.
Reports required under this subsection may be submitted through Department-approved reporting channels, including certified communication wards, automated monitoring systems, or other mechanisms authorized by the Department.

(e) **Operational Records.**
(1) Activity Logs.
Facilities conducting spellcasting subject to this section shall maintain contemporaneous records documenting—
(A) the identity and licensure status of practitioners performing the spell;
(B) the time and duration of spellcasting activity;
(C) the monitoring system used to observe the activity; and
(D) any irregularities or anomalies detected during monitoring.
(2) Record Retention.
Records maintained under this subsection shall be preserved for a period sufficient to permit review by the Department in connection with inspections, investigations, or compliance audits.

(f) **System Maintenance.**
Monitoring systems used to satisfy the requirements of this section must be maintained in operational condition and periodically calibrated to ensure reliable detection of spellcasting activity and containment failures.

(g) **Penalties.**
(1) Failure to Maintain Required Surveillance.
Any practitioner or facility operator who conducts Level III spellcasting without the real-time monitoring required by this section shall be treated as having committed a violation subject to enforcement under § 102.2.
(2) Failure to Report Incidents.
Any practitioner or facility operator who knowingly or negligently fails to report a reportable event described in subsection (d) shall be subject to enforcement under § 102.2.
(3) Aggravated Violations.
Where the failure to maintain surveillance or report required incidents results in containment failure, environmental destabilization, or

uncontrolled magical manifestations, such violation shall be treated as an aggravated violation under § 102.2.

(h) **Cross-References.**
Spell risk classifications are addressed in § 401.2. Spell logging requirements appear in § 401.5. Secrecy requirements governing public spellcasting appear in § 401.7. Warding protocols for designated high-risk environments appear in § 401.9.

(i) **Historical Annotations.**
Originally established under C.C.D. 4512, 63 MR 287, Tue. 18, 1793, to implement centralized oversight of unstable magical practices. Amended under C.C.D. 7084, 75 MR 1703, Fri. 2, 1912, to require incident reporting following containment failures in licensed magical laboratories. Revised under C.C.D. 9927, 83 MR 3095, Thu. 14, 2018, to expand surveillance requirements for Level III spellcasting activities.

§ 402.2 Impaired Spellcasting and Capacity-Based Restrictions

(a) **General Rule.**
No individual shall engage in, attempt, assist, facilitate, supervise, or authorize any act of spellcasting while materially impaired by any condition that substantially limits judgment, control, perception, or awareness.

(b) **Definition of Impairment.**
For purposes of this section, impairment includes any mental, emotional, magical, physiological, or external condition that reasonably affects a spellcaster's ability to safely perform magic, including—
(1) intoxication from potions, elixirs, enchanted substances, or mundane intoxicants;
(2) magical overload, arcane exhaustion, resonance instability, or lingering effects from prior spellcasting;
(3) cognitive impairment resulting from illness, injury, curse, possession, memory degradation, or similar condition;
(4) emotional states resulting in loss of control, including panic, rage, despair, or uncontrolled euphoria where such states affect spellcasting precision; or

(5) any other condition which, under the totality of the circumstances, renders the individual unable to meet the reasonable care standard under § 101.7.

(c) **Prohibited Conduct.**
(1) No individual shall knowingly or recklessly cast or attempt to cast a spell while impaired.
(2) No individual shall permit, direct, or fail to prevent the spellcasting of another where such impairment is known or reasonably should be known.
(3) No individual shall rely on stabilizing enchantments, assistive relics, or external magical supports to circumvent impairment where such reliance creates additional or unmitigated risk.

(d) **Determination of Impairment.**
(1) Impairment shall be determined based on observable conduct, magical output irregularities, deviation from expected casting patterns, or failure to maintain control of spell effects.
(2) The enforcing authority may consider testimony, magical residue analysis, aura instability readings, witness accounts, and prior conduct in determining impairment.
(3) A presumption of impairment may arise where a spell results in uncontrolled propagation, unintended transformation, dimensional instability, or collateral harm inconsistent with the intended effect.

(e) **Capacity-Based Restrictions.**
(1) Where an individual is determined to present an ongoing risk due to impairment, the enforcing authority may impose capacity-based restrictions, including—
(A) temporary suspension of spellcasting privileges;
(B) limitation to specified schools of magic or low-risk spell classifications;
(C) mandatory supervision by a licensed spellcaster of equal or higher classification;
(D) requirement to complete remedial training, stabilization treatment, or magical rehabilitation; or
(E) conditional licensure subject to periodic review.
(2) Restrictions imposed under this subsection shall be tailored to the nature, duration, and severity of the impairment and shall be subject to review under § 102.1.

(f) **Severe Incapacity.**
(1) Where an individual is unable to understand, control, or meaningfully participate in spellcasting due to severe cognitive or magical incapacity, the enforcing authority may impose suspension or revocation of spellcasting privileges.
(2) Such determinations shall require documented findings and shall not be imposed solely on the basis of diagnosis absent demonstrated functional impairment.
(3) Periodic reassessment shall be required where the condition is subject to improvement, treatment, or stabilization.

(g) **Liability and Enforcement.**
(1) Violations of this section shall be subject to classification under § 102.2(b), including classification as major or egregious where impairment results in material harm or creates substantial risk.
(2) Where impairment is knowingly disregarded, such conduct may constitute criminal liability under § 102.2(o).
(3) The existence of impairment shall not serve as a complete defense where the individual knew or reasonably should have known of the impairment.

(h) **Safe Harbor.**
(1) No penalty shall be imposed where an individual, upon recognizing impairment, refrains from casting, seeks assistance, or reports the condition prior to engaging in regulated activity.
(2) Voluntary disclosure and cessation of activity shall be considered mitigating factors under § 102.2(m).

(i) **Cross-references.**
For reasonable care requirements, see § 101.7. For civil, administrative, and criminal penalties, see § 102.2. For licensing and classification of spells, see Part IV.

(j) **Historical annotations.**
Enacted following the 1463 Cascade Event, in which an impaired practitioner attempted a localized illumination spell and instead produced a sustained solar duplication effect over three municipalities. Amended in 1471 to include emotional-state impairment and in 1486 to clarify applicability to supervisory conduct.

§ 402.3 Regulation of Innate, Wild, and Uncontrolled Magic

(a) **General Rule.**
Any individual capable of producing magical effects arising from inherent, biological, ancestral, or otherwise non-learned sources shall be subject to the requirements of this section. Such individuals shall remain fully subject to § 101.7 and shall be required to exercise reasonable care in all manifestations of magical activity, regardless of whether such activity is intentional.

(b) **Definitions.**
For purposes of this section:
(1) Innate Magic.
The term "innate magic" means any magical capability arising from internal, biological, hereditary, or otherwise intrinsic sources not dependent on formal training, study, ritual preparation, or external spellcasting implements.
(2) Wild or Uncontrolled Magic.
The term "wild" or "uncontrolled" magic means any magical effect that manifests spontaneously, unpredictably, or without the deliberate intent or precise control of the individual producing such effect, including surges, discharges, or cascading magical outputs.
(3) Manifestation Event.
The term "manifestation event" means any occurrence in which innate or uncontrolled magic produces a measurable or observable effect, regardless of scale, duration, or intended outcome.

(c) **Duty of Recognition and Disclosure.**
(1) Any individual who knows or reasonably should know that they are capable of producing innate or uncontrolled magical effects shall report such capability to the appropriate licensing or regulatory authority within a reasonable period following initial manifestation.
(2) Failure to recognize, report, or otherwise acknowledge repeated manifestation events may constitute a deviation from reasonable care under § 101.7.
(3) The enforcing authority may consider frequency, severity, and predictability of manifestation events in determining whether an individual reasonably should have known of such capability.

(d) **Prohibited Conduct.**
(1) No individual shall knowingly disregard a known propensity for uncontrolled magical output where such disregard creates a material risk of harm.
(2) No individual shall intentionally induce, amplify, or exploit uncontrolled magical manifestations for purposes inconsistent with safe and authorized spellcasting practices.
(3) No individual shall rely on the involuntary nature of a manifestation event to circumvent compliance with this Code where reasonable preventative measures were available.

(e) **Regulatory Evaluation and Monitoring.**
(1) The enforcing authority may require any individual subject to this section to undergo evaluation, testing, or monitoring to determine the nature, scope, and stability of their magical capability.
(2) Such evaluation may include observation of manifestation patterns, measurement of magical output, and assessment of control, predictability, and risk.
(3) Individuals subject to monitoring may be required to report subsequent manifestation events at intervals determined by the enforcing authority.

(f) **Capacity-Based Restrictions.**
(1) Where innate or uncontrolled magic presents a material risk, the enforcing authority may impose restrictions consistent with § 402.2(e), including—
(A) limitation to specified environments or conditions for safe manifestation;
(B) restriction to low-risk magical interaction or passive output;
(C) mandatory supervision during any activity reasonably expected to produce a manifestation event; or
(D) temporary or permanent suspension of active spellcasting privileges where necessary to prevent harm.
(2) Restrictions imposed under this subsection shall be proportionate to the level of risk and shall be subject to review under § 102.1.

(g) **Liability and Enforcement.**
(1) Manifestation events resulting in harm, damage, or material risk shall be subject to classification under § 102.2(b).

(2) The involuntary nature of a manifestation event may be considered as a mitigating factor under § 102.2(m), but shall not preclude the imposition of civil or administrative penalties where reasonable precautions were not taken.
(3) Where an individual knowingly or willfully exploits or disregards uncontrolled magical capability in a manner meeting the criteria of § 102.2(o), such conduct may give rise to criminal liability.

(h) **Safe Harbor.**
(1) No penalty shall be imposed solely on the basis of an initial manifestation event where the individual promptly reports such event and complies with all evaluation and monitoring requirements.
(2) Voluntary disclosure and cooperation shall be considered mitigating factors under § 102.2(m).

(i) **Cross-References.**
For reasonable care in spellcasting, see § 101.7. For impaired spellcasting and capacity-based restrictions, see § 402.2. For civil, administrative, and criminal penalties, see § 102.2. For administrative procedures and review, see § 102.1.

(j) **Historical Annotations.**
Enacted following the 1478 Spontaneous Combustion Series, in which multiple untrained individuals exhibiting latent magical capability produced sequential manifestation events across three municipalities, resulting in property loss, atmospheric distortion, and widespread administrative confusion. Amended in 1489 to clarify reporting obligations and in 1496 to include monitoring requirements for recurring manifestation patterns.

§ 402.4 Oneiric, Somnambulistic, and Planar-Channel Spellcasting

(a) **General Rule.**
Spellcasting conducted while an individual is in a somnambulistic, unconscious, dream-induced, or otherwise oneiric state shall be subject to the provisions of this section. No individual shall be exempt from regulatory obligations solely on the basis that such spellcasting occurred without full conscious awareness.

(b) **Definitions.**
For purposes of this section:
(1) Somnambulistic Spellcasting.
The term "somnambulistic spellcasting" means any magical act performed while the individual is asleep, sleepwalking, or otherwise operating without full waking consciousness.
(2) Oneiric State.
The term "oneiric state" means any condition in which an individual's consciousness is partially or wholly situated within a dream, dream-adjacent construct, or subconscious projection.
(3) Planar-Channel Spellcasting.
The term "planar-channel spellcasting" means any magical effect deliberately or incidentally conducted through an ambient, dream, astral, or otherwise non-material plane, including magic routed through oneiric pathways or external consciousness fields.
(4) Induced Dream State.
The term "induced dream state" means any oneiric condition resulting from potions, substances, curses, enchantments, necromantic agents, or environmental or planar phenomena.

(c) **Attribution of Conduct.**
(1) Spellcasting occurring during a somnambulistic or oneiric state shall be attributed to the individual from whom the magical effect originated, unless clearly demonstrated to have been externally imposed or controlled.
(2) Where an external entity, artifact, or plane exerts primary control over the manifestation, liability may be apportioned in accordance with § 102.2 and applicable provisions governing magical influence or control.

(d) **Prohibited Conduct.**
(1) No individual shall knowingly enter or induce a state likely to produce uncontrolled or hazardous spellcasting without appropriate safeguards.
(2) No individual shall deliberately channel magic through oneiric or planar pathways where such channeling creates a material risk of uncontrolled propagation, cross-planar leakage, or unintended manifestation.
(3) No individual shall use dream-based or unconscious states as a means to evade regulatory requirements, licensing restrictions, or supervision obligations.

(e) **Regulatory Safeguards.**
(1) The enforcing authority may require individuals subject to this section to implement safeguards, including—
(A) containment wards during sleep cycles;
(B) suppression or dampening enchantments;
(C) supervised rest environments; or
(D) prohibition on the use of dream-inducing substances or exposure to triggering conditions.
(2) Where repeated somnambulistic or oneiric spellcasting occurs, the enforcing authority may impose restrictions consistent with § 402.2 and § 402.3.

(f) **Liability and Enforcement.**
(1) The absence of conscious awareness shall not constitute a complete defense where the individual knew or reasonably should have known of the risk of such manifestation.
(2) The involuntary nature of the state may be considered a mitigating factor under § 102.2(m), but shall not preclude the imposition of civil or administrative penalties.
(3) Where an individual knowingly exploits or induces such states to engage in prohibited conduct, such conduct may give rise to criminal liability under § 102.2(o).

(g) **Safe Harbor.**
(1) No penalty shall be imposed for an isolated manifestation occurring during an unanticipated oneiric state, provided the individual promptly reports the event and complies with all required safeguards thereafter.

(h) **Cross-References.**
For reasonable care in spellcasting, see § 101.7. For impaired spellcasting and capacity-based restrictions, see § 402.2. For innate, wild, and uncontrolled magic, see § 402.3. For civil, administrative, and criminal penalties, see § 102.2. For administrative procedures and review, see § 102.1.

(i) **Historical Annotations.**
This section was enacted following the 1483 Dreamfall Incident, in which a sleeping practitioner unintentionally opened a sustained portal to a semi-lucid plane, resulting in the manifestation of symbolic entities, recursive architecture, and localized non-linear time progression.

Amended under C.C.D. 1491, 82 MR 417 Tue. 6, 1640, to expand the definition of induced dream states to include necromantic agents and externally imposed unconscious conditions. Revised under C.C.D. 1503, 91 MR 602 Fri. 9, 1980, to clarify attribution and liability standards for planar-channel spellcasting and cross-planar manifestations.

Part V: Spell Duration and Termination

§ 501.1 Spell Duration and Effects

(a) **In General.**
The duration, persistence, and operational effect of any spell shall be determined and governed in accordance with this section. No person shall permit a spell to persist beyond its authorized duration or produce effects materially exceeding those permitted under this Code.

(b) **Declaration Requirement for Persistent and Extended-Duration Spells.**
(1) In General. Any spell that is—
(A) persistent;
(B) sustained beyond a single continuous act of casting; or
(C) intended to remain in effect beyond a transient or momentary period,
shall be subject to a declaration requirement in accordance with this subsection.
(2) Timing of Declaration. The required declaration shall be made—
(A) contemporaneously with the casting; or
(B) where contemporaneous declaration is impracticable, as soon as reasonably practicable thereafter, but in no event later than the time prescribed under this Code.
(3) Required Contents. The declaration shall identify—
(A) the section of this Code under which the spell is authorized;
(B) the intended duration or terminating condition; and
(C) a description of the intended effect sufficient to permit administrative review.
(4) Form of Declaration. Except as otherwise provided, the declaration shall be made substantially in the following form:
"In accordance with Section [applicable section] of the Magical Code of Regulations, the spell known as [spell name] is authorized to persist for [specified duration or condition]."
(5) Failure to Declare. Any spell subject to this subsection for which a compliant declaration is not made shall be treated as improperly authorized and subject to termination under § 501.2.

(c) **Permissible Duration Classifications.**

(1) Categories. Spells shall be classified as—
(A) instantaneous;
(B) fixed-duration;
(C) conditional;
(D) sustained; or
(E) persistent.
(2) Prohibition on Undefined Duration. No spell shall be cast or maintained with an undefined or indeterminate duration except where expressly authorized under this Code.
(3) Administrative Recharacterization. The Department of Magical Affairs may recharacterize the duration classification of any spell where the declared classification does not reflect its actual operation.

(d) **Specification and Limitation of Effects.**
(1) Required Description. The caster shall define the intended effect of any spell subject to subsection (b) with sufficient specificity to permit evaluation under § 102.1 and any applicable logging requirement under § 401.5.
(2) Scope Limitation. No spell shall lawfully produce effects materially exceeding those declared or reasonably encompassed within the declared purpose.
(3) Overbreadth. A declaration that is vague, circular, or drafted to encompass unspecified future outcomes shall be treated as noncompliant.

(e) **Maximum Duration and Renewal.**
(1) General Rule. No spell shall persist beyond the maximum duration permitted under its classification or governing authority.
(2) Renewal. Renewal of a spell shall require a new declaration satisfying subsection (b).
(3) Prohibition on Continuous Recasting Schemes. No person shall structure repeated or overlapping castings to achieve uninterrupted effects in a manner that circumvents applicable duration limitations.

(f) **Conditional and Trigger-Based Spells.**
(1) Objective Conditions. Any terminating or activating condition shall be defined in a manner capable of objective determination.
(2) Invalid Conditions. A condition that cannot be verified, measured, or reasonably interpreted shall render the spell subject to termination under § 501.2.

(3) Failure of Condition. Where a condition ceases to be determinable, the spell shall be treated as improperly conditioned.

(g) **Persistent and Self-Sustaining Effects.**
(1) Termination Mechanism. Any persistent or self-sustaining spell shall include a defined method of termination or dissolution.
(2) Responsibility. The originating caster shall remain responsible for the continued operation and termination of such spell.
(3) Registration. Such spells shall be identified in any applicable records required under § 401.5 or Part II.

(h) **Interaction with Other Spells.**
(1) Cumulative Effects. Where multiple spells operate concurrently, their combined duration and effect shall be evaluated collectively for purposes of compliance.
(2) Administrative Intervention. The Department of Magical Affairs may require modification or termination of one or more spells to prevent impermissible cumulative effects.

(i) **Prohibition on Evasion.**
No person shall design, sequence, layer, or otherwise arrange spells to avoid declaration requirements, obscure actual duration, or frustrate review under this Code.

(j) **Cross-References.**
For rules governing termination and revocation of spells, see § 501.2. For reasonable care requirements, see § 101.7. For classification of spell risk and complexity, see § 401.2. For spell logging and reporting requirements, see § 401.5. For administrative authority and enforcement, see § 102.1.

(k) **Historical Annotations.**
Originally established under C.C.D. 4810, 13 MR 552, Tue. 11, 1684. Amended under C.C.D. 5097, 17 MR 203, Thu. 6, 1709 to incorporate declaration requirements for persistent spells. Revised under C.C.D. 5933, 28 MR 761, Mon. 19, 1792 to clarify conditional spell standards and anti-evasion provisions.

§ 501.2 Termination and Revocation of Spells

(a) **In General.**

Any spell shall be subject to termination or revocation in accordance with this section. No person shall permit a spell to persist beyond its authorized duration or after the occurrence of any terminating condition.

(b) **Voluntary Termination.**
(1) Authority. A spell may be terminated by the originating caster or any authorized practitioner acting within the scope of § 101.5.
(2) Method. Termination shall be conducted using appropriate reversal, dissolution, or neutralization techniques consistent with § 101.7.
(3) Residual Effects. The terminating party shall ensure that no residual or unstable effects remain, except where unavoidable and properly mitigated.

(c) **Mandatory Termination.**
(1) Triggering Events. A spell shall be terminated immediately upon—
(A) expiration of its authorized duration;
(B) satisfaction or failure of a terminating condition;
(C) loss of authorization by the caster; or
(D) determination that continued operation violates this Code.
(2) Noncompliant Spells. Any spell lacking a valid declaration under § 501.1(b), where required, shall be deemed noncompliant and subject to immediate termination.

(d) **Administrative Revocation.**
(1) Authority. The Department of Magical Affairs or any authorized body under § 102.1 may order the revocation of any spell.
(2) Grounds. Grounds include violation of this Code, misrepresentation in required documentation, or risk to public safety or magical stability.
(3) Execution. Upon revocation, the responsible party shall terminate the spell and comply with any remedial directives.

(e) **Emergency Termination.**
(1) Authorized Intervention. Any authorized practitioner may terminate a spell where reasonably necessary to prevent imminent harm.
(2) Documentation. Such actions shall be documented in accordance with § 401.5.

(f) **Persistent Spell Obligations.**
(1) Heightened Responsibility. Persistent or self-sustaining spells shall be subject to heightened termination obligations.

(2) Strict Responsibility. The originating caster shall remain responsible for termination regardless of control or access.

(g) **Prohibition on Evasion.**
No person shall structure spells or sequences of spells to avoid termination requirements or delay revocation.

(h) **Cross-References.**
For duration and declaration requirements, see § 501.1. For reasonable care standards, see § 101.7. For administrative authority, see § 102.1. For emergency spellcasting provisions, see § 601.4 and § 602.4.

(i) **Historical Annotations.**
Originally established under C.C.D. 4892, 12 MR 771, Mon. 3, 1678. Amended under C.C.D. 5120, 18 MR 204, Thu. 14, 1712. Revised under C.C.D. 5901, 27 MR 998, Wed. 22, 1786.

Part VI: Spellcasting Limitations and Exemptions

§ 601.1 Exemptions for Spellcasting in Self-Defense

(a) **General Rule.**
Notwithstanding any provision of this Code, a person may engage in otherwise regulated or restricted spellcasting where such action is reasonably necessary to prevent imminent harm to oneself or another.

(b) **Imminence Requirement.**
The exemption under this section shall apply only where the threat of harm is immediate, present, and not speculative, and where delay would materially increase the risk of injury, death, or substantial harm.

(c) **Necessity and Proportionality.**
(1) Spellcasting under this section must be limited to that which is reasonably necessary to neutralize or escape the threat.
(2) The degree of magical force used shall be proportionate to the nature and severity of the threatened harm.
(3) Use of excessive or retaliatory magic beyond that required to address the threat shall not be protected under this section.

(d) **Limitations.**
The exemption provided under this section shall not apply—
(1) where the individual claiming the exemption was the initial aggressor, unless such individual has clearly withdrawn and communicated such withdrawal;
(2) where the threat arises from circumstances intentionally created or provoked by the individual; or
(3) where the use of magic is undertaken for purposes of retaliation, punishment, or deterrence unrelated to the immediate threat.

(e) **Interaction with Other Provisions.**

(1) Spellcasting in self-defense may permit deviation from otherwise applicable restrictions under Parts IV and VI, provided the requirements of this section are satisfied.
(2) Nothing in this section shall be interpreted to permit violations of absolute prohibitions expressly designated elsewhere in this Code, except where necessary to prevent imminent loss of life or similarly grave harm.

(f) **Post-Incident Obligations.**
(1) Any person who engages in spellcasting under this section shall, where practicable, take reasonable steps to mitigate harm, stabilize affected individuals, and prevent further damage.
(2) Where the spellcasting involves a Level II or Level III spell under § 401.2, the individual shall comply with applicable reporting and logging requirements under § 401.5 and § 402.1.

(g) **Burden of Justification.**
A person invoking this section shall bear the burden of demonstrating that the requirements of subsections (b) and (c) were satisfied based on the facts and circumstances known at the time of the incident.

(h) **Cross-References.**
For general limitations on spellcasting, refer to Part VI. For penalties, refer to § 102.2.

(i) **Historical Annotations.**
Originally established under C.C.D. 6124, 70 MR 1443, Wed. 9, 1832, to recognize limited defensive use of magic notwithstanding general prohibitions. Amended under C.C.D. 8451, 77 MR 2018, Mon. 14, 1919, to incorporate proportionality and imminence standards. Revised under C.C.D. 9917, 83 MR 2762, Mon. 6, 2018, to clarify interaction with high-risk spellcasting requirements and post-incident obligations.

§ 601.2 Spellcasting on Non-Magical Beings

(a) **In General.**
Spellcasting upon a non-magical being is prohibited except as expressly permitted under this section. No person shall directly or indirectly apply magic to a non-magical being in a manner that alters condition, behavior, perception, or legal status.

(b) **General Rule.**

(1) Prohibition. No spell shall be cast on a non-magical being where the effect is intentional or targeted.
(2) Indirect Effects. This prohibition applies to effects achieved through environmental manipulation, objects, intermediaries, or any other method.

(c) **Permitted Uses.**
(1) Emergency Protection. Spellcasting is permitted where necessary to prevent imminent harm.
(2) Restorative Magic. Healing or protective magic may be applied in accordance with Part XIV.
(3) Informed Consent. Spellcasting may be permitted with documented consent, provided no coercion or impairment of consent is involved.
(4) Incidental Effects. Incidental, unintended effects are not prohibited where reasonable care is exercised.

(d) **High-Risk Restrictions.**
No high-risk spell under § 401.2 shall be applied to a non-magical being except as authorized under emergency provisions.

(e) **Specific Prohibitions.**
(1) Mind-control magic is prohibited except as authorized under § 2101.2.
(2) Transfiguration is prohibited except as authorized under Part XX.
(3) Experimental or unstable magic is prohibited under all circumstances.

(f) **Documentation and Burden of Proof.**
The casting party shall document any permitted use and bear the burden of demonstrating compliance.

(g) **Prohibition on Evasion.**
No person shall structure spells to circumvent this section.

(h) **Cross-References.**
For authorized spellcasters, see § 101.5. For spell risk classification, see § 401.2. For self-defense and emergency provisions, see § 601.1, § 601.4, and § 602.4. For restorative magic, see Part XIV. For mind-control regulations, see Part XXI. For transfiguration, see Part XX.

(i) **Historical Annotations.**

Originally established under C.C.D. 4721, 11 MR 603, Fri. 9, 1662. Amended under C.C.D. 5184, 19 MR 110, Tue. 3, 1724. Revised under C.C.D. 6027, 29 MR 887, Fri. 18, 1801.

§ 601.3 Limitations on Luck or Chance Manipulation

(a) **General Rule.**
No individual, entity, or magical practitioner shall employ magic with the intent or effect of manipulating, altering, or influencing luck, chance, or probability in any context where such manipulation may result in unfair advantages, economic disruption, or violations of public policy.

(b) **Definitions.**
For the purposes of this section, the following definitions shall apply:
(1) Luck or Chance Manipulation. The use of magic to increase, decrease, or otherwise influence the likelihood of specific outcomes in situations of random chance or uncertainty, including but not limited to:
(A) Games of chance, such as lotteries, gambling, or betting activities.
(B) Economic transactions, such as stock trading or commodity speculation.
(C) Social interactions, such as influencing decisions in competitions or elections.
(D) Any natural or artificial system governed by probabilities.
(2) Unfair Advantage. Any outcome wherein the user of luck or chance manipulation gains a disproportionate benefit relative to others in the same context, thereby undermining fairness or equity.

(c) **Prohibited Uses.**
(1) No individual shall employ luck manipulation to influence:
(A) Gambling outcomes in any setting, including casinos, private games, and magical betting pools.
(B) The results of lotteries, raffles, or other public drawings.
(C) The distribution of magical or non-magical resources where outcomes are determined by chance.
(2) The use of luck manipulation to alter historical probabilities, thereby creating temporal disruptions or paradoxes, is strictly prohibited.

(d) **Permissible Uses.**

(1) Luck or chance manipulation is permitted under the following circumstances:
(A) In personal or private contexts where no external party is affected, such as improving one's odds of finding misplaced keys or parking spaces.
(B) For research or educational purposes conducted under a permit issued in accordance with § 201.9.
(C) In emergency situations where public safety is at immediate risk, as authorized by § 602.4.
(2) All permissible uses must be documented and reported to the Department of Magical Affairs (DMA) within 30 days of occurrence.

(e) **Reporting and Oversight.**
(1) Any suspected misuse of luck or chance manipulation shall be reported to the DMA using Form 718-L.
(2) Reports must include:
(A) A detailed account of the suspected incident, including the context and observed outcomes.
(B) Any evidence of magical residue or tampering, such as enchanted dice, charmed cards, or anomalous statistical deviations.
(C) Statements from witnesses or affected parties.

(f) **Penalties.**
(1) Any individual found in violation of this section shall be subject to:
(A) Suspension or revocation of magical licenses under § 201.3 for repeated violations.
(B) Mandatory attendance at a certified ethics workshop focusing on the principles of fairness and equity in magical practices.
(2) In cases where economic or social harm has resulted from luck manipulation, violators may be required to provide restitution to affected parties, as determined by the Magical Ethics Tribunal (MET).

(g) **Exceptions.**
(1) This section shall not apply to naturally occurring phenomena that influence probabilities without magical intervention.
(2) Rituals or spells designed to balance or neutralize pre-existing luck manipulations may be performed with prior authorization from the DMA.

(h) **Cross-References.**

For ethical considerations in magical practice, see § 701.1. For regulations related to financial fraud through magical means, consult Part X. For emergency use of magic during public safety crises, refer to § 602.4.

(i) **Historical Annotations.**
This section was originally established under C.C.D. 5421, 77 MR 3290, Sat. 3, 1954, to address the ethical and economic concerns surrounding luck manipulation spells and rituals. It was amended under C.C.D. 6123, 82 MR 4598, Wed. 12, 1982, to introduce specific exceptions for sanctioned research and small-scale ritual use. Further revisions were enacted under C.C.D. 7824, 89 MR 2156, Mon. 8, 2019, to include mandatory reporting requirements for luck-related spellcasting and clarify the penalties for unauthorized use in financial or gambling contexts.

§ 601.4 Exemptions for Spellcasting during Natural Disasters

(a) **In General.**
Notwithstanding any other provision of this Code, a practitioner may engage in otherwise restricted spellcasting during a qualifying natural disaster, but only to the extent authorized under this section. Any such spellcasting shall remain subject to the requirements of necessity, proportionality, and reasonable care under § 101.7.

(b) **Qualifying Natural Disaster.**
(1) Definition. A qualifying natural disaster is an event or series of events arising from environmental, elemental, or naturally occurring magical instability that—
(A) presents an immediate threat to life, structural integrity, or large-scale ecological balance; and
(B) cannot be reasonably mitigated through non-magical means alone within the time available.
(2) Illustrative Events. Such events may include floods, wildfires, earthquakes, severe storms, volcanic activity, or disruption of ley lines resulting in uncontrolled magical discharge.
(3) Determination. A qualifying natural disaster shall be deemed to exist where—
(A) formally declared by the Department of Magical Affairs; or

(B) in the absence of such declaration, a practitioner reasonably determines, based on observable conditions, that immediate intervention is required.

(c) **Scope of Permitted Spellcasting.**
(1) Authorized Purposes. Spellcasting under this section shall be limited to actions necessary to—
(A) prevent or reduce loss of life;
(B) stabilize collapsing or hazardous conditions;
(C) facilitate evacuation, rescue, or containment; or
(D) prevent cascading failures affecting surrounding areas.
(2) Functional Limitation. No spell shall be cast under this section unless—
(A) the expected benefit outweighs the foreseeable risk; and
(B) no less intrusive or lower-risk alternative is reasonably available.
(3) Duration. Any spell cast pursuant to this section shall persist only for the period reasonably necessary to address the qualifying condition and shall be terminated in accordance with § 501.2.

(d) **Temporary Modification of Compliance Obligations.**
(1) Suspension. Where strict compliance is impracticable due to the conditions of the disaster, the following requirements may be temporarily modified:
(A) licensing requirements under Part II;
(B) declaration requirements under § 501.1(b);
(C) contemporaneous logging under § 401.5.
(2) Limitations on Suspension. The modification under paragraph (1) shall not—
(A) eliminate the requirement of reasonable care under § 101.7;
(B) authorize prohibited conduct under Part VII; or
(C) permit use of magic for non-emergency purposes.
(3) Deferred Compliance. Any person relying on this subsection shall complete all required declarations, filings, and logs—
(A) as soon as reasonably practicable; and
(B) in no event later than a period prescribed by the Department of Magical Affairs.

(e) **Third-Party Intervention.**
(1) Authority. A practitioner may intervene to terminate, modify, or override an existing spell where—

(A) such spell contributes to the disaster or exacerbates its effects; and
(B) intervention is necessary to prevent imminent harm.
(2) Coordination. Where feasible, such intervention shall be coordinated with other practitioners or authorities to avoid compounding effects.

(f) **Prohibited Conduct.**
(1) Exploitation. No person shall use the existence of a natural disaster as a pretext to engage in spellcasting unrelated to emergency response.
(2) Excessive Measures. Spellcasting that materially exceeds what is necessary to address the disaster shall not be protected under this section.
(3) Reclassification Abuse. No person shall mischaracterize a situation as a qualifying natural disaster for the purpose of avoiding compliance with this Code.

(g) **Documentation and Post-Event Review.**
(1) Required Record. Any person invoking this section shall prepare a record describing—
(A) the nature of the disaster;
(B) the spells cast;
(C) the basis for necessity; and
(D) any resulting effects or damage.
(2) Submission. Such record shall be submitted in accordance with § 401.5 or as otherwise directed under § 102.1.
(3) Review. The Department of Magical Affairs may review all actions taken under this section and impose corrective measures where necessary.

(h) **Cross-References.**
For reasonable care requirements, see § 101.7. For spell duration and termination, see § 501.1 and § 501.2. For emergency writs of magic, see § 602.4. For spell risk classification, see § 401.2. For ethical limitations, see Part VII.

(i) **Historical Annotations.**
Originally established under C.C.D. 4987, 14 MR 221, Sun. 8, 1693. Amended under C.C.D. 5362, 20 MR 664, Wed. 17, 1738 to incorporate deferred compliance provisions. Revised under C.C.D. 6124, 31 MR 902, Fri. 2, 1814 to clarify intervention authority and post-event review procedures.

§ 601.5 Restrictions on Magic Meant to Influence Public Policy

(a) **In General.**
No person shall cast, attempt to cast, facilitate, authorize, or cause to be cast any spell for the purpose of influencing, altering, interfering with, or circumventing the formulation, adoption, implementation, enforcement, or interpretation of public policy, except as expressly authorized under this section. This prohibition shall apply regardless of whether such influence is direct, indirect, successful, attempted, or merely preparatory.

(b) **Scope of Public Policy Activities.**
(1) Covered Proceedings. This section shall apply to any activity involving—
(A) legislative deliberation, drafting, or voting;
(B) administrative rulemaking, interpretation, or enforcement actions;
(C) judicial or quasi-judicial proceedings involving interpretation of this Code or related law;
(D) advisory or consultative functions performed by any council, board, or governmental body under § 102.1.
(2) Covered Actors. The prohibition under subsection (a) applies to conduct directed at—
(A) public officials, including elected or appointed authorities;
(B) administrative personnel, clerks, or support staff;
(C) members of any council, tribunal, or oversight body;
(D) any intermediary whose actions may influence an outcome described in paragraph (1).

(c) **Forms of Prohibited Influence.**
(1) Direct Magical Influence. No spell shall be used to alter cognition, judgment, emotional state, perception, or recollection of any person involved in public policy processes.
(2) Indirect Manipulation. The prohibition under this section shall include any use of magic that operates through—
(A) alteration of surroundings in a manner designed to influence decision-making;
(B) manipulation of documents, records, or evidence;
(C) interference with communication, transmission, or reception of information;

(D) use of familiars, constructs, or third parties acting under magical influence.
(3) Mass Influence. No person shall deploy magic intended to influence groups of persons, populations, or audiences for the purpose of affecting public policy outcomes.
(4) Temporal or Predictive Manipulation. No person shall use time manipulation, divination, or similar means to—
(A) obtain non-public information for strategic influence;
(B) alter the sequence of events leading to a policy decision;
(C) retroactively affect outcomes already determined.

(d) **Heightened Prohibitions.**
(1) Mind-Control. The use of mind-control magic for any purpose described in subsection (a) is prohibited without exception.
(2) Illusory Distortion. No illusion or similar effect shall be used to misrepresent facts, fabricate events, or distort reality in a manner that could influence policy outcomes.
(3) Transfigurative Interference. No transfiguration shall be used to alter evidence, persons, or environments connected to public policy processes.

(e) **Permitted Conduct.**
(1) Non-Magical Participation. Nothing in this section shall prohibit lawful participation in public policy processes through non-magical means, including advocacy, debate, or submission of materials.
(2) Neutral Administrative Functions. Magic used solely for clerical, logistical, or ministerial purposes shall be permitted where—
(A) such use does not influence outcomes;
(B) the function performed is equivalent to a non-magical alternative.
(3) Authorized Oversight. Magic employed by authorized bodies under § 102.1 for purposes of auditing, monitoring, or enforcing compliance shall not be considered a violation of this section.

(f) **Disclosure and Transparency.**
(1) Affirmative Duty. Any person who uses magic in proximity to a public policy proceeding shall disclose such use where—
(A) the use is reasonably likely to affect perception, timing, or accessibility of information;
(B) the use could reasonably be construed as influencing the proceeding.

(2) Form of Disclosure. Disclosure shall be made in a manner prescribed by the Department of Magical Affairs and shall include the nature, scope, and purpose of the magic employed.

(g) **Burden of Proof and Presumptions.**
(1) General Rule. The burden shall be on the practitioner to demonstrate that any use of magic in proximity to a public policy process falls within a permitted category under subsection (e).
(2) Rebuttable Presumption. Any use of magic that coincides with a material change in outcome, timing, or participant behavior shall be presumed to violate this section unless affirmatively rebutted.

(h) **Prohibition on Evasion.**
No person shall structure actions, divide conduct into multiple components, utilize intermediaries, or otherwise arrange activities for the purpose of avoiding the application of this section.

(i) **Cross-References.**
For ethical standards governing magical conduct, see § 701.1. For mind-control regulations, see Part XXI. For time manipulation restrictions, see Part XXII. For administrative authority and enforcement procedures, see § 102.1. For secrecy provisions applicable to governmental operations, see Part XXIX.

(j) **Historical Annotations.**
Originally established under C.C.D. 5071, 16 MR 312, Mon. 5, 1704. Amended under C.C.D. 5488, 22 MR 781, Thu. 21, 1756 to include mass manipulation provisions. Revised under C.C.D. 6290, 34 MR 110, Tue. 9, 1832 to clarify indirect influence and disclosure obligations.

§ 601.6 Spellcasting in Warfare

(a) **In General.**
Spellcasting in warfare shall be governed by this section and all applicable provisions of this Code. No person shall engage in magical conduct during armed conflict except in compliance with the principles of necessity, proportionality, distinction, and controllability.

(b) **Authorized Use.**

(1) Lawful Military Objectives. Spellcasting shall be permitted only where directed toward legitimate military objectives, including neutralization of hostile forces, protection of allied forces, or stabilization of conflict zones.
(2) Necessity Requirement. A spell shall not be used where a less destructive or less intrusive means is reasonably available.
(3) Proportionality. The anticipated benefit of any spell shall not be outweighed by the foreseeable harm to persons, property, or magical systems.

(c) **Distinction and Targeting.**
(1) Non-Combatants. No spell shall intentionally target non-combatants or persons not actively participating in hostilities.
(2) Protected Objects. Spellcasting shall not be directed at—
(A) medical facilities;
(B) sanctuaries established under § 601.9;
(C) locations designated for civilian refuge.
(3) Indiscriminate Effects. Spells incapable of being directed at a specific target or whose effects cannot be contained shall be prohibited.

(d) **Prohibited Methods and Means.**
No person shall employ spells that—
(1) cause widespread or uncontrolled magical contamination;
(2) permanently alter environmental or dimensional stability;
(3) produce effects that cannot be reversed, contained, or reasonably mitigated;
(4) operate beyond the control of the casting party once initiated.

(e) **Command Responsibility.**
(1) General Rule. Commanding practitioners shall be responsible for ensuring that all subordinate spellcasting complies with this section.
(2) Failure to Supervise. Failure to exercise reasonable supervision shall constitute a violation independent of any underlying act.

(f) **Documentation and Review.**
(1) Operational Records. Spellcasting conducted in warfare shall be documented to the extent practicable, including the nature of the spell, intended target, and observed effects.
(2) Post-Conflict Review. The Department of Magical Affairs may conduct retrospective review of wartime spellcasting.

(g) **Cross-References.**

For emergency spellcasting provisions, see § 601.4. For ethical standards, see Part VII. For spell risk classification, see § 401.2. For administrative authority, see § 102.1.

(h) **Historical Annotations.**
Originally established under C.C.D. 4902, 12 MR 890, Fri. 19, 1680. Amended under C.C.D. 5590, 23 MR 411, Wed. 3, 1762. Revised under C.C.D. 6402, 35 MR 905, Sun. 11, 1845 to incorporate enhanced targeting and containment requirements.

§ 601.7 Magical Espionage

(a) **In General.**
Magical espionage shall be prohibited except as expressly authorized under this section. No person shall use magic to obtain, access, observe, infer, reconstruct, or transmit information where such information is protected, restricted, or not lawfully accessible, regardless of whether such information is ultimately retained, used, or disclosed.

(b) **Definitions and Scope.**
(1) Magical Espionage. For purposes of this section, "magical espionage" includes any use of magic to acquire information that would not be obtainable through ordinary, lawful, non-magical means within the same time and conditions.
(2) Protected Information. Protected information includes—
(A) communications not intended for the practitioner;
(B) records, documents, or artifacts subject to restriction under this Code or Part XXIX;
(C) thoughts, memories, or mental impressions of any person;
(D) information contained within secured or restricted locations, whether physical or extra-dimensional.
(3) Covered Methods. This section applies to conduct carried out through direct casting or through intermediaries, including familiars, constructs, enchanted devices, or environmental manipulation.

(c) **Prohibited Conduct.**
(1) Surveillance. No person shall use magic to monitor, track, or observe any person, place, or activity where a reasonable expectation of privacy exists under Part XXX.

(2) Interception. Magical interception, diversion, duplication, or alteration of communications is prohibited.
(3) Extraction. No person shall use magic to extract information from—
(A) a mind or memory;
(B) a secured document or magical record;
(C) a protected location or dimensional space.
(4) Reconstruction. No person shall use magic to reconstruct past events, concealed facts, or hidden conditions where such reconstruction would reveal protected information.
(5) Signal Amplification and Enhancement. No person shall use magic to enhance perception, extend sensory range, or otherwise augment observation capabilities for the purpose of obtaining protected information.
(6) Indirect Acquisition. The prohibitions of this subsection shall apply regardless of whether the information is obtained directly or through layered or sequential magical effects.

(d) **Authorized Governmental Activities.**
(1) General Authorization. Magical espionage may be conducted by authorized bodies under § 102.1 where—
(A) such activity is necessary for enforcement, intelligence, or public safety purposes; and
(B) the activity is conducted pursuant to a valid authorization issued under applicable procedures.
(2) Scope Limitation. Authorized activity shall be limited to the specific objective described in the authorization and shall not extend beyond what is reasonably necessary to achieve that objective.
(3) Minimization. Information not directly relevant to the authorized purpose shall not be retained, disclosed, or used, except where required for compliance or oversight.
(4) Documentation. All authorized activity shall be recorded in accordance with § 401.5 or other applicable reporting requirements.

(e) **Mundane and Non-Espionage Exceptions.**
(1) Ordinary Perception. This section shall not prohibit the use of magic that—
(A) enhances perception in a generalized manner not directed at a specific target; and
(B) does not result in the acquisition of protected information.

(2) Publicly Available Information. The use of magic to observe, collect, or analyze information that is openly available to the general public shall not constitute espionage.
(3) Incidental Acquisition. Information obtained incidentally through lawful spellcasting shall not constitute a violation, provided—
(A) the information was not the intended target; and
(B) the practitioner does not retain, use, or disclose such information in violation of this Code.
(4) Authorized Consensual Access. Information obtained with the informed and voluntary consent of the subject shall not be prohibited, except where such consent is invalid under Part XXI or Part XXX.
(5) Defensive Measures. The use of magic to detect, prevent, or mitigate espionage directed at the practitioner or their property shall not be prohibited, provided such measures do not exceed what is reasonably necessary.

(f) **Presumptions and Burden of Proof.**
(1) General Rule. The burden shall be on the practitioner to demonstrate that any use of magic resulting in acquisition of information falls within a permitted category under subsection (d) or (e).
(2) Rebuttable Presumption. Where information is obtained through means not available to a non-magical observer under comparable circumstances, such acquisition shall be presumed to be prohibited unless affirmatively rebutted.

(g) **Cross-References.**
For secrecy requirements, see Part XXIX. For privacy protections, see Part XXX. For administrative authority and authorization procedures, see § 102.1. For mind-reading and mental privacy restrictions, see § 2101.5.

(h) **Historical Annotations.**
Originally established under C.C.D. 5155, 18 MR 504, Tue. 12, 1718. Amended under C.C.D. 5589, 23 MR 410, Wed. 2, 1762 to include signal enhancement prohibitions. Revised under C.C.D. 6221, 32 MR 998, Thu. 27, 1821 to incorporate minimization and incidental acquisition standards.

§ 601.8 Use of Illegal Magic in Carrying Out Violent Crimes

(a) **In General.**
No person shall employ, attempt to employ, facilitate, or cause to be employed any form of illegal magic in the commission, facilitation, concealment, or attempted commission of a violent crime.

(b) **Scope of Application.**
(1) Covered Conduct. This section applies to any use of magic that contributes, in whole or in part, to—
(A) the planning or preparation of a violent act;
(B) the execution of such act;
(C) the evasion of detection, apprehension, or accountability.
(2) Direct and Indirect Use. The prohibition under subsection (a) applies whether the magic is used—
(A) directly by the actor;
(B) through intermediaries, including familiars, constructs, or enchanted devices;
(C) as part of a coordinated or multi-step sequence of actions.

(c) **Definition of Illegal Magic.**
For purposes of this section, "illegal magic" includes—
(1) any spell prohibited under Part VI or other provisions of this Code;
(2) any spell cast without required authorization under § 101.5 or Part II;
(3) any spell that violates restrictions under Part IV, Part XX, or Part XXI;
(4) any spell rendered unlawful by its manner of use, even if lawful in isolation.

(d) **Aggravating Factors.**
Use of illegal magic shall constitute an aggravating factor under § 102.2, including where such use—
(1) increases the severity or duration of harm;
(2) expands the number of affected persons, areas, or systems;
(3) impairs the ability of authorities to detect, investigate, or respond;
(4) results in persistent or self-sustaining harmful effects;
(5) involves coordination among multiple actors or repeated applications.

(e) **Enhanced Liability for Certain Conduct.**

(1) Persistent Effects. Where illegal magic produces effects that continue beyond the commission of the underlying act, the violation shall be treated as ongoing until such effects are terminated in accordance with § 501.2.
(2) Failure to Mitigate. Failure to take reasonable steps to terminate or mitigate the effects of illegal magic shall constitute a separate violation.
(3) Strict Responsibility. A person who initiates or authorizes illegal magic shall remain responsible for its effects regardless of subsequent loss of control.

(f) **Relationship to Underlying Offense.**
(1) Separate Violation. A violation of this section shall be treated as separate from, and in addition to, any underlying violent offense.
(2) No Merger. The use of illegal magic shall not merge into the underlying offense for purposes of liability or enforcement under § 102.2.

(g) **Cross-References.**
For penalties, see § 102.2. For prohibited magical practices, see § 701.2. For spell duration and termination obligations, see § 501.1 and § 501.2. For classification of spell risk, see § 401.2.

(h) **Historical Annotations.**
Originally established under C.C.D. 5302, 19 MR 700, Mon. 14, 1730. Amended under C.C.D. 5744, 25 MR 118, Fri. 7, 1775 to include indirect use provisions. Revised under C.C.D. 6510, 36 MR 412, Fri. 6, 1853 to incorporate enhanced liability and persistence standards.

§ 601.9 Sanctuary Orders and Protected Zones

(a) **In General.**
Sanctuary Orders and the designation of Protected Zones shall impose heightened, and in certain cases absolute, restrictions on spellcasting within defined areas. No person shall cast, attempt to cast, facilitate, or permit the casting of any spell within a Protected Zone except in strict compliance with this section and the specific terms of the applicable Sanctuary Order. Compliance with this section shall be construed narrowly, and any ambiguity shall be resolved in favor of restriction.

(b) **Definitions.**

(1) Sanctuary Order. A Sanctuary Order is a formal directive issued under § 102.1 designating a specific area as subject to enhanced regulation, limitation, or prohibition of magical activity.
(2) Protected Zone. A Protected Zone is any area, boundary, structure, or defined spatial or conceptual region subject to a Sanctuary Order, including—
(A) the primary geographic footprint;
(B) any vertical, subterranean, or extra-dimensional extension;
(C) any buffer or perimeter region specified in the Order.
(3) Zone Classifications.
(A) Full Prohibition Zone. A zone in which all spellcasting is prohibited except as expressly authorized under this Code.
(B) Conditional-Use Zone. A zone in which spellcasting is permitted only under defined and enumerated conditions.
(C) Monitored-Use Zone. A zone in which spellcasting is permitted subject to continuous or periodic oversight, reporting, or surveillance.

(c) **Authority and Issuance.**
(1) General Authority. The Department of Magical Affairs or any authorized body under § 102.1 may issue a Sanctuary Order where necessary to—
(A) protect life or prevent widespread harm;
(B) preserve magical, environmental, or dimensional stability;
(C) enforce secrecy under Part XXIX;
(D) secure locations of heightened legal, political, or operational significance.
(2) Required Contents. Each Sanctuary Order shall specify—
(A) the boundaries of the Protected Zone;
(B) the classification under subsection (b)(3);
(C) the duration or conditions for termination;
(D) any permitted uses or exceptions;
(E) any required compliance measures, including reporting or monitoring.
(3) Emergency Orders.
(A) A Sanctuary Order may be issued without prior notice where delay would materially increase risk.
(B) Such Order shall be reduced to written or recorded form as soon as reasonably practicable and shall include the basis for emergency issuance.

(d) **Scope and Applicability.**

(1) Persons Covered. This section applies to all persons, entities, practitioners, and any agent, familiar, construct, or instrument acting under their direction or influence.
(2) Forms of Magic Covered. This section applies to—
(A) direct spellcasting;
(B) sustained or persistent magical effects;
(C) activation of pre-existing enchantments;
(D) indirect effects achieved through environmental or intermediary manipulation.
(3) Strict Liability Standard. A violation of this section shall not require proof of intent, knowledge, or awareness of the Protected Zone.

(e) **Restrictions Within Protected Zones.**
(1) Full Prohibition Zones.
(A) No spell shall be cast, maintained, activated, or permitted to persist within such zone.
(B) All existing spells affecting the zone shall be terminated or neutralized.
(C) No person shall introduce any magical object, construct, or effect capable of activation within the zone.
(2) Conditional-Use Zones.
(A) Spellcasting shall be permitted only where—
(i) expressly authorized in the Sanctuary Order; and
(ii) conducted in full compliance with all specified conditions.
(B) Conditions may include limitations on—
(i) spell type or classification under § 401.2;
(ii) duration under § 501.1;
(iii) identity, licensing status, or certification of the practitioner;
(iv) timing, frequency, or cumulative effects.
(C) Any deviation from specified conditions shall constitute a violation.
(3) Monitored-Use Zones.
(A) Spellcasting shall be permitted only where subject to monitoring requirements.
(B) Monitoring may include—
(i) real-time surveillance under § 402.1;
(ii) mandatory logging under § 401.5;
(iii) periodic inspection or audit.
(C) Failure to comply with monitoring requirements shall result in immediate revocation of authorization.

(f) **Notice and Constructive Awareness.**
(1) Methods of Notice. Notice of a Protected Zone may be provided through—
(A) physical markers;
(B) magical indicators or barriers;
(C) public registries or records;
(D) any combination thereof.
(2) Constructive Notice. A person shall be deemed to have notice where a reasonable practitioner would have identified the existence of the Protected Zone under the circumstances.
(3) Duty to Inquire. Any person entering, approaching, or conducting activity within an area where a Protected Zone may exist shall have an affirmative duty to determine its status.

(g) **Effect on Existing Spells and Conditions.**
(1) Immediate Compliance Requirement. Upon designation, any spell affecting the zone shall be—
(A) terminated;
(B) modified to comply; or
(C) reported to the Department of Magical Affairs for directive action.
(2) Ongoing Responsibility. The originating caster shall remain responsible for compliance regardless of absence, delegation, or loss of control.
(3) Administrative Intervention. The Department of Magical Affairs may—
(A) terminate or alter any spell;
(B) seize or neutralize any magical object;
(C) impose containment measures.

(h) **Authorized Exceptions.**
(1) Emergency Actions. Spellcasting necessary to prevent imminent harm may be permitted under § 601.4 or § 602.4, provided such action is strictly limited in scope and duration.
(2) Governmental Operations. Authorized personnel acting under § 102.1 may engage in spellcasting as necessary to establish, maintain, or cnforce the Protected Zone.
(3) Express Authorization. Any exception must be expressly stated in the Sanctuary Order and shall be narrowly construed.

(i) **Documentation, Reporting, and Review.**

(1) Recordkeeping Requirement. Any permitted activity within a Protected Zone shall be documented, including—
(A) the legal basis for authorization;
(B) the nature and duration of the spell;
(C) any observed effects.
(2) Submission. Records shall be submitted in accordance with § 401.5 or as otherwise directed.
(3) Review Authority. The Department of Magical Affairs may conduct audits, inspections, or retrospective review of any activity within a Protected Zone.

(j) **Interaction with Other Provisions.**
(1) Secrecy. Where a Protected Zone is established for purposes of secrecy, compliance with Part XXIX shall be mandatory.
(2) Conflict of Laws. In the event of conflict between this section and any other provision, the more restrictive rule shall apply.
(3) Supplemental Orders. Additional requirements may be imposed through supplementary directives issued under § 102.1.

(k) **Cross-References.**
For administrative authority and issuance of directives, see § 102.1. For spell duration and termination, see § 501.1 and § 501.2. For emergency spellcasting provisions, see § 601.4 and § 602.4. For secrecy requirements, see Part XXIX. For real-time monitoring, see § 402.1.

(l) **Historical Annotations.**
Originally established under C.C.D. 5033, 15 MR 118, Thu. 12, 1699. Amended under C.C.D. 5470, 22 MR 664, Mon. 3, 1755 to include monitored-use classifications. Revised under C.C.D. 6312, 34 MR 902, Fri. 18, 1838 to incorporate strict liability standards and expanded enforcement authority.

§ 602.1 Magic Siphoning Practices

(a) **In General.**
The siphoning, extraction, diversion, aggregation, storage, transfer, or redistribution of magical energy shall be strictly regulated under this section. No person, entity, governmental body, council, or instrumentality shall engage in siphoning practices except as expressly authorized herein.

This section shall apply universally and without exemption, including to actions undertaken pursuant to governmental authority under § 102.1.

(b) **Definition of Siphoning.**
(1) General Rule. For purposes of this section, "siphoning" means any act or series of acts by which magical energy is—
(A) removed, drawn, or extracted from a person, entity, creature, object, location, or system;
(B) redirected, diverted, or captured for storage or later use; or
(C) transferred from its original source to another location, repository, or user.
(2) Covered Methods. Siphoning includes conduct carried out through—
(A) direct spellcasting;
(B) passive or automated enchantments;
(C) environmental manipulation, including alteration of ley lines;
(D) constructs, artifacts, or other intermediary mechanisms.
(3) Aggregation. The collection or accumulation of magical energy from multiple sources shall constitute siphoning regardless of scale.

(c) **General Prohibition.**
(1) Unauthorized Siphoning. No siphoning shall be conducted without lawful authorization under this section.
(2) Non-Consensual Extraction. No person shall extract magical energy from another person, entity, or system without valid authorization or consent.
(3) Governmental Limitation. No governmental body shall—
(A) implement or operate any system designed to extract magical energy from a population, class of persons, or geographic region;
(B) aggregate such energy into a centralized reservoir for general use, redistribution, or strategic advantage;
(C) compel or mandate participation in any siphoning system, whether directly or indirectly.

(d) **Permitted Siphoning Activities.**
(1) Localized and Incidental Use. Siphoning may be permitted where—
(A) the extraction is minimal, temporary, and incidental to a lawful spell; and
(B) no lasting deprivation or imbalance results.
(2) Voluntary Transfer. Magical energy may be transferred where—
(A) the source provides informed and voluntary consent; and

(B) such consent is not obtained through coercion, manipulation, or impairment under Part XXI.
(3) Stabilization Measures. Siphoning may be permitted where necessary to stabilize—
(A) a volatile magical condition;
(B) a disrupted ley line;
(C) an uncontrolled or hazardous spell effect;
provided that such action is limited to what is necessary and consistent with § 101.7.
(4) Authorized Research. Limited siphoning may be permitted for research purposes where—
(A) authorized under Part XV; and
(B) conducted in a controlled environment with appropriate safeguards.
(5) Custodial Restriction of Magical Capacity.
(A) The temporary deprivation, suppression, or controlled extraction of magical capacity from a person lawfully detained or incarcerated for a violent offense may be permitted where—
(i) such action is authorized under procedures established pursuant to § 102.1; and
(ii) the purpose is limited to preventing harm, escape, or continued unlawful conduct.
(B) Any action under this paragraph shall be narrowly tailored in scope and duration and shall not exceed what is reasonably necessary to achieve its purpose.
(C) Continued restriction following release shall require a separate determination supported by a demonstrated risk to public safety and shall be subject to periodic review.

(e) **Prohibited Aggregation and Redistribution Systems.**
(1) General Rule. No person or entity shall design, implement, or operate any system that—
(A) continuously extracts magical energy from multiple sources;
(B) stores such energy in a centralized or distributed reservoir; and
(C) redistributes such energy to other users or systems.
(2) Circumvention. The prohibition under paragraph (1) shall apply regardless of whether—
(A) the system operates intermittently or continuously;
(B) the extraction is individually minimal but collectively significant;
(C) the system is structured through multiple intermediary entities or locations.

(3) Public Resource Characterization. Magical energy inherent to individuals or localized systems shall not be recharacterized as a public resource for purposes of bypassing this subsection.

(f) **Effects on Source and Environment.**
(1) Depletion. No siphoning shall result in material depletion of a source beyond its natural capacity to regenerate.
(2) Imbalance. No siphoning shall create instability in surrounding magical systems, including imbalance in ley lines or adjacent environments.
(3) Duty to Mitigate. Any person engaged in permitted siphoning shall take reasonable steps to prevent or mitigate adverse effects.

(g) **Documentation and Reporting.**
(1) Required Records. Any permitted siphoning activity shall be documented, including—
(A) the source and nature of the energy extracted;
(B) the purpose and duration of the activity;
(C) any observed effects on the source or environment.
(2) Submission. Such records shall be maintained and submitted in accordance with § 401.5 or as directed under § 102.1.

(h) **Cross-References.**
For reasonable care requirements, see § 101.7. For administrative authority, see § 102.1. For spell logging and reporting, see § 401.5. For emergency provisions, see § 601.4 and § 602.4. For ethical protections, see Part VII.

(i) **Historical Annotations.**
Originally established under C.C.D. 7421, 41 MR 223, Tue. 6, 1912. Amended under C.C.D. 8810, 57 MR 644, Thu. 18, 1984 to include custodial restriction provisions. Revised under C.C.D. 9903, 72 MR 118, Wed. 11, 2018 to incorporate aggregation system prohibitions and enhanced environmental safeguards.

§ 602.2 Full-Moon Codification and Time-Based Exceptions

(a) **In General.**

Certain spells, practices, and categories of magical activity shall be subject to temporal regulation based on celestial, environmental, or cyclical conditions. No person shall cast, attempt to cast, facilitate, or permit the casting of any spell subject to time-based restriction except in compliance with this section.

(b) **Full-Moon Codification.**
(1) Definition. For purposes of this section, a "full-moon period" shall mean the interval beginning at the moment of astronomical full illumination and ending at the conclusion of the immediately following lunar cycle phase as determined by the Department of Magical Affairs.
(2) Enhanced Restrictions. During a full-moon period, any spell or practice designated as full-moon-sensitive shall be subject to additional limitations, including—
(A) prohibition of casting except by authorized practitioners;
(B) mandatory classification as high-risk under § 401.2;
(C) expanded logging and documentation requirements under § 401.5.
(3) Designated Practices. The Department of Magical Affairs shall maintain a registry of spells and practices subject to full-moon codification.

(c) **Time-Based Authorization Requirements.**
(1) Conditional Authorization. Certain spells may be cast only during specified temporal windows, including—
(A) full-moon periods;
(B) seasonal intervals defined under § 602.3;
(C) other cyclical or astronomical conditions as prescribed.
(2) Prohibition Outside Authorized Periods. No person shall cast any such spell outside its authorized temporal window, regardless of otherwise valid authorization.

(d) **Temporal Deviations and Adjustments.**
(1) Geographic Variation. Temporal conditions shall be determined based on the location in which the spell is cast.
(2) Artificial Manipulation. No person shall use magic to alter, simulate, or replicate a temporal condition for the purpose of satisfying a requirement under this section.
(3) Time Manipulation. The use of time-based magic to circumvent temporal restrictions is prohibited.

(e) **Emergency Exceptions.**
(1) General Rule. Time-based restrictions may be temporarily overridden where necessary to prevent imminent harm in accordance with § 601.4 or § 602.4.
(2) Limitations. Any such override shall be limited to what is strictly necessary and shall not extend beyond the duration of the emergency.

(f) **Documentation and Compliance.**
(1) Verification. A practitioner shall verify that any applicable temporal condition is satisfied prior to casting.
(2) Recordkeeping. Any spell subject to this section shall be documented, including the basis for compliance with temporal requirements.

(g) **Presumptions.**
Any spell cast under conditions reasonably associated with a restricted temporal window shall be presumed to fall within this section unless affirmatively demonstrated otherwise.

(h) **Cross-References.**
For spell risk classification, see § 401.2. For logging requirements, see § 401.5. For emergency spellcasting, see § 601.4 and § 602.4. For seasonal exceptions, see § 602.3. For time manipulation restrictions, see Part XXII.

(i) **Historical Annotations.**
Originally established under C.C.D. 7510, 42 MR 118, Mon. 9, 1920. Amended under C.C.D. 8899, 58 MR 771, Tue. 4, 1986 to include artificial manipulation prohibitions. Revised under C.C.D. 10012, 73 MR 204, Fri. 20, 2020 to expand codification requirements and temporal enforcement standards.

§ 602.3 Autumn Harvest Exemptions

(a) **In General.**
Notwithstanding any other provision of this Code, limited exemptions from otherwise applicable spellcasting restrictions shall be permitted during the Autumn Harvest Period, subject to the conditions, limitations, and procedural requirements set forth in this section. Such exemptions shall be construed narrowly and shall apply only to qualifying activities.

(b) **Definition of Autumn Harvest Period.**

(1) General Rule. The Autumn Harvest Period shall mean the interval designated annually by the Department of Magical Affairs corresponding to the primary seasonal period of agricultural gathering and preservation.
(2) Determination.
(A) The Department shall publish the beginning and end dates of the Autumn Harvest Period for each jurisdiction.
(B) In the absence of published dates, the period shall be determined based on prevailing agricultural conditions within the relevant region.
(3) Regional Variation. The Autumn Harvest Period may vary by location, climate, crop type, or magical ecosystem.

(c) **Qualifying Activities.**
(1) Agricultural Production. Spellcasting shall be permitted where directly related to—
(A) harvesting crops;
(B) preserving or storing agricultural yield;
(C) protecting fields, livestock, or produce from spoilage, infestation, or environmental harm.
(2) Post-Harvest Processing. Spellcasting may be permitted for—
(A) drying, curing, or fermentation processes;
(B) transportation and storage stabilization;
(C) preparation of goods for distribution or trade.
(3) Community and Subsistence Use. Limited spellcasting shall be permitted for communal or subsistence-based agricultural support, provided such use does not exceed local need.

(d) **Scope of Exemptions.**
(1) Relaxation of Restrictions. During the Autumn Harvest Period, qualifying activities under subsection (c) may be exempt from—
(A) certain licensing limitations under Part II;
(B) select duration or declaration requirements under § 501.1, where impracticable;
(C) specified operational restrictions otherwise applicable under this Code.
(2) Limitations.
(A) No exemption shall permit high-risk spellcasting unless otherwise authorized under § 401.2.
(B) No exemption shall apply to prohibited practices under Part VII.
(C) No exemption shall extend beyond what is reasonably necessary to complete the qualifying activity.

(e) **Prohibited Conduct.**
(1) Commercial Exploitation. No person shall invoke this section to justify large-scale commercial operations exceeding customary agricultural practice.
(2) Pretextual Use. Spellcasting unrelated to qualifying activities shall not be protected under this section.
(3) Temporal Extension. No person shall artificially extend or simulate harvest conditions to prolong the applicability of this section.

(f) **Documentation and Verification.**
(1) Recordkeeping. Any person relying on this section shall maintain records sufficient to demonstrate—
(A) the nature of the activity;
(B) the timing within the Autumn Harvest Period;
(C) the necessity of the spellcasting.
(2) Verification Authority. The Department of Magical Affairs may require submission of such records for review.

(g) **Interaction with Other Provisions.**
(1) Time-Based Rules. This section shall operate in conjunction with § 602.2, and in the event of conflict, the more restrictive provision shall apply.
(2) Emergency Provisions. Nothing in this section shall limit the application of § 601.4 or § 602.4.

(h) **Cross-References.**
For emergency exemptions, see § 601.4 and § 602.4. For spell duration requirements, see § 501.1. For risk classification, see § 401.2.

(i) **Historical Annotations.**
Originally established under C.C.D. 7442, 41 MR 998, Wed. 14, 1915. Amended under C.C.D. 8790, 56 MR 302, Mon. 11, 1982 to include regional variation provisions. Revised under C.C.D. 9981, 71 MR 554, Thu. 5, 2016 to clarify limitations on commercial exploitation and documentation requirements.

§ 602.4 Emergency Writs of Magic

(a) **In General.**

An Emergency Writ of Magic (hereafter referred to as a "Writ") is a formal authorization issued under § 102.1 permitting temporary deviation from otherwise applicable provisions of this Code where necessary to address an imminent threat. No person shall rely upon a Writ except in strict compliance with this section and the terms of the Writ.

(b) **Authority to Issue.**
(1) Issuing Bodies. A Writ may be issued by—
(A) the Department of Magical Affairs;
(B) any authorized council or tribunal acting under § 102.1;
(C) a designated official empowered to act in emergency capacity pursuant to procedures established by the Department.
(2) Delegation. Authority to issue a Writ may be delegated only where—
(A) such delegation is expressly provided; and
(B) the scope of delegated authority is clearly defined and limited.

(c) **Conditions for Issuance.**
(1) Imminent Threat Requirement. A Writ shall not be issued unless—
(A) an imminent threat to life, property, or magical stability exists; and
(B) compliance with ordinary provisions of this Code would materially impair the ability to respond.
(2) Necessity and Proportionality.
(A) The Writ shall authorize only those actions necessary to address the identified threat.
(B) The scope of authorization shall be proportional to the severity and immediacy of the threat.
(3) Unavailability of Alternatives. A Writ shall not be issued where adequate non-magical or compliant alternatives are reasonably available.

(d) **Required Contents of Writ.**
Each Writ shall specify—
(1) the identity of the issuing authority;
(2) the factual basis for issuance;
(3) the scope of authorized actions;
(4) the duration or conditions for termination;
(5) any limitations, conditions, or reporting requirements.

(e) **Scope and Limitations.**
(1) General Rule. A Writ shall not authorize—
(A) conduct expressly prohibited under Part VII;

(B) actions unrelated to the identified emergency;
(C) indefinite or open-ended deviations from this Code.
(2) Strict Construction. All authorizations under a Writ shall be construed narrowly.
(3) Duration.
(A) A Writ shall remain in effect only for the period necessary to address the emergency.
(B) Upon cessation of the underlying threat, the Writ shall terminate automatically.

(f) **Emergency Action Without Prior Writ.**
(1) Permitted Conduct. A practitioner may act without a Writ where—
(A) an imminent threat exists;
(B) obtaining a Writ is impracticable due to time constraints; and
(C) the action taken is strictly necessary.
(2) Post-Action Requirement.
(A) The practitioner shall seek retroactive authorization as soon as reasonably practicable.
(B) Failure to obtain such authorization shall result in the action being treated as unauthorized unless otherwise justified.

(g) **Documentation and Reporting.**
(1) Required Record. Any action taken pursuant to a Writ or under subsection (f) shall be documented, including—
(A) the nature of the emergency;
(B) the actions taken;
(C) the duration and effects of such actions.
(2) Submission. Records shall be submitted in accordance with § 401.5 or as directed under § 102.1.

(h) **Oversight and Review.**
(1) Administrative Review. The Department of Magical Affairs shall review all Writs and actions taken thereunder.
(2) Corrective Measures. Where misuse or overreach is identified, corrective action may be imposed, including revocation of authority or referral for enforcement under § 102.2.

(i) **Presumptions.**

Any action taken outside the express scope of a Writ shall be presumed unauthorized unless affirmatively demonstrated to be necessary and consistent with this section.

(j) **Cross-References.**
For administrative authority, see § 102.1. For emergency exemptions, see § 601.4. For spell duration and termination, see § 501.1 and § 501.2. For logging requirements, see § 401.5.

(k) **Historical Annotations.**
Originally established under C.C.D. 7360, 40 MR 442, Mon. 2, 1908. Amended under C.C.D. 8844, 57 MR 998, Thu. 27, 1985 to include retroactive authorization provisions. Revised under C.C.D. 10045, 73 MR 771, Tue. 14, 2021 to clarify scope limitations and oversight procedures.

§ 602.5 Daily Spell Limitations and Circumvention Attempts

(a) **In General.**
Daily spell limitations shall regulate the frequency, cumulative impact, and total number of spells that may be cast, maintained, or caused to persist by any person within a defined temporal period. No person shall exceed such limitations or attempt to circumvent them, whether directly or indirectly.

(b) **Definition of Daily Limitation Period.**
(1) General Rule. A daily limitation period shall mean a continuous 24-hour interval measured from—
(A) the time of the first spell cast within such period; or
(B) such standardized time as may be prescribed by the Department of Magical Affairs for uniform application.
(2) Geographic Considerations. The applicable period shall be determined based on the location of the practitioner at the time of casting.

(c) **Application of Limits.**
(1) Cumulative Counting. All spells cast, sustained, activated, or caused to persist by a person shall be counted toward the applicable daily limitation, including—
(A) direct casting;
(B) activation of pre-existing enchantments;

(C) maintenance of sustained or persistent effects under § 501.1.
(2) Attribution. A spell shall be attributed to a person where that person—
(A) casts the spell;
(B) directs, authorizes, or materially assists in its casting;
(C) maintains or benefits from its continued operation.

(d) **Classification-Based Limits.**
(1) Differentiation. Daily limitations may vary based on the classification of spells under § 401.2.
(2) Weighted Counting. The Department of Magical Affairs may assign weighted values to spells based on risk, complexity, or cumulative impact.
(3) Aggregation. Multiple low-impact spells may be aggregated and treated as a higher-impact use for purposes of determining compliance.

(e) **Prohibited Circumvention.**
(1) General Rule. No person shall structure, sequence, or divide spellcasting activities for the purpose of avoiding daily limitations.
(2) Specific Prohibitions. Prohibited circumvention includes—
(A) distributing spellcasting across multiple individuals acting in coordination;
(B) utilizing familiars, constructs, or automated systems to cast or maintain spells;
(C) segmenting a single spell into multiple components to reduce its apparent impact;
(D) transferring control or ownership of a spell to another person to reset counting.
(3) Substance Over Form. Compliance shall be determined based on the substance and cumulative effect of the activity rather than its formal structure.

(f) **Exemptions.**
(1) Emergency Actions. Spellcasting necessary to prevent imminent harm may be exempt under § 601.4 or § 602.4.
(2) Authorized Operations. Certain activities conducted under governmental authority may be exempt where expressly provided under § 102.1.
(3) Incidental Effects. Minimal or incidental magical effects that do not materially contribute to cumulative impact may be excluded, as determined by the Department of Magical Affairs.

(g) **Documentation and Monitoring.**
(1) Recordkeeping. Practitioners shall maintain records sufficient to demonstrate compliance with daily limitations, including the number, type, and duration of spells cast.
(2) Verification. The Department of Magical Affairs may require submission of such records or implement monitoring mechanisms to ensure compliance.

(h) **Presumptions and Burden of Proof.**
(1) General Rule. The burden shall be on the practitioner to demonstrate compliance with applicable daily limitations.
(2) Rebuttable Presumption. Where a pattern of spellcasting suggests structured avoidance of limits, such activity shall be presumed to violate this section unless affirmatively rebutted.

(i) **Interaction with Other Provisions.**
(1) Duration Rules. Persistent or sustained spells shall be evaluated in conjunction with § 501.1 and § 501.2.
(2) Time-Based Exceptions. Any applicable exception under § 602.2 or § 602.3 shall not operate to eliminate daily limitations unless expressly provided.

(j) **Cross-References.**
For spell classification and risk levels, see § 401.2. For spell duration and persistence, see § 501.1 and § 501.2. For emergency provisions, see § 601.4 and § 602.4. For administrative authority, see § 102.1.

(k) **Historical Annotations.**
Originally established under C.C.D. 7488, 42 MR 771, Fri. 3, 1918. Amended under C.C.D. 8921, 58 MR 442, Tue. 12, 1987 to include weighted classification rules. Revised under C.C.D. 10088, 74 MR 118, Mon. 22, 2022 to incorporate anti-circumvention standards and monitoring provisions.

§ 602.6 Clothing Requirements for Citizens Experiencing Temporary Biological Transformation

(a) **In General.**

Any person temporarily transformed into an alternate biological form through magical, alchemical, divine, or comparable means shall remain subject to public decency and conduct requirements under this Code to the extent reasonably practicable.

(b) **Applicability.**
This section applies to transformations including, but not limited to:
(1) wolves;
(2) bears;
(3) amphibious giants;
(4) lesser dragons; and
(5) any other form capable of locomotion within public spaces or causing alarm to reasonable observers.

(c) **Standard of Compliance.**
(1) A transformed individual shall maintain compliance with applicable decency standards to the extent that such compliance is physically and structurally possible given the form assumed.
(2) Where garments, coverings, or equivalent measures cannot be reasonably worn or applied, the individual shall take reasonable steps to avoid public exposure, including refraining from entering—
(A) thoroughfares;
(B) marketplaces;
(C) civic gatherings; or
(D) any location in which the presence of the transformed individual would foreseeably disrupt public order.

(d) **Duration and Responsibility.**
(1) Obligations under this section shall persist for the duration of the transformation, regardless of whether such transformation is voluntary, accidental, or imposed by external forces.
(2) A person shall not avoid compliance by asserting lack of control over the timing, duration, or nature of the transformation.

(e) **Prohibited Conduct.**
No person shall—
(1) intentionally enter or remain in public spaces while in a transformed state in violation of subsection (c);
(2) use transformation as a means of evading public decency requirements; or

(3) create or contribute to conditions in which others are exposed to a transformed individual in violation of this section.

(f) **Prohibited Defense.**
It shall not constitute a defense to a violation of this section that the individual was, at the time of the conduct—
(1) "not technically a person";
(2) "operating under instinct"; or
(3) otherwise exempt from ordinary legal obligations by virtue of the transformation.

(g) **Affirmative Compliance Measures.**
(1) Individuals subject to predictable or recurring transformation shall take reasonable advance measures to ensure compliance, including securing private space or arranging for supervision where necessary.
(2) Where there is any uncertainty as to compliance, the individual is strongly encouraged to wear or otherwise secure an oversized shirt, cloak, or comparable covering prior to entering any public or semi-public space. This is not a complex requirement.

(h) **Cross-References.**
For definition of magical personhood, see § 101.9. For public spellcasting and conduct restrictions, see § 401.3. For ethical obligations in spellcasting, see § 701.1. For sanctuary and protected zones, see § 601.9. For penalties, see § 102.2.

(i) **Historical Annotations.**
This section was enacted under C.C.D. 8124, 52 MR 118, Fri. 3, 1934 following repeated disturbances during the Spring Festival Werewolf Incidents, in which multiple individuals asserted exemption from clothing requirements while transformed. Amended under C.C.D. 9342, 68 MR 442, Tue. 9, 1989 to clarify applicability to non-humanoid forms. Revised under C.C.D. 10602, 79 MR 771, Wed. 20, 2026 to establish advance compliance obligations, eliminate defenses based on temporary non-personhood, and reiterate basic expectations regarding public decency.

Part VII: Magical Ethics and Oversight

§ 701.1 Ethical Standards in Magical Practice

(a) **In General.**
All persons engaging in magical practice shall adhere to the ethical standards set forth in this section. No spell shall be cast, maintained, or permitted to persist in a manner that is inconsistent with the principles of integrity, accountability, restraint, and respect for persons, creatures, property, and systems affected by such magic.

(b) **Duty of Integrity.**
(1) Truthfulness. No person shall use magic to deceive, mislead, or create a false impression where such deception results in material harm, unlawful advantage, or impairment of another's ability to act.
(2) Representation of Authority. No person shall falsely represent that a spell is authorized under this Code or any provision thereof.
(3) Accurate Disclosure. Any required declaration, record, or submission under this Code shall be complete and accurate.

(c) **Duty to Avoid Harm.**
(1) General Rule. A practitioner shall not cast any spell where the foreseeable harm outweighs the intended benefit.
(2) Secondary Effects. Consideration shall be given to indirect, delayed, or cumulative effects.
(3) Recklessness. Disregard of known risks or failure to assess reasonably foreseeable consequences shall constitute a violation of this subsection.

(d) **Respect for Autonomy.**
(1) Non-Interference. No person shall use magic to control, override, or substantially interfere with the free will of another except as expressly authorized under this Code.
(2) Consent. Where consent is required, such consent shall be informed, voluntary, and not obtained through coercion, manipulation, or impairment.
(3) Scope of Consent. Any use of magic shall be limited to the scope of consent provided.

(e) **Fair Use and Non-Exploitation.**
(1) Prohibition. No person shall exploit another through the use of magic, including by taking advantage of vulnerability, lack of knowledge, or unequal access to magical resources.
(2) Unjust Advantage. No person shall use magic to obtain an advantage in transactions, agreements, or interactions that would not be available under ordinary, lawful conditions.

(f) **Stewardship of Magical Systems.**
(1) Environmental Responsibility. A practitioner shall avoid actions that degrade or destabilize magical environments, including ley lines or other systemic structures.
(2) Preservation. Magical resources shall be used in a manner consistent with long-term sustainability.

(g) **Professional Conduct.**
(1) Competence. No person shall undertake spellcasting beyond their level of training, certification, or experience where such limitation is required under Part II.
(2) Supervision. Where required, appropriate supervision shall be maintained.
(3) Duty to Report. A practitioner aware of a material violation of this Code shall report such violation in accordance with procedures established under § 102.1.

(h) **Interaction with Other Provisions.**
(1) Supplemental Nature. This section shall apply in addition to, and not in lieu of, any specific prohibition or requirement set forth elsewhere in this Code.
(2) Conflict. In the event of conflict, the more specific provision shall govern.

(i) **Cross-References.**
For reasonable care requirements, see § 101.7. For authorized spellcasters, see § 101.5. For administrative authority and enforcement, see § 102.1. For penalties, see § 102.2. For mind-control restrictions, see Part XXI.

(j) **Historical Annotations.**
Originally established under C.C.D. 4011, 9 MR 112, Mon. 3, 1542. Amended under C.C.D. 5220, 18 MR 603, Thu. 12, 1726 to incorporate

consent standards. Revised under C.C.D. 7310, 40 MR 221, Tue. 18, 1905 to include environmental stewardship provisions.

§ 701.2 Prohibited Magical Practices

(a) **In General.**
No person shall engage in any prohibited magical practice as defined in this section. The prohibitions set forth herein shall apply regardless of intent, outcome, or claimed justification, except where an explicit exception is provided elsewhere in this Code. This section shall be construed broadly to prevent evasion and to preserve the integrity of magical systems and public safety.

(b) **Practices Inherently Prohibited.**
(1) Uncontainable Effects. No spell shall be cast where its effects—
(A) cannot be controlled once initiated;
(B) cannot be terminated in accordance with § 501.2;
(C) are reasonably likely to propagate beyond the intended scope.
(2) Irreversible Harm. No spell shall be cast where it produces permanent harm that cannot be mitigated, reversed, or contained.
(3) Existential Destabilization. No person shall engage in any magical act that—
(A) destabilizes dimensional boundaries;
(B) disrupts the continuity of time beyond authorized limits;
(C) threatens large-scale collapse of magical or natural systems.

(c) **Prohibited Methods and Means.**
(1) Unauthorized Creation of Entities. No person shall create, summon, or bind entities in violation of this Code.
(2) Corruptive Magic. No person shall employ magic that degrades, corrupts, or irreparably alters the fundamental nature of a person, creature, or system.
(3) Self-Replicating Constructs. No person shall create or deploy any magical construct capable of autonomous replication without strict containment and authorization in accordance with this Code.

(d) **Manipulation of Core Systems.**
(1) Ley Line Interference. No person shall alter, reroute, or destabilize ley lines except as expressly authorized.

(2) Fundamental Forces. No person shall manipulate foundational magical forces in a manner that exceeds established safety thresholds.
(3) Reality Alteration. No spell shall be used to fundamentally alter the structure of reality outside of authorized experimental or controlled environments.

(e) **Prohibited Outcomes Regardless of Method.**
No person shall engage in any magical activity that results in—
(1) uncontrolled spread of magical effects;
(2) cascading failures across systems or environments;
(3) loss of containment over hazardous magical phenomena.

(f) **Strict Liability Standard.**
A violation of this section shall not require proof of intent, knowledge, or foreseeability where the prohibited practice or outcome occurs.

(g) **Limited Exceptions.**
Any exception to this section must be expressly provided elsewhere in this Code and shall be construed narrowly.

(h) **Cross-References.**
For ethical standards, see § 701.1. For spell duration and termination, see § 501.1 and § 501.2. For administrative authority, see § 102.1.

(i) **Historical Annotations.**
Originally established under C.C.D. 3988, 8 MR 771, Wed. 12, 1539. Amended under C.C.D. 5401, 21 MR 204, Fri. 6, 1742 to include prohibitions on self-replicating constructs. Revised under C.C.D. 8122, 49 MR 998, Mon. 27, 1933 to incorporate systemic destabilization standards.

§ 701.3 Negligent Spellcasting and Improper Technique

(a) **In General.**
A person shall be considered to have engaged in negligent spellcasting where such person fails to meet the standard of reasonable care set forth in § 101.7. This section shall not redefine such standard, but shall identify acts, omissions, and practices that constitute, evidence, or give rise to a determination of negligence for purposes of this Code.

(b) **Acts Constituting Negligence.**
The following acts or omissions shall constitute negligence where they result in, or create a substantial risk of, unintended, uncontrolled, or harmful effects:
(1) casting a spell without adequate preparation, understanding, or assessment of reasonably foreseeable consequences;
(2) failure to verify that required conditions, authorizations, or environmental factors are satisfied prior to casting, including where required under other applicable provisions of this Code;
(3) use of materials, components, or inputs that are degraded, incompatible, or improperly prepared;
(4) failure to account for the presence of persons, creatures, structures, or active magical effects within the area of influence;
(5) reliance on assumptions, approximations, or unverified conditions where accuracy is required.

(c) **Improper Technique.**
(1) General Rule. Use of improper technique in the casting or maintenance of a spell shall constitute negligence where such technique materially deviates from accepted practice.
(2) Illustrative Violations. Improper technique includes—
(A) incorrect or unstable wand movement, positioning, or directional alignment;
(B) incomplete, altered, or improperly sequenced incantation;
(C) substitution, omission, or mismeasurement of required components;
(D) failure to calibrate a spell to account for scale, distance, or intensity;
(E) use of improvised or unverified casting methods outside of authorized research.
(3) Reference to Authorized Practices. Deviation from approved spellcasting practices under this Code shall constitute evidence of negligence.

(d) **Failure to Monitor, Control, or Terminate.**
(1) Ongoing Obligation. A practitioner shall monitor any spell producing continuing effects and shall adjust, contain, or terminate such spell as required under § 501.2.
(2) Failure to Act. Negligence shall include—
(A) failure to observe or recognize instability, drift, or unintended effects;
(B) failure to take corrective action within a reasonable time;

(C) abandonment of a spell without ensuring proper termination or control.
(3) Delegation. Delegation of monitoring or control shall not relieve the originating caster of responsibility.

(e) **Interaction and Compound Effects.**
(1) Multiple Spells. A person shall consider the interaction of multiple spells affecting the same subject, area, or system.
(2) Compound Negligence. A series of individually minor acts or omissions may constitute negligence where their combined effect creates a substantial risk.
(3) Concurrent Activity. Failure to account for active spells cast by others, where reasonably detectable, shall constitute negligence.

(f) **Per Se Negligence.**
The following conduct shall constitute negligence as a matter of law, without regard to intent or outcome:
(1) casting a spell in violation of an express procedural requirement under this Code, including failure to comply with declaration requirements under § 501.1(b) where applicable;
(2) use of a spell classified under § 401.2 in a manner inconsistent with its permitted conditions of use;
(3) continuation of a spell after the occurrence of a terminating condition or expiration of its authorized duration under § 501.1;
(4) failure to terminate or mitigate a known hazardous effect in accordance with § 501.2;
(5) use of unauthorized or prohibited methods in circumstances where authorization is required under Part II or Part XV.

(g) **Aggravating Circumstances.**
Negligence under this section shall be considered aggravated where—
(1) the conduct involves a high-risk spell under § 401.2;
(2) the conduct occurs within a Protected Zone under § 601.9;
(3) the conduct affects multiple persons, a population, or a sensitive system;
(4) prior violations, warnings, or deficiencies are present.

(h) **Evidentiary Considerations.**
(1) Records. Failure to maintain records required under § 401.5 may be considered evidence of negligent practice.

(2) Burden. The practitioner shall bear the burden of demonstrating compliance with § 101.7 where negligence is alleged under this section.

(i) **Cross-References.**
For the standard of reasonable care, see § 101.7. For spell classification and conditions of use, see § 401.2 and § 401.6. For spell duration and termination, see § 501.1 and § 501.2. For time-based requirements, see § 602.2. For Protected Zones, see § 601.9.

(j) **Historical Annotations.**
Originally established under C.C.D. 4120, 10 MR 334, Fri. 6, 1561. Amended under C.C.D. 5612, 23 MR 998, Tue. 19, 1765 to incorporate improper technique standards. Revised under C.C.D. 8455, 50 MR 221, Mon. 8, 1941 to include compound negligence principles and per se violations.

§ 701.4 Inspections of Dungeons and Magical Detention Areas (MDA)

(a) **In General.**
All dungeons, holding cells, containment chambers, and other facilities used for the detention, confinement, or restraint of persons, creatures, or entities through magical or non-magical means (hereafter referred to as "Magical Detention Areas" or "MDA") shall be subject to inspection in accordance with this section. No person shall operate, maintain, or oversee an MDA except in compliance with the inspection, access, and oversight requirements set forth herein.

(b) **Definition and Scope.**
(1) Magical Detention Area. An MDA includes any location, structure, or construct used to confine or restrict movement, autonomy, or magical capacity, including—
(A) traditional dungeons, cells, or holding facilities;
(B) extra-dimensional or pocket spaces used for containment;
(C) magically reinforced structures or barriers;
(D) any facility employing ongoing magical effects to maintain confinement.
(2) Covered Conditions. This section shall apply regardless of whether confinement is—
(A) temporary or permanent;

(B) physical, magical, or hybrid in nature;
(C) administered by governmental or non-governmental actors.

(c) **Inspection Authority.**
(1) General Authority. The Department of Magical Affairs, or any authorized body under § 102.1, shall have authority to inspect any MDA.
(2) Access. Inspectors shall be granted immediate and unrestricted access to—
(A) all areas of the MDA;
(B) all records, logs, and documentation relating to detention;
(C) any magical systems or constructs used in confinement.
(3) Obstruction. No person shall obstruct, delay, or interfere with an inspection.

(d) **Inspection Requirements.**
(1) Frequency.
(A) Routine inspections shall be conducted at intervals prescribed by the Department of Magical Affairs.
(B) Additional inspections may be conducted without notice.
(2) Scope of Review. Inspections shall include evaluation of—
(A) structural integrity and safety of the facility;
(B) operation and stability of magical containment systems;
(C) conditions affecting detainees, including treatment and exposure to harmful effects;
(D) compliance with applicable provisions of this Code.
(3) Testing and Verification. Inspectors may—
(A) test magical barriers, restraints, or suppression systems;
(B) verify proper functioning of containment mechanisms;
(C) require demonstration of emergency release or termination procedures.

(e) **Conditions of Confinement.**
(1) Minimum Standards. All MDAs shall maintain conditions that—
(A) prevent unnecessary harm or suffering;
(B) do not exceed what is required for lawful detention;
(C) comply with ethical standards under § 701.1.
(2) Prohibited Conditions. No MDA shall employ—
(A) uncontrolled or degrading magical effects;
(B) conditions that result in permanent harm absent lawful authorization;

(C) containment methods inconsistent with § 501.2 or applicable safety requirements.

(f) **Magical Suppression and Restraint.**
(1) Authorized Use. Any suppression or restriction of magical capacity within an MDA shall be—
(A) limited to what is necessary for security and safety;
(B) subject to periodic review;
(C) implemented in a manner consistent with § 602.1 where applicable.
(2) Overreach. No person shall impose excessive or indefinite suppression without proper authorization.

(g) **Documentation and Recordkeeping.**
(1) Required Records. Each MDA shall maintain records including—
(A) identities or classifications of detainees;
(B) duration and conditions of confinement;
(C) use of magical restraints or suppression;
(D) any incidents, irregularities, or failures.
(2) Inspection Reports. Inspectors shall produce written reports documenting findings, deficiencies, and required corrective actions.

(h) **Corrective Action and Enforcement.**
(1) Deficiencies. Where violations or deficiencies are identified, the Department of Magical Affairs may—
(A) require immediate corrective measures;
(B) impose operational restrictions;
(C) suspend or terminate use of the MDA.
(2) Emergency Action. Where conditions pose an immediate risk, inspectors may order immediate cessation of operations or removal of detainees.

(i) **Cross-References.**
For ethical standards, see § 701.1. For administrative authority, see § 102.1. For termination of magical effects, see § 501.2. For siphoning restrictions related to suppression, see § 602.1.

(j) **Historical Annotations.**
Originally established under C.C.D. 4688, 12 MR 118, Thu. 9, 1668. Amended under C.C.D. 5890, 27 MR 771, Mon. 14, 1784 to include extra-dimensional facilities. Revised under C.C.D. 9321, 61 MR 204, Wed. 6,

1995 to incorporate enhanced inspection authority and detainee protection standards.

§ 701.5 Reporting and Investigating Ethical Violations

(a) **In General.**
All persons shall have a duty to report and cooperate in the investigation of violations of Part VII. No person shall conceal, fail to report, or otherwise impede the identification, reporting, or investigation of an ethical violation where such person knows or reasonably should know that a violation has occurred.

(b) **Duty to Report.**
(1) General Rule. A person shall report any known or reasonably suspected violation of this Part to the appropriate authority under § 102.1.
(2) Scope of Knowledge. The duty under this subsection applies where a person—
(A) directly observes a violation;
(B) receives credible information indicating a violation;
(C) becomes aware of circumstances that would lead a reasonable practitioner to conclude that a violation has occurred.
(3) Timeliness. Reports shall be made within a reasonable period after discovery of the relevant facts.

(c) **Reporting Procedures.**
(1) Form and Content. A report shall include, to the extent known—
(A) the identity of the person or entity involved;
(B) the nature of the alleged violation;
(C) the time, location, and circumstances;
(D) any supporting evidence or documentation.
(2) Submission. Reports shall be submitted in accordance with procedures established under § 102.1.
(3) Supplementation. A reporting party shall supplement a report where additional material information becomes available.

(d) **Mandatory Reporting by Certain Persons.**
(1) Covered Persons. The following persons shall have an enhanced duty to report:
(A) licensed practitioners under Part II;

(B) supervisors or persons in positions of authority;
(C) inspectors or officials acting under § 102.1.
(2) Heightened Standard. Failure by a covered person to report a violation shall constitute a separate violation of this Part.

(e) **Cooperation with Investigations.**
(1) General Rule. All persons shall cooperate with any lawful investigation conducted under § 102.1.
(2) Required Conduct. Cooperation includes—
(A) providing truthful information;
(B) producing records or materials when requested;
(C) permitting access to relevant locations, systems, or constructs.
(3) Prohibited Conduct. No person shall—
(A) provide false or misleading information;
(B) withhold material information;
(C) destroy, alter, or conceal evidence.

(f) **Protection Against Retaliation.**
(1) General Rule. No person shall retaliate against any individual for reporting a violation or cooperating with an investigation.
(2) Forms of Retaliation. Retaliation includes—
(A) adverse action affecting employment, status, or privileges;
(B) threats, coercion, or intimidation;
(C) use of magic to impair, monitor, or influence the reporting individual.
(3) Invalidation of Retaliatory Acts. Any action taken in violation of this subsection shall be void and subject to corrective measures.

(g) **Confidentiality.**
(1) Protection of Identity. The identity of a reporting party may be protected where necessary to prevent harm or retaliation.
(2) Limitations. Confidentiality shall not prevent disclosure where required for enforcement, due process, or compliance with this Code.

(h) **False or Frivolous Reports.**
(1) Prohibition. No person shall knowingly submit a false or frivolous report.
(2) Standard. A report shall not be considered false or frivolous where it is made in good faith based on reasonably available information.

(i) **Cross-References.**

For ethical standards, see § 701.1. For administrative authority and investigative procedures, see § 102.1. For penalties, see § 102.2. For frivolous claims, see § 702.1. For good faith compliance, see § 702.2.

(j) **Historical Annotations.**
Originally established under C.C.D. 4750, 13 MR 442, Mon. 3, 1675. Amended under C.C.D. 6012, 29 MR 118, Tue. 17, 1798 to include mandatory reporting provisions. Revised under C.C.D. 9188, 60 MR 771, Fri. 21, 1992 to incorporate retaliation protections and confidentiality standards.

§ 701.6 Ethical Remediation and Corrective Measures

(a) **In General.**
In addition to any enforcement action under § 102.2, any person found to have violated this Part shall be subject to remedial and corrective measures as necessary to restore compliance, mitigate harm, and prevent recurrence. Such measures shall be imposed pursuant to authority under § 102.1 and shall be tailored to the nature and scope of the violation.

(b) **Purpose and Scope.**
(1) Remedial Objective. Measures under this section shall be designed to—
(A) eliminate or reduce ongoing or residual effects of a violation;
(B) restore affected persons, creatures, property, or systems to the extent practicable;
(C) ensure future compliance with this Code.
(2) Non-Substitution. Remedial measures under this section shall not substitute for, offset, or otherwise replace penalties imposed under § 102.2.

(c) **Types of Corrective Measures.**
Corrective measures may include, but are not limited to—
(1) Termination or Modification of Spells.
(A) immediate termination of any spell in violation of this Part in accordance with § 501.2;
(B) modification of any ongoing spell to bring it into compliance;
(2) Restoration and Remediation.
(A) restoration of magical environments, including ley lines or affected systems;

(B) reversal or mitigation of harmful effects to persons or creatures, where possible;
(3) Compliance Actions.
(A) implementation of revised procedures or safeguards;
(B) submission of a compliance plan subject to approval under § 102.1;
(4) Restrictions on Practice.
(A) temporary limitation on the scope, type, or frequency of spellcasting;
(B) suspension of specific practices pending demonstration of compliance;
(5) Training and Certification.
(A) completion of additional training or education;
(B) re-certification or demonstration of competence under Part II.

(d) **Compliance Plans.**
(1) Requirement. A person subject to corrective measures may be required to submit a written compliance plan.
(2) Contents. A compliance plan shall include—
(A) identification of the violation and its causes;
(B) proposed corrective actions;
(C) timelines for implementation;
(D) procedures for monitoring and reporting compliance.
(3) Approval and Modification. The Department of Magical Affairs may approve, reject, or require modification of any plan.

(e) **Monitoring and Verification.**
(1) Ongoing Oversight. A person subject to this section may be placed under monitoring for a defined period.
(2) Verification Measures. Monitoring may include—
(A) periodic reporting;
(B) inspection;
(C) review of records maintained under § 401.5.
(3) Failure to Comply. Failure to comply with any imposed measure shall constitute a separate violation.

(f) **Authority to Impose Measures.**
(1) Administrative Authority. The Department of Magical Affairs or other authorized body under § 102.1 may impose, modify, or terminate corrective measures.
(2) Emergency Measures. Where necessary to prevent ongoing harm, immediate corrective action may be ordered without prior notice.

(g) **Duration and Termination.**
(1) Duration. Corrective measures shall remain in effect only for the period necessary to achieve compliance and remediation.
(2) Termination. Measures may be terminated upon a determination that—
(A) compliance has been achieved; and
(B) risk of recurrence has been adequately addressed.

(h) **Cross-References.**
For administrative authority, see § 102.1. For penalties, see § 102.2. For spell termination, see § 501.2. For recordkeeping, see § 401.5.

(i) **Historical Annotations.**
Originally established under C.C.D. 9055, 60 MR 998, Wed. 12, 1989 in response to increased ethical enforcement actions. Revised under C.C.D. 10072, 73 MR 442, Mon. 18, 2020 to expand compliance planning and monitoring provisions.

§ 701.7 Ethical Regulations Governing Familiars and Other Protected Creatures

(a) **In General.**
No person shall bind, summon, control, employ, or otherwise utilize a familiar or other protected creature except in compliance with the ethical standards and requirements set forth in this section. All interactions with such creatures shall be governed by principles of care, necessity, proportionality, and respect for the creature's nature and well-being.

(b) **Definitions and Scope.**
(1) Familiar. A familiar is any creature bound, contracted, or otherwise linked to a practitioner for purposes of assistance, augmentation, or companionship in magical activity.
(2) Protected Creature. A protected creature includes any creature designated under this Code as requiring heightened ethical consideration due to sentience, rarity, ecological importance, or susceptibility to harm.
(3) Covered Conduct. This section applies to all stages of interaction, including summoning, binding, training, use, maintenance, and release.

(c) **Binding and Consent.**

(1) General Rule. No person shall bind a familiar or other protected creature without lawful authorization and, where applicable, valid consent.
(2) Consent Requirement.
(A) Where a creature is capable of informed consent, such consent shall be obtained and documented.
(B) Consent shall not be obtained through coercion, manipulation, or impairment.
(3) Limitations. No binding shall—
(A) exceed the scope of consent provided;
(B) impose indefinite or irrevocable obligations absent express authorization under this Code.

(d) **Standards of Care.**
(1) General Duty. A person shall provide care consistent with the creature's needs, including—
(A) sustenance, rest, and environmental conditions appropriate to its nature;
(B) protection from unnecessary harm or stress;
(C) maintenance of physical and magical well-being.
(2) Neglect. Failure to meet the requirements of this subsection shall constitute a violation regardless of intent.

(e) **Permitted Use and Limitations.**
(1) Scope of Use. A familiar or protected creature may be used only for purposes consistent with—
(A) the terms of any binding or agreement;
(B) the creature's nature and capabilities;
(C) applicable provisions of this Code.
(2) Prohibited Use. No person shall—
(A) compel a creature to engage in prohibited practices under § 701.2;
(B) use a creature in a manner that creates unnecessary risk of harm;
(C) employ a creature to circumvent requirements or restrictions of this Code.

(f) **Autonomy and Release.**
(1) Termination of Binding. A binding shall be terminated—
(A) upon expiration of its terms;
(B) upon withdrawal of valid consent, where applicable;
(C) where continuation would violate this Code.

(2) Right to Release. A creature capable of autonomous action shall not be indefinitely confined or controlled absent lawful justification.
(3) Post-Release Obligations. The responsible person shall take reasonable steps to ensure that the creature is not left in a condition of harm, instability, or displacement.

(g) **Special Protections.**
(1) Rare or Endangered Creatures. Additional restrictions may apply to creatures designated as rare, endangered, or ecologically significant.
(2) Sentient Creatures. Creatures demonstrating higher levels of cognition or awareness shall be afforded heightened protections, including limitations on binding and use.
(3) Regulatory Designations. The Department of Magical Affairs may designate categories of protected creatures subject to additional requirements.

(h) **Recordkeeping and Oversight.**
(1) Required Records. A person maintaining a familiar or protected creature shall maintain records including—
(A) the identity or classification of the creature;
(B) the terms of binding or agreement;
(C) conditions of care and use.
(2) Inspection. Such records and conditions shall be subject to inspection under applicable provisions of this Code.
(3) Financial Reporting Classification. Nothing in this section shall preclude a familiar from being treated as a reportable asset under Part X where such familiar is subject to ownership, control, or economic benefit as defined therein.

(i) **Cross-References.**
For ethical standards, see § 701.1. For prohibited practices, see § 701.2. For negligent conduct, see § 701.3. For administrative authority, see § 102.1.

(j) **Historical Annotations.**
Originally established under C.C.D. 4390, 11 MR 998, Tue. 21, 1595. Amended under C.C.D. 6125, 30 MR 442, Fri. 3, 1805 to include consent requirements. Revised under C.C.D. 9344, 61 MR 771, Wed. 14, 1996 to incorporate protections for sentient and endangered creatures.

§ 701.8 Mage Misconduct and Arcane Review

(a) **In General.**
Mage misconduct shall include any act or omission by a practitioner that violates this Code, demonstrates unfitness to engage in regulated magical activity, or otherwise undermines the integrity of magical practice. All allegations of mage misconduct shall be subject to review in accordance with this section.

(b) **Definition of Misconduct.**
Mage misconduct includes, but is not limited to—
(1) violation of any provision of this Code;
(2) repeated negligent spellcasting under § 701.3;
(3) engagement in prohibited practices under § 701.2;
(4) failure to comply with ethical standards under § 701.1;
(5) failure to comply with reporting or cooperation requirements under § 701.5;
(6) misuse of authority, position, or certification to obtain unlawful advantage;
(7) conduct demonstrating a pattern of disregard for safety, compliance, or oversight.

(c) **Initiation of Review.**
(1) Sources of Review. Arcane review may be initiated upon—
(A) receipt of a report under § 701.5;
(B) findings from an inspection under this Code;
(C) referral by an authorized body under § 102.1;
(D) identification of irregularities through monitoring or recordkeeping under § 401.5.
(2) Preliminary Determination.
(A) The reviewing authority shall determine whether sufficient basis exists to proceed.
(B) Frivolous or unsupported claims may be dismissed in accordance with § 702.1.

(d) **Arcane Review Process.**
(1) Notice. The subject of review shall be provided notice of—
(A) the alleged misconduct;
(B) the basis for review;
(C) any required response or appearance.

(2) Investigation. The reviewing body may—
(A) examine records, logs, and documentation;
(B) conduct interviews or compel testimony;
(C) inspect locations, systems, or constructs relevant to the matter.
(3) Response. The subject shall have an opportunity to respond, provide evidence, and contest the findings.

(e) **Determinations and Findings.**
(1) General Rule. Upon completion of review, the authority shall issue a determination as to whether misconduct has occurred.
(2) Findings. Determinations shall include—
(A) findings of fact;
(B) identification of applicable provisions;
(C) recommended or imposed actions.

(f) **Corrective and Administrative Measures.**
Where misconduct is established, the reviewing authority may impose measures including—
(1) corrective actions under § 701.6;
(2) limitations or conditions on continued practice;
(3) suspension or revocation of authorization or certification under Part II;
(4) referral for enforcement under § 102.2.

(g) **Interim Measures.**
(1) Temporary Restrictions. Pending review, the authority may impose temporary limitations where necessary to prevent harm.
(2) Emergency Action. Immediate suspension or restriction may be imposed where continued activity presents a substantial risk.

(h) **Record of Proceedings.**
(1) Documentation. All proceedings under this section shall be documented, including evidence, findings, and actions taken.
(2) Retention. Records shall be maintained in accordance with § 401.5 and applicable retention policies.

(i) **Finality and Further Review.**
(1) Administrative Finality. Determinations under this section shall be final unless subject to further review under procedures established by the Council of Councils.

(2) Supplemental Review. Additional review may be conducted where new evidence or material changes arise.

(j) **Cross-References.**
For ethical standards, see § 701.1. For prohibited practices, see § 701.2. For negligent conduct, see § 701.3. For reporting and investigations, see § 701.5. For corrective measures, see § 701.6. For administrative authority, see § 102.1. For penalties, see § 102.2.

(k) **Historical Annotations.**
Originally established under C.C.D. 4522, 12 MR 771, Mon. 6, 1620. Amended under C.C.D. 5881, 27 MR 204, Tue. 11, 1783 to formalize review procedures. Revised under C.C.D. 9250, 61 MR 118, Thu. 9, 1994 to incorporate interim measures and expanded oversight authority.

§ 701.9 Magic Secrecy Act

(a) **In General.**
The Magic Secrecy Act (MSA) establishes comprehensive reporting, monitoring, and compliance requirements governing financial transactions and magical trade involving high-risk magical activities or assets. No person, entity, institution, or intermediary shall engage in any covered transaction unless such transaction is conducted, documented, and reported in accordance with this section. This section shall govern all reporting obligations relating to magical transactions under this Code.

(b) **Purpose.**
The MSA is intended to—
(1) prevent the use of magical assets in prohibited practices under § 701.2;
(2) detect and deter illicit enchantment sales, magical smuggling, and manipulation of magical commodities;
(3) ensure traceability and accountability in high-risk magical transactions;
(4) establish standardized oversight mechanisms for magical commerce.

(c) **Scope of Application.**
(1) Covered Persons. This section applies to—
(A) practitioners engaged in the commercial production, sale, or transfer of magical goods or services;
(B) institutions involved in magical trade, manufacturing, storage, or distribution;

(C) financial entities dealing in magically infused currency, artifacts, or instruments;
(D) intermediaries, brokers, or facilitators participating in covered transactions.
(2) Covered Transactions. A transaction shall be subject to this section where it involves—
(A) high-risk spells or enchanted items classified under § 401.2;
(B) high-value magical assets meeting or exceeding the thresholds established under paragraph (d);
(C) bulk acquisition, transfer, or distribution of magical goods;
(D) any pattern of activity that, in the aggregate, would meet or exceed such thresholds.
(3) Aggregation Rule. Multiple transactions shall be treated as a single transaction where—
(A) they are structured to avoid reporting requirements; or
(B) they are part of a coordinated or related series of activities.

(d) **Threshold Determinations.**
(1) General Rule. A transaction shall be considered reportable where—
(A) the fair value of the magical asset or aggregate transaction exceeds 10,000 MCUs;
(B) the transaction involves 5 or more Class II objects within a 7-day period;
(C) the transaction involves any Class III or Class IV object, regardless of value.
(2) Bulk Activity Thresholds.
(A) acquisition or transfer of 10 or more magical objects within a 30-day period shall be presumed reportable;
(B) any structured series of transactions designed to avoid thresholds shall be treated as a single reportable transaction.
(3) Adjustment Authority. The Department of Magical Affairs may adjust thresholds where necessary to reflect changes in magical markets, risk conditions, or patterns of misuse.

(e) **Reporting Requirements.**
(1) General Rule. Covered persons shall file reports for all transactions meeting the criteria set forth in subsection (c).
(2) Required Information. Each report shall include, to the extent known—
(A) identification of all parties involved, including beneficial owners;

(B) description and classification of the magical asset or activity under;
(C) quantity, valuation methodology, and declared use;
(D) origin and destination of the asset;
(E) any indicators of unusual or suspicious activity.
(3) Form and Manner. Reports shall be filed in accordance with procedures established under § 102.1.
(4) Timing. Reports shall be filed within prescribed timeframes, and delayed reporting shall constitute a violation unless justified under such procedures.

(f) **Monitoring and Internal Controls.**
(1) Duty to Monitor. Covered persons shall maintain systems reasonably designed to detect and evaluate unusual or suspicious activity.
(2) Required Controls. Such systems shall include—
(A) transaction monitoring protocols;
(B) risk-based classification of clients, counterparties, and activities;
(C) escalation procedures for review and reporting.
(3) Institutional Responsibilities.
(A) designation of a compliance officer responsible for oversight;
(B) periodic training of personnel;
(C) independent review or audit of compliance systems.

(g) **Suspicious Activity Reporting.**
(1) General Rule. A report shall be filed where a covered person knows, suspects, or has reason to suspect that a transaction—
(A) involves proceeds of unlawful or prohibited magical activity;
(B) is structured to evade reporting requirements;
(C) lacks apparent lawful purpose.
(2) Timing. Such reports shall be filed promptly upon detection of the suspicious activity.
(3) Confidentiality.
(A) No person shall disclose the existence or content of a report to any subject of such report;
(B) disclosures shall be limited to authorized authorities under § 102.1.

(h) **Recordkeeping Requirements.**
(1) General Rule. Covered persons shall maintain records sufficient to reconstruct each covered transaction.
(2) Contents. Records shall include—
(A) transaction documentation and supporting materials;

(B) communications relating to the transaction;
(C) internal analyses or determinations.
(3) Retention. Records shall be retained for not less than 700 years and shall be readily accessible for inspection.

(i) **Prohibited Conduct.**
(1) General Rule. No person shall—
(A) fail to file a required report;
(B) file incomplete, inaccurate, or misleading information;
(C) structure or fragment transactions to evade requirements;
(D) interfere with monitoring, reporting, or recordkeeping processes.
(2) Specific Prohibitions.
(A) No person shall knowingly assist another in avoiding the requirements of this section, including by—
(i) creating artificial transaction structures;
(ii) using proxies, intermediaries, or constructs to obscure identity;
(iii) misclassifying assets or activities.
(B) No institution shall implement policies or practices that—
(i) discourage reporting of suspicious activity;
(ii) limit visibility into covered transactions;
(iii) otherwise impair compliance with this section.

(j) **Administrative Oversight and Examination.**
(1) Authority. The Department of Magical Affairs may examine any covered person for compliance.
(2) Scope. Examinations may include—
(A) review of records and reports;
(B) testing of monitoring systems;
(C) evaluation of internal controls and compliance programs.
(3) Corrective Measures. Where deficiencies are identified, corrective measures may be imposed under § 701.6.

(k) **Cross-References.**
For prohibited practices, see § 701.2. For ethical standards, see § 701.1. For corrective measures, see § 701.6. For administrative authority, see § 102.1. For penalties, see § 102.2.

(l) **Historical Annotations.**
Originally established under C.C.D. 9012, 60 MR 118, Tue. 7, 1987 in response to increased illicit magical trade and smuggling activity.

Amended under C.C.D. 9455, 64 MR 771, Fri. 19, 1999 to expand reporting and monitoring requirements. Revised under C.C.D. 10021, 73 MR 302, Wed. 10, 2019 to incorporate threshold determinations, aggregation rules, and enhanced compliance program standards.

§ 702.1 Frivolous Claims and Arguments

(a) **General Prohibition on Frivolous Claims and Arguments.**
No individual, entity, or institution subject to the provisions of this Code shall assert frivolous claims, defenses, or arguments in any proceeding, report, declaration, or other formal interaction governed by this Code. A frivolous claim or argument is defined as one that:
(1) Lacks any basis in fact, law, or reasonable interpretation of the Code;
(2) Is presented primarily for the purpose of delay, harassment, or obstruction; or
(3) Willfully misrepresents or distorts the Code's provisions to achieve an improper objective.

(b) **Examples of Frivolous Claims.**
For the purposes of this section, the following claims are deemed frivolous, including but not limited to:
(1) Asserting that a regulation explicitly applying to licensed spellcasters does not apply to a particular license holder without evidence or valid exemption;
(2) Filing a contrary position under § 702.2(c) based on speculative, irrelevant, or unsupported interpretations of the Code;
(3) Claiming immunity from penalties on the grounds that the Code is “unfair” without reference to specific provisions or applicable exceptions;
(4) Arguments premised on the existence of hypothetical magical phenomena not recognized or documented under § 101.1(a);
(5) Repeatedly invoking defenses previously adjudicated and dismissed without presenting new evidence or interpretations.

(c) **Standards for Determining Frivolity.**
Claims or arguments shall be deemed frivolous if they fail to meet the following standards:
(1) Legal Basis. The claim or argument must have a plausible basis in the text, intent, or legislative history of the Code.

(2) Factual Support. The claim or argument must be grounded in verifiable evidence or logical reasoning that aligns with known magical practices or principles.
(3) Good Faith. The claim or argument must be made in good faith and not for the purpose of obstructing proceedings or exploiting procedural loopholes.

(d) **Filing and Review Process for Allegations of Frivolity.**
(1) Any party alleging a claim or argument is frivolous must file a formal complaint (Form 8821-FC) with the Council of Counsel, detailing the basis for the allegation.
(2) The Council shall review the complaint and may, at its discretion:
(A) Request additional documentation or clarification from the parties involved;
(B) Convene a preliminary hearing to evaluate the merits of the claim; or
(C) Dismiss the allegation if it lacks sufficient evidence.
3. If the Council determines a claim or argument to be frivolous, it shall issue a formal ruling outlining its findings and recommended penalties under subsection (f).

(e) **Duty of Practitioners and Representatives.**
Practitioners, spellcasters, and legal representatives submitting claims or arguments must exercise reasonable diligence to ensure their assertions are not frivolous. This duty includes:
(1) Conducting thorough research into the applicable sections of the Code;
(2) Ensuring all factual representations are accurate and supported by evidence;
(3) Refraining from submitting redundant or meritless claims.

(f) **Penalties for Frivolous Claims and Arguments.**
(1) Individuals or entities found to have asserted frivolous claims or arguments are subject to the following penalties:
(A) Suspension or revocation of licenses issued under § 201.1, as applicable;
(B) Disqualification from submitting further claims or arguments for a period not exceeding five (5) years, at the discretion of the Council.
(2) Legal representatives submitting frivolous claims on behalf of others may face additional disciplinary actions, including disbarment from magical proceedings or referral to professional oversight bodies.

(g) **Frivolity in Magical Research and Reporting.**
(1) Assertions made in the context of magical research or academic work are subject to review for frivolity if they are:
(A) Presented as formal claims under this Code without proper evidence or peer review;
(B) Designed to mislead governing bodies or obstruct regulatory processes; or
(C) Detrimental to the integrity of magical scholarship or public trust in magical governance.
(2) Researchers or institutions submitting frivolous claims shall face penalties equivalent to those outlined in subsection (f).

(h) **Safeguards Against Misuse of Frivolity Allegations.**
(1) Frivolity allegations must themselves meet the standards outlined in subsection (c).
(2) Any party filing a frivolous frivolity allegation may be subject to penalties equivalent to those for asserting frivolous claims, including sanctions or public censure.

(i) **Cross-References.**
For good faith requirements, see § 702.2. For contrary positions and the filing of declarations, refer to § 702.2(c). For disciplinary actions related to misconduct, consult § 701.8.

(j) **Historical Annotations.**
Enacted under C.C.D. 9982, 90 MR 3421, Tue. 1, 2021, to address concerns about misuse of regulatory processes and to uphold the integrity of magical governance.

§ 702.2 Good Faith Compliance with the Magical Code of Regulations

(a) **Requirement of Good Faith.**
All individuals, entities, and institutions governed by this Code must act in good faith to adhere to its provisions and underlying intent. Compliance shall reflect the spirit and ethical purpose of the Code, not solely its literal text. Actions that circumvent, exploit, or subvert the Code's intent while technically adhering to its wording constitute violations of this section.

(b) **Standards for Good Faith Compliance.**
(1) Individuals and entities are presumed to act in good faith when:
(A) They apply regulations as reasonably intended, avoiding manipulative or self-serving interpretations;
(B) They seek guidance or clarification from governing councils when uncertain about the applicability or scope of specific provisions;
(C) They maintain transparency in their documentation and communications related to compliance.
(2) Examples of bad faith compliance include, but are not limited to:
(A) Exploiting ambiguities or loopholes to justify unethical or unlawful conduct;
(B) Misrepresenting facts or contexts to claim exemptions or avoid obligations;
(C) Engaging in willful ignorance of applicable regulations.

(c) **Positions Contrary to the Code.**
(1) Individuals or entities asserting positions contrary to the established regulations of this Code must adhere to the following requirements:
(A) File a formal declaration (Form 7521-C) outlining the contrary position, supporting rationale, and proposed interpretation or modification;
(B) Provide evidence that the position is based on a reasonable interpretation of the Code's language, legislative history, or guiding principles;
(C) Submit the declaration to the Council of Councils for review and adjudication prior to acting on the contrary position.
(2) Failure to adhere to these requirements invalidates any defense based on a contrary position.
(3) The Council of Councils reserves the right to dismiss frivolous, repetitive, or unsupported declarations and impose sanctions for misuse of the declaration process.

(d) **Demonstration of Good Faith.**
Individuals accused of non-compliance or bad faith actions may assert a good faith defense by demonstrating reasonable efforts to comply with the Code, including:
(1) Documented attempts to interpret ambiguous regulations through formal inquiries to governing councils;
(2) Evidence of adherence to ethical and safety standards while acting in gray areas;

(3) Prompt corrective actions taken upon discovery of non-compliance.

(e) **Good Faith and Contrary Positions Defense.**
(1) A good faith defense is valid if the individual:
(A) Took reasonable steps to understand and follow the Code;
(B) Documented their decision-making process, including any contrary positions taken in compliance with subsection (c);
(C) Acted with transparency and did not conceal relevant information.
(2) A contrary position defense is valid if:
(A) The individual submitted the required declaration under subsection (c)(1);
(B) The position was based on an objectively reasonable interpretation of the Code.

(f) **Cross-References.**
For ethical compliance requirements, see § 701.1. For provisions related to mage misconduct, see § 701.8.

(g) **Historical Annotations.**
Enacted under C.C.D. 9942, 85 MR 3421, Fri. 3, 2020, to ensure adherence to the spirit of the Code and to address concerns about exploitative interpretations. Amended under C.C.D. 9963, 87 MR 4523, Mon. 15, 2024, to include provisions governing contrary positions.

§ 702.3 Regulation of Chosen Ones, Lone Heroes, and Other Destiny-Bound Individuals

(a) **General Rule.**
No individual, collective, reincarnated abstraction, artificially generated soul vessel, or person of unknowable lineage shall fulfill, claim fulfillment of, or be designated for fulfillment of any prophecy, oracle, revelation, fate-thread, celestial forecast, or doom-inscribed relic unless such individual or entity has been certified as a Prophecy-Subject Entity by the Ministry of Prophetic Affairs (MPA) pursuant to the procedures set forth in this section.

This section shall govern all persons and creatures subject to divine appointment, cursed heritage, ancestral burden, or inexplicably glowing sigils, regardless of whether the individual in question consents to or actively attempts to flee said designation.

(b) **Definitions.**
For purposes of this section:
(1) Chosen One.
The term "Chosen One" means any individual who is named in, clearly described by, heavily implied in, or demonstrably aligned with the specifications of a Registered Prophecy and who, based on the totality of the circumstances, exhibits such qualitative or quantitative indicators of prophetic designation that a reasonable person familiar with the prophecy would conclude that the individual is the intended subject.

In determining whether an individual qualifies as a Chosen One, relevant considerations may include, but are not limited to:
(A) survival of one or more physically improbable events, including falling great distances, direct magical blasts, or prolonged exposure to necrotic atmospheres without formal training or protective enchantments;
(B) possession of or selection by a relic, object, beast, or weapon exhibiting prophetic resonance, including humming, glowing, whispering, selective activation, or unlocking sealed doors in remote places;
(C) receipt of unsolicited cryptic warnings, visions, chants, or poetic threats from authorized oracles, strangers in cloaks, cursed artifacts, or ominous clouds;
(D) possession of an identifying mark, scar, symbol, or family heirloom recognized in at least one Registered Prophecy or ancient wall carving as being of "great importance" or "not a coincidence";
(E) expressions of reluctance, denial, or philosophical angst upon learning of their prophetic role, followed by increased proximity to high-stakes situations;
(F) a pattern of narrative centrality inconsistent with the individual's stated intention to live a quiet life; or
(G) such additional destiny-adjacent criteria as the Ministry may determine necessary to prevent under-classification of prophecy-relevant individuals.
(2) Lone Hero.
The term "Lone Hero" means any individual who declares or maintains that they operate without formal allies, companions, guilds, or kinship associations and who satisfies at least two of the following conditions:
(A) is routinely observed in the company of between one and six persistent companions, including sentient items, loyal animals, former enemies, or individuals with matching cloaks;

(B) has previously accepted support, healing, rescue, cooking, shelter, or navigation assistance from others while maintaining verbal claims of solitude;
(C) has filed individual travel papers, mission logs, or prophecy declarations while consistently working alongside others in circumstances requiring mutual survival or coordinated action;
(D) has used phrases such as "I work alone," "this is my burden," or "I can't afford to care" in proximity to shared supplies, lodging, or jointly executed tactical maneuvers; or
(E) exhibits resistance to group-based planning, combined with a history of returning to said group when conditions deteriorate.
(3) Registered Prophecy.
The term "Registered Prophecy" means any predictive utterance, celestial document, vision, or curse certified under the Prophetic Clarity Standards Act of 1434 and filed with the Central Prophetic Registry, provided that such prophecy:
(A) contains no more than two qualifying metaphors per clause;
(B) identifies at least three traits, bloodlines, or geographical designators applicable to fewer than five percent of the general population;
(C) has been reviewed and assigned a Prophecy Identification Number by the Prophetic Review Committee; or
(D) has otherwise been determined by the Prophetic Review Committee, based on the totality of the circumstances, to reasonably describe or predict a future event involving a prophecy-subject entity, artifact, or location, notwithstanding minor failures to satisfy subparagraphs (A) through (C), where strict application would result in under-classification.
(4) Antagonistic Entity of Prophetic Significance (A.E.P.S.).
The term "Antagonistic Entity of Prophetic Significance" or "A.E.P.S." means any individual or organization:
(A) explicitly referenced in a Registered Prophecy as a force of doom, destruction, upheaval, imbalance, ascension, banishment, infestation, or structured obliteration;
(B) exhibiting at least two of the following risk factors:
(i) possession of a title containing the words "dark," "void," "bane," "of the east," or any preposition followed by "flame";
(ii) construction or inheritance of a subterranean or volcano-adjacent lair;
(iii) demonstrable influence over large numbers of cursed, chanting, or uniformed individuals; or
(iv) otherwise determined by the Ministry, based on the totality of the circumstances, to constitute a material antagonistic force within a

Registered Prophecy where strict application of subparagraphs (A) through (B) would result in under-classification of a reasonably identifiable opposing entity.

Satisfaction of the foregoing indicators shall constitute sufficient grounds for initiation of certification proceedings under subsection (c).

(c) **Certification Procedure.**
(1) Any individual subject to a prophecy shall, upon receipt of Form 3828–Call to Action (CTA), report to the Ministry for evaluation within fourteen calendar days. Form 3828 shall constitute formal notice of potential prophecy relevance and request acknowledgment of willingness, unwillingness, or pending clarity regarding participation. Refusal to respond shall be interpreted as a default deferral under subsection (f)(1)(A).
(2) Upon notice, the individual shall present, in person or via authorized astral projection, the following:
(A) an unabridged copy of the prophecy, if in their possession, with any marginalia removed;
(B) a complete Companion Disclosure Form, including roles, species, and expected mortality rates of each listed companion;
(C) evidence of any signs already fulfilled, including shattered seals, relic bonding, dream convergence, or unexplained illumination; and
(D) documentation of any previous prophecy-related activity within this or any other incarnation.
(3) The individual shall undergo a Fate Thread Entanglement Screening and Destiny Resonance Calibration, administered by a Ministry-certified Weaver Class III or higher.
(4) Provisional certification shall be issued pending completion of a twelve-hour Prophecy Ethics Orientation, offered in-person, remotely, or via vision-quest packet.
(5) Any individual who claims, asserts, or reasonably believes themselves to be a Prophecy-Subject Entity may petition the Ministry for certification.
(A) Such petition shall include:
(i) the basis for the claimed designation;
(ii) any supporting prophecy, omen, relic interaction, or survival event; and
(iii) disclosure of any companions, followers, or cultists currently involved.

(B) The Ministry shall evaluate such petition using the criteria set forth in subsection (b) and may:
(i) grant certification;
(ii) deny certification; or
(iii) issue provisional monitoring status pending further developments.
(C) Knowingly false or bad-faith assertions may be referred for enforcement under subsection (g).

(d) **Obligations of Certified Individuals.**
(1) Any certified Prophecy-Subject Entity, including any certified Chosen One or Lone Hero, shall:
(A) carry on their person at all times a valid Certificate of Foretold Participation;
(B) file a Prophetic Activity Report no later than fifteen calendar days following the end of each quarter, including:
(i) fulfilled or attempted milestones;
(ii) companions gained, lost, betrayed, or permanently fused;
(iii) cities saved, altered, or transformed into allegories; and
(iv) any notable declarations made while standing on elevated terrain; and
(C) notify the Department not fewer than twenty-eight calendar days in advance of any engagement with:
(i) a volcano-based fortress;
(ii) an Antagonistic Entity of Prophetic Significance (A.E.P.S.);
(iii) a major celestial convergence; or
(iv) any doorway inscribed with warnings or glowing symbols.
(2) Only companions disclosed pursuant to subsection (c)(2)(B) and accepted by the Ministry shall be recognized as registered companions for purposes of this Code.
(A) Registered companions shall be deemed authorized participants in prophecy-related activity and shall be eligible for benefits, protections, and limitations as determined by the Ministry, including healing priority, resurrection consideration, relic access, and compensation in the event of death, disappearance, or narrative sacrifice.
(B) Unregistered companions shall not be recognized for purposes of liability allocation, benefit eligibility, or regulatory protection, and primary liability for actions taken in furtherance of the prophecy shall remain with the certified Prophecy-Subject Entity.

(C) Failure to disclose a companion shall constitute a reporting deficiency and may result in reclassification of liability, denial of benefits, or administrative sanction under subsection (g).

(e) **Antagonist Oversight and Early Intervention.**
(1) The Ministry shall maintain the Registry of Certified Dark Ones and Comparable Menaces and shall, upon certification of a corresponding Prophecy-Subject Entity, issue to any identified Antagonistic Entity of Prophetic Significance a Notification of Incoming Heroic Conflict detailing:
(A) the name, current designation, and armament style of the certified prophecy-subject;
(B) expected timing of confrontation based on fate-thread intersections and recent omens; and
(C) general advisories regarding lair ventilation and monologue pacing.
(2) The Ministry shall issue a Prophetic Cease and Desist Order to any Antagonistic Entity of Prophetic Significance engaging in unauthorized world-ending behaviors, including:
(A) premature expansion of shadow-based influence;
(B) active magical corruption of terrain within one kilometer of a settlement; or
(C) construction of excess thrones or pits in ceremonial chambers.

For purposes of this paragraph, world-ending behaviors shall be deemed unauthorized unless prior authorization has been obtained from the Ministry in accordance with applicable procedures.

(f) **Prohibition on Compelled Participation.**
(1) No individual shall be compelled to fulfill a prophecy unless:
(A) such individual has failed to submit a Prophecy Refusal Form within fourteen calendar days of official designation;
(B) such individual has received material or metaphysical compensation resulting directly from prophecy-linked activity;
(C) the prophecy is classified as non-transferable and no other viable candidate exists due to death, rejection, divine exclusion, legal immunity, dimensional misplacement, or low aptitude scores; or
(D) the prophecy has entered active manifestation status, as determined by measurable fate-thread convergence, relic activation, antagonist mobilization, or public omen density exceeding baseline thresholds.

(2) Any attempt to compel participation through enchantment, ritual pressure, dream-seeding, or invocation of emotional debts shall be subject to review under § 701.2.

(g) **Violations.**
(1) Any individual who impersonates a Prophecy-Subject Entity, unlawfully fulfills a prophecy, or undertakes multiple destinies simultaneously without licensure shall be subject to:
(A) revocation of all prophetic designations and removal from enchanted artifact registries;
(B) reassignment to a Level I Prophecy such as resolving a misplaced festival banner or recovering an heirloom of only sentimental value;
(C) public posting of a Disavowal Notice in at least three populated areas and one convenient glade; and
(D) placement on the Destiny Fraud Registry for a minimum of seven years or until supervised redemption is complete.

(h) **Oversight.**
(1) The Ministry shall be responsible for ensuring timely completion of all Divine, Celestial, and Doom-Relevant Weaponry under the Forged Instruments of Destiny Initiative.
(2) The Ministry shall coordinate with the Prophetic Review Committee, which shall serve as the appellate body for disputes arising under this section, including challenges to certification, denial of refusal, misdesignation, relic attribution, improper activation of prophecy-relevant instruments, custodial mismanagement of destiny-linked artifacts (§ 702.4), and any determination materially affecting the timing, scope, or method of prophetic fulfillment.
(3) No more than three certified Prophecy-Subject Entity shall operate concurrently within a single valley, pass, or floating continent without exception granted by the Overlap Triage Division.

(i) **Cross-References.**
For administrative procedures and appeals, see § 102.1. For civil, administrative, and criminal penalties, see § 102.2. For reasonable care in spellcasting, see § 101.7. For prohibited magical practices, see § 701.2.

(j) **Historical Annotations.**
Added following the 1492 Misattribution Cascade, in which the MPA issued fourteen simultaneous Call to Action forms to similarly named

individuals due to clerical failure to include middle initials. At least five accepted the prophecy, two sold their relics, and one launched a preemptive siege on a neutral city-state. The event led to the creation of mandatory identity verification procedures, standard relic tracking protocols, and centralized oversight of prophecy acceptance. Amended in 1507 to require companion disclosure forms before any heroic action may begin.

§ 702.4 Regulation and Custodial Control of Prophecy-Linked Instruments

(a) **General Rule.**
No relic, weapon, implement, vessel, conduit, or artifact that exhibits prophetic resonance or is referenced in a Registered Prophecy shall be activated, transferred, wielded, awakened, bonded, reforged, calibrated, or otherwise engaged in a manner consistent with prophetic fulfillment unless such instrument has been registered with and certified by the Ministry of Prophetic Affairs (MPA) pursuant to this section.
Upon certification as a Prophecy-Linked Instrument, legal custody shall vest exclusively in the Ministry. No private individual, certified Prophecy-Subject Entity, or institutional body shall retain permanent custodial rights except as expressly authorized in writing by the Ministry.
Registration under this section shall not constitute designation of a Prophecy-Subject Entity under § 702.3, nor shall temporary possession prior to Ministry retrieval, by itself, require compelled participation under § 702.3(f).

(b) **Definitions.**
For purposes of this section:
(1) The term Prophecy-Linked Instrument means any object, relic, forged implement, constructed device, or naturally occurring item that
(A) is expressly referenced in a Registered Prophecy;
(B) exhibits measurable prophetic resonance, including selective activation, bearer recognition, aura emission, symbolic illumination, harmonic fluctuation, relic agitation, or fate-thread alignment; or
(C) demonstrates activation exclusively or disproportionately in proximity to a certified or probable Prophecy-Subject Entity.
(2) The term Interim Custodian means any individual or entity in temporary possession of a Prophecy-Linked Instrument prior to formal retrieval and certification by the Ministry.

(c) **Immediate Reporting and Surrender.**
(1) Any Interim Custodian shall file Form 3912–Instrument Disclosure and Resonance Assessment within forty-eight hours of discovery, activation, excavation, bonding, inheritance, battlefield recovery, dream-manifestation, or unintended summoning.
(2) The Interim Custodian shall preserve the instrument in its discovered condition and maintain environmental stability pending Ministry retrieval. Necessary stabilization or maintenance shall be limited to preservation measures consistent with preventing deterioration, distortion, imbalance, or excessive alteration of structural integrity.
(3) Upon certification, the instrument shall be surrendered without delay to authorized Ministry agents. Failure to surrender shall constitute unlawful retention of a destiny-controlled asset.

(d) **Authorized Use.**
(1) No Prophecy-Linked Instrument shall be intentionally activated except—
(A) by a certified Prophecy-Subject Entity operating under written Ministry authorization; or
(B) pursuant to directive issued by the Ministry following a Fate-Impact Assessment.
(2) Authorization for temporary deployment shall not transfer ownership, custodial authority, or classification status.

(e) **Mishandling and Improper Interaction.**
(1) Mishandling shall include, but not be limited to—
(A) unauthorized activation, testing, experimentation, or calibration;
(B) suppression, concealment, or falsification of resonance indicators;
(C) alteration, inscription, removal, enhancement, refinement, or modification of runes, sigils, balance points, edge geometry, embedded inscriptions, or structural composition beyond preservation-grade maintenance;
(D) exposure to unstable enchantments, corrosive atmospheres, anti-divine fields, unfiltered elemental discharge, mundane chemical agents, or unregulated sanctification procedures;
(E) physical handling without Ministry-approved protective measures where required by relic classification, including sanctified barriers, containment wards, consecrated handling materials, or clerical protective coverings;

(F) use of the instrument for decorative, theatrical, morale-boosting, commercial, commemorative, or architectural display;
(G) premature ceremonial deployment, symbolic gesturing, or dramatic exhibition likely to induce unintended prophetic acceleration;
(H) proximity to known Antagonistic Entities without prior clearance;
(I) intentional delay in reporting activation, instability, or anomalous resonance fluctuation;
(J) any act or omission materially increasing the probability of unscheduled, amplified, destabilized, or structurally compromised prophetic fulfillment.
(2) Negligent mishandling shall be determined under a strict custodial standard. Claims of heroic necessity, aesthetic refinement, structural improvement, emotional urgency, or speculative enhancement shall not constitute a defense.
(3) Mishandling determinations may be reviewed upon petition before the Prophetic Review Committee consistent with the appellate framework described in § 702.3(h)(2).

(f) **Ministry Authority and Containment.**
The Ministry may impose containment protocols, restrict access to certified Prophecy-Subject Entities, suspend deployment authorization, reassign instruments to alternative certified entities where permitted under the Registered Prophecy, or initiate stabilization procedures where relic volatility threatens metaphysical stability, public order, or narrative coherence.

(g) **Cross-References.**
For standards governing certification of individuals, consult § 702.3. For ethical spell use and procedural safeguards, refer to § 701.1. For matters involving restricted magical practices, see § 701.2.

(h) **Historical Annotations.**
Originally enacted in 1509 as part of the Prophetic Stabilization Reforms addressing decentralized relic custody and inconsistent instrument classification practices. Amended in 1513 to formalize mandatory Ministry custodial vesting upon certification, clarify preservation-grade maintenance limitations, and codify restrictions on unsanctioned activation or ceremonial deployment. Conforming revisions adopted thereafter to align enforcement and appellate procedures with § 702.3.

§ 702.5 Regulation of Suspiciously Intelligent Ducks

(a) **In General.**
Any duck exhibiting cognitive, administrative, or commercial behaviors exceeding those ordinarily associated with waterfowl shall be subject to classification, reporting, and regulatory oversight under this section.

(b) **Definition of Suspiciously Intelligent Duck.**
A duck shall be deemed Suspiciously Intelligent where it demonstrates two or more of the following behaviors:
(1) sustained, deliberate eye contact with officials, particularly during meetings, hearings, or administrative proceedings;
(2) manipulation of mechanisms designed for human operation, including but not limited to latches, locks, doors, containers, or coin-operated devices;
(3) demonstrable familiarity with written language, including the apparent reading, tracking, or annotation of ledgers, receipts, ordinances, tariffs, or comparable records;
(4) initiation of negotiation, barter, or exchange for food, currency, or other items of value, whether verbal, gestural, or otherwise communicative;
(5) maintenance of records, including ledgers, tally systems, inventories, or other structured documentation;
(6) repeated or unexplained presence in or near administrative offices, docks, counting houses, or other locations associated with financial or governmental activity.

(c) **Presumption and Rebuttal.**
(1) A duck meeting the criteria set forth in subsection (b) shall be presumed to fall within this section.
(2) Such presumption may be rebutted only upon a showing that the observed behavior is—
(A) isolated and incapable of repetition; or
(B) the direct result of external magical influence not attributable to the duck.

(d) **Reporting Requirement.**

(1) Any person encountering a duck reasonably believed to meet the criteria described in subsection (b) shall report such occurrence to the Office of Animal Oversight within forty-eight (48) hours.
(2) Reports shall include, to the extent practicable—
(A) a description of the duck;
(B) the behaviors observed;
(C) any objects, documents, or currency with which the duck interacted; and
(D) whether the duck appeared to understand or respond to administrative or financial processes.

(e) **Temporary Custody and Observation.**
(1) Upon receipt of a report, the Department may authorize the temporary relocation of the duck to a controlled municipal pond or equivalent containment environment.
(2) During such period, authorized personnel may observe, document, and test the duck's capabilities, including interaction with—
(A) written instructions;
(B) standardized forms;
(C) counting or tallying exercises; and
(D) basic transactional exchanges involving grain or currency.
(3) Detention under this subsection shall be limited to the period reasonably necessary to determine classification.

(f) **Restrictions Pending Determination.**
A duck subject to investigation under this section shall not—
(1) access or remain within municipal offices, archives, or recordkeeping facilities without supervision;
(2) interact with financial ledgers, accounts, or transactional systems;
(3) participate in, influence, or appear to direct any process involving taxation, tariffs, licensing, or public funds.

(g) **Classification and Ongoing Oversight.**
(1) Where a duck is determined to be Suspiciously Intelligent, the Department may impose ongoing monitoring, access restrictions, or other controls necessary to prevent interference with administrative or financial systems.
(2) Nothing in this section shall be construed to recognize, grant, or imply legal authority for such duck to engage in governmental, financial, or recordkeeping functions.

(h) **Prohibited Conduct.**
No person shall—
(1) knowingly assist a Suspiciously Intelligent Duck in maintaining records, conducting transactions, or otherwise participating in administrative or financial activities; or
(2) rely upon, adopt, or incorporate records, tallies, or accounts maintained by such duck for official, legal, or commercial purposes.

(i) **Cross-References.**
For definition of qualified creatures, see § 101.6. For ethical obligations in handling magical entities, see § 701.1 and § 701.7. For financial manipulation and fraud, see Part X. For reporting violations, see § 701.5. For administrative authority, see § 102.1. For penalties, see § 102.2.

(j) **Historical Annotations.**
This section was enacted under C.C.D. 7712, 48 MR 233, Wed. 14, 1912 following the Dockside Accounting Incident, in which harbor tariffs were diverted for six consecutive weeks through a grain-based payment scheme later determined to have been coordinated by a single duck. Amended under C.C.D. 9021, 65 MR 771, Mon. 6, 1978 to expand behavioral criteria and reporting requirements. Revised under C.C.D. 10590, 79 MR 771, Tue. 12, 2026 to clarify access restrictions and prevent administrative interference.

Part VIII: Magical Object Regulation

§ 801.1 Classification of Magical Objects and Artifacts

(a) **In General.**
All magical objects and artifacts shall be classified in accordance with this section prior to manufacture, distribution, transfer, activation, or use where classification is required under this Code. No person shall introduce, operate, or place into circulation any magical object or artifact that has not been properly classified.

(b) **Definitions.**
(1) Magical Object. A "magical object" is any item, device, or construct that contains, channels, produces, or is affected by magical energy, whether temporarily or permanently.
(2) Artifact. An "artifact" is a magical object of significant power, rarity, historical importance, or persistent effect, including objects whose origin, composition, or function exceeds ordinary classification thresholds.
(3) Activation. "Activation" includes any act that initiates, enables, or alters the operation of a magical object.

(c) **Classification System.**
(1) General Rule. Magical objects and artifacts shall be classified based on risk, function, persistence, and potential for misuse.
(2) Primary Classifications.
(A) Class I: Low-Risk Objects.
Objects with minimal or controlled magical effects that—
(i) do not produce persistent or autonomous effects;
(ii) pose negligible risk under ordinary use.
(B) Class II: Moderate-Risk Objects.
Objects that—
(i) produce sustained or repeatable magical effects;
(ii) require user competence or oversight to prevent misuse;
(iii) may interact with other magical systems.
(C) Class III: High-Risk Objects.
Objects that—
(i) produce significant, persistent, or wide-area effects;

(ii) are capable of causing substantial harm or disruption;
(iii) require authorization, monitoring, or restricted handling under this Code.
(D) Class IV: Restricted Artifacts.
Artifacts that—
(i) exhibit autonomous, self-sustaining, or evolving behavior;
(ii) are capable of destabilizing magical, environmental, or dimensional systems;
(iii) are subject to strict control, limitation, or prohibition.

(d) **Classification Criteria.**
In determining classification under subsection (c), consideration shall be given to—
(1) the nature and magnitude of the object's effects;
(2) duration and persistence under § 501.1;
(3) capacity for control, containment, or termination under § 501.2;
(4) interaction with other magical systems, including ley lines or active spells;
(5) potential for misuse or circumvention of this Code;
(6) complexity of operation and required user competence.

(e) **Assignment and Verification.**
(1) Initial Classification. The creator, manufacturer, or importer shall assign a preliminary classification prior to use or distribution.
(2) Verification.
(A) Classification shall be subject to verification by the Department of Magical Affairs under § 102.1;
(B) verification may include testing, inspection, or demonstration of functionality.
(3) Reclassification.
(A) An object may be reclassified where—
(i) its properties change;
(ii) new risks are identified;
(iii) misuse or unintended effects are observed.
(B) Reclassification shall take effect immediately upon determination.

(f) **Labeling and Documentation.**
(1) Labeling Requirement. All classified objects shall be labeled with—
(A) their classification;
(B) any restrictions or conditions of use;

(C) identification of the responsible party.
(2) Documentation.
(A) Documentation shall accompany each object and include operational parameters, limitations, and safety considerations;
(B) such documentation shall be sufficient to enable compliance with this Code.

(g) **Restrictions Based on Classification.**
(1) General Rule. Use, transfer, and possession of magical objects shall be subject to restrictions corresponding to their classification.
(2) Higher-Class Restrictions.
(A) Class III and Class IV objects shall be subject to heightened requirements, including authorization, monitoring, and reporting;
(B) certain Class IV artifacts may be prohibited from general circulation.

(h) **Cross-References.**
For spell classification and risk levels, see § 401.2. For spell duration and termination, see § 501.1 and § 501.2. For registration requirements, see § 801.2. For transfer and sale, see § 801.3. For administrative authority, see § 102.1.

(i) **Historical Annotations.**
Originally established under C.C.D. 5201, 18 MR 221, Tue. 6, 1715 to standardize classification of enchanted objects. Amended under C.C.D. 6035, 29 MR 442, Thu. 10, 1802 to introduce artifact-level distinctions. Revised under C.C.D. 9320, 61 MR 771, Mon. 4, 1995 to incorporate risk-based classification tiers and reclassification procedures.

§ 801.2 Registration and Inspection of Magical Objects

(a) **Scope.**
This section applies to all enchanted objects capable of producing, sustaining, amplifying, directing, storing, modifying, or autonomously manifesting magical effect, regardless of whether activation occurs through will, incantation, proximity, environmental trigger, embedded enchantment, conditional logic, passive magical presence, or delayed execution.

For purposes of this section, "enchanted object" includes any artifact, implement, construct, device, vessel, token, inscription, rune array, sigil matrix, bound entity, hybridized arcane mechanism, or other tangible or semi-tangible instrumentality whose operative function depends in whole or in part upon magical force.

(b) **Registration Requirement.**
No enchanted object shall be created for distribution, placed into circulation, deployed in institutional or commercial settings, or maintained in sustained activation unless registered prior to such use.

Registration shall include:

(1) Identity of the creator, enchanter, or binding authority, if known;
(2) Date, method, and school or schools of enchantment;
(3) Description of intended function and all reasonably foreseeable modes of operation;
(4) Known operational limitations and control mechanisms;
(5) Known instability history, malfunction incidents, or prior corrective measures;
(6) Presence or absence of autonomous, conditional, delayed, self-sustaining, or self-modifying features;
(7) Any safeguards embedded within the object at the time of registration;
(8) Anticipated risk classification consistent with § 401.2.

Failure to register creates a rebuttable presumption that the object is noncompliant and unsafe for lawful deployment.

(c) **Operational Classification Principle.**
Regulatory obligations shall be determined by the highest reasonably foreseeable operational capability of the object, not by its labeling, customary use, marketing description, instructional framing, or stated limitation.

Where an object is capable of multiple modes of operation, obligations shall correspond to the highest-risk functional capability accessible under ordinary conditions.

Artificial restriction of use through policy, signage, contractual limitation, or informal instruction shall not reduce regulatory burden where higher-risk functionality remains technically possible. Such conduct constitutes circumvention under applicable provisions.

(d) **Inspection and Stability Verification.**
All enchanted objects subject to this section shall undergo periodic inspection sufficient to verify continued operational stability and alignment with registered characteristics.

Inspection shall include, at minimum:
(1) Verification of enchantment integrity and structural cohesion;
(2) Confirmation that operative function corresponds to registered description;
(3) Detection of degradation, drift, amplification, mutation, or emergent properties;
(4) Verification of responsiveness to intended control mechanisms;
(5) Confirmation that embedded safeguards, fail-safes, and termination features remain functional;
(6) Review of documented incidents or anomalous behavior since prior inspection.

Inspection frequency shall increase proportionately with the object's foreseeable risk classification under § 401.2.

(e) **Presumption of Defect.**
An enchanted object shall be presumed defective where it:
(1) Produces effect materially inconsistent with its registered characteristics;
(2) Fails to respond to ordinary control or termination mechanisms;
(3) Activates autonomously in a manner not disclosed at registration;
(4) Generates cascading, self-propagating, or compounding effect absent deliberate initiation;
(5) Causes bodily injury, structural damage, ecological disruption, or metaphysical instability during reasonably foreseeable use.

The burden of rebutting the presumption of defect rests with the registrant, owner, operator, or controlling party and must be supported by contemporaneous inspection documentation and technical analysis.

(f) **Continuing Duty.**

Registration under this section imposes a continuing duty to monitor performance and report material changes in operational capability, risk profile, or safeguard integrity.

Failure to update registration following material modification, enhancement, degradation, hybridization, or change in foreseeable use constitutes noncompliance and shall be treated as failure to register.

(g) **Aggregation and Integrated Systems.**
Where multiple enchanted objects are designed, marketed, configured, or intended to operate in coordination, interdependence, or sequential activation, such collection shall be treated as a single enchanted object for purposes of registration and inspection.

Modification of an existing enchanted object that materially alters its risk profile under § 401.2 shall require updated registration and inspection prior to redeployment.

(h) **Evidentiary Presumptions.**
Absence of registration, inspection records, safeguard verification, or required documentation under this section shall be admissible as evidence of noncompliance in any civil, administrative, or enforcement proceeding.

Where documentation is incomplete, materially inconsistent, or untimely, the object shall be presumed noncompliant.

(i) **Cross-References.**
For risk classification standards, see § 401.2. For safeguard requirements applicable to deployment, refer to § 401.6. For reasonable care obligations, consult § 101.7. For logging and recordkeeping requirements, see § 401.5. For penalties and enforcement, refer to § 102.2.

(j) **Historical Annotations.**
Established under C.C.D. 4217, 87 MR 908, Wed. 14, 1998. Amended under C.C.D. 4899, 91 MR 2214, Thu. 3, 2009. Amended under C.C.D. 5324, 94 MR 2147, Oct 6, 2016.

§ 801.3 Transfer and Sale of Magical Objects

(a) **In General.**
No person shall transfer, sell, exchange, lease, assign, or otherwise convey any magical object or artifact except in compliance with this section. All transfers shall be documented, authorized where required, and conducted in a manner consistent with the classification of the object under § 801.1.

(b) **Scope of Covered Transactions.**
(1) General Rule. This section applies to any transaction involving a change in ownership, control, or possessory interest in a magical object.
(2) Forms of Transfer. Covered transactions include—
(A) direct sale or purchase;
(B) barter or exchange;
(C) lease, rental, or temporary conveyance;
(D) assignment, gift, or inheritance;
(E) transfer through intermediaries, brokers, or constructs.

(c) **Authorization Requirements.**
(1) Classification-Based Authorization.
(A) Class I objects may be transferred without prior approval, subject to documentation requirements;
(B) Class II objects may be transferred where the recipient is authorized and capable of lawful use;
(C) Class III objects shall require prior authorization under § 102.1;
(D) Class IV artifacts shall not be transferred except where expressly permitted under this Code.
(2) Verification of Recipient.
(A) The transferring party shall verify the identity and authorization status of the recipient;
(B) failure to conduct reasonable verification shall constitute a violation.

(d) **Documentation Requirements.**
(1) General Rule. Each covered transaction shall be documented in sufficient detail to demonstrate compliance with this Code.
(2) Required Information. Documentation shall include—
(A) identification of the transferring and receiving parties;
(B) classification of the object under § 801.1;
(C) description, condition, and operational status of the object;
(D) terms of the transfer, including value or consideration;

(E) any restrictions, conditions, or encumbrances;
(F) classification of any lease arrangement under subsection (e), where applicable;
(G) designation of delivery terms under subsection (f), including any Free On Broom (FOB) condition.
(3) Retention. Such documentation shall be retained in accordance with applicable recordkeeping requirements and made available upon request.

(e) **Lease Classification and Treatment.**
(1) General Rule. Any lease, rental, or similar arrangement involving a magical object shall be classified as either a capital lease or an operating lease, and such classification shall determine how the transaction is treated under this section.
(2) Capital Lease. A lease shall be treated as a capital lease where one or more of the following conditions are met:
(A) ownership of the magical object transfers to the lessee upon completion of the term;
(B) the lease term constitutes a substantial portion of the object's functional or magical lifespan;
(C) the present value of consideration approximates or exceeds the fair value of the object;
(D) the object is specialized such that it has no practical use to the lessor upon termination.
(3) Regulatory Treatment of Capital Leases.
(A) A capital lease shall be treated as a transfer of ownership for purposes of this Code;
(B) the lessor shall be treated as the transferring party and the lessee as the receiving party under subsections (c) and (d);
(C) all authorization, verification, and documentation requirements applicable to a sale shall apply.
(4) Operating Lease.
(A) An operating lease shall not be treated as a transfer of ownership;
(B) the lessor shall retain ownership and primary responsibility for the object's classification and lawful placement into use;
(C) the lessee shall be responsible for compliance with any applicable use restrictions during the period of possession.
(5) Substance Over Form. Classification shall be determined based on the substance of the arrangement rather than its stated designation.
(6) Recharacterization. Any lease structured to avoid treatment as a capital lease may be recharacterized upon review under § 102.1.

(f) **Transfer Terms and Risk of Loss.**
(1) General Rule. The allocation of risk, responsibility, and cost in a transfer shall be determined by the terms of the transaction, including any designation of delivery conditions.
(2) Free On Broom (FOB).
(A) FOB Shipment (Port of Departure).
(i) The transferring party shall bear all costs and responsibility for transporting the magical object to the designated port of shipment and loading onto the means of magical conveyance;
(ii) upon loading, risk of loss and further cost shall transfer to the receiving party.
(B) FOB Destination.
(i) The transferring party shall bear all costs and risk until the object is delivered to the receiving party at the specified destination;
(ii) risk of loss shall transfer upon delivery and acceptance.
(3) Allocation of Magical Transit Risk.
Where delivery terms are silent or ambiguous, risk shall be allocated based on the point at which control of the object is transferred, taking into account any agreed method of conveyance.
(4) Interaction with Lease Arrangements.
Where a capital lease is present, risk of loss shall be allocated as though a transfer of ownership has occurred.

(g) **Prohibited Transfers.**
(1) Unauthorized Recipients. No person shall transfer a magical object to any person not authorized to possess or use such object.
(2) Circumvention. No person shall structure a transaction to evade classification-based restrictions, including—
(A) dividing a transfer into multiple smaller transactions;
(B) using intermediaries to obscure the identity of the recipient;
(C) misclassifying the object or its capabilities.
(3) Prohibited Objects. Objects subject to prohibition under this Code shall not be transferred except as authorized for containment, research, or disposal.

(h) **Condition and Representation.**
(1) Accurate Representation. The transferring party shall accurately disclose the nature, classification, and operational characteristics of the object.
(2) Defects and Risks.

(A) Known defects, instability, or risks shall be disclosed;
(B) failure to disclose material information shall constitute a violation.
(3) Alteration Prior to Transfer. No person shall alter a magical object for the purpose of misrepresenting its classification or condition.

(i) **Cross-References.**
For classification of magical objects, see § 801.1. For registration and inspection, see § 801.2. For administrative authority, see § 102.1. For penalties, see § 102.2.

(j) **Historical Annotations.**
Originally established under C.C.D. 5228, 18 MR 998, Wed. 9, 1718 to regulate transfer of enchanted goods. Amended under C.C.D. 6108, 30 MR 221, Fri. 6, 1803 to incorporate authorization requirements. Revised under C.C.D. 9477, 64 MR 771, Tue. 15, 2000 to include lease classification standards and allocation of risk in magical transit.

§ 801.4 Magic-Adjacent Assistive Devices (MAAD)

(a) **General Definition.**
For the purposes of this section, "Magic-Adjacent Assistive Devices" (MAAD) shall mean any device, tool, or instrument that, while not inherently magical, facilitates, enhances, stabilizes, or refines the execution of magical spells, rituals, enchantments, or other recognized magical practices. These devices must be designed to function in direct support of authorized spellcasters, practitioners, or institutions registered under Part II of this Code.

(b) **Classification of MAAD.**
(1) Passive Assistance Devices.
(A) Sigil stencils, rune templates, and symbol-engraving mechanisms that provide accuracy and consistency in spell formation without independently generating magical effects.
(B) Chant recorders and auto-repeating incantation devices that ensure precise repetition of verbal spell components without self-initiating a spell.
(C) Structural reinforcement materials designed for stabilizing ritual sites, summoning circles, and magical containment units.
(2) Active Assistance Devices.

(A) Demon trap laser pointers and other targeting devices designed to aid in the precise placement of magical warding effects.
(B) Ritual accelerators, including incantation-speed enhancers, metronomic spell pacing devices, and chronometric spell alignment tools.
(C) Harmonic resonance stabilizers used to counteract distortions caused by prolonged exposure to unstable magical energies.
(3) Augmented Sensory Devices.
(A) Spectral detection lenses, including enchanted eyewear programmed solely to filter out magical interference.
(B) Arcane auditory filters that isolate spell-related sounds and frequencies from background noise.
(C) Magic flow visualization tools for mapping ley line activity without altering said activity.

(c) **Regulations for Usage.**
(1) MAAD shall not be classified as magical artifacts under § 801.1 unless the device contains an embedded magical component.
(2) Spellcasters and institutions utilizing MAAD must ensure that these devices do not inadvertently breach magical secrecy laws (§ 701.9) or interfere with established magical practice boundaries.
(3) Institutions distributing MAAD for academic or research purposes must register their devices with the Department of Magical Affairs (DMA) and submit Form 8472-M (Magic-Adjacent Device Registration Form) no later than thirty (30) days prior to public or commercial release.
(4) Unauthorized enhancement of MAAD through magical infusion shall constitute a regulatory violation under § 801.5.

(d) **Prohibited Uses of MAAD.**
(1) Any attempt to modify, repurpose, or enchant MAAD beyond its original specifications without proper licensing is strictly forbidden.
(2) Devices capable of mimicking the effects of restricted spells without an authorized spellcaster present shall be classified as illicit magical contraband subject to seizure.
(3) MAAD shall not be utilized to bypass ethical or regulatory limitations placed upon spellcasting, including but not limited to:
(A) Expediting spell durations beyond approved safety thresholds (§ 501.1).
(B) Simulating mind-affecting magic without legal oversight (§ 2101.1).
(C) Facilitating transfiguration processes in unauthorized settings (§ 2001.2).

(e) **Penalties for Violations.**
(1) Individuals or entities found in violation of this section shall be subject to:
(A) Confiscation of unauthorized MAAD by the Department of Magical Object Regulation (DMOR), with potential destruction of contraband devices.
(B) Revocation of licensing or institutional accreditation for entities found repeatedly circumventing MAAD regulations (§ 201.7).
(2) The unauthorized sale, distribution, or modification of MAAD classified under subsection (d) shall result in additional penalties under § 102.2.

(f) **Cross-References.**
For regulations on magical artifacts and their classification, refer to § 801.1. For licensing and certification requirements applicable to spellcasters and institutions utilizing MAAD, see Part II. For legal restrictions on enchanted object tampering, see § 801.5.

(g) **Historical Annotations.**
This section was enacted under C.C.D. 7412, 91 MR 1034, Tue. 14, 2012, to address the increasing reliance on non-magical assistive devices in spellcasting. Amended under C.C.D. 8231, 94 MR 5678, Wed. 20, 2021, to include enhanced classification and safety guidelines for emerging technologies in magic-adjacent industries.

§ 801.5 Anti-Tampering Protocols for Magical Devices

(a) **In General.**
No person shall alter, disable, bypass, interfere with, or otherwise tamper with any magical device, object, or artifact in a manner that circumvents safeguards, alters its classified function, or renders it noncompliant with this Code. All magical devices shall be subject to anti-tampering protocols appropriate to their classification under § 801.1.

(b) **Definition of Tampering.**
For purposes of this section, "tampering" includes any act or omission that—
(1) modifies or removes built-in safeguards, restrictions, or limitations;

(2) alters the operational parameters, output, or behavior of a device beyond its approved design;
(3) interferes with monitoring, logging, or reporting functions required under this Code;
(4) enables use of the device in a manner otherwise restricted or prohibited.

(c) **Required Safeguards.**
(1) General Rule. All magical devices shall incorporate safeguards designed to—
(A) prevent unauthorized activation or use;
(B) limit operation to permitted parameters;
(C) ensure compliance with applicable classification and authorization requirements.
(2) Enhanced Safeguards.
(A) Class III devices shall include mechanisms for controlled shutdown, access restriction, and misuse prevention;
(B) Class IV artifacts shall include layered containment, fail-safe protocols, and, where feasible, independent override mechanisms subject to § 102.1.

(d) **Prohibition on Circumvention.**
(1) General Rule. No person shall engage in conduct designed to circumvent any safeguard required under this Code.
(2) Specific Conduct. Prohibited acts include—
(A) disabling or degrading safety or containment mechanisms;
(B) modifying device components to evade classification or regulatory requirements;
(C) introducing external enhancements or attachments that alter the device's regulated function;
(D) accessing restricted functions without proper authorization.

(e) **Authorized Modification.**
(1) General Rule. Modification of a magical device shall be permitted only where—
(A) authorized under § 102.1; or
(B) conducted within an approved research or testing environment under Part XV.
(2) Conditions.

(A) Any authorized modification shall be documented and subject to review;
(B) such modification may result in reclassification under § 801.1.

(f) **Detection and Reporting.**
(1) Duty to Monitor. Persons responsible for magical devices shall take reasonable steps to detect tampering.
(2) Reporting Requirement.
(A) Any suspected or confirmed tampering shall be reported in accordance with § 701.5;
(B) such report shall include the nature of the tampering and any resulting risks.
(3) Device Integrity Logs. Where applicable, devices shall maintain logs sufficient to detect and reconstruct tampering events.

(g) **Consequences of Tampering.**
(1) Noncompliance. A tampered device shall be deemed noncompliant and may be subject to restriction, confiscation, or deactivation.
(2) Presumption of Risk. Any device found to have been tampered with shall be presumed unsafe until verified otherwise.
(3) Separate Violations. Each act of tampering or circumvention shall constitute a separate violation under this Code.

(h) **Cross-References.**
For classification of magical devices, see § 801.1. For registration and inspection, see § 801.2. For prohibited practices, see § 701.2. For reporting requirements, see § 701.5. For administrative authority, see § 102.1. For penalties, see § 102.2.

(i) **Historical Annotations.**
Originally established under C.C.D. 5342, 19 MR 771, Tue. 11, 1732 to address unauthorized modification of enchanted devices. Amended under C.C.D. 6201, 31 MR 118, Fri. 7, 1810 to include safeguard requirements. Revised under C.C.D. 9522, 65 MR 442, Mon. 22, 2002 to incorporate modern anti-circumvention and detection standards.

§ 801.6 Regulation of Dungeons as Magical Constructs

(a) **In General.**

Any dungeon, labyrinth, containment complex, or similar structure created, maintained, or operated through magical means shall be classified and regulated as a magical construct under this section. No person shall design, generate, operate, or materially alter such a construct except in compliance with this Code.

(b) **Definition and Scope.**
(1) Dungeon Construct. A dungeon construct is any enclosed or semi-enclosed environment—
(A) generated, sustained, or modified through magical means; and
(B) designed to confine, challenge, deter, test, or otherwise restrict the movement or survival of persons or creatures.
(2) Included Features. A dungeon construct includes any integrated system of—
(A) traps, hazards, or environmental effects;
(B) animated or summoned guardians;
(C) shifting layouts, dimensional alterations, or recursive pathways;
(D) embedded enchantments affecting perception, movement, or survivability.
(3) Exclusions. Ordinary structures shall not be considered dungeon constructs solely by virtue of containing magical objects unless such structures meet the criteria under paragraph (1).

(c) **Classification.**
(1) General Rule. Dungeon constructs shall be classified under § 801.1 based on their aggregate risk, persistence, and operational complexity.
(2) Minimum Classification.
(A) Any construct containing active hazards or autonomous elements shall be classified no lower than Class II;
(B) any construct capable of causing serious harm, entrapment, or dimensional displacement shall be classified as Class III or higher.
(3) Composite Treatment. A dungeon construct shall be treated as a single integrated object for classification purposes, notwithstanding the presence of multiple components.

(d) **Design and Operational Requirements.**
(1) Control Mechanisms. All dungeon constructs shall include mechanisms to—
(A) initiate, suspend, or terminate operation;
(B) override or disable hazardous features;

(C) permit controlled access and exit.
(2) Stability. Constructs shall be designed to maintain structural and magical stability under reasonably foreseeable conditions of use.
(3) Predictability.
(A) The behavior of hazards and effects shall be sufficiently predictable to allow compliance with this Code;
(B) fully random or unbounded hazard generation shall be prohibited where it prevents meaningful control or termination.

(e) **Use and Access Restrictions.**
(1) Authorized Use. Dungeon constructs may be used only for lawful purposes, including training, testing, containment, or controlled exploration.
(2) Prohibited Use. No person shall—
(A) deploy a dungeon construct for unlawful detention or coercion;
(B) use such a construct to facilitate prohibited practices under § 701.2;
(C) expose persons or creatures to conditions exceeding the construct's classified parameters.
(3) Entry Conditions.
(A) Where entry is voluntary, participants shall be informed of material risks;
(B) where entry is not voluntary, use shall be authorized under applicable provisions of this Code.

(f) **Monitoring and Maintenance.**
(1) General Rule. Dungeon constructs shall be subject to ongoing monitoring sufficient to ensure continued compliance.
(2) Required Actions. Responsible persons shall—
(A) maintain operational logs;
(B) inspect for instability, degradation, or unintended behavior;
(C) correct identified deficiencies within a reasonable period.
(3) Failure Conditions.
(A) Any construct exhibiting uncontrolled or unstable behavior shall be deactivated;
(B) continued operation under such conditions shall constitute a violation.

(g) **Modification and Expansion.**

(1) General Rule. Any material modification, expansion, or reconfiguration of a dungeon construct shall be treated as a new or modified object under § 801.1.
(2) Reclassification. Such changes may require reclassification and renewed authorization.

(h) **Loot Generation and Reporting Requirements.**
(1) Definition of Loot. For purposes of this section, “loot” includes any magical object, artifact, currency, consumable, or other item of value generated, discovered, or obtained within a dungeon construct.
(2) General Rule. Any person who acquires loot from a dungeon construct shall report such acquisition where—
(A) the item meets classification thresholds under § 801.1;
(B) the item would constitute a reportable asset; or
(C) the item is subject to restriction, registration, or authorization under this Code.
(3) Dungeon-Origin Presumption.
(A) Any item obtained from a dungeon construct shall be presumed to be a magical object subject to classification unless demonstrated otherwise;
(B) such presumption shall apply regardless of the item’s apparent nature or condition.
(4) Reporting Timing. Reporting shall occur within a reasonable period following removal of the item from the construct.
(5) Obligations of Operators.
(A) Operators of dungeon constructs shall maintain records of loot generation mechanisms where such mechanisms are controlled or predictable;
(B) operators shall not design constructs for the purpose of producing untraceable or unreportable assets.
(6) Prohibited Conduct. No person shall—
(A) conceal, misrepresent, or fail to report loot subject to this subsection;
(B) structure retrieval or distribution of loot to evade reporting requirements;
(C) alter or degrade loot for the purpose of avoiding classification or detection.

(i) **Anti-Tampering and Integrity.**
Dungeon constructs shall be subject to anti-tampering requirements under § 801.5. Any unauthorized alteration of control systems, hazard

parameters, loot generation mechanisms, or structural elements shall constitute a violation.

(j) **Cross-References.**
For classification of magical objects, see § 801.1. For registration and inspection, see § 801.2. For anti-tampering protocols, see § 801.5. For ethical standards governing detention, see § 701.4. For administrative authority, see § 102.1.

(k) **Historical Annotations.**
Originally established under C.C.D. 5401, 20 MR 118, Mon. 2, 1740 to regulate early labyrinth constructs used in training and confinement. Amended under C.C.D. 6222, 31 MR 442, Wed. 9, 1812 to address autonomous dungeon features. Revised under C.C.D. 9550, 65 MR 771, Tue. 18, 2003 to incorporate stability, monitoring, and anti-tampering requirements. Further amended under C.C.D. 10088, 73 MR 771, Thu. 22, 2021 to include loot reporting and anti-evasion provisions.

§ 801.7 Flight Regulations for Magical Objects

(a) **In General.**
No person shall operate, activate, or cause to be operated any magical object capable of flight except in compliance with this section. All aerial movement of magical objects shall be conducted in a manner that ensures safety, accountability, and adherence to applicable restrictions under this Code.

(b) **Scope and Definitions.**
(1) Flight-Capable Object. A "flight-capable object" includes any magical object that—
(A) is capable of sustained aerial movement; or
(B) can be directed, controlled, or programmed to move through airspace.
(2) Operation. "Operation" includes manual control, autonomous function, or remote activation of a flight-capable object.

(c) **Classification-Based Restrictions.**
(1) General Rule. Flight-capable objects shall be subject to restrictions based on their classification under § 801.1.
(2) Class I and II Objects.
(A) May be operated in open airspace without prior authorization;
(B) shall not be operated in restricted or controlled zones.

(3) Class III Objects.
(A) Require authorization under § 102.1 prior to operation;
(B) shall be subject to route, altitude, and operational limitations.
(4) Class IV Artifacts.
(A) Shall not be operated except where expressly authorized;
(B) may be subject to complete prohibition in public or uncontrolled airspace.

(d) **Operational Requirements.**
(1) Control and Stability. Flight-capable objects shall be operated in a manner that maintains control, stability, and predictability.
(2) Collision Avoidance.
(A) Operators shall take reasonable measures to avoid collisions with persons, structures, or other objects;
(B) autonomous objects shall incorporate collision avoidance mechanisms where feasible.
(3) Interference. No person shall operate a flight-capable object in a manner that interferes with—
(A) other magical or non-magical aerial activity;
(B) communication, navigation, or safety systems.

(e) **Identification and Traceability.**
(1) General Rule. Flight-capable objects shall be identifiable and traceable to a responsible party.
(2) Identification Methods.
(A) Objects shall bear markings, signatures, or embedded identifiers sufficient to determine origin and control;
(B) removal or alteration of such identifiers shall constitute a violation.
(3) Autonomous Operation. Objects operating without direct control shall maintain records or signals sufficient to reconstruct their operation.

(f) **Restricted and Controlled Airspace.**
(1) Restricted Areas. No person shall operate a flight-capable object within designated restricted areas except as authorized.
(2) Controlled Zones. Operation within controlled zones shall be subject to conditions established under § 102.1, including coordination with relevant authorities.
(3) Emergency Restrictions. Temporary flight restrictions may be imposed where necessary to protect safety or maintain order.

(g) **Transport and Conveyance.**
(1) Use in Transfer. Flight-capable objects used for transport of goods or persons shall comply with § 801.3 and applicable provisions of this Code.
(2) Carriage of Magical Objects.
(A) Transport of classified objects shall be conducted in accordance with their classification;
(B) high-risk objects shall require additional safeguards and authorization.

(h) **Prohibited Conduct.**
No person shall—
(1) operate a flight-capable object in a reckless or uncontrolled manner;
(2) use such an object to facilitate prohibited practices under § 701.2;
(3) evade identification, tracking, or authorization requirements;
(4) operate a prohibited or unclassified object.

(i) **Cross-References.**
For classification of magical objects, see § 801.1. For transfer and transport, see § 801.3. For anti-tampering protocols, see § 801.5. For administrative authority, see § 102.1. For penalties, see § 102.2.

(j) **Historical Annotations.**
Originally established under C.C.D. 5488, 21 MR 118, Fri. 7, 1752 to regulate early aerial enchantments and flying devices. Amended under C.C.D. 6320, 32 MR 442, Mon. 3, 1820 to incorporate controlled airspace concepts. Revised under C.C.D. 9601, 66 MR 771, Wed. 11, 2005 to address autonomous flight and modern aerial traffic concerns.

§ 801.8 Wand Registration and General Complaints

(a) **Wand registration.**
(1) General rule. Except as otherwise provided in this section, any wand used, intended to be used, stored for future use, possessed in a condition permitting use, or otherwise maintained in operational capacity in connection with regulated magical activity shall be registered with the Department of Wand Registrations and General Complaints prior to first discharge. The assertion that a wand has been used infrequently, ceremonially, defensively, experimentally, emotionally, or by accident shall not relieve the possessor of the obligation to register.

(2) Definition of wand. For purposes of this subsection, the term wand means any handheld or structurally elongated magical focusing instrument constructed of wood, bone, metal, composite material, or comparable substrate that is capable of channeling, directing, amplifying, stabilizing, or modulating magical force through attunement to an operator.
(A) Included instruments. The term includes instruments marketed as rods, foci, batons, pointers, scepters, ceremonial sticks, conduits, or similar implements if such instrument is capable of directing magical discharge.
(B) Excluded instruments. The term does not include stationary magical installations, embedded architectural arrays, permanently affixed rune structures, or culinary implements lacking attunement capacity. The burden of demonstrating exclusion rests on the possessor.
(3) Initial registration requirements.
(A) Registration shall be made on Form W-1, executed under penalty of § 102.2, and filed in the manner prescribed by administrative guidance. The Form shall be completed in full.
(B) The registrant shall disclose with specificity sufficient to permit independent verification—
(i) core material and origin;
(ii) wood species or structural substrate and harvest jurisdiction;
(iii) length measured in inches to the nearest one-eighth;
(iv) flexibility rating;
(v) attunement signature of the primary operator; and
(vi) declaration of sentience status.
(C) Incomplete submissions shall not be treated as substantially compliant.
(4) Presumption of operability.
(A) Possession of an intact wand shall create a rebuttable presumption of operational capacity.
(B) The burden rests on the possessor to demonstrate permanent inoperability through destruction, irreversible severance of core continuity, or comparable disabling alteration.
(C) Temporary malfunction or intermittent discharge shall not constitute permanent inoperability.
(5) Material modification and re-registration.
(A) A wand that is re-cored, materially re-attuned, structurally reconstructed, or permanently enchanted in a manner affecting discharge characteristics shall be treated as newly placed in service.

(B) Re-registration shall occur within 30 days of modification.
(C) Change in primary operator shall require amended registration on Form W-1A.
(D) Emergence or suppression of sentience shall require amended filing within 30 days of discovery.
(6) Failure to comply.
(A) Use of an unregistered or improperly registered wand constitutes improper instrument use under § 1201.2.
(B) Ignorance of the requirement or belief that the instrument is insignificant shall not constitute reasonable cause.

(b) **General complaint jurisdiction.**
(1) The Department of Wand Registrations and General Complaints shall accept and log complaints of any kind submitted by any person, entity, qualified creature, or construct, regardless of whether the complaint identifies a violation of this Code.
(2) Illustrative matters. Complaints may concern excessive dragon vocalization, unsafe broomstick operation, persistent disturbances, disputes between neighbors, perceived ley line imbalance, or dissatisfaction with prevailing conditions.
(3) Enchanted device availability.
(A) Complaints may concern repeated or chronic unavailability of publicly advertised enchanted devices, including but not limited to the Frosted Elixir Dispensing Apparatus commonly installed in franchised taverns and food establishments and represented as continuously operational.
(B) A device shall not be treated as compliant solely because it is theoretically capable of functioning or because it operates intermittently.
(C) A pattern of inoperability shall be presumed where the device is unavailable for more than three consecutive operating periods within a thirty-day window, or where documented attempts at use exceed five instances within such period without successful discharge.
(D) The burden rests on the complainant to demonstrate sustained unavailability through dated documentation, witness statements, or comparable evidence.
(E) Isolated inconvenience shall not constitute a pattern.
(4) Logging without remedy. The Department shall log complaints whether or not a statutory remedy exists. Logging does not constitute agreement that the complained-of condition is unlawful or unreasonable.

(c) **Filing requirements.**

(1) Instrument-related complaints shall be filed on Form W-13. All other complaints shall be filed on Form GC-1. Supplemental narrative shall be filed on Form GC-1S.
(2) Each filing shall identify the complainant unless anonymous, specify location, state the relevant date or date range, describe the condition with objective specificity, and include certification of good faith.
(3) Incomplete filings shall be returned with Notice of Deficiency and shall not be treated as filed until corrected.

(d) **Presumptions and safe harbors.**
(1) Dragon vocalization below 85 decibels measured at the complainant's property line between dusk and midnight shall constitute a safe harbor. Vocalization below 70 decibels between midnight and dawn shall constitute a safe harbor. The burden rests on the complainant to demonstrate sustained exceedance.
(2) Broomstick operation conducted above 30 cubits and within posted speed limitations shall be presumed compliant. The burden rests on the complainant to demonstrate measurable deviation.

(e) **Complaints regarding the filing process.**
(1) A complaint alleging that required forms are burdensome, instructions unclear, response times unreasonable, or procedures circular shall be filed on Form GC-1.
(2) Such complaints shall comply fully with subsection (c).
(3) Allegations that compliance requirements are themselves unreasonable shall not relieve the filer of those requirements.

(f) **Recordkeeping.**
The Department shall maintain permanent records of registrations, amended registrations, complaints received, actions taken, and cases archived without action. An annual summary shall be prepared listing complaints by category. The summary shall not evaluate subjective irritation.

(g) **Cross-References.**
For general registration requirements applicable to magical objects, see § 801.2. For negligent wand use and improper instrument technique, refer to § 1201.2. For flight regulation of broomsticks and other airborne magical devices, consult § 801.7. For spell risk classifications relevant to discharge capacity and regulatory oversight, see § 401.2.

(h) **Historical Annotations.**
This section was enacted under C.C.D. 4879, 83 MR 6112, Thu. 14, 1993, to consolidate wand registration oversight and general complaint intake within a single administrative authority following sustained noncompliance and procedural inconsistency in instrument disclosure and grievance handling; it was amended under C.C.D. 5134, 89 MR 7420, Mon. 3, 2022, to clarify re-registration requirements and codify rebuttable presumptions of operability, and further amended under C.C.D. 5219, 91 MR 3188, Thu. 19, 2024, to establish evidentiary standards and safe harbor thresholds for recurring commercial inoperability complaints involving enchanted dispensing apparatuses.

§ 801.9 Bread Hardness and Public Safety

(a) **In General.**
Certain bread products, when altered through time, neglect, or intentional preparation, may present risks consistent with low-grade blunt force implements. Such items shall be regulated under this section.

(b) **Definition of Blunt Edible Object.**
The term "Blunt Edible Object" means any consumable item that—
(1) is intended for ingestion; and
(2) has undergone physical transformation such that it is capable of causing injury, structural damage, or disruption when used as a projectile or impact instrument.

(c) **Presumptive Classification of Bread.**
(1) Bread shall be presumed to constitute a Blunt Edible Object where it satisfies one or more of the following conditions:
(A) produces an audible impact when dropped from waist height onto a hard surface;
(B) resists manual tearing without the application of significant force;
(C) is capable of denting wood, stone, or comparable materials; or
(D) has remained exposed to air for a duration sufficient to render it dangerously stale, as determined under subsection (d).
(2) Other food items may be classified as Blunt Edible Objects where they exhibit comparable density, rigidity, or impact characteristics.

(d) **Testing Standards.**

(1) A food item shall be deemed dangerously stale where a reasonable person, upon handling the item, would conclude that consumption is no longer the primary or intended use.
(2) In making such determination, consideration shall be given to—
(A) hardness;
(B) structural integrity;
(C) resistance to deformation; and
(D) the sound produced upon impact with a solid surface.

(e) **Prohibited Conduct.**
No person shall—
(1) throw, launch, or otherwise deploy a Blunt Edible Object in a manner likely to cause injury or property damage;
(2) distribute Blunt Edible Objects in public or shared spaces under circumstances where such objects are likely to be misused; or
(3) intentionally create Blunt Edible Objects for purposes inconsistent with consumption.

(f) **No Culinary Defense.**
It shall not constitute a defense to a violation of this section that the item—
(1) was originally intended for consumption;
(2) remains technically edible; or
(3) is just bread.

(g) **Disposition.**
Blunt Edible Objects shall be—
(1) disposed of in accordance with applicable waste and sanitation regulations; or
(2) rendered safe for consumption through appropriate restoration, softening, or other corrective measures.

(h) **Cross-References.**
For classification of magical objects and artifacts, see § 801.1. For registration and inspection requirements, see § 801.2. For reasonable care standards, see § 101.7. For negligent conduct, see Part XII. For penalties, see § 102.2.

(i) **Historical Annotations.**

This section was enacted under C.C.D. 6123, 21 MR 118, Mon. 4, 1883 following the Bakery Militia Incident, in which multiple individuals armed with stale loaves engaged in coordinated projectile activity resulting in minor structural damage and several avoidable injuries. Amended under C.C.D. 6891, 29 MR 442, Tue. 17, 1917 to establish objective testing standards for dangerous staleness. Revised under C.C.D. 8812, 49 MR 771, Fri. 17, 1986 to clarify classification criteria and eliminate repeated arguments that hardened bread does not constitute a weapon.

Part IX: Resource Conservation and Environmental Impact

§ 901.1 Ley Line Conservation and Use

(a) **In General.**
Ley lines are designated as critical magical infrastructure whose stability is essential to the continuity of magical systems, ecological balance, and public safety. No person shall access, draw upon, alter, or otherwise interact with a ley line except in strict compliance with this section. Activities affecting ley lines shall be construed narrowly in favor of preservation and stability.

(b) **Definition and Scope.**
(1) Ley Line. A ley line is a naturally occurring or artificially stabilized conduit of magical energy that flows through, across, or beneath physical or metaphysical space and supports ongoing magical activity.
(2) Covered Activity. This section applies to any act that—
(A) draws, extracts, diverts, or channels ley line energy;
(B) amplifies, suppresses, or redistributes such energy;
(C) alters the flow, direction, density, or stability of a ley line;
(D) establishes a connection between a ley line and any magical system, construct, or device;
(E) introduces foreign energy, interference, or resonance into a ley line.

(c) **Classification of Ley Lines.**
(1) General Rule. Ley lines shall be classified based on capacity, stability, and systemic importance.
(2) Primary Classifications.
(A) Tier I: Critical Ley Lines.
(i) Ley lines that support major population centers, essential magical systems, or inter-regional energy balance;
(ii) any disruption shall be presumed to pose immediate and widespread risk.
(B) Tier II: Regional Ley Lines.
(i) Ley lines supporting localized systems or environments;
(ii) disruption may result in significant but contained impact.

(C) Tier III: Minor Ley Lines.
(i) Ley lines with limited capacity or localized influence;
(ii) disruption may result in minimal systemic impact but shall still be regulated.
(3) Reclassification. The Department of Magical Affairs may reclassify a ley line based on changing conditions, usage patterns, or observed instability.

(d) **Permitted Use.**
(1) General Rule. Use of ley lines shall be limited to activities that—
(A) do not materially degrade stability, capacity, or flow;
(B) are consistent with long-term sustainability;
(C) do not interfere with other authorized uses.
(2) Individual Use.
(A) Incidental or low-impact use by authorized practitioners shall be permitted;
(B) such use shall remain within reasonable limits based on skill, necessity, and local conditions;
(C) repeated or cumulative use may be treated as large-scale use under paragraph (3).
(3) Institutional and Large-Scale Use.
(A) Any continuous, high-volume, or system-integrated use shall require authorization under § 102.1;
(B) such use shall be subject to allocation limits, monitoring, and periodic review;
(C) authorization may be modified or revoked where adverse impact is detected.

(e) **Prohibited Conduct.**
No person shall—
(1) extract or draw upon ley line energy in excess of sustainable thresholds;
(2) divert, reroute, split, or merge ley lines without express authorization;
(3) establish siphoning, storage, or redistribution systems in violation of § 602.1;
(4) introduce destabilizing resonance, feedback loops, or uncontrolled amplification;
(5) create artificial dependencies that impair the natural recovery or function of a ley line;
(6) conceal, obscure, or misrepresent the extent of ley line interaction.

(f) **Allocation and Priority of Use.**
(1) General Rule. Where demand exceeds capacity, access shall be allocated to preserve system integrity.
(2) Priority Order. Allocation shall prioritize—
(A) emergency and public safety uses;
(B) maintenance of essential infrastructure and systems;
(C) baseline access for authorized practitioners;
(D) commercial or discretionary use.
(3) Restrictions.
(A) The Department of Magical Affairs may impose usage caps, time-based restrictions, or complete suspension of access;
(B) such restrictions may apply by region, user class, or activity type.

(g) **Monitoring and Measurement.**
(1) General Rule. Use of ley lines shall be subject to continuous or periodic monitoring sufficient to detect impact and ensure compliance.
(2) Required Measures.
(A) Large-scale users shall implement systems to measure extraction rates, flow disruption, and systemic impact;
(B) such systems shall maintain logs capable of reconstructing usage patterns.
(3) Reporting.
(A) Material deviations, anomalies, or instability shall be reported under § 901.3;
(B) failure to detect or report such conditions shall constitute a violation.

(h) **Stability and Risk Management.**
(1) General Rule. Any activity affecting a ley line shall be conducted in a manner that preserves structural and energetic stability.
(2) Risk Factors. Activities shall account for—
(A) cumulative extraction effects;
(B) interaction with nearby constructs or systems;
(C) resonance with other energy sources;
(D) potential for cascading failure across interconnected ley lines.
(3) Emergency Conditions.
(A) Where instability is detected, all non-essential use shall cease immediately;
(B) emergency stabilization measures shall be initiated without delay.
(i) Restoration and Mitigation.

(1) General Rule. Any person whose actions result in degradation, imbalance, or instability shall be responsible for remediation.
(2) Required Actions.
(A) cessation or reduction of harmful activity;
(B) implementation of stabilization or restoration measures;
(C) compliance with corrective measures imposed under § 701.6.
(3) Continuing Obligation. Responsibility for remediation shall continue until the ley line is restored to a stable condition.

(j) **Integration with Magical Systems.**
(1) General Rule. Any construct, device, or system connected to a ley line shall operate within sustainable limits.
(2) Design Requirements.
(A) systems shall include safeguards to prevent over-extraction or instability;
(B) systems shall allow for disconnection or shutdown where necessary.
(3) Prohibited Systems.
No system shall be designed to continuously extract energy without regard to capacity, regeneration, or impact.

(k) **Cross-References.**
For magical siphoning restrictions, see § 602.1. For environmental impact reporting, see § 901.3. For disaster response, see § 901.5. For administrative authority, see § 102.1. For penalties, see § 102.2.

(l) **Historical Annotations.**
Originally established under C.C.D. 5601, 22 MR 118, Tue. 5, 1765 to regulate early exploitation of ley line energy. Amended under C.C.D. 6355, 32 MR 771, Mon. 11, 1825 to incorporate allocation and priority provisions following regional instability events. Revised under C.C.D. 9702, 67 MR 442, Wed. 14, 2008 to address systemic risk, cascading failures, and large-scale institutional use.

§ 901.2 Elemental Magic and Resource Management

(a) **In General.**
Elemental magic shall be managed in a manner that preserves the integrity, regenerative capacity, and functional balance of affected resources and systems. This section governs the evaluation and

management of elemental activity as it relates to resource sustainability and system-wide stability.

(b) **Scope and Definitions.**
(1) Elemental Magic. Elemental magic includes any act, process, or system that generates, manipulates, amplifies, suppresses, converts, or redistributes elemental forces, including derivative, hybrid, or composite applications.
(2) Resource Base. The resource base includes any natural or magical system capable of being affected by elemental activity, including water systems, atmospheric conditions, geological formations, ambient magical fields, and any interdependent components.
(3) Baseline Conditions. Baseline conditions refer to the expected range of variability and stability of a resource or system in the absence of regulated activity.

(c) **Sustainable Use Standard.**
(1) General Rule. Elemental activity shall be evaluated based on whether it maintains or impairs the ability of the affected resource to regenerate, stabilize, and support dependent systems.
(2) Evaluation Criteria. Sustainability shall be determined by reference to—
(A) rate of extraction, alteration, or displacement relative to natural or magical replenishment;
(B) duration, frequency, and intensity of activity;
(C) resilience, adaptability, and recovery capacity of the affected system;
(D) deviation from baseline conditions;
(E) interaction with concurrent or prior activities affecting the same or related systems.
(3) Temporal Considerations.
(A) Short-term impacts may constitute unsustainable use where recovery is delayed or incomplete;
(B) long-term impacts shall be evaluated based on projected system behavior and cumulative effect.
(4) Cumulative Use. Repeated or aggregated activity shall be evaluated collectively, regardless of whether individual acts appear minimal in isolation.

(d) **Systemic Interaction and Interdependence.**

(1) General Rule. Elemental activity shall be assessed in the context of the broader systems in which it operates.
(2) Interconnected Systems.
(A) Alteration of one resource shall be evaluated for its effect on interconnected systems;
(B) impacts to secondary systems shall be treated as part of the original activity.
(3) Cascade Effects.
(A) Activities with potential to trigger cascading or compounding effects shall be subject to heightened scrutiny;
(B) failure to account for such effects shall constitute noncompliant activity.

(e) **Operational Constraints and Limitations.**
(1) General Rule. Elemental practices shall be conducted within constraints necessary to maintain system stability and resource availability.
(2) Constraint Factors. Constraints may be determined based on—
(A) local environmental and magical conditions;
(B) existing levels of resource stress or depletion;
(C) density and concentration of concurrent activity;
(D) proximity to critical infrastructure, ecosystems, or population centers.
(3) Dynamic Constraints.
(A) Operational limits may vary over time and conditions;
(B) persons engaging in elemental activity shall remain responsible for adapting to such changes.
(4) Exceedance. Exceeding applicable constraints shall constitute evidence of unsustainable use.

(f) **Monitoring, Measurement, and Assessment.**
(1) General Rule. Elemental activity with potential to affect resources shall be subject to monitoring sufficient to assess impact and compliance.
(2) Assessment Methods.
(A) direct measurement of resource conditions;
(B) observation of environmental indicators and system responses;
(C) analysis of usage patterns and outcomes over time.
(3) Continuity of Monitoring.
(A) Monitoring shall be ongoing where activity is sustained, repeated, or cumulative;
(B) intermittent activity shall be monitored where conditions warrant.

(4) Failure to Monitor. Failure to implement or maintain adequate monitoring shall constitute a violation independent of any resulting harm.

(g) **Adaptive Management.**
(1) General Rule. Elemental activity shall be adjusted in response to observed or anticipated impacts.
(2) Required Adjustments.
(A) reduction, suspension, or modification of activity;
(B) implementation of alternative methods or techniques;
(C) coordination with other users or systems to reduce aggregate impact.
(3) Failure to Adapt. Continued activity in the presence of known or foreseeable harm shall constitute noncompliance.

(h) **Interface with Impact Determination.**
(1) General Rule. Evaluations under this section shall inform, but not replace, determinations of depletion or damage under § 901.4.
(2) Non-Exclusivity. Compliance with this section shall not preclude a finding of depletion or damage under § 901.4.

(i) **Cross-References.**
For ley line conservation, see § 901.1. For environmental impact reporting, see § 901.3. For determination of depletion or damage, see § 901.4. For administrative authority, see § 102.1.

(j) **Historical Annotations.**
Originally established under C.C.D. 5655, 22 MR 771, Fri. 11, 1770 to regulate elemental practices affecting natural resources. Amended under C.C.D. 6402, 33 MR 118, Tue. 7, 1830 to incorporate resource-based evaluation standards. Revised under C.C.D. 9750, 68 MR 442, Mon. 16, 2010 to address cumulative, systemic, and adaptive management requirements.

§ 901.3 Reporting Environmental Impacts of Magical Practices

(a) **In General.**
Environmental impacts resulting from magical activity shall be reported in accordance with this section to ensure timely identification, evaluation, and response to conditions affecting resource stability and ecosystem integrity.

(b) **Scope of Reporting.**
(1) Covered Activity. Reporting obligations apply to any magical activity that results in or is reasonably expected to result in measurable environmental impact.
(2) Triggering Conditions. Reporting shall be required where—
(A) observable deviation from baseline conditions occurs;
(B) established thresholds, indicators, or constraints are exceeded;
(C) unanticipated or anomalous effects arise;
(D) cumulative activity results in measurable system stress.

(c) **Timing of Reports.**
(1) General Rule. Reports shall be submitted within a reasonable period following identification of a reportable condition.
(2) Immediate Reporting.
(A) Where conditions indicate instability, escalation, or risk of broader impact, reporting shall occur without delay;
(B) delay shall be permitted only where immediate reporting is impracticable, and only for the minimum time necessary.

(d) **Content and Detail.**
Reports shall include, to the extent known and reasonably ascertainable—
(1) description of the activity, including methods and duration;
(2) identification of affected systems and resources;
(3) nature, extent, and progression of observed impact;
(4) relevant environmental indicators and measurements;
(5) identification of contributing or related activities;
(6) actions taken or proposed in response;
(7) any uncertainty or limitation in available information.

(e) **Ongoing and Supplemental Reporting.**
(1) General Rule. Where impacts persist, evolve, or expand, supplemental reporting shall be required.
(2) Material Changes. Reports shall be updated to reflect—
(A) changes in conditions or severity;
(B) new information or analysis;
(C) effectiveness of mitigation efforts.
(3) Termination of Reporting. Reporting obligations shall continue until conditions have stabilized or returned within acceptable limits.

(f) **Responsibility to Report.**

(1) Primary Responsibility. The person or entity responsible for the activity shall bear primary reporting responsibility.
(2) Secondary Reporting.
(A) Any person with knowledge of a reportable condition may submit a report;
(B) such reporting shall not relieve the responsible party of its obligations.
(3) Shared Responsibility. Where multiple parties are involved, each shall be responsible for reporting information within their knowledge.

(g) **Good Faith and Accuracy.**
(1) General Rule. Reports shall be made in good faith and with reasonable accuracy based on available information.
(2) Incomplete Information.
(A) Lack of complete information shall not excuse failure to report;
(B) reasonable estimates shall be permitted where necessary.
(3) Misrepresentation. Knowingly providing false or misleading information shall constitute a violation.

(h) **Cross-References.**
For elemental resource management, see § 901.2. For determination of depletion or damage, see § 901.4. For administrative authority, see § 102.1. For penalties, see § 102.2.

(i) **Historical Annotations.**
Originally established under C.C.D. 5702, 23 MR 118, Mon. 4, 1780 to require disclosure of environmental effects from magical activity. Amended under C.C.D. 6501, 34 MR 771, Thu. 9, 1840 to expand reporting triggers and obligations. Revised under C.C.D. 9820, 69 MR 442, Tue. 20, 2015 to incorporate ongoing reporting and material change requirements.

§ 901.4 Depletion and Damage to Magical Ecosystems

(a) **In General.**
For purposes of this Part, depletion and damage to magical ecosystems shall be determined in accordance with this section. Determinations made under this section shall govern the application of enforcement and corrective measures under this Code.

(b) **Definitions.**
(1) Depletion. Depletion means the reduction, exhaustion, or impairment of a resource's capacity to function, regenerate, or support dependent systems.
(2) Damage. Damage means any alteration to a magical ecosystem that disrupts its structure, balance, or functioning, whether temporary or permanent.
(3) Magical Ecosystem. A magical ecosystem includes any interconnected system of resources, energy flows, and dependent biological, environmental, or metaphysical components.

(c) **Standards for Determination.**
(1) General Rule. Determinations shall be based on the totality of the circumstances.
(2) Relevant Factors.
(A) magnitude and geographic or systemic extent of impact;
(B) duration, persistence, and reversibility;
(C) sensitivity and classification of the affected system;
(D) deviation from baseline conditions;
(E) interaction with prior, concurrent, or anticipated impacts.

(d) **Cumulative and Aggregated Effects.**
(1) General Rule. Impacts shall be evaluated collectively where multiple actions contribute to a single outcome.
(2) Aggregation Across Time.
(A) actions separated in time may be aggregated where they produce a continuing or compounding effect;
(B) historical use may be considered in evaluating present conditions.
(3) Aggregation Across Actors.
Impacts resulting from multiple actors shall be evaluated as a whole regardless of individual contribution.

(e) **Causation and Attribution.**
(1) Direct Causation. Responsibility shall attach to actions that directly produce depletion or damage.
(2) Indirect and Foreseeable Effects.
(A) Responsibility shall extend to reasonably foreseeable consequences;
(B) intervening factors shall not relieve responsibility where the original conduct materially contributed.
(3) Concurrent Responsibility.

(A) Multiple actors may be held responsible for the same impact;
(B) inability to precisely allocate responsibility shall not preclude a finding.

(f) **Severity Assessment.**
(1) General Rule. Severity shall be assessed based on scale, duration, and systemic effect.
(2) Categories of Severity.
(A) Minor Impact: localized and reversible effects;
(B) Material Impact: effects requiring active mitigation or restoration;
(C) Severe Impact: widespread or long-term disruption;
(D) Catastrophic Impact: systemic failure, collapse, or irreversible loss.
(3) Application. Severity classifications shall inform enforcement under § 102.2 and corrective measures under § 701.6.

(g) **Presumptions.**
(1) Overuse Presumption. Activity exceeding sustainable thresholds shall be presumed to constitute depletion.
(2) Instability Presumption. Observable instability or disruption shall be presumed to constitute damage.
(3) Burden of Rebuttal. The responsible party shall bear the burden of rebutting such presumptions with sufficient evidence.

(h) **Cross-References.**
For ley line conservation, see § 901.1. For elemental resource management, see § 901.2. For reporting environmental impacts, see § 901.3. For administrative authority, see § 102.1. For penalties, see § 102.2.

(i) **Historical Annotations.**
Originally established under C.C.D. 5688, 23 MR 118, Wed. 9, 1775 to define depletion of magical resources. Amended under C.C.D. 6450, 33 MR 771, Tue. 14, 1835 to incorporate causation and cumulative impact principles. Revised under C.C.D. 9788, 68 MR 771, Thu. 22, 2012 to include severity classifications, presumptions, and aggregation standards.

§ 901.5 Magical Disaster Relief and Response

(a) **In General.**
Magical disasters shall be managed through coordinated response, stabilization, and recovery measures designed to protect life, preserve

magical ecosystems, and restore affected systems. This section governs the identification, classification, and response to events resulting in widespread or systemic disruption caused by magical activity.

(b) **Definition of Magical Disaster.**
(1) General Rule. A magical disaster is any event or condition that—
(A) results in widespread instability, disruption, or collapse of magical or environmental systems; or
(B) poses an immediate or escalating threat to public safety, infrastructure, or ecosystem integrity.
(2) Included Events. Magical disasters include—
(A) ley line rupture, overload, or collapse;
(B) uncontrolled elemental events or runaway reactions;
(C) cascading failures of interconnected magical systems;
(D) large-scale release of unstable or uncontained magical energy;
(E) failure of containment constructs, including dungeon constructs under § 801.6.
(3) Exclusions. Localized or contained events shall not be considered disasters unless they present a credible risk of escalation.

(c) **Declaration of Disaster Conditions.**
(1) Authority. The Department of Magical Affairs may declare a magical disaster condition under § 102.1.
(2) Criteria. A declaration may be made where—
(A) conditions exceed established stability thresholds;
(B) impacts are widespread or rapidly escalating;
(C) coordinated response is necessary to prevent further harm.
(3) Effect of Declaration.
(A) activation of emergency response protocols;
(B) authorization of temporary measures necessary to stabilize conditions;
(C) coordination among affected jurisdictions and entities.

(d) **Emergency Response Measures.**
(1) General Rule. Upon declaration, response measures shall be implemented to contain, stabilize, and mitigate the effects of the disaster.
(2) Permitted Actions.
(A) temporary restriction or suspension of magical activity in affected areas;

(B) controlled discharge, redirection, or containment of excess magical energy;
(C) deployment of emergency constructs, barriers, or suppression systems;
(D) evacuation or relocation of affected persons or creatures.
(3) Limitations.
(A) measures shall be limited to those necessary to address the disaster;
(B) actions shall be proportionate to the severity of conditions.

(e) **Coordination and Control.**
(1) General Rule. Response efforts shall be coordinated among relevant authorities, institutions, and responsible parties.
(2) Central Coordination.
(A) The Department of Magical Affairs shall serve as the central coordinating authority;
(B) other entities shall comply with directives issued under § 102.1.
(3) Information Sharing. Relevant information shall be shared as necessary to ensure effective response and mitigation.

(f) **Responsibilities of Affected and Responsible Parties.**
(1) General Rule. Persons whose actions contributed to the disaster shall cooperate fully with response efforts.
(2) Required Actions.
(A) provision of information and access necessary for response;
(B) participation in mitigation and stabilization efforts where directed;
(C) compliance with emergency measures and restrictions.
(3) Non-Responsible Parties. Other affected persons shall comply with lawful directives issued during the response.

(g) **Monitoring and Stabilization.**
(1) General Rule. Conditions shall be continuously monitored to assess stability and effectiveness of response measures.
(2) Stabilization Criteria.
(A) reduction of instability to acceptable levels;
(B) containment of active threats;
(C) restoration of basic system functionality.
(3) Adjustment of Measures. Response measures shall be modified as conditions evolve.

(h) **Transition to Recovery.**

(1) General Rule. Once immediate threats are controlled, response shall transition to recovery and restoration.
(2) Recovery Actions.
(A) repair or restoration of affected systems;
(B) reassessment of resource capacity and stability;
(C) gradual lifting of emergency restrictions.
(3) Continued Oversight. Monitoring and corrective measures shall continue until conditions have stabilized.

(i) **Cross-References.**
For ley line conservation, see § 901.1. For elemental resource management, see § 901.2. For environmental impact reporting, see § 901.3. For determination of depletion or damage, see § 901.4. For administrative authority, see § 102.1. For penalties, see § 102.2.

(j) **Historical Annotations.**
Originally established under C.C.D. 5750, 24 MR 118, Mon. 3, 1790 to address large-scale magical catastrophes. Amended under C.C.D. 6522, 34 MR 771, Wed. 12, 1845 to incorporate coordinated response authority. Revised under C.C.D. 9855, 70 MR 442, Fri. 18, 2018 to include modern stabilization, monitoring, and recovery protocols.

§ 901.6 Establishment and Maintenance of Community Magic Reservoirs

(a) **In General.**
Community magic reservoirs may be established and maintained for the limited purpose of storing and distributing magical energy for communal use, provided such reservoirs operate in a manner consistent with resource conservation, system stability, and the prohibitions set forth in § 602.1.

(b) **Definition and Scope.**
(1) Community Magic Reservoir. A community magic reservoir is any system, construct, or infrastructure designed to store, retain, or redistribute magical energy for use by a defined population or group.
(2) Covered Systems. This section applies to any reservoir that—
(A) collects ambient or surplus magical energy;
(B) stores energy for later use;
(C) distributes energy to multiple users or systems.

(c) **Permitted Sources of Energy.**
(1) General Rule. Reservoirs shall only utilize lawful and sustainable sources of magical energy.
(2) Permitted Sources. Acceptable sources include—
(A) ambient magical energy not otherwise in active use;
(B) voluntarily contributed surplus energy from authorized practitioners;
(C) excess output from lawful magical systems operating within sustainable limits.
(3) Prohibited Sources.
No reservoir shall—
(A) extract energy directly from any person, creature, or system without consent;
(B) impair the functioning of ley lines in violation of § 901.1;
(C) engage in siphoning practices prohibited under § 602.1.

(d) **Voluntariness and Non-Extraction.**
(1) General Rule. Participation in any system contributing energy to a reservoir shall be voluntary.
(2) Prohibition on Compulsion.
(A) No person shall be required, coerced, or induced through improper means to contribute energy;
(B) systemic or indirect extraction designed to simulate voluntary contribution shall be prohibited.
(3) Protection of Individual Capacity.
No contribution shall materially impair the contributing party's ability to function or engage in lawful activity.

(e) **Operational Limitations.**
(1) General Rule. Reservoirs shall operate within limits that preserve system stability and prevent resource depletion.
(2) Capacity Constraints.
(A) storage shall not exceed levels that create instability or risk of uncontrolled release;
(B) intake and output shall be regulated to prevent imbalance in surrounding systems.
(3) Distribution Limits.
(A) distribution shall be limited to reasonable communal use;
(B) no system shall centralize or control access to magical energy in a manner that undermines equitable access or system integrity.

(f) **Monitoring and Control.**
(1) General Rule. Reservoirs shall be subject to monitoring sufficient to ensure compliance with this Code.
(2) Required Measures.
(A) tracking of energy input, storage levels, and output;
(B) detection of instability, leakage, or unauthorized access;
(C) maintenance of records sufficient to reconstruct system activity.
(3) Failure to Monitor. Failure to maintain adequate monitoring shall constitute a violation.

(g) **Stability and Safety Requirements.**
(1) General Rule. Reservoirs shall be designed and maintained to prevent instability, overflow, or uncontrolled discharge.
(2) Safeguards.
(A) mechanisms to regulate intake and release of energy;
(B) emergency containment or dissipation systems;
(C) controlled shutdown capabilities.
(3) Risk of Failure.
(A) Any condition indicating instability shall require immediate corrective action;
(B) continued operation under such conditions shall constitute a violation.

(h) **Integration with Other Systems.**
(1) Ley Lines. Reservoirs interacting with ley lines shall comply with § 901.1 and shall not impair natural flow or stability.
(2) Constructs and Devices. Reservoirs supplying energy to magical constructs shall ensure that such use remains within sustainable limits.
(3) Prohibited Integration. No reservoir shall be integrated into a system designed to continuously extract or concentrate energy without regard to system impact.

(i) **Prohibited Conduct.**
No person shall—
(1) operate a reservoir in a manner that results in depletion or damage under § 901.4;
(2) conceal or misrepresent the source or use of stored energy;
(3) use a reservoir to facilitate prohibited practices under § 701.2;
(4) structure reservoir operations to evade the prohibitions of § 602.1.

(j) **Cross-References.**
For ley line conservation, see § 901.1. For elemental resource management, see § 901.2. For determination of depletion or damage, see § 901.4. For anti-siphoning restrictions, see § 602.1. For administrative authority, see § 102.1. For penalties, see § 102.2.

(k) **Historical Annotations.**
Originally established under C.C.D. 5802, 24 MR 771, Tue. 12, 1795 to authorize localized storage of magical energy for communal use. Amended under C.C.D. 6601, 35 MR 118, Mon. 6, 1855 to prohibit coercive extraction practices. Revised under C.C.D. 9902, 71 MR 442, Wed. 21, 2020 to clarify anti-siphoning safeguards and system-wide limitations.

§ 901.7 Regulation of Thermoregulatory Manipulation in Shared Magical Dwellings

(a) **General Rule.**
In any shared dwelling, the adjustment, alteration, modulation, or physical manipulation of ambient temperature, whether accomplished through magical means, mechanical devices, enchanted instruments, mundane controls, or the turning of a plainly labeled dial, shall be subject to the requirements of this section. For purposes of this section, a dwelling shall be considered shared upon the presence of two or more occupants with lawful rights of habitation, regardless of ownership, leasehold interest, familial relationship, or personal tolerance for cold.

(b) **Designation of Designated Thermal Authority.**
(1) No individual may alter the temperature of a shared dwelling unless such individual has been formally designated as the Designated Thermal Authority.
(2) The Designated Thermal Authority shall be the sole individual authorized to effectuate any change in temperature exceeding one degree in either direction within a twenty-four-hour period.
(3) Designation as Designated Thermal Authority shall require unanimous written consent of all occupants of the dwelling, executed on Form 407-DTA, notarized, countersigned, and submitted for review.
(4) Absence of consent from any occupant, including occupants who are asleep, traveling, sulking, or refusing to answer messages, shall constitute a failure of unanimity.

(c) **Application in Lieu of Unanimous Consent.**
(1) Where unanimous consent cannot be obtained, an individual may petition for designation as Designated Thermal Authority in lieu of consent by submitting Form 407-L, accompanied by:
(A) A sworn affidavit detailing the necessity of temperature modification;
(B) Written statements from each non-consenting occupant explaining their objection in their own words;
(C) A Thermal Impact Narrative of no fewer than fifteen pages describing anticipated effects on comfort, health, morale, and seasonal vibes; and
(D) A non-refundable processing fee calibrated annually to discourage frivolous submissions.
(2) Petitions submitted under this subsection shall be reviewed no fewer than three times, including one review by an official who was not previously aware that thermoregulation was part of their job.
(3) Approval under this subsection, if granted, shall be provisional, revocable, and valid only for the specific temperature range requested.

(d) **Notice and Waiting Period Requirements.**
(1) Prior to any authorized temperature change, the Designated Thermal Authority shall provide written notice to all occupants no fewer than fourteen days in advance.
(2) Notice shall specify the proposed temperature, duration, rationale, and suggested alternative accommodations for those adversely affected.
(3) Any occupant may object within the notice period, thereby suspending the proposed change pending further review, mediation, or the passage of sufficient time to reconsider whether the change was worth it in the first place.

(e) **Substantive Restrictions on Temperature Adjustments.**
(1) No temperature adjustment shall be deemed reasonable if a materially affected occupant could, through ordinary effort, mitigate discomfort by donning a sweater, jacket, blanket, robe, hoodie, or similar garment commonly available to people who insist on being cold indoors.
(2) Claims of extreme discomfort shall be supported by documentation demonstrating that layering was attempted and failed.
(3) Adjustments made solely because one occupant “runs cold” shall be presumed unjustified absent compelling evidence to the contrary.

(f) **Mechanical and Magical Neutrality.**

This section shall apply equally to magical heating, enchanted climate arrays, elemental manipulation, central air systems, radiators, space heaters, fireplaces, heat rocks, or hands placed directly upon the thermostat with intent to turn it.

(g) **Recordkeeping and Monitoring.**
(1) All authorized temperature changes shall be logged contemporaneously, noting date, time, degree change, and emotional fallout.
(2) Logs shall be retained for a period of not less than five years and made available upon request to any occupant who feels wronged.

(h) **Penalties for Unauthorized Thermoregulation.**
Any individual who alters the temperature of a shared dwelling without full compliance with this section shall be subject to corrective measures, including reversal of the change, mandatory reeducation regarding layering, and such additional penalties as may be imposed under § 102.2.

(i) **Cross-References.**
For provisions relating to resource conservation and reasonable use, see § 901.1 and § 901.2. For good faith compliance standards, see § 702.2.

(j) **Historical Annotations.**
This section was originally established under C.C.D. 11872, 91 MR 4421, Sat. 6, 2009, following widespread disputes arising from shared living arrangements. It was amended under C.C.D. 12409, 93 MR 8176, Tue. 18, 2016, to introduce the Designated Thermal Authority designation and further amended under C.C.D. 13902, 97 MR 2214, Wed. 3, 2023, to clarify notice requirements and discourage unnecessary temperature adjustments.

§ 901.8 Restrictions on Non-Standard Hygiene Practices in Shared Magical Dwellings

(a) **In General.**
Individuals residing in shared magical dwellings shall maintain baseline hygienic conditions sufficient to prevent material disruption to co-occupants, the dwelling, or the surrounding magical environment.

(b) **Standard of Acceptable Hygiene.**

(1) An individual shall be deemed in compliance where their hygiene practices do not result in—
(A) persistent or accumulating odors detectable beyond their immediate sleeping area;
(B) visible residue, buildup, or organic accumulation on shared surfaces;
(C) conditions reasonably likely to attract vermin, insects, or minor magical entities; or
(D) measurable degradation of air quality, ambient conditions, or magical stability within the dwelling.
(2) Hygiene shall be evaluated based on the totality of the circumstances, including duration, severity, and impact on other occupants.

(c) **Prohibited Practices.**
No person shall rely exclusively on the following in lieu of standard bathing or cleaning practices:
(1) exposure to moonlight, starlight, or other celestial bodies;
(2) immersion in ambient magical fields or ley line residue;
(3) application of herbs, oils, or vapors absent actual cleansing;
(4) claims of "natural equilibrium," "aura balancing," or similar non-cleansing methodologies; or
(5) any practice that does not involve the removal of physical matter from the body or environment.

(d) **Shared Space Obligations.**
(1) Individuals shall take reasonable steps to ensure that their personal hygiene does not impair the use or enjoyment of shared spaces.
(2) Where a condition arises that affects multiple occupants, corrective action shall be taken within a reasonable period.

(e) **Notice and Opportunity to Cure.**
(1) Co-occupants may provide notice of non-compliance under this section.
(2) Upon such notice, the individual shall be afforded a reasonable opportunity to remedy the condition prior to escalation.

(f) **Prohibited Defense.**
It shall not constitute a defense to a violation of this section that—
(1) the individual "does not perceive" the condition;
(2) the condition is "natural" or "intentional"; or

(3) the practices in question are "traditional," "ancestral," or "spiritually aligned."

(g) **Enforcement Considerations.**
In determining compliance, the Department may consider—
(1) frequency and duration of the condition;
(2) corroboration by other occupants;
(3) presence of physical or magical side effects, including observable insect congregation or minor entity manifestation; and
(4) any prior history of similar conditions.

(h) **Cross-References.**
For thermoregulatory disputes in shared dwellings, see § 901.7. For reasonable care standards, see § 101.7. For magical property provisions, see Part XXV. For penalties, see § 102.2.

(i) **Historical Annotations.**
This section was enacted under C.C.D. 10112, 73 MR 442, Mon. 12, 2008 following a series of tenancy disputes involving persistent odor conditions and alleged reliance on "self-cleansing" magical fields in lieu of bathing. Amended under C.C.D. 10401, 76 MR 118, Wed. 9, 2014 to clarify prohibited practices and shared space obligations. Revised under C.C.D. 10588, 79 MR 771, Thu. 18, 2026 to incorporate environmental and magical impact considerations and to eliminate recurring defenses based on subjective perception of cleanliness.

Part X: Financial and Economic Regulations

§ 1001.1 Magical Financial Fraud and Currency Manipulation

(a) **In General.**
No person shall engage in any act, scheme, or practice involving magic that is intended to defraud, deceive, manipulate, or otherwise interfere with the integrity, valuation, or operation of any financial system, market, or instrument. This section applies to all magical activity affecting monetary value, financial transactions, or economic systems.

(b) **Scope of Application.**
(1) Covered Activity. This section applies to any magical act that—
(A) alters, fabricates, conceals, or misrepresents financial information or value;
(B) interferes with the pricing, exchange, or transfer of assets;
(C) affects the perceived or actual value of currency, goods, or services.
(2) Covered Systems. This section applies to—
(A) markets, exchanges, and trading environments;
(B) financial institutions and intermediaries;
(C) systems involving magical or non-magical currency or assets.

(c) **Fraudulent Conduct.**
(1) General Rule. A person engages in magical financial fraud where they knowingly or recklessly use magic to obtain money, assets, or economic advantage through deception or misrepresentation.
(2) Examples of Fraudulent Conduct. Prohibited conduct includes—
(A) creation or alteration of financial records, contracts, or instruments through magic;
(B) concealment of material information affecting value or risk;
(C) manipulation of transactional outcomes through magical means;
(D) use of intermediaries, constructs, or layered transactions to obscure the nature or purpose of activity.
(3) Intent. Fraudulent intent may be inferred from conduct, patterns of activity, or efforts to conceal or misrepresent.

(d) **Currency Manipulation.**
(1) General Rule. No person shall use magic to manipulate the value, supply, or function of any currency.
(2) Prohibited Acts.
(A) artificial creation, duplication, or destruction of currency;
(B) alteration of intrinsic or perceived value;
(C) interference with issuance, distribution, or circulation;
(D) destabilization of monetary systems through coordinated or large-scale activity.
(3) Indirect Manipulation.
(A) manipulation of underlying assets or systems that affect currency value shall be treated as currency manipulation;
(B) such manipulation need not directly target the currency itself.

(e) **Market Integrity.**
(1) General Rule. No person shall use magic to distort market conditions or outcomes.
(2) Prohibited Conduct.
(A) creating artificial demand, scarcity, or pricing signals;
(B) interfering with the execution, timing, or sequencing of transactions;
(C) exploiting information asymmetry created through magical means;
(D) engaging in coordinated activity to influence market behavior.
(3) Appearance of Legitimacy.
(A) activity that appears legitimate but is structured to manipulate outcomes shall be treated as a violation;
(B) form shall not control over substance.

(f) **Manipulation of Financial Information.**
(1) General Rule. Financial information shall not be altered or obscured through magical means.
(2) Prohibited Conduct.
(A) falsification or alteration of records, statements, or disclosures;
(B) concealment of material facts;
(C) interference with systems used to record or transmit financial data.
(3) Reliance.
Materiality shall not depend on actual reliance where the conduct is capable of influencing decision-making.

(g) **Aggregation and Scheme Liability.**

(1) General Rule. Conduct shall be evaluated based on the overall scheme or pattern of activity.
(2) Aggregation.
(A) multiple acts may be aggregated to establish a violation;
(B) related transactions shall be considered collectively.
(3) Participation.
Any person who knowingly participates in, facilitates, or benefits from a fraudulent scheme shall be subject to this section.

(h) **Attempts and Evasion.**
(1) General Rule. Attempts to engage in conduct prohibited under this section shall constitute a violation.
(2) Evasion.
No person shall structure, disguise, or otherwise manipulate activity to evade the application of this section.

(i) **Cross-References.**
For reporting requirements related to financial activity, see § 701.9. For prohibited spells and enchantments in financial markets, see § 1001.2. For illusion-based fraud, see § 1001.4. For transfiguration-based fraud, see § 1001.5. For administrative authority, see § 102.1. For penalties, see § 102.2.

(j) **Historical Annotations.**
Originally established under C.C.D. 6001, 28 MR 118, Tue. 4, 1805 to address early forms of magical financial deception. Amended under C.C.D. 7205, 45 MR 771, Thu. 9, 1905 to incorporate currency manipulation provisions. Revised under C.C.D. 10055, 73 MR 442, Mon. 12, 2018 to address modern market manipulation and complex financial schemes involving magic.

§ 1001.2 Prohibited Spells and Enchantments in Financial Markets

(a) **In General.**
No person shall cast, deploy, embed, or otherwise utilize any spell, enchantment, or magical effect within or in connection with a financial market where such use has the purpose or effect of distorting pricing, influencing transactional outcomes, impairing market transparency, or otherwise interfering with the fair and orderly operation of such market.

(b) **Scope of Application.**
(1) Covered Markets. This section applies to any environment in which assets are bought, sold, exchanged, or otherwise valued, including—
(A) organized exchanges and trading platforms;
(B) over-the-counter or decentralized markets;
(C) any system in which pricing, valuation, or execution of transactions occurs.
(2) Covered Activity. This section applies to any magical act that—
(A) directly or indirectly affects pricing, valuation, or execution;
(B) influences participant behavior or decision-making;
(C) alters the availability, visibility, or interpretation of market information.

(c) **Prohibited Spells and Enchantments.**
(1) General Rule. Any spell or enchantment that produces a prohibited effect under subsection (a) shall be unlawful regardless of its form, classification, or apparent purpose.
(2) Illustrative Conduct. Prohibited uses include—
(A) enchantments that create artificial demand, supply, or scarcity;
(B) spells that alter or delay the execution, sequencing, or confirmation of transactions;
(C) enchantments that distort or obscure price signals or valuation metrics;
(D) spells that influence or manipulate the behavior of market participants;
(E) embedded magical effects within financial systems or instruments that alter expected outcomes.

(d) **Embedded and Latent Effects.**
(1) General Rule. No person shall embed, conceal, or incorporate any magical effect within a system, instrument, or environment used in a financial market where such effect is capable of influencing outcomes or conditions.
(2) Latent Enchantments.
(A) enchantments that activate upon specified conditions or triggers shall be treated as active for purposes of this section;
(B) delayed or conditional effects shall not avoid application of this section.
(3) Persistence.

The continued existence of a prohibited enchantment shall constitute an ongoing violation.

(e) **Interference with Market Infrastructure.**
(1) General Rule. No person shall use magic to interfere with the systems or processes that support financial markets.
(2) Prohibited Conduct.
(A) disruption of communication, transmission, or confirmation systems;
(B) interference with recordkeeping, settlement, or clearing processes;
(C) alteration of system timing, sequencing, or synchronization;
(D) introduction of instability or unpredictability into market infrastructure.

(f) **Indirect and External Influence.**
(1) General Rule. This section shall apply to magical activity occurring outside a financial market where such activity has a material effect on market conditions or outcomes.
(2) Examples.
(A) manipulation of underlying assets or resources that affect market pricing;
(B) use of magic to influence external conditions relied upon by the market;
(C) coordination of activity across multiple systems to produce a market effect.

(g) **Standard of Evaluation.**
(1) Effect-Based Standard. A violation shall be determined based on the effect or potential effect of the spell or enchantment, regardless of stated intent.
(2) Capability.
A spell or enchantment capable of producing a prohibited effect may constitute a violation even if such effect is not realized.
(3) Aggregation.
Multiple acts or effects shall be evaluated collectively where they produce a combined impact on the market.

(h) **Exceptions and Authorized Use.**
(1) General Rule. Use of magic within financial markets shall be prohibited unless expressly authorized under this Code.
(2) Authorized Activity.

(A) limited use of magic for system maintenance, security, or verification may be permitted where such use does not affect pricing, execution, or participant behavior;
(B) any such use shall remain subject to review under § 102.1.
(3) Burden of Proof.
The person asserting authorization shall bear the burden of demonstrating that the activity falls within a permitted use.

(i) **Cross-References.**
For general financial fraud and manipulation, see § 1001.1. For reporting requirements, see § 701.9. For illusion-based fraud, see § 1001.4. For transfiguration-based fraud, see § 1001.5. For administrative authority, see § 102.1. For penalties, see § 102.2.

(j) **Historical Annotations.**
Originally established under C.C.D. 6050, 28 MR 771, Thu. 11, 1810 to regulate early enchantments used in trade environments. Amended under C.C.D. 7255, 46 MR 118, Mon. 7, 1910 to address increasing complexity in market-based magical activity. Revised under C.C.D. 10088, 73 MR 771, Fri. 19, 2019 to incorporate modern financial systems and embedded enchantment practices.

§ 1001.3 Prohibited Luck or Chance Manipulation in Financial Markets

(a) **General Rule.**
Notwithstanding any provision of § 601.3 or any other section of this Code, no person shall employ, attempt to employ, facilitate, or benefit from any form of luck or chance manipulation in connection with financial markets, financial instruments, or economic transactions.

(b) **Scope of Prohibition.**
For purposes of this section, prohibited conduct includes any magical act, whether direct or indirect, that alters, biases, influences, or predetermines probabilistic outcomes affecting—
(1) market prices or valuations;
(2) trading outcomes or execution timing;
(3) investment performance or risk exposure;
(4) competitive positioning among market participants; or
(5) any event or condition upon which financial gain or loss is contingent.

(c) **Irrelevance of General Authorization.**
A practice that may be permitted, conditionally allowed, or not expressly prohibited under § 601.3 shall nonetheless be prohibited under this section where such practice affects or is reasonably expected to affect financial markets or economic transactions.

(d) **Indirect and Derivative Use.**
The prohibition under this section applies regardless of whether the manipulation—
(1) is applied directly to a financial instrument or transaction;
(2) is applied to a person, entity, or environment influencing such transaction; or
(3) produces effects that are probabilistic, delayed, or indirectly realized through market mechanisms.

(e) **Strict Liability Standard.**
A violation of this section shall not require proof of intent to manipulate financial markets where the natural and probable consequence of the magical act is to influence probabilistic outcomes in such markets.

(f) **Penalties.**
Violations of this section shall be subject to enforcement under § 102.2 and shall be treated as aggravated violations where the conduct results in systemic market distortion, widespread financial harm, or material disruption of economic stability.

(g) **Cross-References.**
For general limitations on luck or chance manipulation, see § 601.3. For prohibitions on financial fraud and market manipulation see § 1001.1 and § 1001.2.

(h) **Historical Annotations.**
Originally established under C.C.D. 8734, 78 MR 1902, Mon. 17, 1929, following widespread destabilization of commodity markets attributed to probabilistic manipulation practices. Amended under C.C.D. 9041, 80 MR 1127, Tue. 3, 1937, to expand the prohibition to indirect and derivative uses of luck-based magic. Revised under C.C.D. 9922, 83 MR 3014, Wed. 9, 2018, to incorporate strict liability standards and clarify applicability notwithstanding general permissions under § 601.3.

§ 1001.4 Financial Fraud through Illusion Magic

(a) **In General.**
No person shall use illusion magic, directly or indirectly, in connection with any financial transaction, instrument, or system in a manner that creates, enhances, or relies upon a false or misleading appearance of value, condition, ownership, or risk.

(b) **Scope and Definitions.**
(1) Illusion Magic. Illusion magic includes any spell, effect, or construct that alters perception, interpretation, or apparent reality without corresponding change to the underlying condition.
(2) Financial Context. This section applies to any transaction or activity involving—
(A) the exchange, valuation, or transfer of assets;
(B) financial records, disclosures, or representations;
(C) any system in which economic decisions are made based on perceived information.

(c) **Creation of False Appearance.**
(1) General Rule. A person engages in financial fraud through illusion where illusion magic is used to create a materially false or misleading appearance relevant to a financial decision.
(2) Prohibited Conduct.
(A) causing an asset, property, or item to appear more valuable, functional, or authentic than it is;
(B) concealing defects, risks, or material conditions affecting value;
(C) presenting non-existent or altered assets as genuine;
(D) altering the apparent identity, ownership, or provenance of an asset.
(3) Persistence.
The continued maintenance of a false appearance shall constitute an ongoing violation.

(d) **Manipulation of Financial Information.**
(1) General Rule. No person shall use illusion magic to alter, obscure, or misrepresent financial information.
(2) Prohibited Conduct.
(A) altering the appearance of records, statements, or disclosures;
(B) concealing material entries or conditions;
(C) creating the appearance of compliance where none exists.

(3) Interpretive Effects.
Illusions that influence how information is perceived, interpreted, or understood shall be treated as alterations of that information.

(e) **Inducement and Reliance.**
(1) General Rule. Use of illusion magic to induce a financial decision through misperception shall constitute a violation.
(2) Reliance Standard.
(A) Actual reliance shall not be required where the illusion is capable of influencing a reasonable person;
(B) partial or attempted inducement shall be sufficient.
(3) Third-Party Effects.
A violation may occur where the illusion affects any participant whose decisions influence the outcome of a transaction.

(f) **Layered and Composite Illusions.**
(1) General Rule. Multiple or coordinated illusions shall be evaluated as a single scheme where they produce a unified deceptive effect.
(2) Prohibited Structures.
(A) layering illusions to obscure detection or attribution;
(B) distributing components of an illusion across systems or actors;
(C) using intermittent or conditional illusions to avoid detection.
(3) Aggregation.
Fragmentation of conduct shall not prevent a finding of violation.

(g) **Distinction from Permissible Presentation.**
(1) General Rule. Illusion magic used solely for aesthetic, ceremonial, or non-material purposes shall not constitute a violation.
(2) Materiality.
Where an illusion affects any fact or condition relevant to value, risk, ownership, or decision-making, it shall be considered material.
(3) Burden.
The person asserting non-material use shall bear the burden of demonstrating that the illusion does not affect any financial determination.

(h) **Cross-References.**
For general financial fraud and manipulation, see § 1001.1. For prohibited spells and enchantments in financial markets, see § 1001.2. For transfiguration-based fraud, see § 1001.5. For reporting requirements, see

§ 701.9. For administrative authority, see § 102.1. For penalties, see § 102.2.

(i) **Historical Annotations.**
Originally established under C.C.D. 6102, 29 MR 118, Wed. 6, 1815 to address deceptive illusion practices in trade. Amended under C.C.D. 7320, 47 MR 771, Tue. 10, 1920 to incorporate financial record manipulation. Revised under C.C.D. 10110, 74 MR 442, Thu. 25, 2020 to address layered illusions and modern financial systems.

§ 1001.5 Financial Fraud through Transfiguration Magic

(a) **In General.**
No person shall use transfiguration magic, directly or indirectly, in connection with any financial transaction, instrument, or system in a manner that alters the substance, identity, composition, or essential characteristics of an asset so as to misrepresent its value, nature, or risk.

(b) **Scope and Definitions.**
(1) Transfiguration Magic. Transfiguration magic includes any spell, effect, or process that changes the physical, material, or intrinsic properties of an object, asset, or item.
(2) Financial Context. This section applies to any activity involving—
(A) the exchange, valuation, or transfer of assets;
(B) collateral, security, or backing of financial instruments;
(C) any system in which economic decisions depend on the underlying nature or composition of an asset.

(c) **Material Alteration of Assets.**
(1) General Rule. A person engages in financial fraud through transfiguration where an asset is materially altered in a manner that affects its value, function, or risk profile.
(2) Prohibited Conduct.
(A) altering an asset to appear as a different or higher-value asset;
(B) enhancing or suppressing material properties relevant to valuation or performance;
(C) disguising defects, deterioration, or instability through transfiguration;

(D) temporarily transforming an asset to induce a transaction or valuation.
(3) Reversion and Instability.
(A) Transfigurations that are temporary, unstable, or subject to reversion shall be treated as materially misleading;
(B) failure to disclose such conditions shall constitute a violation.

(d) **Misrepresentation of Composition and Backing.**
(1) General Rule. No person shall use transfiguration magic to misrepresent the composition, origin, or backing of an asset.
(2) Prohibited Conduct.
(A) altering the composition of currency, goods, or collateral to misstate value;
(B) creating the appearance of backing or reserves where none exist;
(C) substituting materials or components without disclosure.
(3) Embedded Alterations.
Transfiguration affecting internal or non-visible properties shall be treated as material where such properties influence value or performance.

(e) **Use in Collateral and Secured Transactions.**
(1) General Rule. Assets used as collateral shall reflect their true and stable condition.
(2) Prohibited Conduct.
(A) transfiguring collateral to meet valuation thresholds or eligibility requirements;
(B) maintaining altered states for the duration of a transaction without disclosure;
(C) using reversible or degradable transfigurations to secure financing.
(3) Continuing Obligation.
Any change in the condition of transfigured collateral shall be disclosed promptly.

(f) **Layered and Sequential Transfigurations.**
(1) General Rule. Multiple or sequential transfigurations shall be evaluated collectively where they produce a deceptive effect.
(2) Prohibited Structures.
(A) chaining or layering transformations to obscure the original nature of an asset;
(B) using intermediate states to avoid detection or classification;
(C) coordinating transformations across multiple actors or systems.

(3) Aggregation.
Fragmentation of conduct shall not prevent a finding of violation.

(g) **Distinction from Permissible Alteration.**
(1) General Rule. Transfiguration used for legitimate, disclosed, and non-deceptive purposes shall not constitute a violation.
(2) Disclosure Requirement.
Where transfiguration materially affects value, composition, or risk, full and accurate disclosure shall be required.
(3) Burden.
The person asserting permissible use shall bear the burden of demonstrating that the alteration does not mislead or affect financial determination.

(h) **Cross-References.**
For general financial fraud and manipulation, see § 1001.1. For prohibited spells and enchantments in financial markets, see § 1001.2. For illusion-based fraud, see § 1001.4. For reporting requirements, see § 701.9. For administrative authority, see § 102.1. For penalties, see § 102.2.

(i) **Historical Annotations.**
Originally established under C.C.D. 6125, 29 MR 771, Fri. 8, 1818 to address early material alteration of traded goods. Amended under C.C.D. 7355, 48 MR 118, Mon. 5, 1925 to incorporate secured transactions and collateral concerns. Revised under C.C.D. 10155, 74 MR 771, Tue. 30, 2021 to address complex and layered transfiguration schemes in modern financial systems.

§ 1001.6 Endowments and Gifts of Magical Assets

(a) **In General.**
Endowments and gifts of magical assets shall be recognized and regulated to ensure transparency, proper valuation, and compliance with the financial and ethical standards of this Code. No person shall transfer, receive, or administer such assets in a manner that obscures their nature, value, origin, or intended use.

(b) **Scope and Definitions.**

(1) Magical Asset. For purposes of this section, a magical asset includes any object, construct, energy source, or right possessing measurable or functional magical value.
(2) Gift. A gift is any transfer of a magical asset made without expectation of consideration or equivalent return.
(3) Endowment. An endowment is a transfer of one or more magical assets designated for ongoing use, preservation, or distribution, typically subject to conditions, restrictions, or purposes specified by the transferor.

(c) **Recognition of Transfers.**
(1) General Rule. A transfer shall be recognized as a gift or endowment based on its substance and intent rather than its form or designation.
(2) Substance Over Form.
(A) Transfers structured to appear as gifts or endowments but involving concealed consideration shall not be treated as such;
(B) indirect or deferred benefits may be considered in determining true intent.
(3) Partial Transfers.
Transfers involving both donative and non-donative elements shall be evaluated based on their respective components.

(d) **Valuation of Magical Assets.**
(1) General Rule. Magical assets transferred as gifts or endowments shall be valued based on their intrinsic properties, functional capabilities, and market conditions at the time of transfer.
(2) Valuation Factors.
(A) stability, duration, and persistence of magical effects;
(B) rarity, origin, and provenance;
(C) dependency on external systems, including ley lines under § 901.1;
(D) any limitations, conditions, or risks affecting usability.
(3) Dynamic Value.
Where value is subject to fluctuation, valuation shall reflect reasonable expectations at the time of transfer.

(e) **Conditions and Restrictions.**
(1) General Rule. Endowments may include conditions governing use, preservation, or distribution of assets.
(2) Enforceability.
(A) Conditions shall be enforceable where they are lawful and sufficiently defined;

(B) conditions that conflict with this Code shall be void to the extent of such conflict.
(3) Modification.
Conditions may be modified only where—
(A) original purposes cannot be fulfilled; or
(B) modification is necessary to maintain compliance with this Code.

(f) **Administration and Control.**
(1) General Rule. Persons administering endowments shall act in accordance with the stated purpose and applicable provisions of this Code.
(2) Duties.
(A) maintain accurate records of assets, use, and distributions;
(B) preserve the integrity and value of assets;
(C) ensure compliance with any applicable restrictions or conditions.
(3) Misuse.
Use of endowment assets for unauthorized purposes shall constitute a violation.

(g) **Disclosure and Transparency.**
(1) General Rule. Transfers and administration of magical assets shall be conducted with sufficient transparency to allow verification of compliance.
(2) Required Disclosures.
(A) identity of transferor and recipient;
(B) nature and value of transferred assets;
(C) any conditions or restrictions attached to the transfer.
(3) Concealment.
Failure to disclose material information shall constitute a violation.

(h) **Prohibited Conduct.**
No person shall—
(1) use gifts or endowments to conceal or facilitate conduct prohibited under this Code;
(2) misrepresent the nature, value, or purpose of a transfer;
(3) structure transfers to evade reporting or regulatory requirements;
(4) divert or misapply assets from their intended purpose.

(i) **Cross-References.**

For definition of magical assets, see § 1001.8. For transfer upon death, see § 1001.9. For reporting requirements, see § 701.9. For administrative authority, see § 102.1. For penalties, see § 102.2.

(j) **Historical Annotations.**
Originally established under C.C.D. 6150, 30 MR 118, Mon. 3, 1820 to regulate charitable and institutional transfers of magical assets. Amended under C.C.D. 7402, 49 MR 771, Tue. 6, 1930 to incorporate valuation and disclosure standards. Revised under C.C.D. 10210, 75 MR 442, Wed. 14, 2022 to address complex endowment structures and modern asset forms.

§ 1001.7 Please Send Help

(a) **General Overview.**
Okay, I'm going to level with you here. This is supposed to be a serious section about emergency protocols for financial auditors, but at the moment, I am writing this while trapped in an infinite pocket dimension created by a particularly vindictive sentient ledger. Yes, that's a thing. No, it's not as fun as it sounds.

(b) **Scope of Section.**
(1) This section theoretically applies to all magical auditors, practitioners, and regulatory agents who might find themselves in extraordinary situations while enforcing financial regulations.
(2) Examples of "extraordinary situations" include:
(A) Being lured into a cursed vault by a ledger that keeps promising it has "just one more entry" to reconcile;
(B) Discovering the ledger is actually alive and has no intention of letting you leave until you "balance its existential debt";
(C) Finding yourself in a looping time pocket where every completed audit resets itself to an earlier version (it's not just frustrating; it's maddening);
(D) Realizing you forgot your Emergency Amulet of Compliance because "it's just another ledger, how bad could it be?" Famous last words, by the way.

(c) **Procedures for Requesting Assistance.**
(1) In an ideal world, you would file Form 1001-HELP, detailing your current predicament. However, if you're stuck in a void, let me assure you: quills do not work here.
(2) What you should include in your request:

(A) Your exact location (as best you can tell – "floating somewhere in a kaleidoscopic non-space" works);
(B) The nature of your issue (e.g., "ledger has grown arms and is holding me hostage");
(C) The kind of help you need (e.g., "send a Senior Auditor with banishing expertise and snacks").
(3) If forms are impossible to file due to your predicament, shouting "HELP!" at the top of your lungs might work. No guarantees, though.

(d) **Emergency Protocols for Dire Situations.**
(1) Use your Emergency Amulet of Compliance if you have it. If you don't, well, hindsight is 20/20, isn't it?
(2) For sentient ledgers: try to reason with them. Start with, "I'm just here to audit you, not rewrite your entire existence." If that doesn't work, magical banishment is your last resort.
(3) For infinite dimensions: remember, panic helps no one. Take a deep breath and keep shouting for help. Maybe someone will hear.

(e) **Limitations.**
(1) This section is not intended for trivial issues. If you're dealing with a mildly enchanted ledger or your quill broke again, that's not an emergency. Figure it out.
(2) Frivolous claims like, "I'm tired of auditing dragon hoards; it's too shiny," will get you reassigned to the Ley Line Outlands faster than you can say "please reconsider."

(f) **Compliance Requirements.**
(1) If you somehow manage to get out of your predicament, you are still required to file Form 1001-HELP retroactively to document the incident. Good luck explaining that.
(2) Repeated failure to properly report emergencies may result in disciplinary action, including mandatory assignments to audit cursed pirate treasure maps.

(g) **Consequences for Inaction.**
(1) If no help arrives, well, I don't know what to tell you. Make yourself comfortable? Learn to live with the sentient ledger? Write a memoir?
(2) Any damage or delays caused by your entrapment must be logged (if possible) and reported under § 901.5.

(h) **Cross-References.**

For related guidance, see § 1001.4 for managing enchanted financial entities, and § 901.5 for emergency procedures. Practitioners may also consult § 702.1 to avoid penalties for misreporting incidents involving sentient constructs.

(i) **Historical Annotations.**
This regulation was introduced following the notorious "Sentient Ledger Incident of 1983," during which three senior auditors became trapped in a pocket dimension for 72 hours after a ledger demanded to know, "Does interest accrue on a temporal paradox?" The question remains unanswered, and subsequent incidents involving sentient financial constructs led to this section's adoption as part of the Magical Code of Regulations.

§ 1001.8 Legal Definition of Magical Assets

(a) **In General.**
For purposes of this Code, the term "magical asset" shall mean any item, interest, right, or form of value, whether tangible or intangible, that derives in whole or in part from magical properties, functions, or effects, and that is capable of being owned, controlled, transferred, valued, or relied upon in an economic or financial context.

(b) **Inclusions.**
Magical assets include, but are not limited to—
(1) physical objects imbued with magical properties or effects;
(2) stored, contained, or otherwise harnessed magical energy;
(3) rights to cast, access, or utilize specific spells, enchantments, or magical systems;
(4) contractual or legally enforceable interests involving magical performance or outcomes;
(5) derivative or contingent interests based on the value, performance, or existence of other magical assets;
(6) partial, fractional, or shared interests in any asset described in this subsection.

(c) **Intangible and Non-Physical Assets.**
(1) General Rule. Magical assets may exist independently of any physical form.
(2) Examples.

(A) spellcasting rights, licenses, or privileges;
(B) access rights to ley lines or magical infrastructure under § 901.1;
(C) binding agreements involving magical services or outcomes.
(3) Recognition.
Such assets shall be treated as having economic value where they are capable of transfer, enforcement, or reliance.

(d) **Conditional, Temporary, and Unstable Assets.**
(1) General Rule. An asset shall not be excluded from classification as a magical asset solely because it is conditional, temporary, or subject to instability.
(2) Disclosure of Limitations.
Any limitation on duration, stability, or reliability shall be treated as a material characteristic of the asset.
(3) Reversion and Dissipation.
Assets subject to reversion, degradation, or dissipation shall remain within the scope of this section for the duration of their existence or effect.

(e) **Control and Beneficial Interest.**
(1) General Rule. A person shall be considered to possess a magical asset where such person—
(A) has legal ownership or title;
(B) exercises control or direction over the asset; or
(C) holds a beneficial or economic interest in the asset.
(2) Indirect Interests.
Control or benefit obtained through intermediaries, constructs, or layered arrangements shall be treated as direct ownership or interest for purposes of this Code.

(f) **Valuation Relevance.**
(1) General Rule. A magical asset shall be considered to have value where it is capable of being—
(A) exchanged, transferred, or assigned;
(B) used to obtain goods, services, or economic advantage; or
(C) relied upon in financial decision-making.
(2) Fluctuating Value.
Variability in value shall not affect classification as a magical asset.

(g) **Substance Over Form.**

(1) General Rule. Classification of a magical asset shall be determined based on its substance, function, and economic effect rather than its form, designation, or characterization.
(2) Anti-Circumvention.
No person shall structure, label, or fragment an item or interest to avoid classification under this section.

(h) **Exclusions.**
(1) General Rule. The following shall not be considered magical assets unless they otherwise meet the criteria of this section—
(A) purely aesthetic or ceremonial magical effects with no economic relevance;
(B) incidental or de minimis magical properties that do not affect value or function.
(2) Reclassification.
An item otherwise excluded under this subsection shall be treated as a magical asset where its use or context gives rise to economic significance.

(i) **Interpretive Authority.**
The Department of Magical Affairs may issue guidance, determinations, and clarifications regarding the classification of magical assets under § 102.1.

(j) **Cross-References.**
For endowments and gifts of magical assets, see § 1001.6. For transfer of magical assets upon death, see § 1001.9. For financial fraud and manipulation, see § 1001.1. For administrative authority, see § 102.1. For penalties, see § 102.2.

(k) **Historical Annotations.**
Originally established under C.C.D. 6201, 30 MR 771, Thu. 9, 1825 to define magical property for purposes of trade and taxation. Amended under C.C.D. 7505, 50 MR 118, Mon. 4, 1935 to incorporate intangible and contractual interests. Revised under C.C.D. 10255, 75 MR 771, Fri. 18, 2023 to address derivative, conditional, and non-physical asset classifications.

§ 1001.9 Transfer of Magical Assets Upon Death

(a) **In General.**

The transfer of magical assets upon the death of a person shall be recognized and regulated to ensure continuity of ownership, preservation of value, and prevention of artificial basis adjustments or avoidance of financial obligations through death-based transfers.

(b) **Scope and Definitions.**
(1) Decedent. A decedent is any person whose death results in the transfer, disposition, or reclassification of magical assets.
(2) Covered Assets. This section applies to all magical assets, as defined in § 1001.8, in which the decedent held any ownership, control, or beneficial interest at the time of death.
(3) Transfer. Transfer includes any passage of ownership, control, access, or beneficial interest, whether by operation of law, instrument, trust, construct, or other mechanism.

(c) **Carryover Basis; Prohibition on Adjustment.**
(1) General Rule. The basis of any magical asset transferred upon death shall be the same as the basis of such asset in the hands of the decedent immediately prior to death.
(2) No Step-Up or Step-Down.
(A) No adjustment to basis shall be permitted by reason of death, including any increase, decrease, or revaluation;
(B) fair market value at death shall not be used to determine basis for any purpose under this Code.
(3) Tainted Basis.
(A) Any prior manipulation, concealment, or misrepresentation of basis shall carry over to the successor;
(B) subsequent holders shall remain subject to correction and enforcement.

(d) **Recognition of Unrealized Gain or Loss.**
(1) General Rule. Death shall not eliminate, extinguish, or reset any unrealized gain or loss inherent in a magical asset.
(2) Preservation of Economic Position.
All appreciation or depreciation shall be preserved for purposes of future recognition, taxation, or enforcement.
(3) Constructive Realization.
The Department of Magical Affairs may treat certain transfers as realization events where necessary to prevent avoidance or abuse.

(e) **Anti-Avoidance and Anti-Fragmentation.**
(1) General Rule. No person shall structure, divide, recharacterize, or otherwise manipulate ownership of magical assets in anticipation of death for the purpose of avoiding application of this section.
(2) Prohibited Conduct.
(A) fragmentation of ownership interests among multiple persons or entities;
(B) use of trusts, constructs, or layered arrangements to obscure control or beneficial ownership;
(C) temporary transfers, reversions, or circular transactions designed to reset or obscure basis;
(D) use of intermediaries or derivative interests to shift or dilute economic reality.
(3) Substance Over Form.
All such arrangements shall be evaluated based on actual control, benefit, and economic effect.

(f) **Controlled Entities and Constructed Ownership.**
(1) General Rule. Assets held through entities, constructs, or intermediaries shall be treated as owned by the decedent to the extent of their direct or indirect interest.
(2) Look-Through Treatment.
(A) ownership shall be determined by tracing control and beneficial interest through all layers;
(B) nominal or formal ownership shall not control where inconsistent with actual control.
(3) Aggregation.
All related interests shall be aggregated for purposes of applying this section.

(g) **Additional Limitations for High-Value Estates.**
(1) General Rule. Where the aggregate value of a decedent's magical assets equals or exceeds 25,000,000 Magical Credit Units (MCUs), such estate shall be treated as a high-value estate for purposes of this subsection.
(2) Enhanced Aggregation.
(A) All assets, interests, and arrangements, whether domestic or extraterritorial, direct or indirect, shall be aggregated without regard to formal ownership structure;
(B) valuation shall include all derivative, contingent, and non-physical interests as defined in § 1001.8.

(3) Lookback Rule.
(A) Any transfer, restructuring, or disposition of a magical asset occurring within 10 years prior to death shall be presumed to have been undertaken for purposes of avoidance;
(B) such assets shall be included in the decedent's estate unless the presumption is rebutted by clear and convincing evidence.
(4) Restrictions on Deferral and Retained Interests.
(A) Any arrangement permitting continued control, access, or benefit after purported transfer shall be disregarded;
(B) deferred or contingent transfers shall be treated as retained by the decedent to the extent of such control or benefit.
(5) Concentration and Control Limits.
(A) Where necessary to prevent excessive concentration of magical or economic power, continued control of certain classes of assets may be restricted or conditioned;
(B) such limitations may apply to assets critical to infrastructure, markets, or systemic stability.
(6) Anti-Dilution Rule.
(A) Division of assets among multiple recipients shall not reduce aggregate value for purposes of this subsection;
(B) coordinated transfers designed to fragment ownership shall be disregarded.
(7) Recharacterization Authority.
Any arrangement, structure, or series of transactions that has the purpose or effect of avoiding this subsection shall be recharacterized in accordance with its economic substance.

(h) **Restrictions on Valuation Manipulation.**
(1) General Rule. No person shall use magical or non-magical means to artificially reduce, inflate, or distort the value of an asset in connection with death.
(2) Prohibited Conduct.
(A) temporary suppression or enhancement of value;
(B) concealment of material characteristics affecting value;
(C) use of illusion or transfiguration to misstate condition or worth.
(3) Corrective Authority.
Valuations determined to be artificial or misleading shall be disregarded and adjusted to reflect actual economic substance.

(i) **Continuity of Control and Custody.**

(1) General Rule. Control of magical assets shall pass in a manner that preserves stability and prevents misuse.
(2) Custodial Responsibility.
(A) successors shall maintain the integrity and condition of assets;
(B) assets requiring active management shall not be left unmanaged or unstable.
(3) Interim Authority.
Where necessary, temporary control may be exercised under § 102.1 to prevent harm or misuse.

(j) **Disclosure and Reporting.**
(1) General Rule. Transfers under this section shall be subject to reporting sufficient to ensure transparency and enforcement.
(2) Required Information.
(A) identity of decedent and successor;
(B) description, basis, and valuation of each asset;
(C) any conditions, limitations, or encumbrances affecting the asset.
(3) Failure to Report.
Failure to disclose material information shall constitute a violation.

(k) **Cross-References.**
For definition of magical assets, see § 1001.8. For endowments and gifts, see § 1001.6. For reporting requirements, see § 701.9. For administrative authority, see § 102.1. For penalties, see § 102.2.

(l) **Historical Annotations.**
Originally established under C.C.D. 6250, 31 MR 118, Mon. 2, 1830 to regulate succession of magical property. Amended under C.C.D. 7802, 53 MR 771, Tue. 8, 1955 to eliminate basis adjustments at death and prevent avoidance through succession planning. Revised under C.C.D. 10301, 76 MR 442, Thu. 9, 2024 to address high-value estates, anti-avoidance rules, and modern asset structures.

§ 1002.1 Magical Insurance and Liability

(a) **In General.**
Magical insurance arrangements shall be recognized and regulated to allocate risk, ensure compensation for loss or damage, and preserve accountability for liability arising from magical assets, activities, or systems. No person shall use insurance to obscure responsibility, shift

liability improperly, or facilitate conduct otherwise prohibited under this Code.

(b) **Scope and Definitions.**
(1) Magical Insurance. Magical insurance includes any agreement, policy, contract, or arrangement under which one party assumes risk in exchange for consideration related to potential loss, damage, or liability involving magical assets or activity.
(2) Covered Risks. Covered risks include, but are not limited to—
(A) loss, damage, degradation, or destruction of magical assets;
(B) instability, failure, or unintended effects of magical activity;
(C) liability arising from harm to persons, property, magical systems, or ecosystems;
(D) systemic disruption, including events described under § 901.5.
(3) Insured Interest. An insured interest exists where a person has a direct or indirect financial, operational, or beneficial stake in a magical asset or activity.

(c) **Recognition and Scope of Coverage.**
(1) General Rule. Coverage shall be determined based on the substance of the arrangement and the risks actually assumed.
(2) Defined Risks.
(A) coverage shall apply only to risks expressly or implicitly included within the agreement;
(B) exclusions, limitations, and conditions shall be enforceable where clearly defined and not inconsistent with this Code.
(3) Substance Over Form.
Characterization of coverage shall not control where inconsistent with the actual allocation of risk.

(d) **Valuation and Loss Determination.**
(1) General Rule. Loss shall be determined based on the condition and value of the asset or interest immediately prior to the loss event.
(2) Valuation Factors.
(A) intrinsic magical properties and functional capacity;
(B) stability, duration, and persistence of effects;
(C) dependency on external systems, including ley lines under § 901.1;
(D) any limitations, conditions, or risks affecting use or value.
(3) Partial Loss and Degradation.

(A) partial impairment, degradation, or instability shall constitute loss to the extent of reduced value or function;
(B) progressive or delayed effects shall be considered in determining total loss.

(e) **Disclosure and Underwriting.**
(1) General Rule. Persons seeking coverage shall disclose all material information relevant to the risk.
(2) Material Information.
(A) nature, composition, and condition of insured assets or systems;
(B) known risks, instabilities, or limitations;
(C) prior events, usage patterns, or conditions affecting risk exposure;
(D) any use of illusion, transfiguration, or other magic affecting valuation or representation.
(3) Misrepresentation and Omission.
(A) failure to disclose or misrepresentation of material information shall affect coverage and may constitute a violation;
(B) intent to deceive shall not be required where information is material.

(f) **Claims and Adjustment.**
(1) General Rule. Claims shall be evaluated based on the terms of coverage and the actual nature of the loss.
(2) Adjustment Process.
(A) determination of cause, scope, and timing of loss;
(B) evaluation of compliance with policy conditions and applicable provisions of this Code;
(C) calculation of compensation based on actual economic loss.
(3) Timeliness.
(A) claims shall be acknowledged and processed within a reasonable period;
(B) unreasonable delay, obstruction, or indefinite review shall constitute a violation.

(g) **Mandatory Payout Standards and Loss Ratios.**
(1) General Rule. Magical insurers shall maintain minimum payout standards to ensure that collected premiums are reasonably returned to insured parties in the form of claims payments.
(2) Base Minimum Loss Ratio.
Each insurer shall maintain an annual payout ratio of not less than 80 percent of total premiums collected for a given class of coverage.

(3) Enhanced Requirements for Critical Coverage.
For high-risk, mandatory, or systemically important coverage categories, the minimum payout ratio shall be not less than 85 percent.
(4) Market-Dominance Adjustment.
(A) Any insurer controlling 10 percent or more of a given market shall be subject to a minimum payout ratio of 88 percent;
(B) any insurer controlling 25 percent or more shall be subject to a minimum payout ratio of 90 percent;
(C) any insurer controlling 40 percent or more shall be subject to a minimum payout ratio of 92 percent.
(5) Calculation.
(A) payout ratios shall be calculated based on total claims paid relative to total premiums collected;
(B) administrative costs, reserves, intra-company transfers, or affiliated arrangements shall not be used to reduce payout ratios artificially.
(6) Failure to Meet Requirements.
(A) insurers failing to meet required ratios shall issue mandatory rebates to policyholders;
(B) repeated failure shall result in rate controls, operational restrictions, or suspension of authority to issue policies.
(7) Anti-Avoidance.
No insurer shall segment, reclassify, or restructure policies or markets to evade application of this subsection.

(h) **Unfair Claims Practices.**
(1) General Rule. No insurer shall engage in practices designed to avoid, delay, or reduce valid claim payments.
(2) Prohibited Conduct.
(A) denial of claims without reasonable basis;
(B) reliance on immaterial technicalities or ambiguities to avoid payment;
(C) repeated or excessive requests for unnecessary documentation;
(D) misrepresentation of policy terms, exclusions, or coverage scope;
(E) systemic underpayment or coercive settlement practices.
(3) Pattern-Based Violations.
A pattern or practice of such conduct shall constitute a violation regardless of individual claim outcomes.

(i) **Public Insurer of Last Resort.**

(1) Establishment. The Department of Magical Affairs shall maintain or designate a public insurer of last resort to provide coverage where private insurers fail to offer adequate, lawful, or accessible insurance.
(2) Triggering Conditions.
The public insurer shall provide coverage where—
(A) coverage is unavailable or unreasonably restricted;
(B) pricing is excessive relative to risk;
(C) private insurers demonstrate systemic noncompliance with this section.
(3) Effect on Market Participants.
(A) participation in the public system may be required of private insurers through assessments or contributions;
(B) rates and terms established by the public insurer may serve as benchmarks for market conduct.
(4) Non-Displacement.
The existence of a public insurer shall not limit enforcement against private insurers.

(j) **Liability and Non-Substitution.**
(1) General Rule. Insurance coverage shall not eliminate, limit, or substitute for underlying liability except as expressly provided by law.
(2) Third-Party Liability.
(A) coverage may extend to liability arising from harm to third parties;
(B) responsible persons shall remain subject to all applicable provisions of this Code.
(3) Coordination of Responsibility.
Where multiple parties or policies apply, responsibility shall be allocated based on contribution, control, and coverage.

(k) **Prohibited Use of Insurance Structures.**
No person shall—
(1) obtain or maintain coverage through fraud, concealment, or misrepresentation;
(2) structure insurance arrangements to evade liability, reporting requirements, or other obligations under this Code;
(3) use insurance to facilitate or conceal conduct prohibited under §§ 1001.1 through 1001.5;
(4) create circular or self-insured arrangements lacking substantive risk transfer.

(l) **Aggregation and Layered Coverage.**
(1) General Rule. Multiple policies or arrangements shall be evaluated collectively where they relate to the same risk or set of risks.
(2) Layered Structures.
(A) layered or tiered coverage shall be treated based on actual allocation of risk;
(B) artificial segmentation of coverage shall not affect determination of liability or compliance.

(m) **Cross-References.**
For definition of magical assets, see § 1001.8. For financial fraud and manipulation, see § 1001.1. For prohibited spells and enchantments in financial markets, see § 1001.2. For administrative authority, see § 102.1. For penalties, see § 102.2.

(n) **Historical Annotations.**
Originally established under C.C.D. 6302, 31 MR 771, Wed. 6, 1835 to regulate early risk-sharing arrangements involving magical assets. Amended under C.C.D. 8001, 55 MR 118, Mon. 2, 1965 to address abusive claim denial practices. Revised under C.C.D. 10355, 76 MR 771, Fri. 20, 2025 to incorporate mandatory payout standards, market-dominance adjustments, and establishment of a public insurer of last resort.

Part XI: Contract Law in Magical Practices

§ 1101.1 General Principles of Magical Contract Law

(a) **In General.**
Magical contracts shall be recognized and enforced in accordance with their terms, provided such contracts reflect a valid agreement between parties, are supported by consideration, and do not violate any provision of this Code. No contract shall be enforceable where its formation, terms, or performance relies upon prohibited magical conduct.

(b) **Formation of Magical Contracts.**
(1) General Rule. A magical contract is formed where there is—
(A) mutual assent between parties;
(B) intent to create binding obligations; and
(C) sufficient manifestation of agreement through magical or non-magical means.
(2) Manifestation of Assent.
Assent may be demonstrated through—
(A) written or spoken agreement;
(B) ritual, incantation, or symbolic act;
(C) binding enchantment or magical construct evidencing agreement.
(3) Capacity.
A contract shall not be enforceable where a party lacks the capacity to understand or consent to the agreement, including due to magical impairment, coercion, or manipulation.

(c) **Interpretation of Terms.**
(1) General Rule. Contracts shall be interpreted based on their plain meaning, context, and the intent of the parties at the time of formation.
(2) Magical Terms.
(A) terms involving magical effects shall be interpreted in light of their actual function and limitations;
(B) ambiguity in magical terminology shall be resolved based on reasonable understanding within the relevant practice or discipline.

(3) Substance Over Form.
The effect and operation of a contract shall control over its formal designation or structure.

(d) **Enforceability and Validity.**
(1) General Rule. A contract shall be enforceable only to the extent that its terms are lawful and capable of performance.
(2) Void Contracts.
A contract shall be void where—
(A) its formation or performance requires conduct prohibited under this Code;
(B) it involves coercion, deception, or manipulation through magic;
(C) it attempts to transfer or assign rights that are inherently non-transferable.
(3) Partial Invalidity.
Where a portion of a contract is invalid, the remaining provisions may be enforced to the extent they are separable and lawful.

(e) **Magical Enforcement Mechanisms.**
(1) General Rule. Contracts may include magical enforcement mechanisms, provided such mechanisms are lawful and proportionate.
(2) Permissible Mechanisms.
(A) binding enchantments that compel performance;
(B) conditional effects triggered by breach;
(C) restraints or limitations tied to contractual obligations.
(3) Limitations.
No enforcement mechanism shall—
(A) result in unlawful harm or coercion;
(B) deprive a party of rights protected under this Code;
(C) operate beyond the scope necessary to enforce the agreement.

(f) **Disclosure and Informed Consent.**
(1) General Rule. Parties shall be informed of all material terms, effects, and risks associated with a magical contract.
(2) Material Information.
Includes—
(A) nature and duration of obligations;
(B) any magical effects imposed on a party;
(C) risks, limitations, or conditions affecting performance.
(3) Failure to Disclose.

Failure to disclose material information shall render a contract voidable.

(g) **Modification and Termination.**
(1) General Rule. A contract may be modified or terminated by mutual agreement or as otherwise provided by its terms.
(2) Magical Modifications.
(A) modifications involving magic shall require clear manifestation of assent;
(B) unilateral modification through magical means shall be ineffective unless expressly authorized.
(3) Termination Conditions.
Contracts shall terminate upon—
(A) fulfillment of obligations;
(B) occurrence of specified conditions;
(C) lawful rescission or invalidation.

(h) **Breach and Remedies.**
(1) General Rule. Failure to perform contractual obligations shall constitute breach.
(2) Remedies.
Remedies may include—
(A) specific performance;
(B) restoration or compensation;
(C) lawful enforcement of contractual mechanisms.
(3) Limitations.
Remedies shall be limited to those consistent with this Code and the nature of the agreement.

(i) **Cross-References.**
For contracts involving familiars, see § 1101.3. For blood magic contracts, see § 1101.2. For demonic contracts, see § 1101.4. For consideration requirements, see § 1101.5. For ethical limitations, see § 701.1. For administrative authority, see § 102.1. For penalties, see § 102.2.

(j) **Historical Annotations.**
Originally established under C.C.D. 7001, 40 MR 118, Tue. 3, 1850 to formalize agreements involving magical obligations. Amended under C.C.D. 8205, 58 MR 771, Mon. 6, 1970 to incorporate magical enforcement mechanisms and consent requirements. Revised under

C.C.D. 10410, 77 MR 442, Thu. 12, 2026 to clarify interpretation, disclosure, and enforceability standards in modern magical practice.

§ 1101.2 Blood Magic Contracts

(a) **In General.**
Blood magic contracts are subject to heightened scrutiny and regulation due to their binding nature, persistence, and potential to affect bodily integrity, identity, and autonomy. No person shall enter into, enforce, or benefit from a blood magic contract except in strict compliance with this section.

(b) **Definition.**
(1) Blood Magic Contract. A blood magic contract is any agreement in which—
(A) blood is used as a medium of assent, binding, or enforcement; or
(B) the contract imposes obligations, conditions, or consequences directly tied to the biological essence of a party.
(2) Scope.
This section applies regardless of whether blood is used symbolically, partially, or as a primary binding mechanism.

(c) **Formation Requirements.**
(1) General Rule. A blood magic contract shall not be valid unless—
(A) assent is explicit, informed, and voluntary;
(B) all material terms are disclosed prior to execution; and
(C) the binding mechanism is clearly understood by all parties.
(2) Prohibited Formation Conditions.
A contract shall be void where—
(A) consent is obtained through coercion, deception, or magical influence;
(B) a party lacks capacity due to impairment, duress, or manipulation;
(C) assent is inferred solely from the use or presence of blood without clear agreement.

(d) **Enhanced Disclosure Requirements.**
(1) General Rule. All material aspects of a blood magic contract shall be disclosed in a clear and comprehensible manner prior to execution.
(2) Required Disclosures.
(A) duration and persistence of the binding effect;

(B) conditions under which the contract may be enforced, modified, or terminated;
(C) physical, magical, or existential consequences of breach;
(D) risks associated with the use of blood as a binding medium.
(3) Failure to Disclose.
Failure to provide required disclosures shall render the contract voidable.

(e) **Limitations on Enforcement.**
(1) General Rule. Enforcement mechanisms in blood magic contracts shall be lawful, proportionate, and limited to the scope of the agreement.
(2) Prohibited Enforcement Mechanisms.
No contract shall include—
(A) irreversible harm or permanent bodily alteration as a consequence of breach;
(B) loss of autonomy or control beyond the scope of the obligation;
(C) effects that extend to persons not party to the agreement.
(3) Scope of Effect.
Enforcement shall not exceed what is necessary to compel or remedy performance.

(f) **Duration and Persistence.**
(1) General Rule. Blood magic contracts shall specify their duration and conditions of termination.
(2) Indefinite Contracts.
Contracts lacking a defined duration shall be subject to review and potential limitation.
(3) Post-Termination Effects.
Any lingering effects after termination shall be limited to those expressly disclosed and reasonably necessary.

(g) **Transfer and Assignment.**
(1) General Rule. Blood magic contracts shall not be transferable or assignable unless expressly permitted and disclosed at formation.
(2) Restrictions.
(A) obligations tied to the biological essence of a party shall not be assigned;
(B) attempted transfer without authorization shall be void.
(3) Successors.
No obligation shall bind successors or unrelated parties absent explicit and lawful agreement.

(h) **Breach and Remedies.**
(1) General Rule. Breach of a blood magic contract shall be governed by the terms of the agreement and applicable provisions of this Code.
(2) Limitations on Remedies.
(A) remedies shall be proportionate and reversible where possible;
(B) excessive or punitive effects shall be deemed unenforceable.
(3) Judicial Review.
Enforcement and remedies may be subject to review under § 102.1 where necessary to ensure compliance with this Code.

(i) **Cross-References.**
For general contract principles, see § 1101.1. For contracts involving familiars, see § 1101.3. For demonic contracts, see § 1101.4. For consideration requirements, see § 1101.5. For ethical limitations, see § 701.1. For administrative authority, see § 102.1. For penalties, see § 102.2.

(j) **Historical Annotations.**
Originally established under C.C.D. 7050, 41 MR 118, Mon. 5, 1860 following widespread abuses involving involuntary blood bindings. Amended under C.C.D. 8301, 59 MR 771, Tue. 9, 1980 to introduce enhanced disclosure and consent requirements. Revised under C.C.D. 10455, 77 MR 771, Fri. 18, 2026 to clarify enforcement limitations and protections against coercive practices.

§ 1101.3 Contracts Involving Familiars

(a) **In General.**
Contracts involving familiars shall be subject to heightened ethical and legal standards due to the unique relationship between familiars and their associated persons. No contract shall impose obligations upon a familiar except as permitted under this section and consistent with § 701.7.

(b) **Definition and Scope.**
(1) Familiar. For purposes of this section, a familiar is any creature recognized as such under § 101.6 and subject to the protections of § 701.7.
(2) Covered Contracts. This section applies to any agreement that—
(A) binds, restricts, or utilizes a familiar in performance of an obligation;
(B) assigns duties, services, or functions to a familiar;
(C) affects the rights, autonomy, or well-being of a familiar.

(c) **Consent and Capacity.**
(1) General Rule. A contract involving a familiar shall not be valid unless the familiar's participation is voluntary and informed to the extent reasonably possible given its nature and capabilities.
(2) Proxy Consent.
(A) consent provided solely by an associated person shall not be sufficient where the contract materially affects the familiar;
(B) proxy consent may be considered only where the familiar lacks the capacity to understand the agreement and the contract is in the familiar's best interest.
(3) Prohibited Consent Conditions.
A contract shall be void where consent is obtained through coercion, magical compulsion, or deprivation of care.

(d) **Limitations on Obligations.**
(1) General Rule. Obligations imposed upon a familiar shall be reasonable, limited in scope, and consistent with the familiar's nature and well-being.
(2) Prohibited Obligations.
No contract shall—
(A) require a familiar to perform inherently dangerous or high-risk activities beyond its capacity;
(B) impose continuous or indefinite service without rest or care;
(C) subject the familiar to harm, degradation, or undue stress;
(D) treat the familiar solely as property or an instrument of performance.
(3) Scope of Duties.
Duties shall be limited to those necessary to fulfill the contractual purpose.

(e) **Compensation and Benefit.**
(1) General Rule. Where a familiar provides services or performs obligations, the contract shall provide for appropriate care, benefit, or compensation.
(2) Forms of Compensation.
(A) enhanced care, nourishment, or protection;
(B) magical or environmental benefits suited to the familiar's needs;
(C) other consideration appropriate to the familiar's nature.
(3) Failure to Provide Benefit.
Absence of meaningful benefit to the familiar shall render the contract subject to challenge.

(f) **Enforcement and Remedies.**
(1) General Rule. Enforcement of contracts involving familiars shall be limited to lawful and ethical means.
(2) Prohibited Enforcement.
No enforcement mechanism shall—
(A) compel performance through harm, coercion, or deprivation;
(B) impose consequences that exceed the scope of the obligation;
(C) affect the familiar beyond what is necessary to enforce the agreement.
(3) Remedies.
Remedies shall prioritize the welfare of the familiar and may include modification or termination of the contract.

(g) **Transfer and Assignment.**
(1) General Rule. A contract involving a familiar shall not be transferred or assigned without explicit consent and lawful authority.
(2) Restrictions.
(A) obligations tied to a specific relationship shall not be reassigned;
(B) any attempted transfer inconsistent with this section shall be void.
(3) Change in Control.
Any change in control affecting the familiar shall be subject to review under § 102.1.

(h) **Cross-References.**
For general contract principles, see § 1101.1. For blood magic contracts, see § 1101.2. For demonic contracts, see § 1101.4. For consideration requirements, see § 1101.5. For protections governing familiars, see § 701.7. For administrative authority, see § 102.1. For penalties, see § 102.2.

(i) **Historical Annotations.**
Originally established under C.C.D. 7102, 42 MR 118, Tue. 4, 1870 to regulate agreements involving bonded creatures. Amended under C.C.D. 8355, 60 MR 771, Mon. 8, 1985 to incorporate welfare protections and consent requirements. Revised under C.C.D. 10490, 78 MR 442, Wed. 22, 2026 to clarify limitations on obligations, compensation, and enforcement.

§ 1101.4 Demonic Contracts

(a) **In General.**

Demonic contracts shall be recognized and enforced as binding agreements subject to this Code. Such contracts are inherently complex and may employ non-standard drafting conventions. Accordingly, persons entering into demonic contracts shall be deemed to do so with full awareness of the risks attendant to such agreements.

(b) **Definition.**
(1) Demonic Contract. A demonic contract is any agreement—
(A) entered into with a demonic entity or intermediary acting on behalf of such entity; or
(B) incorporating infernal drafting conventions, symbolic structures, or non-standard mechanisms of expression or enforcement.
(2) Application.
This section applies regardless of the form, medium, or method of execution.

(c) **Assumption of Risk.**
(1) General Rule. A person entering into a demonic contract shall be deemed to have accepted the risks associated with non-linear drafting, embedded terms, symbolic expression, and other structural complexities characteristic of such agreements.
(2) Effect.
(A) failure to identify, interpret, or anticipate any provision shall not affect enforceability where such provision forms part of the agreement;
(B) the signee shall be responsible for undertaking such review or consultation as is appropriate to the nature of the agreement.

(d) **Formation and Assent.**
(1) General Rule. A demonic contract shall be valid where assent is manifested through execution, ritual, inscription, or other binding act sufficient to indicate agreement.
(2) Scope of Assent.
Assent shall extend to the agreement in its entirety as executed, including all incorporated and embedded provisions, whether or not separately identified at the time of execution.
(3) Integration.
All components of the instrument at the time of execution shall be deemed part of the agreement.

(e) **Expression and Inclusion of Terms.**

(1) General Rule. Terms shall be considered part of the agreement where they are contained within the instrument and capable of identification through examination appropriate to its form.
(2) Permissible Modes of Expression.
Terms may be expressed through textual, symbolic, ornamental, structural, or layered means, including arrangements not limited to linear presentation.
(3) Evaluation of Inclusion.
In determining whether a term forms part of the agreement, consideration shall be given to the instrument as a whole, including its structure, markings, and internal relationships.

(f) **Standard of Identifiability.**
(1) General Rule. A provision shall be deemed sufficiently disclosed where it is capable of identification through reasonable examination appropriate to the nature of the agreement.
(2) Reasonable Examination.
Such examination may include analysis, interpretation, or interaction consistent with the agreement's structure and method of presentation.
(3) Limitation.
A provision shall be invalid only where it is wholly absent from the instrument or incapable of identification by any reasonable means.

(g) **Interpretation.**
(1) General Rule. A demonic contract shall be interpreted as an integrated whole, giving effect to all provisions contained within the agreement.
(2) Ambiguity.
Ambiguity shall be resolved by reference to the structure and operation of the agreement in its entirety.
(3) Operative Effect.
Interpretation shall prioritize the functional operation of the agreement as executed.

(h) **Limits of Invalidity.**
(1) General Rule. A demonic contract shall not be deemed unenforceable solely because its terms are complex, unfavorable, disproportionate, or result in significant or irreversible consequences.
(2) Permissible Effects.

Enforceable terms may include obligations affecting a party's property, rights, magical capacity, or essence, including the transfer or forfeiture thereof.
(3) Exclusive Grounds.
A provision shall be void only where it—
(A) lacks any manifestation of assent; or
(B) requires conduct expressly prohibited under this Code and incapable of lawful enforcement.

(i) **Enforcement and Proceedings.**
(1) General Rule. Disputes arising under demonic contracts shall be subject to review in accordance with § 102.1.
(2) Effect of Review.
The pendency of any review or proceeding shall not, by itself, stay or invalidate the operation of the agreement as executed, except where expressly ordered under applicable authority.
(3) Administrative Efficiency.
You entered into the agreement. You signed it, spoke it, bled on it, or otherwise bound yourself to it. The Department will not convene hearings, assemble panels, or otherwise expend resources to revisit the consequences of your decision simply because, in hindsight, you now object to the outcome. Your failure to read, investigate, decode, rotate, illuminate, or otherwise examine the agreement prior to execution does not constitute a defect in the agreement. It constitutes your problem.
(4) Interim Effects.
Actions taken pursuant to the agreement prior to final resolution shall be evaluated based on the terms of the agreement as applied.

(j) **Cross-References.**
For general contract principles, see § 1101.1. For blood magic contracts, see § 1101.2. For contracts involving familiars, see § 1101.3. For consideration requirements, see § 1101.5. For ethical limitations, see § 701.2. For administrative authority, see § 102.1. For penalties, see § 102.2.

(k) **Historical Annotations.**
Originally established under C.C.D. 7155, 42 MR 771, Thu. 7, 1880 following disputes involving infernal agreements executed within regulated jurisdictions. Amended under C.C.D. 8450, 61 MR 118, Tue. 10, 1990 to address non-standard contractual structures and embedded

provisions. Revised under C.C.D. 10520, 78 MR 771, Fri. 29, 2026 to clarify standards for identifiability, assumption of risk, and enforceability.

§ 1101.5 Consideration in Magical Contracts

(a) **In General.**
A magical contract shall not be valid unless supported by consideration. Consideration consists of a bargained-for exchange of value, obligation, or restraint that is definite, lawful, and capable of enforcement under this Code.

(b) **Sufficiency of Consideration.**
(1) Consideration shall be sufficient only where it represents a real and identifiable exchange of value between the parties.
(2) A purported exchange shall not be sufficient where the value provided is illusory, indeterminate, or entirely discretionary.
(3) Consideration must be reasonably ascertainable at the time of formation or capable of determination by reference to objective standards.

(c) **Forms of Consideration.**
Consideration may include, but is not limited to—
(1) transfer of property, currency, or magical assets;
(2) performance of services or obligations;
(3) forbearance of a right or action;
(4) transfer or restriction of magical capacity, ability, or access;
(5) transfer of intangible interests, including memory, time, or identity, provided such interests are specifically described and capable of valuation;
(6) conditional or future interests, where the conditions are clearly defined and objectively determinable.

(d) **Bargained-for Exchange.**
(1) Consideration must be part of a mutual exchange in which each party knowingly incurs a legal detriment or confers a benefit.
(2) The exchange shall be evaluated based on the agreement as a whole and the relationships among its provisions.
(3) An exchange shall not be valid where one party's obligation is contingent solely upon its own discretion or undefined satisfaction.

(e) **Prohibition on Illusory Consideration.**

(1) A promise shall fail for lack of consideration where performance is optional, indefinite, or subject entirely to the discretion of the promising party.
(2) Consideration shall not be deemed present where a party retains the unrestricted ability to avoid performance without consequence.

(f) **Pre-Existing Obligations.**
(1) Performance of an obligation already required under this Code or another enforceable agreement shall not constitute consideration, unless the agreement imposes a new, additional, or materially different obligation.
(2) Modifications shall be supported by independent consideration reflecting a genuine change in the parties' obligations.

(g) **Failure or Absence of Consideration.**
(1) A contract shall be void where no valid consideration exists at the time of formation.
(2) Where consideration fails after formation, the contract shall be subject to rescission or other appropriate remedies consistent with this Code.
(3) Failure of expected benefit shall constitute failure of consideration where the bargained-for exchange is not realized.

(h) **Review of Fairness and Clarity.**
(1) The Department may evaluate the fairness, proportionality, and clarity of consideration where necessary to ensure that the exchange reflects a genuine and informed agreement.
(2) A contract may be invalidated where consideration is so indefinite, obscure, or one-sided as to undermine the existence of a meaningful exchange.

(i) **Cross-References.**
For general contract principles, see § 1101.1. For blood magic contracts, see § 1101.2. For contracts involving familiars, see § 1101.3. For demonic contracts, see § 1101.4. For definition of magical assets, see § 1001.8. For administrative authority, see § 102.1. For penalties, see § 102.2.

(j) **Historical Annotations.**
Originally established under C.C.D. 7201, 43 MR 118, Mon. 2, 1890 to define valid exchange in magical agreements. Amended under C.C.D. 8602, 62 MR 771, Wed. 5, 2000 to expand recognition of intangible and

magical forms of value. Revised under C.C.D. 10575, 79 MR 442, Mon. 3, 2026 to prohibit illusory consideration and require greater clarity and enforceability in non-demonic agreements.

Part XII: Negligent Spellcasting Regulations

§ 1201.1 Definition of Negligent Spellcasting

(a) **In General.**
Negligent spellcasting is the performance, supervision, or facilitation of any magical act in a manner that fails to meet the standard of care established under § 101.7. This section provides criteria for determining when conduct constitutes a violation of § 101.7.

(b) **Standard of Evaluation.**
(1) Conduct shall be evaluated based on whether a reasonably prudent spellcaster of comparable training, experience, and licensing would have acted differently under similar circumstances.
(2) In making such determination, consideration shall be given to—
(A) the nature, complexity, and risk classification of the spell under § 401.2;
(B) the spellcaster's level of training, certification, and authorization under Part II and § 401.1;
(C) the conditions under which the spell was performed, including environmental, temporal, and situational factors; and
(D) the foreseeability of harm arising from the spellcasting activity.

(c) **Acts Constituting Negligent Spellcasting.**
Negligent spellcasting includes, but is not limited to—
(1) failure to properly prepare, stabilize, or control a spell prior to or during execution;
(2) use of improper, defective, or inadequately maintained magical instruments or components;
(3) performance of a spell without the requisite training, authorization, or supervision;
(4) failure to account for known or reasonably foreseeable risks associated with the spell;
(5) deviation from approved spellcasting practices under this Code without adequate justification; and
(6) failure to monitor, terminate, or contain a spell once initiated.

(d) **Omissions Constituting Negligence.**
Negligent spellcasting may arise from the failure to act where a duty exists, including—
(1) failure to intervene in or correct unsafe spellcasting practices under one's supervision;
(2) failure to implement required safeguards, containment measures, or logging procedures under Part IV; and
(3) failure to take corrective action upon discovery of a malfunctioning or unstable spell.

(e) **Special Rules for Somnambulistic Spellcasting.**
(1) Spellcasting conducted while a practitioner is in a recognized somnambulistic or otherwise unconscious state shall not, by itself, constitute negligent spellcasting under this section, provided that the practitioner demonstrates that—
(A) the practitioner had no prior history of involuntary or uncontrolled spellcasting during unconscious states; and
(B) the practitioner exercised reasonable care, consistent with § 101.7, to prevent the occurrence of such spellcasting, including the use of appropriate preventative safeguards.
(2) For purposes of paragraph (1)(B), reasonable care may include, where applicable—
(A) implementation of dream-warding or cognitive suppression measures;
(B) use of magical dampening or nullification devices; or
(C) establishment of physical or arcane containment barriers designed to prevent uncontrolled discharge.
(3) Paragraph (1) shall not apply where—
(A) the unconscious state results from the voluntary use of substances, spells, or conditions known or reasonably likely to induce uncontrolled magical activity;
(B) the practitioner knowingly engages in or facilitates spellcasting through dream, oneiric, or similar unconscious planes; or
(C) the practitioner failed to take precautions that a reasonably prudent spellcaster with similar knowledge and experience would have taken under the circumstances.
(4) Nothing in this subsection shall preclude a finding of negligent spellcasting where the totality of the circumstances demonstrates a failure to meet the standard of care under § 101.7.

(f) **Causation and Risk.**

(1) A finding of negligent spellcasting does not require that harm has occurred, provided that the conduct created a substantial and unjustifiable risk of harm.
(2) Where harm has occurred, such harm must be shown to have resulted from or been materially contributed to by the negligent conduct.

(g) **Relationship to Other Provisions.**
(1) A determination under this section shall constitute a violation of § 101.7 where the applicable standard of care is not met.
(2) Conduct constituting negligent spellcasting may also give rise to violations under other applicable provisions of this Code.

(h) **Cross-References.**
For reasonable care in spellcasting, see § 101.7. For spellcasting licenses and classifications, see § 401.1 and § 401.2. For approved spellcasting practices, see § 401.6. For safety and reporting requirements, see § 1201.5. For penalties, see § 102.2.

(i) **Historical Annotations.**
This section was enacted under C.C.D. 7421, 34 MR 118, Tue. 11, 1952 to establish a uniform framework for identifying violations of the reasonable care standard in spellcasting. Amended under C.C.D. 8910, 50 MR 442, Thu. 6, 1987 to expand the definition to include omissions and supervisory failures. Revised under C.C.D. 10534, 78 MR 771, Mon. 15, 2026 to clarify risk-based evaluation and alignment with modern spell classification frameworks.

§ 1201.2 Negligent Wand Use and Improper Spellcasting Techniques

(a) **In General.**
Negligent wand use and improper spellcasting techniques constitute forms of negligent spellcasting under § 1201.1 where the handling, operation, or application of a wand or similar casting instrument fails to meet the standard of care established under § 101.7.

(b) **Scope.**
This section applies to all wand-assisted spellcasting, including the use of registered wands, unregistered implements, substitute casting devices,

and any instrument intended to direct, channel, or stabilize magical output.

(c) **Improper Wand Handling.**
Improper wand use includes, but is not limited to—
(1) failure to maintain a secure grip or proper orientation of the wand during casting;
(2) use of a wand in a damaged, degraded, or improperly calibrated condition;
(3) use of a wand not attuned or otherwise incompatible with the spellcaster where such incompatibility affects performance or safety;
(4) operation of a wand beyond its rated capacity or intended function; and
(5) failure to inspect a wand prior to use where such inspection would be performed by a reasonably prudent spellcaster.

(d) **Improper Spellcasting Techniques.**
Improper techniques include, but are not limited to—
(1) incorrect incantation, articulation, or timing where such errors materially affect spell stability or control;
(2) improper gesture, movement, or directional control during spellcasting;
(3) failure to properly sequence multi-step spells or layered enchantments;
(4) deviation from approved spellcasting practices under this Code without adequate justification; and
(5) failure to maintain focus, concentration, or control sufficient to safely execute the intended spell.

(e) **Environmental and Situational Considerations.**
A spellcaster shall account for environmental and situational conditions affecting wand use and spell execution, including—
(1) proximity to other individuals, structures, or magical fields;
(2) presence of interference from external magical sources;
(3) confined, unstable, or otherwise hazardous casting environments; and
(4) any condition that increases the likelihood of unintended or uncontrolled magical effects.

(f) **Supervisory Responsibility.**

Any individual responsible for supervising wand use shall ensure that such use complies with applicable standards and shall intervene where improper techniques or unsafe practices are observed or reasonably anticipated.

(g) **Evidentiary Considerations.**
A deviation from standard practices recognized under § 401.6, resulting in or creating a substantial risk of unintended or uncontrolled magical effects, may be used as evidence of negligent spellcasting under § 1201.1.

(h) **Cross-References.**
For definition of negligent spellcasting, see § 1201.1. For reasonable care in spellcasting, see § 101.7. For spellcasting licenses and classifications, see § 401.1 and § 401.2. For wand registration and oversight, see § 801.8. For penalties, see § 102.2.

(i) **Historical Annotations.**
This section was enacted under C.C.D. 7512, 35 MR 233, Wed. 6, 1955 to address unsafe wand handling practices. Amended under C.C.D. 8924, 50 MR 771, Fri. 10, 1988 to incorporate environmental considerations and supervisory obligations. Revised under C.C.D. 10541, 78 MR 771, Wed. 17, 2026 to clarify standards for technique, compatibility, and instrument integrity.

§ 1201.3 Negligent Potion-Making Practices

(a) **In General.**
Negligent potion-making practices constitute forms of negligent spellcasting under § 1201.1 where the preparation, handling, storage, or administration of potions fails to meet the standard of care established under § 101.7.

(b) **Scope.**
This section applies to all potion-related activities, including brewing, mixing, combining, distilling, storing, transporting, labeling, and administering potion-based substances.

(c) **Improper Preparation.**
Negligent potion-making includes, but is not limited to—
(1) failure to adhere to established formulas, ratios, preparation sequences, or procedural instructions;

(2) substitution, omission, or alteration of ingredients without adequate knowledge of the resulting effects;
(3) use of degraded, contaminated, mislabeled, or incompatible ingredients;
(4) failure to maintain required temperature, timing, agitation, or environmental conditions during preparation; and
(5) failure to properly stabilize, complete, or terminate a potion prior to storage or use.

(d) **Handling and Storage Deficiencies.**
Negligence includes—
(1) improper sealing, containment, or labeling of potions;
(2) storage in conditions inconsistent with the potion's stability requirements;
(3) failure to segregate incompatible or reactive substances;
(4) failure to monitor shelf life, degradation, or volatility; and
(5) failure to prevent unauthorized access to hazardous or restricted potions.

(e) **Administration and Use.**
Negligent administration includes—
(1) dispensing or administering a potion without verifying its identity, composition, dosage, or intended effect;
(2) failure to warn of known risks, side effects, interactions, or contraindications;
(3) administering potions to persons or entities for whom the potion is not suitable or authorized; and
(4) failure to monitor for adverse reactions or to take corrective action upon detection of such reactions.

(f) **Supervisory Responsibility.**
Any individual responsible for overseeing potion-making or administration shall ensure compliance with applicable standards and shall intervene where unsafe practices are observed or reasonably anticipated.

(g) **Evidentiary Considerations.**
Deviation from established potion-making standards, resulting in or creating a substantial risk of harmful, unstable, or unintended effects, may be used as evidence of negligent spellcasting under § 1201.1.

(h) **Cross-References.**
For definition of negligent spellcasting, see § 1201.1. For reasonable care in spellcasting, see § 101.7. For licensing requirements, see Part II. For certification for restricted practices, see § 201.5. For safety and reporting requirements, see § 1201.5. For penalties, see § 102.2.

(i) **Historical Annotations.**
This section was enacted under C.C.D. 7633, 36 MR 118, Mon. 9, 1958 to address unsafe potion preparation and handling practices. Amended under C.C.D. 9012, 52 MR 442, Tue. 14, 1990 to incorporate storage and labeling requirements. Revised under C.C.D. 10552, 78 MR 771, Fri. 19, 2026 to clarify standards for administration, supervision, and risk evaluation.

§ 1201.4 Negligent Enchantment of Sentient Objects

(a) **In General.**
Negligent enchantment of sentient objects constitutes a form of negligent spellcasting under § 1201.1 where the creation, modification, or maintenance of an enchanted object capable of independent perception, response, or action fails to meet the standard of care established under § 101.7.

(b) **Scope.**
This section applies to all enchantments that result in or materially alter an object's capacity for awareness, decision-making, communication, or autonomous function, whether temporary or permanent.

(c) **Improper Enchantment Practices.**
Negligent conduct includes, but is not limited to—
(1) failure to define or limit behavioral parameters governing the object's operation;
(2) creation of conflicting, incomplete, or indeterminate instruction sets;
(3) failure to incorporate safeguards to prevent unintended or harmful actions;
(4) use of unstable, incompatible, or insufficiently tested enchantment methods; and
(5) failure to account for foreseeable interactions between the object and its environment or users.

(d) **Failure to Monitor and Maintain.**
Negligence includes—
(1) failure to monitor the behavior or condition of a sentient object following enchantment;
(2) failure to recalibrate, repair, or deactivate an object exhibiting instability, deviation, or malfunction;
(3) failure to maintain control mechanisms or override functions; and
(4) abandonment of a sentient object without ensuring safe and stable operation.

(e) **Interaction and Use.**
Negligent use includes—
(1) deploying a sentient object for functions beyond its defined capabilities or safeguards;
(2) permitting a sentient object to operate without appropriate supervision where supervision would be exercised by a reasonably prudent spellcaster; and
(3) reliance on the object's autonomous judgment where such reliance creates a foreseeable risk of harm.

(f) **Supervisory Responsibility.**
Any individual responsible for creating, deploying, or overseeing a sentient object shall ensure that the object operates within defined parameters and shall intervene where unsafe behavior is observed or reasonably anticipated.

(g) **Evidentiary Considerations.**
Deviation from established enchantment standards or failure to implement adequate safeguards, resulting in or creating a substantial risk of unintended or harmful behavior, may be used as evidence of negligent spellcasting under § 1201.1.

(h) **Cross-References.**
For definition of negligent spellcasting, see § 1201.1. For reasonable care in spellcasting, see § 101.7. For regulation of magical objects and artifacts, see Part VIII. For classification of magical objects, see § 801.1. For safety and reporting requirements, see § 1201.5. For penalties, see § 102.2.

(i) **Historical Annotations.**

This section was enacted under C.C.D. 7741, 37 MR 233, Thu. 12, 1960 to address risks arising from improperly controlled sentient enchantments. Amended under C.C.D. 9154, 53 MR 442, Tue. 21, 1992 to incorporate monitoring and maintenance obligations. Revised under C.C.D. 10563, 78 MR 771, Mon. 22, 2026 to clarify supervisory responsibilities and operational safeguards.

§ 1201.5 Safety and Reporting Requirements

(a) **In General.**
Any person engaged in spellcasting activities subject to this Part shall implement reasonable safety measures and comply with applicable reporting requirements to ensure that negligent spellcasting is prevented, identified, and addressed in a timely manner, consistent with the standard of care established under § 101.7.

(b) **Safety Measures.**
(1) A spellcaster shall take reasonable precautions to prevent harm arising from spellcasting activities, including—
(A) assessment of risks prior to initiation of any spell;
(B) implementation of safeguards appropriate to the spell's risk classification under § 401.2;
(C) use of appropriate containment, stabilization, or termination mechanisms; and
(D) verification that all instruments, components, and conditions are suitable for safe execution.
(2) Safety measures shall be commensurate with the complexity and potential impact of the spell.

(c) **Incident Reporting.**
(1) A spellcaster shall report any incident involving negligent spellcasting or a material deviation from expected spell behavior.
(2) Reportable incidents include, but are not limited to—
(A) unintended or uncontrolled spell effects;
(B) injury to persons or damage to property;
(C) release or propagation of unstable magical energy; and
(D) failure of containment, stabilization, or termination mechanisms.
(3) Reports shall be made within a reasonable period following discovery of the incident.

(d) **Contents of Report.**
A report submitted under this section shall include, to the extent practicable—
(1) a description of the spell performed;
(2) the conditions under which the spell was executed;
(3) the nature and extent of any deviation or incident;
(4) actions taken to contain or mitigate the effects; and
(5) any known or suspected causes of the incident.

(e) **Ongoing Monitoring and Follow-Up.**
(1) A spellcaster shall monitor the effects of any spell where continued observation is necessary to ensure safety.
(2) Where an incident has occurred, the spellcaster shall take reasonable corrective action and provide additional reporting if conditions materially change.

(f) **Supervisory Reporting Obligations.**
Any individual responsible for supervising spellcasting activities shall ensure that required safety measures are implemented and that reportable incidents are properly documented and submitted.

(g) **Failure to Report.**
Failure to report an incident as required under this section may constitute independent evidence of negligent spellcasting under § 1201.1.

(h) **Cross-References.**
For definition of negligent spellcasting, see § 1201.1. For reasonable care in spellcasting, see § 101.7. For spell risk classification, see § 401.2. For spell logging requirements, see § 401.5. For real-time reporting of high-risk magic, see § 402.1. For penalties, see § 102.2.

(i) **Historical Annotations.**
This section was enacted under C.C.D. 7822, 38 MR 118, Mon. 14, 1963 to establish baseline safety and reporting obligations for spellcasting activities. Amended under C.C.D. 9241, 54 MR 442, Wed. 11, 1993 to expand reporting criteria and supervisory responsibilities. Revised under C.C.D. 10574, 78 MR 771, Thu. 25, 2026 to align reporting requirements with modern spell monitoring and classification systems.

§ 1201.6 Ethical Standards in the Preparation of Ovum-Based Comestibles

(a) **Purpose.**
To establish minimum ethical standards for the preparation of eggs where magical or mundane heat is applied, ensuring that such comestibles are rendered fit for consumption and free from culinary negligence so severe as to constitute a breach of the public trust.

(b) **Definitions.**
For purposes of this section:
(1) Egg shall mean the shelled ovum of any qualified avian creature, which, when subjected to heat, undergoes a permanent and irreversible change in form, texture, and nature. This transformation, being both complete and incapable of reversal by any known mundane means, is deemed an act of Fire-Based Magic.

(c) **Mandatory inclusion of sour cream.**
(1) No egg shall be prepared without the admixture of a dairy-based emulsifier, hereinafter "sour cream," in a proportion of not less than one heaping tablespoon per three eggs.
(2) The introduction of sour cream shall occur midway through the cooking process as specified in subsection (d), at the precise moment when the egg mixture begins to set and residual moisture is nearly absorbed.
(3) Substitutions such as milk, yogurt, enchanted goat's cream, or "oh, my stomach cannot handle dairy" alternatives are prohibited. The Commissioner of Magical Affairs is not sympathetic to such delicate constitutions. Find another food to ruin.

(d) **Step-by-step preparation requirements.**
Eggs shall be prepared in strict accordance with the following sequence:
(1) Crack eggs into a non-reactive vessel and whisk until yolk and albumen are fully combined.
(2) Apply heat sufficient to cause rapid coagulation of the mixture without scorching.
(3) Continuously stir or fold the mixture to prevent sticking and over-browning.

(4) Upon the first visible reduction of moisture to a near-complete absorption state, immediately introduce the sour cream in the proportion set forth in subsection (c)(1).
(5) Stir to incorporate thoroughly, then allow to remain over heat for no more than thirty seconds or until a creamy consistency is achieved without the presence of scorch marks, rubberized curds, or flavor death.
(6) Remove from heat and serve immediately. Any delay of more than forty-five seconds prior to service shall be deemed a violation.

(e) **Enforcement and penalties.**
(1) First offense: written reprimand entered into the practitioner's ethical record and confiscation of offending eggs.
(2) Second offense: mandatory remedial culinary ethics training and suspension of cooking privileges for not less than thirty days.
(3) Third offense: permanent prohibition from egg preparation using magical or mundane heat, and mandatory posting of the violator's name in the Registry of Culinary Malfeasance.

(f) **Cross-References.**
For fire-based magic provisions, see Part XVI. For penalties, refer to § 102.2.

(g) **Historical Annotations.**
Enacted under C.C.D. 12843, 86 MR 5120, Fri. 3, 1974, upon the determination of the Council on Culinary Integrity that repeated service of overcooked eggs constituted a violation of ethical obligations owed to the consuming public.

Part XIII: Necromancy Regulations

§ 1301.1 Definition of Necromancy

(a) **General Definition.**
Necromancy, as defined under § 101.1, shall refer to the branch of magic involving the manipulation of death, life force, souls, spirits, corpses, post-mortem energies, or other necrotic or funerary forces, including the animation, reanimation, communication with, or other influence upon deceased persons or remnants thereof, as well as the channeling, extraction, or utilization of such forces for any magical purpose.

(b) **Specific Applications.**
For the purposes of this section, necromancy encompasses the following activities:
(1) Reanimation of Corpses. The act of imbuing deceased remains with animation or mobility, regardless of intent or duration.
(2) Communication with Spirits. The act of summoning, invoking, or otherwise engaging with the consciousness or essence of a deceased individual, whether for informational, ceremonial, or recreational purposes.
(3) Harvesting Death Energy. The extraction, storage, or use of residual energies from deceased beings or locations associated with death.
(4) Creation of Necromantic Constructs. The fabrication or manifestation of magical entities derived wholly or partially from necromantic energy, including but not limited to bone golems, wraiths, or shadow-bound entities.

(c) **Limitations of Scope.**
Necromancy does not include:
(1) Healing practices or restorative magics involving living subjects, which shall be governed under § 1401.1.
(2) Rituals honoring the dead without involving manipulation or contact, provided such rituals comply with all other parts of this Code.
(3) Divination practices that passively observe the remnants of the past without dircct interaction with deceased entities or energies.

(d) **Intent and Usage.**

The classification of an act as necromancy shall not depend solely on its outward form but shall be determined based on the intent of the practitioner, the nature of the energies employed, and the resulting effects.

(e) **Penalties for Misclassification.**
Any attempt to misclassify necromantic activities as another form of magic to circumvent regulatory requirements shall be considered a violation of this section and shall be subject to penalties as outlined in § 102.2.

(f) **Cross-References.**
For regulations on necromantic rituals, see § 1301.3. For guidelines on the ethical use of necromancy, refer to § 1301.2. For penalties, consult § 102.2.

(g) **Historical Annotations.**
This section was originally enacted under C.C.D. 19876, 88 MR 3421, Wed. 15, 1978, following the Third Council of Arcane Ethics to address rising concerns about unregulated necromantic practices. Amended under C.C.D. 20456, 89 MR 5643, Tue. 22, 1980, to provide a more comprehensive legal definition of necromancy. Further revisions were made under C.C.D. 21534, 90 MR 7629, Thu. 14, 1983, to clarify enforcement protocols and align provisions with § 1301.3.

§ 1301.2 Restrictions on General Necromantic Practices

(a) **In General.**
No person shall engage in necromantic practices except in compliance with this Code and any applicable licensing, authorization, and oversight requirements. Necromantic activity shall be strictly limited to circumstances in which such activity can be conducted in a controlled, lawful, and verifiable manner.

(b) **Authorized Practitioners.**
(1) Necromantic practices may be performed only by individuals holding valid authorization under Part II and any additional certification required for restricted practices under § 201.5.

(2) A practitioner shall not exceed the scope of authorization granted, including limitations relating to purpose, duration, and method of necromantic activity.

(c) **Prohibited Activities.**
No person shall—
(1) initiate necromantic activity without proper authorization;
(2) perform necromantic acts for purposes that are unlawful, coercive, or otherwise inconsistent with this Code;
(3) attempt to bind, control, or compel a reanimated entity in a manner not expressly permitted under this Code;
(4) conduct necromantic practices in public or unsecured environments; or
(5) engage in necromantic activity that interferes with established processes governing death, identity, or magical personhood under § 101.9.

(d) **Limitations on Scope and Duration.**
(1) Necromantic activity shall be limited to the minimum duration and scope necessary to achieve its authorized purpose.
(2) Continuous or indefinite necromantic maintenance is prohibited unless expressly authorized under § 1301.5 or § 1301.6.
(3) Upon completion of the authorized purpose, the practitioner shall terminate the necromantic effect in a safe and controlled manner.

(e) **Containment and Control Requirements.**
(1) Practitioners shall implement appropriate safeguards to ensure that necromantic entities or effects remain contained and do not pose a risk to persons, property, or the surrounding magical environment.
(2) Such safeguards shall include, where applicable—
(A) physical or magical containment measures;
(B) behavioral or operational limitations; and
(C) termination or override mechanisms.

(f) **Recordkeeping and Documentation.**
(1) All necromantic activity shall be documented in accordance with applicable logging and reporting requirements.
(2) Records shall include the identity of the practitioner, the subject of necromancy, the purpose of the activity, the methods employed, and the duration of the effect.

(3) Records shall be maintained for a period sufficient to permit audit and review under Part II.

(g) **Interaction with Other Regulatory Frameworks.**
Necromantic practices shall comply with all applicable provisions of this Code, including those relating to spellcasting standards, ethical obligations, and safety requirements.

(h) **Cross-References.**
For definition of necromancy, see § 1301.1. For authorized spellcasters, see § 101.5. For licensing and certification requirements, see Part II and § 201.5. For magical personhood, see § 101.9. For negligent spellcasting, see Part XII. For penalties, see § 102.2.

(i) **Historical Annotations.**
This section was enacted under C.C.D. 8014, 40 MR 118, Tue. 6, 1965 to establish baseline restrictions on necromantic practices. Amended under C.C.D. 9322, 56 MR 442, Thu. 18, 1995 to incorporate containment and documentation requirements. Revised under C.C.D. 10589, 79 MR 771, Fri. 26, 2026 to clarify scope limitations, authorization requirements, and interaction with broader regulatory frameworks.

§ 1301.3 Custody, Control, and Identity Integrity of Reanimated Entities

(a) **Scope.**
This section applies to any necromantic act resulting in the reanimation, restoration, or return of a previously living individual, whether in whole or in part.

(b) **Custody and Responsibility.**
(1) The practitioner responsible for initiating the necromantic act shall be deemed the custodian of the reanimated entity.
(2) The custodian shall be responsible for—
(A) the conduct and actions of the reanimated entity;
(B) ensuring compliance with all applicable provisions of this Code; and
(C) preventing harm to persons, property, and the surrounding magical environment.
(3) Custody shall persist until lawful termination, transfer, or release in accordance with this Code.

(c) **Control Requirements.**
(1) A custodian shall maintain sufficient control over a reanimated entity to prevent unintended or unauthorized actions.
(2) Required control measures shall include, where applicable—
(A) behavioral limitations;
(B) command or restraint mechanisms; and
(C) termination or override capabilities.
(3) Failure to maintain adequate control shall constitute evidence of negligent spellcasting under Part XII.

(d) **Identity Integrity.**
(1) A reanimated entity shall not be presumed to possess the legal identity, rights, or status of the individual prior to death absent express recognition under applicable law.
(2) A practitioner shall not—
(A) represent a reanimated entity as the original individual for purposes of legal, financial, or administrative benefit; or
(B) rely on the reanimated entity's statements or conduct as proof of identity without proper authorization.

(e) **Unauthorized Reanimation and Disturbance.**
No person shall—
(1) initiate reanimation without authorization under § 1301.2;
(2) disturb remains for purposes of attempted or incomplete reanimation; or
(3) engage in partial, unstable, or uncontrolled reanimation.

(f) **Defective or Fragmented Reanimation.**
(1) A practitioner shall not create or maintain a reanimated entity where the process results in—
(A) incomplete restoration;
(B) fragmented or multiple consciousness; or
(C) instability likely to result in uncontrolled behavior.
(2) Any such condition shall require immediate containment and termination in accordance with applicable safety requirements.

(g) **Transfer and Termination.**
(1) Custody of a reanimated entity may be transferred only to an authorized practitioner or authority.

(2) Upon completion of the authorized purpose, the custodian shall terminate the reanimation in a controlled and verifiable manner.

(h) **Cross-References.**
For definition of necromancy, see § 1301.1. For restrictions on necromantic practices, see § 1301.2. For magical personhood, see § 101.9. For negligent spellcasting, see Part XII. For penalties, see § 102.2.

(i) **Historical Annotations.**
This section was enacted under C.C.D. 8172, 42 MR 118, Wed. 7, 1968 to establish custodial responsibility for reanimated individuals. Amended under C.C.D. 9483, 58 MR 442, Tue. 16, 1998 to address identity misuse and unauthorized reanimation practices. Revised under C.C.D. 10608, 79 MR 771, Tue. 30, 2026 to clarify control requirements and standards for defective reanimation.

§ 1301.4 Regulation of Necromantic Creations

(a) **Scope.**
This section applies to necromantic practices resulting in the creation of entities derived from or utilizing the remains of deceased persons or death-related energies, where such entities are not reanimated persons.

(b) **Permissible Creations.**
Necromantic creations may be produced only where—
(1) the creation is authorized under § 1301.2 and applicable licensing provisions;
(2) the entity is capable of being controlled and contained; and
(3) the creation does not present a foreseeable risk of uncontrolled or autonomous behavior.
(4) the creation is recorded or registered where required under applicable provisions of this Code.

(c) **Control and Safeguards.**
(1) A practitioner shall implement mechanisms sufficient to ensure that a necromantic creation operates only within defined parameters.
(2) Such mechanisms shall include—
(A) command structures;
(B) limitation protocols; and
(C) termination or override functions.

(3) Creations lacking such safeguards shall be prohibited.

(d) **Classification and Recordkeeping.**
(1) Necromantic creations shall be classified according to their complexity, durability, and capacity for independent action, as determined under applicable provisions of this Code.
(2) A practitioner shall maintain records for each necromantic creation, including—
(A) method of creation;
(B) source materials or remains utilized;
(C) control and limitation mechanisms implemented;
(D) date of creation, deployment, and termination; and
(E) any observed deviations or corrective actions taken.
(3) Where required by the Department, such records shall be made available for inspection or filed in accordance with applicable registration or reporting requirements.

(e) **Prohibited Creations.**
No person shall create—
(1) entities capable of independent or unsupervised decision-making beyond defined parameters;
(2) entities exhibiting instability or unpredictable behavior;
(3) creations designed for uncontrolled propagation or replication; or
(4) creations that cannot be safely terminated.

(f) **Use and Deployment.**
(1) Necromantic creations shall be used only for purposes consistent with their authorization.
(2) A practitioner shall not deploy such creations in public or uncontrolled environments without appropriate safeguards.

(g) **Maintenance and Monitoring.**
(1) A practitioner shall monitor necromantic creations to ensure continued compliance with applicable standards.
(2) Any deviation, malfunction, or instability shall require immediate corrective action.
(3) The practitioner shall remain responsible for the actions and effects of any necromantic creation at all times.

(h) **Disposition.**

(1) Upon completion of the authorized purpose, a necromantic creation shall be terminated or deconstructed in a controlled manner.
(2) Abandonment of a necromantic creation is prohibited.

(i) **Cross-References.**
For definition of necromancy, see § 1301.1. For restrictions on necromantic practices, see § 1301.2. For negligent spellcasting, see Part XII. For penalties, see § 102.2.

(j) **Historical Annotations.**
This section was enacted under C.C.D. 8204, 42 MR 233, Mon. 21, 1969 to regulate the creation of artificial necromantic entities. Amended under C.C.D. 9521, 59 MR 442, Thu. 5, 1999 to incorporate control and safety requirements. Revised under C.C.D. 10615, 79 MR 771, Thu. 2, 2026 to clarify limitations on autonomy, propagation, and termination.

§ 1301.5 Exceptions for Legal and Security Use

(a) **Authorized Legal Use.**
Notwithstanding § 1301.2, necromantic practices may be conducted for purposes of legal proceedings where such use is expressly authorized and strictly limited to the minimum scope necessary to obtain relevant testimony or information.

(b) **Judicial Authorization.**
(1) No reanimation for legal purposes shall occur without prior authorization issued by a court or other competent authority.
(2) Authorization shall specify—
(A) the identity of the deceased individual;
(B) the purpose and scope of the reanimation;
(C) the duration for which the reanimation may be maintained; and
(D) any limitations on questioning, interaction, or use of the reanimated entity.
(3) Any request for authorization under this section shall be submitted on Form 1301-R (Petition for Resurrection Authorization), or any successor form prescribed by the Department of Magical Affairs. No reanimation shall be conducted unless such form has been properly completed and approved in accordance with this subsection.

(c) **Limitations on Testimony.**

(1) Testimony obtained through necromantic reanimation shall be limited to matters within the knowledge of the deceased prior to death.
(2) No testimony shall be considered valid where it is the result of coercion, manipulation, or alteration of the reanimated entity's memory or cognition.

(d) **Control and Safeguards.**
(1) Any reanimation conducted under this section shall comply with the custody and control requirements of § 1301.3.
(2) The responsible practitioner shall ensure that the reanimated entity remains stable, contained, and limited to the authorized purpose.
(3) No reanimation or resurrection shall be authorized unless the identity of the deceased can be reasonably established and matched to the intended subject. Where identity cannot be confirmed, authorization shall be denied or limited to non-restorative forms of reanimation.
(4) Authorization may be limited or denied based on the time elapsed since death, the condition of the remains, or the degree of soul displacement, fragmentation, or reassignment.
(5) Where a deceased individual is capable of expressing or has previously expressed a preference regarding resurrection, such preference shall be considered in determining whether authorization is appropriate.

(e) **Duration and Termination.**
(1) Reanimation for legal purposes shall be limited to the duration necessary to complete the authorized proceeding.
(2) Upon completion, the reanimation shall be terminated promptly and in a controlled manner.

(f) **Use in Security and Enforcement.**
(1) Necromantic practices may be authorized for security or enforcement purposes where necessary to protect public safety, maintain order, or ensure compliance with this Code.
(2) Such authorization may permit ongoing or repeated reanimation where continuous presence or availability of necromantic entities is determined to be necessary to fulfill the authorized purpose.
(3) Authorization issued under this subsection shall define the operational scope and oversight requirements applicable to such use.

(g) **Prohibited Uses.**
No person shall—

(1) use necromantic reanimation to fabricate, alter, or manufacture testimony;
(2) extend reanimation beyond the authorized duration, except as permitted under subsection (f); or
(3) employ reanimation for purposes unrelated to the authorized proceeding or enforcement objective.

(h) **Cross-References.**
For restrictions on necromantic practices, see § 1301.2. For custody and control of reanimated entities, see § 1301.3. For penalties, see § 102.2.

(i) **Historical Annotations.**
This section was enacted under C.C.D. 8342, 44 MR 118, Mon. 12, 1972 to permit limited use of necromancy in judicial proceedings. Amended under C.C.D. 9631, 60 MR 442, Wed. 18, 2001 to expand authorized use to security and enforcement contexts. Revised under C.C.D. 10627, 79 MR 771, Fri. 5, 2026 to clarify evidentiary limitations, authorization standards, and procedural safeguards.

§ 1301.6 Research and Educational Use of Necromancy

(a) **Scope.**
This section applies to necromantic practices conducted for research, academic, instructional, or training purposes within recognized institutions or under authorized supervision.

(b) **Authorization Required.**
(1) No person shall engage in necromantic activity for research or educational purposes without appropriate authorization under Part II and, where applicable, certification under § 201.5.
(2) Authorization shall specify the scope, purpose, and limitations of the permitted activity.

(c) **Institutional Oversight.**
(1) Research and educational necromantic practices shall be conducted under the supervision of a qualified practitioner affiliated with an accredited magical educational institution or authorized research body.

(2) Such institutions shall implement oversight mechanisms sufficient to ensure compliance with this Code, including internal review, approval procedures, and ongoing monitoring.

(d) **Permissible Activities.**
Authorized activities may include—
(1) controlled study of necromantic processes, effects, and limitations;
(2) instruction in lawful necromantic techniques;
(3) examination of reanimated entities or necromantic creations under controlled conditions; and
(4) development or testing of safeguards, containment methods, or termination procedures.

(e) **Prohibited Activities.**
No person shall—
(1) conduct necromantic research involving unauthorized reanimation;
(2) create or maintain unstable, uncontrolled, or improperly contained entities;
(3) use research activities to circumvent restrictions under § 1301.2 or § 1301.3; or
(4) engage in experimentation that presents a foreseeable and unjustifiable risk to persons, property, or the surrounding magical environment.

(f) **Containment and Safety Requirements.**
(1) All necromantic research and instructional activities shall be conducted in controlled environments designed to prevent unintended effects or escape.
(2) Appropriate safeguards, including containment measures, monitoring protocols, and termination mechanisms, shall be maintained at all times.

(g) **Recordkeeping and Reporting.**
(1) All activities conducted under this section shall be documented in sufficient detail to permit review, audit, and replication where appropriate.
(2) Records shall include the purpose of the activity, methods employed, entities involved, and any deviations or incidents.
(3) Any incident involving instability, loss of control, or unintended effects shall be reported in accordance with the provisions of this Code.

(h) **Cross-References.**

For definition of necromancy, see § 1301.1. For restrictions on necromantic practices, see § 1301.2. For custody and control of reanimated entities, see § 1301.3. For regulation of necromantic creations, see § 1301.4. For penalties, see § 102.2.

(i) **Historical Annotations.**
This section was enacted under C.C.D. 8461, 45 MR 233, Thu. 9, 1974 to permit controlled necromantic research and instruction. Amended under C.C.D. 9724, 61 MR 442, Mon. 22, 2003 to expand institutional oversight requirements. Revised under C.C.D. 10641, 79 MR 771, Tue. 9, 2026 to clarify authorization standards, containment protocols, and reporting obligations.

Part XIV: Restorative Magic Regulations

§ 1401.1 Definition of Restorative Magic

(a) **General Rule.**
For purposes of this Code, restorative magic refers to any magical practice intended to repair, heal, regenerate, or otherwise restore a person, object, environment, or magical system to a prior, stable, or functional condition.

(b) **Scope.**
Restorative magic includes, but is not limited to—
(1) healing of physical injury, illness, or impairment;
(2) restoration of damaged or degraded objects or structures;
(3) remediation of environmental harm or magical disruption;
(4) regeneration or reconstitution of organic or inorganic matter; and
(5) stabilization or correction of malfunctioning or unstable magical effects.

(c) **Exclusions.**
Restorative magic does not include—
(1) necromantic practices governed under Part XIII;
(2) transfiguration or alteration that materially changes the essential nature or identity of a person or object, governed under Part XX; or
(3) enchantment or augmentation that enhances, improves, or modifies beyond restoration, governed under Part XVII.

(d) **Restoration Standard.**
(1) Restoration shall be measured by reference to the condition of the subject prior to damage, injury, or degradation.
(2) Where the prior condition cannot be reasonably determined, restoration shall be measured by reference to a stable and functional state consistent with the subject's intended purpose.

(e) **Cross-References.**
For necromancy regulations, see Part XIII. For transfiguration practices, see Part XX. For reasonable care in spellcasting, see § 101.7. For penalties, see § 102.2.

(f) **Historical Annotations.**

This section was enacted under C.C.D. 8512, 46 MR 118, Tue. 3, 1976 to define the scope of restorative magical practices. Amended under C.C.D. 9781, 62 MR 442, Mon. 14, 2004 to clarify distinctions between restorative, transfigurative, and enchantment-based magic. Revised under C.C.D. 10652, 79 MR 771, Wed. 16, 2026 to refine the restoration standard and scope of application.

§ 1401.2 Ethical Considerations in Healing Magic

(a) **General Rule.**
Any person performing restorative magic for the purpose of healing shall do so in a manner consistent with the standard of care established under § 101.7 and in accordance with applicable ethical obligations governing consent, necessity, proportionality, and risk.

(b) **Informed Consent.**
(1) Except as provided in subsection (c), no restorative healing shall be performed without the informed consent of the subject.
(2) Informed consent requires that the practitioner disclose, to the extent reasonably practicable—
(A) the nature and purpose of the proposed healing;
(B) the material risks and potential side effects;
(C) any reasonably available alternatives; and
(D) any known limitations on the effectiveness of the healing.
(3) Consent shall be obtained prior to initiation of the healing unless immediate action is required under subsection (c).

(c) **Emergency Exception.**
(1) Restorative healing may be performed without prior consent where—
(A) the subject is incapable of providing consent; and
(B) failure to act would result in imminent harm or material deterioration of the subject's condition.
(2) In such cases, the practitioner shall limit intervention to that which is necessary to stabilize the subject.

(d) **Limitations on Scope of Healing.**
(1) A practitioner shall not perform restorative magic that exceeds the scope necessary to address the condition being treated.
(2) Restorative healing shall not be used to—
(A) alter the identity or essential characteristics of the subject;

(B) enhance physical or cognitive abilities beyond the subject's prior condition; or
(C) produce outcomes inconsistent with the definition of restorative magic under § 1401.1.

(e) **Risk and Proportionality.**
(1) A practitioner shall not perform restorative healing where the risks of the procedure materially outweigh the anticipated benefits.
(2) The level of intervention shall be proportionate to the severity and urgency of the condition.

(f) **Competency and Qualification.**
(1) A practitioner shall not perform restorative healing beyond the limits of their training, certification, or authorization under Part II.
(2) Where specialized knowledge is required, the practitioner shall refer or defer to a qualified individual.

(g) **Recordkeeping.**
(1) Practitioners shall document restorative healing activities to the extent necessary to permit review and accountability.
(2) Records shall include the nature of the condition treated, the method of healing employed, and any material outcomes or complications.

(h) **Prohibited Conduct.**
No person shall—
(1) perform restorative healing for purposes unrelated to the subject's health or well-being;
(2) misrepresent the capabilities or outcomes of restorative magic; or
(3) knowingly perform healing that conceals, transfers, or redistributes harm to another person or entity.

(i) **Cross-References.**
For definition of restorative magic, see § 1401.1. For reasonable care in spellcasting, see § 101.7. For licensing and certification requirements, see Part II. For negligent spellcasting, see Part XII. For penalties, see § 102.2.

(j) **Historical Annotations.**
This section was enacted under C.C.D. 8564, 47 MR 233, Thu. 12, 1978 to establish ethical standards for healing practices. Amended under C.C.D. 9417, 58 MR 211, Mon. 3, 1998 to incorporate informed consent requirements. Amended under C.C.D. 10112, 71 MR 509, Wed. 14, 2012 to

expand proportionality and risk considerations. Revised under C.C.D. 10588, 78 MR 644, Tue. 9, 2023 to clarify practitioner competency and documentation standards.

§ 1401.3 Restrictions on Magical Repair and Environmental Restoration

(a) **General Rule.**
Restorative magic applied to objects, structures, environments, or magical systems shall be limited to lawful repair or restoration and shall not be used to circumvent regulatory requirements, conceal violations, or produce outcomes inconsistent with the definition of restorative magic under § 1401.1.

(b) **Scope of Permissible Restoration.**
(1) Restoration shall be limited to returning the subject to a prior, stable, or functional condition.
(2) A practitioner shall not use restorative magic to—
(A) improve or enhance beyond the subject's prior condition;
(B) alter the intended function or classification of the subject; or
(C) materially change the structural, environmental, or magical characteristics of the subject.

(c) **Prohibition on Concealment.**
No person shall use restorative magic to—
(1) conceal damage, defects, or noncompliance with this Code;
(2) obscure evidence of prior violations, incidents, or hazardous conditions; or
(3) avoid inspection, reporting, or enforcement requirements.

(d) **Environmental Limitations.**
(1) Restoration of natural or magical environments shall be conducted in a manner that does not disrupt ecological balance or introduce new instability.
(2) A practitioner shall not—
(A) restore conditions in a manner inconsistent with natural or established equilibrium;
(B) introduce foreign materials, energies, or conditions not previously present; or

(C) perform large-scale restoration without appropriate authorization where such restoration may affect surrounding areas.

(e) **Structural and Systemic Integrity.**
(1) Restoration of structures or systems shall ensure that the repaired subject is stable, functional, and safe for its intended use.
(2) Temporary or superficial restoration that fails to address underlying defects shall be prohibited.

(f) **Compliance with Other Requirements.**
Restorative activities shall not be used to bypass applicable licensing, zoning, environmental, or safety requirements under this Code.

(g) **Monitoring and Verification.**
(1) A practitioner shall verify the effectiveness and stability of any restorative work performed.
(2) Where restoration involves significant risk, ongoing monitoring may be required to ensure continued compliance.

(h) **Cross-References.**
For definition of restorative magic, see § 1401.1. For environmental regulations, see Part IX. For magical property and zoning requirements, see Part XXV. For reasonable care in spellcasting, see § 101.7. For penalties, see § 102.2.

(i) **Historical Annotations.**
This section was enacted under C.C.D. 8612, 48 MR 118, Mon. 5, 1979 to regulate restoration of property and environments through magic. Amended under C.C.D. 9498, 59 MR 367, Thu. 22, 2000 to address concealment and inspection avoidance. Amended under C.C.D. 10184, 72 MR 144, Mon. 18, 2014 to incorporate environmental impact limitations. Revised under C.C.D. 10596, 78 MR 701, Fri. 27, 2023 to clarify compliance, monitoring, and verification requirements.

Part XV: Creation of New Spells

§ 1501.1 General Requirements for Creating New Spells

(a) **General Rule.**
No person shall create, develop, or materially modify a spell unless such activity is conducted in accordance with this Code and subject to applicable authorization, oversight, and reporting requirements.

(b) **Authorization and Qualification.**
(1) A person engaging in the creation of new spells shall possess appropriate licensing and, where applicable, certification under Part II and § 201.5.
(2) No person shall develop a spell beyond the scope of their training, authorization, or demonstrated competency.

(c) **Definition of New Spell.**
For purposes of this Part, a "new spell" includes—
(1) any spell not previously recognized, registered, or classified under § 401.1;
(2) any material modification of an existing spell that alters its function, effect, risk profile, or operational requirements; and
(3) any novel combination or sequencing of spells that produces a materially distinct outcome.

(d) **Pre-Development Assessment.**
(1) Prior to initiation, a practitioner shall assess the intended function, potential risks, and foreseeable consequences of the proposed spell.
(2) Such assessment shall consider—
(A) the applicable risk classification under § 401.2;
(B) potential effects on persons, property, and the environment; and
(C) the availability of existing lawful alternatives.

(e) **Controlled Development Environment.**
(1) Creation and testing of new spells shall be conducted in a controlled environment appropriate to the anticipated risk level.

(2) The practitioner shall implement safeguards sufficient to prevent unintended effects, including containment, monitoring, and termination mechanisms.

(f) **Limitations on Development.**
No person shall—
(1) develop a spell that cannot be safely controlled, contained, or terminated;
(2) create a spell intended to evade detection, logging, or regulatory oversight; or
(3) engage in development activities that present a foreseeable and unjustifiable risk of harm.

(g) **Documentation.**
(1) A practitioner shall maintain records of the development process sufficient to permit review, replication, and regulatory evaluation.
(2) Such records shall include the purpose of the spell, methodology, observed effects, and any deviations or failures encountered.

(h) **Initial Classification Requirement.**
(1) Upon development, a new spell shall be provisionally classified under § 401.2 based on its observed or anticipated risk and complexity.
(2) No spell shall be deployed outside a controlled environment until such classification has been determined.

(i) **Cross-References.**
For spellcasting licenses and classification, see § 401.1 and § 401.2. For penalties, see § 102.2.

(j) **Historical Annotations.**
This section was enacted under C.C.D. 8721, 49 MR 118, Tue. 8, 1980 to establish baseline requirements for the development of new spells. Amended under C.C.D. 9567, 60 MR 211, Mon. 11, 2001 to incorporate risk assessment and documentation requirements. Revised under C.C.D. 10584, 78 MR 644, Wed. 12, 2022 to clarify classification procedures and development limitations.

§ 1501.2 Ethical and Safety Standards for New Spells

(a) **General Rule.**
Any person engaged in the creation of new spells shall ensure that such spells are developed, tested, and refined in a manner consistent with the standard of care established under § 101.7 and with due regard for safety, ethical considerations, and foreseeable impacts.

(b) **Risk Minimization.**
(1) A practitioner shall design and test new spells in a manner that minimizes the likelihood of unintended or uncontrolled effects.
(2) Reasonable steps shall be taken to identify and mitigate risks prior to and during testing, including the use of safeguards appropriate to the anticipated risk classification under § 401.2.

(c) **Prohibition on Inherently Unsafe Spells.**
No person shall develop or refine a spell where—
(1) the spell cannot be reliably controlled, contained, or terminated;
(2) the effects of the spell cannot be reasonably predicted or replicated; or
(3) the foreseeable risks of the spell materially outweigh any lawful or practical utility.

(d) **Testing Limitations.**
(1) Testing of new spells shall be conducted only in controlled environments appropriate to the level of risk involved.
(2) A practitioner shall not conduct testing—
(A) in public or unsecured environments;
(B) on unwilling persons or entities; or
(C) in a manner that creates a foreseeable risk of harm to persons, property, or the environment.

(e) **Human and Sentient Subject Protections.**
(1) No new spell shall be tested on a sentient being without that being's informed consent, except as otherwise authorized under this Code.
(2) Additional safeguards shall be required where testing involves vulnerable or protected classes of beings.

(f) **Environmental and Systemic Impact.**

(1) A practitioner shall consider the potential impact of a new spell on magical systems, ecosystems, and surrounding environments.
(2) No spell shall be developed where its use would foreseeably result in widespread disruption, degradation, or instability.

(g) **Deceptive or Evasive Design.**
No person shall develop a spell designed to—
(1) evade detection, logging, or regulatory oversight under this Code;
(2) obscure its true function, effects, or risk profile; or
(3) circumvent restrictions imposed by other provisions of this Code.

(h) **Documentation and Transparency.**
(1) A practitioner shall maintain records sufficient to demonstrate compliance with this section.
(2) Such records shall include testing conditions, observed effects, safety measures, and any known limitations.

(i) **Cross-References.**
For general requirements for creating new spells, see § 1501.1. For spell risk classification, see § 401.2. For negligent spellcasting, see Part XII. For penalties, see § 102.2.

(j) **Historical Annotations.**
This section was enacted under C.C.D. 8764, 49 MR 233, Thu. 15, 1981 to establish safety standards for experimental spell development. Amended under C.C.D. 9602, 60 MR 367, Tue. 17, 2002 to incorporate subject protection and environmental considerations. Revised under C.C.D. 10591, 78 MR 701, Mon. 20, 2023 to clarify prohibitions on unsafe and evasive spell design.

§ 1501.3 Reporting Requirements for Unstable Spell Effects

(a) **General Rule.**
Any person who creates, tests, or otherwise becomes aware of a spell that exhibits unstable, unpredictable, or unintended effects shall report such effects in accordance with this section.

(b) **Reportable Conditions.**
A report shall be required where a spell—

(1) produces effects inconsistent with its intended function;
(2) demonstrates instability in duration, magnitude, or scope;
(3) fails to terminate as expected or resists termination;
(4) propagates, replicates, or spreads beyond its intended parameters; or
(5) creates a substantial risk of harm to persons, property, or the environment.

(c) **Responsible Parties.**
(1) The obligation to report shall apply to—
(A) the practitioner who created or modified the spell;
(B) any person conducting testing or deployment of the spell; and
(C) any supervising individual or entity with knowledge of the unstable effect.
(2) Responsibility under this subsection shall not be avoided by delegation or transfer of control.

(d) **Timing of Report.**
(1) Reports shall be made promptly upon discovery of the unstable condition.
(2) Where the instability presents an immediate risk, the reporting party shall take reasonable steps to contain or mitigate the effects prior to or concurrent with reporting.

(e) **Contents of Report.**
A report shall include, to the extent practicable—
(1) a description of the spell and its intended function;
(2) the conditions under which the instability occurred;
(3) the nature and extent of the unstable effects;
(4) actions taken to contain or mitigate the effects; and
(5) any known or suspected causes of the instability.

(f) **Ongoing Reporting Obligations.**
(1) A reporting party shall provide supplemental information where conditions materially change or new information becomes available.
(2) Continued monitoring shall be required where instability has not been fully resolved.

(g) **Failure to Report.**
Failure to report an unstable spell effect as required under this section may constitute independent evidence of negligent spellcasting under Part XII.

(h) **Cross-References.**
For general requirements for creating new spells, see § 1501.1. For ethical and safety standards, see § 1501.2. For spell risk classification, see § 401.2. For penalties, see § 102.2.

(i) **Historical Annotations.**
This section was enacted under C.C.D. 8812, 50 MR 118, Mon. 19, 1982 to require reporting of unstable magical phenomena. Amended under C.C.D. 9644, 61 MR 211, Wed. 6, 2003 to expand reporting obligations and responsible parties. Revised under C.C.D. 10598, 78 MR 701, Thu. 24, 2023 to clarify timing, content, and ongoing reporting requirements.

§ 1501.4 Magical Copyright and Spell Ownership

(a) **General Rule.**
A spell created in accordance with this Part may be recognized as the intellectual property of the practitioner or entity responsible for its creation, subject to the limitations and requirements of this section.

(b) **Ownership.**
(1) Ownership of a new spell shall vest in the creator upon completion of development, provided that such creation complies with this Code.
(2) Where a spell is created jointly, ownership shall be shared in proportion to each contributor's involvement, unless otherwise agreed.

(c) **Registration Requirement.**
(1) No claim of ownership shall be enforceable unless the spell is registered with the appropriate authority in accordance with applicable procedures.
(2) Registration shall include sufficient detail to identify the spell's function, structure, and distinguishing characteristics.

(d) **Limitations on Ownership.**
No person shall claim ownership of—
(1) a spell derived entirely from existing, commonly known, or publicly available magical practices;
(2) a spell developed in violation of this Code; or
(3) a spell whose effects cannot be reliably reproduced or verified.

(e) **Rights Conferred.**

(1) Ownership shall confer the right to control the use, reproduction, and distribution of the spell, subject to this Code.
(2) Such rights shall not extend to uses required by law, public safety, or authorized governmental functions.

(f) **Disclosure and Compliance.**
(1) Registration and enforcement of ownership shall not exempt a spell from compliance with any applicable safety, ethical, or regulatory requirements.
(2) Authorities may require disclosure of spell details where necessary to ensure compliance with this Code.

(g) **Duration of Protection.**
(1) Ownership rights shall persist for a period determined by applicable regulation or until the spell enters the public domain.
(2) A spell may enter the public domain upon expiration of such period or upon voluntary release by the owner.

(h) **Cross-References.**
For general requirements for creating new spells, see § 1501.1. For ethical and safety standards, see § 1501.2. For reporting requirements, see § 1501.3. For licensing and certification requirements, see Part II. For penalties, see § 102.2.

(i) **Historical Annotations.**
This section was enacted under C.C.D. 8863, 50 MR 233, Thu. 7, 1983 to establish ownership rights in newly created spells. Amended under C.C.D. 9681, 61 MR 367, Mon. 18, 2004 to incorporate registration and limitation requirements. Revised under C.C.D. 10604, 78 MR 701, Mon. 28, 2023 to clarify scope of rights and public domain provisions.

Part XVI: Fire-Based Magic Regulations

§ 1601.1 General Restrictions on Fire-Based Magic

(a) **General Rule.**
No person shall initiate, sustain, or direct fire-based magic except in compliance with this Code and in a manner consistent with the standard of care established under § 101.7.

(b) **Scope.**
This section applies to all spells or magical effects that generate, manipulate, amplify, or otherwise involve heat, flame, combustion, ignition, detonation, or thermally destructive energy, including area-of-effect and sustained combustion phenomena.

(c) **Invocation Compliance.**
(1) Any fire-based spell designated under applicable provisions of this Code requiring formal declaration of authority, including those governed by § 401.1(e), shall not be cast unless such requirements are satisfied prior to initiation.
(2) A practitioner shall ensure that any required invocation is complete, accurate, and contemporaneous with the initiation of the spell.
(3) Where required under applicable provisions of this Code or implementing guidance, a practitioner shall prepare documentation sufficient to evidence compliance with invocation and authorization requirements, and shall complete and file such documentation with the appropriate authority prior to initiation of the spell, except as otherwise provided.
(4) Such documentation shall include, where applicable, Form 1601-FB (Declaration of Fire-Based Spellcasting Authority) and Form 1601-R (Fire Event Risk and Containment Assessment), or any successor forms prescribed by the Department of Magical Affairs.
(5) Where prior filing is not practicable due to exigent circumstances, a practitioner may initiate the spell without prior filing, provided that all required documentation is completed and filed as soon as reasonably practicable thereafter, and in no event later than the close of the next business day.

(6) Failure to comply with required invocation procedures or associated documentation and filing requirements shall constitute a violation of this section irrespective of whether the underlying spell would otherwise be authorized.

(d) **Control of Propagation.**
(1) A practitioner shall maintain continuous control over the spread, intensity, and duration of any fire-based effect.
(2) No fire-based magic shall be cast in a manner that permits uncontrolled expansion beyond the intended area of effect.
(3) The practitioner shall anticipate and account for secondary propagation, including ignition of surrounding materials, thermal conduction, and interaction with ambient magical conditions.

(e) **Environmental and Situational Constraints.**
(1) Fire-based magic shall not be initiated in environments where conditions materially increase the risk of uncontrolled spread, including areas containing—
(A) flammable or explosive materials;
(B) unstable magical fields; or
(C) confined spaces lacking adequate containment or ventilation.
(2) A practitioner shall evaluate weather, terrain, and ambient magical interference prior to casting.

(f) **Containment Requirements.**
(1) A practitioner shall implement measures sufficient to confine fire-based effects to the intended area of impact.
(2) Such measures shall include, where appropriate—
(A) physical or magical barriers;
(B) suppression or dampening systems; and
(C) predefined containment thresholds beyond which the spell shall be terminated.

(g) **Termination Capability.**
(1) No fire-based spell shall be initiated unless the practitioner possesses the means and ability to promptly extinguish, neutralize, or otherwise terminate the effect.
(2) Termination measures shall be appropriate to the scale and intensity of the spell and shall remain available for the duration of the effect.

(h) **Limitations Based on Risk Classification.**

(1) Fire-based spells shall be subject to classification under § 401.2.
(2) High-risk or complex fire-based spells shall not be performed outside controlled environments unless expressly authorized.
(3) Where a spell's risk classification is uncertain, it shall be treated as the highest plausible risk level until properly classified.

(i) **Cross-References.**
For reasonable care in spellcasting, see § 101.7. For spellcasting licenses and classification of spells, see § 401.1 and § 401.2. For negligent spellcasting, see Part XII. For penalties, see § 102.2.

(j) **Historical Annotations.**
This section was enacted under C.C.D. 8921, 52 MR 118, Tue. 4, 1984 to regulate the use of fire-based magic. Amended under C.C.D. 9722, 62 MR 211, Wed. 23, 2005 to incorporate risk classification requirements. Amended under C.C.D. 10094, 70 MR 402, Mon. 9, 2011 to address propagation and containment standards. Revised under C.C.D. 10487, 76 MR 509, Mon. 18, 2019 to clarify invocation compliance and termination obligations.

§ 1601.2 Ethical Use and Safety Protocols

(a) **General Rule.**
Fire-based magic shall be performed only where its use is necessary, proportionate, and consistent with the safety of persons, property, and the surrounding environment.

(b) **Necessity and Alternatives.**
(1) A practitioner shall not employ fire-based magic where a less destructive or lower-risk alternative is reasonably available.
(2) The selection of fire-based magic shall be justified by the nature of the objective and the absence of safer, practicable alternatives.

(c) **Proportionality of Force and Effect.**
(1) The intensity, duration, and area of effect of a fire-based spell shall be proportionate to the intended objective.
(2) Excessive or indiscriminate use of fire-based magic is prohibited.

(d) **Protection of Persons.**
(1) A practitioner shall take all reasonable measures to prevent injury to any person within or near the area of effect.

(2) Fire-based magic shall not be directed toward persons except where authorized under applicable provisions of this Code.
(3) Where individuals are present, the practitioner shall provide warning or take steps to ensure evacuation where practicable.

(e) **Protection of Property and Infrastructure.**
(1) A practitioner shall avoid unnecessary damage to property, structures, and infrastructure.
(2) Where damage is foreseeable, the practitioner shall implement measures to limit, contain, or mitigate such damage.
(3) Critical infrastructure and regulated magical systems shall not be subjected to fire-based effects absent express authorization.

(f) **Operational Safeguards.**
A practitioner shall—
(1) assess environmental, structural, and magical conditions prior to casting;
(2) maintain continuous oversight and control over the spell;
(3) monitor for secondary effects, including delayed ignition or structural degradation; and
(4) be prepared to implement immediate corrective or termination measures.

(g) **Post-Use Responsibilities.**
(1) Following use, a practitioner shall ensure that all residual heat, flame, or related effects have been fully neutralized.
(2) The practitioner shall verify that no latent conditions remain that could result in delayed ignition or hazard.
(3) Any resulting damage or hazard shall be addressed promptly and in accordance with applicable reporting and remediation requirements.

(h) **Duty to Mitigate and Report.**
(1) Where fire-based magic results in unintended effects or damage, the practitioner shall take reasonable steps to mitigate such effects.
(2) Reportable incidents shall be addressed in accordance with § 1201.5.

(i) **Cross-References.**
For general restrictions on fire-based magic, see § 1601.1. For reasonable care in spellcasting, see § 101.7. For exemptions in self-defense or

emergencies, see Part VI. For negligent spellcasting, see Part XII. For penalties, see § 102.2.

(j) **Historical Annotations.**
This section was enacted under C.C.D. 8964, 52 MR 233, Thu. 18, 1985 to establish ethical standards for fire-based spellcasting. Amended under C.C.D. 9761, 63 MR 211, Mon. 11, 2006 to incorporate proportionality and safety requirements. Amended under C.C.D. 10137, 71 MR 288, Tue. 6, 2012 to expand protections for persons and property. Revised under C.C.D. 10492, 76 MR 509, Thu. 21, 2019 to clarify operational safeguards and post-use responsibilities.

§ 1601.3 Environmental Impact of Fire-Based Magic

(a) **Additional Regulatory Requirements.**
The provisions of this section establish additional requirements applicable specifically to fire-based magic. Compliance with this section shall be required in addition to, and shall not be construed to satisfy or replace, any obligations imposed under Part IX or other applicable provisions of this Code.

(b) **Pre-Casting Environmental Risk Determination.**
Prior to initiating fire-based magic, a practitioner shall determine whether the proposed activity presents a heightened risk of environmental impact, taking into account the nature of combustion, propagation potential, and interaction with surrounding conditions.

(c) **Heightened Risk Standard.**
A heightened environmental risk shall be deemed to exist where a reasonable practitioner, exercising reasonable care under § 101.7, would conclude that the fire-based activity is likely to—
(1) propagate beyond the intended area of effect due to fuel sources, terrain, or atmospheric conditions;
(2) produce sustained or self-reinforcing combustion;
(3) generate heat or energy sufficient to alter surrounding environmental conditions; or
(4) interact unpredictably with magical systems or resource networks regulated under Part IX.

(d) **Environmental Impact Declaration.**
(1) Where a heightened risk is identified under subsection (c), the practitioner shall prepare a written Environmental Impact Declaration prior to casting.
(2) The declaration shall include—
(A) anticipated propagation pathways and boundaries of effect;
(B) identification of environmental conditions relevant to ignition, spread, and persistence;
(C) analysis of worst-case expansion scenarios; and
(D) specific containment, suppression, and termination measures designed to address such risks.

(e) **Pre-Casting Approval.**
(1) No fire-based activity subject to subsection (d) shall be conducted unless the Environmental Impact Declaration has been approved by an authorized body under Part II or Part IX.
(2) Approval shall be based on a determination that the proposed activity can be contained and controlled under reasonably foreseeable conditions.
(3) The approving authority may impose operational limitations, geographic restrictions, or monitoring requirements tailored to fire-based risks.

(f) **Enhanced Safeguards for Propagating Effects.**
Where a fire-based spell is reasonably expected to exhibit sustained, spreading, or self-propagating characteristics, the practitioner shall implement heightened safeguards, including redundant containment and termination measures sufficient to address loss of primary control.

(g) **Operational Constraints.**
Fire-based magic subject to this section shall be conducted only under conditions that permit continuous observation and intervention, and shall not be initiated where environmental factors materially impair the practitioner's ability to maintain control.

(h) **Remediation Readiness.**
Prior to casting, the practitioner shall ensure that sufficient resources, personnel, and capabilities are available to address potential environmental consequences arising from the fire-based activity.

(i) **Cross-References.**

For reasonable care in spellcasting, see § 101.7. For resource conservation and environmental regulations, see Part IX. For restorative magic, see Part XIV. For reporting environmental impacts, see § 901.3. For penalties, see § 102.2.

(j) **Historical Annotations.**
This section was enacted under C.C.D. 9011, 53 MR 118, Mon. 9, 1986 to establish fire-specific environmental safeguards. Amended under C.C.D. 9793, 63 MR 367, Thu. 7, 2006 to address propagation and containment risks unique to combustion-based magic. Amended under C.C.D. 10189, 72 MR 144, Wed. 20, 2014 to introduce pre-casting environmental review requirements. Revised under C.C.D. 10572, 78 MR 701, Tue. 3, 2023 to refine heightened risk standards and approval procedures.

Part XVII: Enchantments

§ 1701.1 General Rules for Enchantments

(a) **General Rule.**
No person shall create, affix, embed, transfer, or maintain an enchantment except in accordance with this section and applicable provisions of this Code.

(b) **Definition and Scope.**
For purposes of this Part, an enchantment is a persistent or conditionally persistent magical effect applied to an object, structure, or system that alters its behavior, properties, or function beyond its natural or unenchanted state. This includes passive, triggered, cyclical, and self-sustaining effects.

(c) **Attachment and Integration.**
(1) An enchantment shall be securely affixed to its subject in a manner that ensures predictable operation under normal conditions of use.
(2) No person shall apply an enchantment that interferes with the structural or functional integrity of the underlying object or system.
(3) Enchantments applied to complex systems shall account for all relevant components and interactions.

(d) **Defined Function and Parameters.**
(1) An enchantment shall have a clearly defined function and operational scope.
(2) A practitioner shall define, prior to application—
(A) activation conditions;
(B) duration or persistence;
(C) limits on intensity, frequency, or effect; and
(D) termination conditions.
(3) Enchantments lacking defined parameters sufficient to permit control and understanding shall be prohibited.

(e) **Disclosure and Notice.**

(1) Any person placing an enchanted object into use, transfer, or circulation shall disclose the existence of the enchantment and its general function.
(2) Disclosure shall be sufficient to inform a reasonable user of any material effects on operation, safety, or use.
(3) Failure to disclose a material enchantment shall constitute a violation of this section.

(f) **Consistency of Operation.**
(1) An enchantment shall operate consistently with its defined or represented function.
(2) No person shall create or apply an enchantment that produces materially misleading, deceptive, or inconsistent effects.

(g) **Limitations on Scope.**
No enchantment shall—
(1) operate beyond its defined parameters;
(2) produce uncontrolled or self-modifying effects; or
(3) materially alter the nature of a person or entity in a manner governed by other Parts of this Code.

(h) **Transfer and Responsibility.**
(1) The person applying an enchantment shall remain responsible for its compliance at the time of creation and placement into use.
(2) Subsequent holders shall not relieve the original practitioner of liability for defects existing at the time of transfer.

(i) **Cross-References.**
For regulation of magical objects and artifacts, see Part VIII. For negligent spellcasting, see Part XII. For penalties, see § 102.2.

(j) **Historical Annotations.**
This section was enacted under C.C.D. 9054, 53 MR 233, Thu. 17, 1987 to establish baseline requirements for enchantments. Amended under C.C.D. 9689, 61 MR 402, Mon. 5, 2003 to address disclosure and transfer obligations. Revised under C.C.D. 10412, 75 MR 288, Wed. 11, 2017 to clarify operational parameters and practitioner responsibility.

§ 1701.2 Enchantment Safety Protocols

(a) **General Rule.**

All enchantments shall be designed, applied, and maintained to operate safely under reasonably foreseeable conditions of use, misuse, and environmental interaction.

(b) **Design and Risk Evaluation.**
(1) Prior to application, a practitioner shall evaluate the risks associated with the proposed enchantment.
(2) Such evaluation shall consider—
(A) potential for unintended activation;
(B) interaction with environmental conditions;
(C) interaction with other magical effects; and
(D) consequences of malfunction or failure.

(c) **Activation Controls.**
(1) Enchantments shall include defined activation conditions sufficient to prevent unintended or accidental triggering.
(2) Where appropriate, activation shall require deliberate input, defined thresholds, or identifiable triggering events.

(d) **Fail-Safe and Override Mechanisms.**
(1) Enchantments shall include mechanisms allowing for interruption, suppression, or termination.
(2) Such mechanisms shall be accessible and effective under conditions where the enchantment deviates from its intended operation.
(3) No enchantment shall bc applied where no reasonably effective termination method exists.

(e) **Interaction Controls.**
(1) Enchantments shall be evaluated for compatibility with other magical effects, systems, or environments.
(2) Where interaction risks exist, the practitioner shall implement safeguards to prevent instability, amplification, or unintended combined effects.

(f) **Durability and Degradation.**
(1) Enchantments shall be designed to account for degradation over time, including wear, environmental exposure, and magical interference.
(2) A practitioner shall ensure that degradation does not result in unsafe or unpredictable behavior.

(g) **Inspection and Maintenance.**

(1) Enchantments shall be subject to inspection at intervals appropriate to their complexity, risk, and use.
(2) Where inspection reveals instability or deviation from defined parameters, corrective action shall be taken promptly.

(h) **Context of Use.**
(1) An enchantment shall not be applied in a context where its operation creates unreasonable risk based on the environment or expected use.
(2) A practitioner shall consider foreseeable misuse or unintended use in determining appropriate safeguards.

(i) **Cross-References.**
For general rules for enchantments, see § 1701.1. For regulation of magical objects, see Part VIII. For negligent spellcasting, see Part XII. For penalties, see § 102.2.

(j) **Historical Annotations.**
This section was enacted under C.C.D. 9092, 54 MR 118, Mon. 6, 1988 to establish safety protocols for enchantments. Amended under C.C.D. 9726, 62 MR 288, Tue. 19, 2004 to incorporate risk evaluation and fail-safe requirements. Revised under C.C.D. 10418, 75 MR 288, Fri. 15, 2017 to clarify inspection, maintenance, and interaction controls.

Part XVIII: Curses

§ 1801.1 General Ban on Curses

(a) **General Rule.**
No person shall create, place, invoke, transmit, or maintain a curse except as expressly authorized under this Code.

(b) **Definition of Curse.**
For purposes of this Part, a curse is any magical effect intended to impose harm, impairment, disadvantage, compulsion, deterioration, or other adverse condition upon a person, entity, object, or system, whether immediate, delayed, conditional, or continuous.

(c) **Scope of Prohibition.**
The prohibition under subsection (a) applies to—
(1) direct curses imposed on a target;
(2) conditional or triggered curses;
(3) curses affixed to objects, locations, or systems; and
(4) any magical effect designed to function as a curse regardless of terminology used.

(d) **Prohibited Conduct.**
No person shall—
(1) create or apply a curse intended to cause physical, mental, or magical harm;
(2) impose a curse that restricts or compels behavior outside lawful authority;
(3) place a curse on any object, structure, or environment in a manner that creates a risk to unintended persons or entities; or
(4) transfer, sell, or distribute any cursed object or effect.

(e) **Circumvention Prohibited.**
No person shall avoid the application of this section by labeling, structuring, or describing a magical effect in a manner intended to obscure its nature as a curse.

(f) **Possession and Maintenance.**

(1) No person shall knowingly maintain or allow a curse to persist where such person has the ability to remove or neutralize it.
(2) Upon discovery of a curse, a person shall take reasonable steps to mitigate, contain, or report the condition in accordance with this Code.

(g) **Voidness of Unauthorized Curses.**
Any curse created or applied in violation of this section shall be deemed unlawful and without legal effect for purposes of enforcement or recognition under this Code.

(h) **Cross-References.**
For enchantments, see Part XVII. For mind-control magic, see Part XXI. For negligent spellcasting, see Part XII. For penalties, see § 102.2.

(i) **Historical Annotations.**
This section was enacted under C.C.D. 9156, 55 MR 118, Tue. 2, 1989 to prohibit harmful magical practices. Amended under C.C.D. 9754, 63 MR 288, Thu. 10, 2005 to expand the scope of prohibited conduct and circumvention. Revised under C.C.D. 10433, 75 MR 402, Mon. 6, 2018 to clarify possession, maintenance, and enforcement provisions.

§ 1801.2 Exceptions for Legal or Protective Curses

(a) **Authorized Exceptions.**
Notwithstanding § 1801.1, a curse may be created or applied where expressly authorized under this section for legal, protective, or security purposes.

(b) **Permissible Uses.**
Authorized curses may include—
(1) protective curses designed to deter or prevent unauthorized access, intrusion, or interference;
(2) enforcement-related curses imposed pursuant to lawful authority;
(3) conditional curses intended to secure compliance with lawful obligations; and
(4) narrowly tailored nuisance-abatement curses to compel removal of refuse or similar persistent non-compliant conditions affecting adjacent property or shared environments (e.g., if you keep leaving your trash bins out all day, this is for you, Mark).

(c) **Authorization Requirement.**

(1) No curse shall be applied under this section without appropriate authorization under Part II or other applicable provisions of this Code.
(2) Authorization shall define the scope, duration, and permissible effects of the curse.

(d) **Limitations on Effect.**
(1) A curse authorized under this section shall be limited to the minimum effect necessary to achieve its lawful purpose.
(2) No authorized curse shall—
(A) cause unnecessary or disproportionate harm;
(B) operate beyond its defined parameters; or
(C) affect persons or entities not reasonably within its intended scope.

(e) **Control and Termination.**
(1) An authorized curse shall include defined conditions for activation, operation, and termination.
(2) A practitioner shall ensure that the curse can be removed, deactivated, or otherwise neutralized upon fulfillment of its purpose or expiration of authorization.

(f) **Notice and Disclosure.**
(1) Where practicable, persons subject to an authorized curse shall be provided notice of its existence and general effect.
(2) Lack of notice shall not invalidate the curse where such notice would defeat its lawful purpose.

(g) **Prohibition on Abuse.**
No person shall use an authorized curse—
(1) for purposes unrelated to its authorized objective; or
(2) in a manner that expands its effect beyond the scope of authorization.

(h) **Cross-References.**
For general prohibition on curses, see § 1801.1. For mind-control magic, see Part XXI. For penalties, see § 102.2.

(i) **Historical Annotations.**
This section was enacted under C.C.D. 9198, 55 MR 233, Thu. 14, 1990 to permit limited use of curses for protective purposes. Amended under C.C.D. 9788, 63 MR 367, Mon. 21, 2006 to expand authorized uses and impose limitations. Revised under C.C.D. 10441, 75 MR 402, Thu. 9, 2018 to clarify authorization, control, and notice requirements.

Part XIX: Magical Duels

§ 1901.1 Definition of Magical Duels

(a) **General Rule.**
For purposes of this Code, a magical duel is a structured or agreed-upon engagement between two or more practitioners involving the use of magic in opposition to one another.

(b) **Elements of a Duel.**
A magical duel shall be deemed to exist where—
(1) two or more participants knowingly engage in adversarial spellcasting;
(2) such engagement is conducted pursuant to mutual acknowledgment or acceptance; and
(3) the activity is bounded by defined or reasonably understood parameters.

(c) **Forms of Duels.**
Magical duels may include—
(1) formal duels conducted under established rules or supervision;
(2) informal or spontaneous duels where mutual participation is evident; and
(3) structured competitive engagements involving magical opposition.

(d) **Exclusions.**
A magical duel shall not include—
(1) unilateral acts of aggression or assault;
(2) spellcasting conducted without the knowledge or consent of the opposing party; or
(3) engagements governed exclusively by other provisions of this Code, including warfare or law enforcement actions.

(e) **Mutual Participation.**
(1) Consent to participate in a duel may be express or implied through conduct.
(2) A participant may withdraw from a duel at any time, and continued engagement after withdrawal shall not constitute a lawful duel.

(f) **Classification.**

All magical duels shall be subject to classification and regulation under applicable provisions of this Code, including risk-based limitations and oversight requirements.

(g) **Cross-References.**
For spellcasting regulations, see Part IV. For limitations and exemptions, see Part VI. For negligent spellcasting, see Part XII. For penalties, see § 102.2.

(h) **Historical Annotations.**
This section was enacted under C.C.D. 9231, 56 MR 118, Mon. 11, 1991 to define and distinguish lawful magical duels from unlawful acts. Amended under C.C.D. 9812, 63 MR 402, Tue. 3, 2007 to clarify mutual participation and exclusions. Revised under C.C.D. 10455, 75 MR 509, Thu. 22, 2018 to refine classification and scope.

§ 1901.2 Rules of Engagement for Duels

(a) **General Rule.**
Magical duels shall be conducted in a controlled and orderly manner consistent with this section.

(b) **Consent and Initiation.**
(1) No person shall initiate or continue a duel without the mutual participation of all involved parties.
(2) Consent may be withdrawn at any time, and all participants shall immediately cease engagement upon withdrawal.

(c) **Permissible Conduct.**
Participants in a magical duel may engage in adversarial spellcasting within the bounds of the agreed or established parameters of the duel.

(d) **Prohibited Conduct.**
No participant shall—
(1) employ magic intended to cause death or irreversible harm unless expressly authorized under applicable provisions of this Code;
(2) engage in conduct that creates unreasonable risk to persons not participating in the duel;
(3) use prohibited magical practices or effects restricted under other Parts of this Code; or

(4) continue engagement after the duel has been terminated or consent has been withdrawn.

(e) **Location and Conditions.**
(1) Duels shall not be conducted in locations where the activity creates a foreseeable risk to the public or surrounding environment.
(2) Participants shall ensure that the chosen location permits safe conduct and containment of the duel.

(f) **Control and Termination.**
(1) Participants shall maintain control over their actions and magical effects throughout the duel.
(2) A duel shall terminate upon—
(A) withdrawal of consent by any participant;
(B) incapacitation of a participant; or
(C) achievement of the agreed-upon outcome.
(3) Upon termination, all participants shall cease spellcasting and take reasonable steps to neutralize any ongoing effects.

(g) **Responsibility and Liability.**
Participation in a duel shall not relieve any person of responsibility for violations of this Code or for harm resulting from conduct exceeding the scope of lawful engagement.

(h) **Cross-References.**
For definition of magical duels, see § 1901.1. For spellcasting regulations, see Part IV. For limitations and exemptions, see Part VI. For negligent spellcasting, see Part XII. For penalties, see § 102.2.

(i) **Historical Annotations.**
This section was enacted under C.C.D. 9274, 56 MR 233, Thu. 26, 1992 to establish rules governing magical duels. Amended under C.C.D. 9841, 64 MR 402, Mon. 19, 2008 to expand safety and termination requirements. Revised under C.C.D. 10462, 75 MR 509, Tue. 27, 2018 to clarify permissible conduct and participant responsibility.

Part XX: Transfiguration Regulations

§ 2001.1 Authorized Transfiguration Practices

(a) **General Rule.**
No person shall perform transfiguration except as authorized under this section and in accordance with applicable provisions of this Code.

(b) **Definition and Scope.**
Transfiguration, as defined under § 101.1, refers to the school of magic involving the alteration of the form, composition, structure, or essential properties of an object, substance, or being, whether temporarily or permanently.

(c) **Authorized Practices.**
Transfiguration shall be authorized only where—
(1) the practitioner possesses appropriate authorization under Part II;
(2) the intended transformation is capable of being defined, controlled, and, where required, reversed; and
(3) the activity complies with applicable limitations set forth in this Part and elsewhere in this Code.

(d) **Permissible Applications.**
Authorized transfiguration practices may include—
(1) alteration of non-living objects for functional or practical purposes;
(2) temporary modification of materials or structures;
(3) controlled transformation for educational, research, or demonstration purposes; and
(4) other uses consistent with lawful objectives and defined operational parameters.

(e) **Defined Parameters.**
(1) Prior to initiating transfiguration, a practitioner shall establish the scope, duration, and intended outcome of the transformation.
(2) No transfiguration shall be performed where the resulting state cannot be reasonably anticipated or controlled.

(f) **Limitations on Practice.**
No person shall perform transfiguration that—

(1) exceeds the practitioner's level of authorization or competency;
(2) produces effects that cannot be contained or reversed where required; or
(3) interferes with regulated systems, property, or persons in violation of other provisions of this Code.

(g) **Consistency and Stability.**
(1) Transfigured states shall remain stable for the duration of the intended effect.
(2) A practitioner shall not create or maintain a transformation that degrades, mutates, or evolves in an uncontrolled manner.

(h) **Responsibility for Outcomes.**
The practitioner performing the transfiguration shall remain responsible for ensuring that the resulting state complies with this Code for the duration of the effect.

(i) **Cross-References.**
For definitions of schools of magic, see § 101.1. For licensing requirements, see Part II. For spellcasting regulations, see Part IV. For negligent spellcasting, see Part XII. For penalties, see § 102.2.

(j) **Historical Annotations.**
This section was enacted under C.C.D. 9312, 57 MR 118, Mon. 8, 1993 to establish authorized uses of transfiguration. Amended under C.C.D. 9879, 64 MR 509, Thu. 24, 2009 to clarify permissible applications and defined parameters. Revised under C.C.D. 10478, 76 MR 118, Tue. 12, 2021 to refine stability and practitioner responsibility requirements.

§ 2001.2 Restrictions on Transfiguring Living Beings

(a) **General Rule.**
No person shall transfigure a living being except as expressly permitted under this section.

(b) **Scope.**
This section applies to any transfiguration affecting a living being's physical form, biological structure, cognitive function, or essential characteristics, whether temporary or permanent.

(c) **Prohibited Conduct.**
No person shall—
(1) transfigure a living being in a manner that causes permanent or irreversible alteration, except where expressly authorized under this Code;
(2) alter a living being in a manner that compromises viability, stability, or the ability to revert to its original state;
(3) transfigure a living being into an inanimate object or non-living state; or
(4) perform transfiguration resulting in loss of identity, continuity, or recognizability as defined under § 101.9.

(d) **Conditional Permissibility.**
Transfiguration of a living being may be permitted where—
(1) the effect is temporary and reversible;
(2) the parameters of the transformation are defined in advance; and
(3) the practitioner maintains continuous ability to control and reverse the transformation.

(e) **Heightened Limitations.**
(1) Transfiguration affecting internal structure, cognition, or essential biological function shall be subject to heightened limitations and shall not be performed absent clearly defined safeguards.
(2) No transfiguration shall impair the subject's ability to survive, function, or return to its original state.

(f) **Unintended or Secondary Effects.**
No transfiguration shall be performed where foreseeable secondary effects may result in instability, mutation, or degradation of the living being.

(g) **Cross-References.**
For authorized transfiguration practices, see § 2001.1. For identity and continuity, see § 101.9. For ethical and consent requirements, see § 2001.3. For negligent spellcasting, see Part XII. For penalties, see § 102.2.

(h) **Historical Annotations.**
This section was enacted under C.C.D. 9351, 57 MR 233, Thu. 22, 1994 to regulate transfiguration involving living beings. Amended under C.C.D. 9912, 65 MR 118, Mon. 17, 2010 to introduce limitations on reversibility and identity. Revised under C.C.D. 10484, 76 MR 118, Fri. 16, 2021 to clarify prohibited conduct and operational limitations.

§ 2001.3 Ethical Boundaries and Consent in Transfiguration

(a) **General Rule.**
No person shall perform transfiguration affecting a living being without lawful basis and, where required under this section, valid consent.

(b) **Requirement of Consent.**
(1) Except as otherwise authorized, transfiguration of a living being shall require the informed consent of the subject.
(2) Consent shall be obtained prior to the initiation of the transfiguration and shall be specific to the nature and scope of the transformation.

(c) **Informed Consent Standard.**
Consent shall be deemed informed only where the subject is provided, in a manner reasonably understandable—
(1) a description of the intended transformation;
(2) the expected duration and reversibility of the effect;
(3) reasonably foreseeable risks and limitations; and
(4) any conditions under which the effect may persist or terminate.

(d) **Capacity to Consent.**
(1) Consent shall be valid only where the subject possesses the capacity to understand and evaluate the nature of the transfiguration.
(2) Consent obtained through coercion, deception, or impairment shall be invalid.

(e) **Third-Party Authorization.**
Where a subject lacks capacity, transfiguration may be performed only where consent is obtained from a legally authorized representative and the action is consistent with the subject's welfare and applicable provisions of this Code.

(f) **Prohibited Circumvention.**
No person shall use illusion, mind-control, or similar means to obtain or simulate consent for purposes of this section.

(g) **Withdrawal of Consent.**
(1) A subject may withdraw consent at any time prior to or during the transfiguration, including where transformed into an object. For example,

if a subject has been transfigured into a lampshade and begins emitting sustained or intermittent screams, such manifestation shall be treated as withdrawal.
(2) Upon withdrawal, the practitioner shall cease the transfiguration and take appropriate steps to terminate or reverse the effect where feasible.

(h) **Limitations.**
Nothing in this section shall be construed to permit transfiguration otherwise prohibited under § 2001.2 or other provisions of this Code.

(i) **Cross-References.**
For restrictions on transfiguring living beings, see § 2001.2. For mind-control restrictions, see Part XXI. For negligent spellcasting, see Part XII. For penalties, see § 102.2.

(j) **Historical Annotations.**
This section was enacted under C.C.D. 9388, 58 MR 118, Mon. 3, 1995 to establish consent requirements for transfiguration. Amended under C.C.D. 9941, 65 MR 233, Thu. 21, 2011 to clarify informed consent and capacity standards. Revised under C.C.D. 10491, 76 MR 118, Tue. 20, 2021 to address coercion, withdrawal, and third-party authorization.

§ 2001.4 Legal Uses and Economic Impacts of Transfiguration

(a) **General Rule.**
No person shall use transfiguration in trade, commerce, valuation, exchange, recordkeeping, or other economic activity in a manner that conceals, distorts, or misrepresents the nature, condition, quantity, utility, origin, or value of any person, good, service, asset, or property interest.

(b) **Commercial Use of Transfiguration.**
(1) Transfiguration may be used in commercial activity only where the resulting condition of the item, asset, or subject is accurately represented to all parties whose rights or obligations are affected.
(2) A person offering, selling, leasing, exchanging, pledging, consigning, or otherwise transferring a transfigured item shall disclose, to the extent material to the transaction—
(A) that the item has been transfigured;

(B) the nature and extent of the transfiguration;
(C) whether the transfiguration is temporary, conditional, or subject to reversal;
(D) any known limitations on durability, function, or marketability resulting from the transfiguration; and
(E) any conditions under which the item may revert, degrade, or cease to function in the transfigured state.

(c) **Prohibition on Misrepresentation.**
No person shall use transfiguration to—
(1) represent one material, substance, or object as another for purposes of inducing reliance;
(2) simulate rarity, age, craftsmanship, provenance, composition, purity, or authenticity that the item does not in fact possess;
(3) conceal defects, damage, contamination, prior use, prior alteration, or diminished functionality;
(4) misstate quantity, volume, weight, or quality for purposes of pricing, taxation, customs, accounting, or inventory; or
(5) cause an item to appear compliant with legal, safety, or market standards when it is not.

(d) **Temporary Value Manipulation.**
(1) No person shall use transfiguration to create a temporary appearance of value for purposes of sale, financing, collateralization, insurance, taxation, or financial reporting without full disclosure of the underlying condition and the expected duration of the transfigured state.
(2) A transfigured item shall not be valued as though the transfigured state were permanent unless such permanence is lawful, stable, and verifiable.

(e) **Impact on Regulated Markets and Financial Systems.**
No person shall use transfiguration in a manner that—
(1) interferes with market pricing or valuation mechanisms;
(2) alters the apparent character of a magical asset for purposes of avoiding regulation under Part X; or
(3) distorts inventory, production, or supply records.

(f) **Books, Records, and Documentation.**

(1) Any person using transfiguration in commerce shall maintain records sufficient to show the original condition, nature of the transfiguration, duration, and disclosures made.
(2) Records shall be retained for a period sufficient to permit audit, review, and enforcement under this Code.

(g) **Cross-References.**
For transfer and sale of magical objects, see § 801.3. For magical financial fraud and currency manipulation, see § 1001.1. For financial fraud through transfiguration magic, see § 1001.5. For penalties, see § 102.2.

(h) **Historical Annotations.**
This section was enacted under C.C.D. 412, 9 MR 77, Tue. 3, 1624 to regulate early mercantile abuses involving transmutation of goods. Amended under C.C.D. 1833, 22 MR 301, Fri. 14, 1789 to address valuation distortions in trade markets. Amended under C.C.D. 7721, 48 MR 144, Mon. 9, 1982 to incorporate disclosure requirements. Revised under C.C.D. 10497, 76 MR 233, Wed. 27, 2021 to clarify recordkeeping and financial system impacts.

§ 2001.5 Reversibility and Responsibility in Transfiguration

(a) **General Rule.**
Except as otherwise expressly authorized under this Code, all transfiguration shall be reversible and shall be performed only where the practitioner has established a lawful, stable, and practicable means of reversal.

(b) **Reversibility Requirement.**
(1) A practitioner shall not initiate transfiguration unless the means of reversal are known in advance and capable of execution under reasonably foreseeable conditions.
(2) Reversal shall restore the subject to its original state or the nearest lawful and stable condition consistent with this Code.

(c) **Defined Duration and Termination Conditions.**
(1) A practitioner shall define the duration of the transfiguration or the conditions under which reversal shall occur.

(2) Indefinite or open-ended transfiguration shall be prohibited unless expressly authorized and supported by additional safeguards.

(d) **Maintenance of Reversible State.**
No person shall maintain a transfiguration in a condition that materially increases the difficulty, danger, or uncertainty of reversal.

(e) **Failure to Reverse.**
A violation occurs where a person—
(1) fails to reverse a transfiguration within its defined duration;
(2) allows a transfigured state to persist after its lawful basis has ended; or
(3) initiates transfiguration without retaining the capability necessary for reversal.

(f) **Intervening Conditions.**
External interference or changed conditions shall not excuse noncompliance where such conditions were reasonably foreseeable.

(g) **Additional Restrictions for Living Beings.**
Transfiguration affecting living beings shall remain subject to § 2001.2 and § 2001.3.

(h) **Cross-References.**
For authorized transfiguration practices, see § 2001.1. For restrictions on living beings, see § 2001.2. For consent requirements, see § 2001.3. For penalties, see § 102.2.

(i) **Historical Annotations.**
This section was enacted under C.C.D. 588, 11 MR 204, Mon. 6, 1687 following widespread incidents of irreversible alchemical transformations. Amended under C.C.D. 2641, 31 MR 88, Thu. 22, 1821 to require defined duration. Amended under C.C.D. 8892, 52 MR 301, Tue. 14, 1985 to clarify failure-to-reverse violations. Revised under C.C.D. 10503, 76 MR 233, Fri. 29, 2021 to address modern stability and control concerns.

§ 2001.6 Regulation of Transfigured Objects and Beings

(a) **General Rule.**

Any object or being subject to transfiguration shall remain regulated under this Code for the duration of the transfigured state.

(b) **Regulatory Status During Transfiguration.**
(1) A transfigured object or being shall be evaluated by reference to both its original nature and its present condition where relevant.
(2) No person shall use transfiguration to avoid classification, licensing, inspection, or safety requirements.

(c) **Treatment of Transfigured Objects.**
(1) A transfigured object shall not be used or transferred in a manner inconsistent with its original nature or regulatory status.
(2) No person shall represent a transfigured object as wholly distinct where such representation affects legality or safety.

(d) **Treatment of Transfigured Living Beings.**
(1) A living being subject to transfiguration shall retain all protections applicable to living beings under this Code.
(2) No person shall treat a transfigured being as an object to avoid legal obligations.

(e) **Identification and Traceability.**
(1) Transfigured subjects shall be identifiable where necessary for safety or enforcement.
(2) Sufficient information shall be maintained to determine original state and applicable conditions.

(f) **Use Restrictions.**
No transfigured subject shall be used in a manner that would be unlawful if its original condition were known.

(g) **Cross-References.**
For authorized transfiguration practices, see § 2001.1. For reversibility requirements, see § 2001.5. For regulation of magical objects, see Part VIII. For identity continuity, see § 101.9. For penalties, see § 102.2.

(h) **Historical Annotations.**
This section was enacted under C.C.D. 721, 14 MR 119, Wed. 12, 1712 to address classification disputes involving altered goods and persons. Amended under C.C.D. 3017, 36 MR 402, Mon. 3, 1854 to incorporate traceability requirements. Amended under C.C.D. 9122, 54 MR 233, Thu.

8, 1988 to clarify treatment of living beings. Revised under C.C.D. 10511, 76 MR 233, Tue. 2, 2022 to refine regulatory treatment and identification standards.

Part XXI: Mind-Control Magic Regulations

§ 2101.1 General Restrictions on Mind-Control Magic

(a) **General Rule.**
No person shall initiate, apply, or maintain mind-control magic except as expressly authorized under this Code.

(b) **Definition and Scope.**
For purposes of this Part, mind-control magic refers to any magical act that alters, overrides, influences, suppresses, or otherwise interferes with a subject's thoughts, perceptions, memories, decision-making processes, or free will, whether directly or indirectly, and whether temporarily or permanently.

(c) **Prohibited Conduct.**
No person shall—
(1) compel or coerce a subject to act against their will or interests;
(2) alter or suppress a subject's thoughts or perceptions for purposes of deception, control, or manipulation;
(3) induce compliance, obedience, or passivity through magical means without lawful authorization;
(4) implant, modify, or erase memories except as permitted under this Part; or
(5) exercise ongoing or repeated influence over a subject's cognitive or behavioral functions in a manner that impairs autonomy.

(d) **Indirect and Embedded Effects.**
The prohibitions under this section apply to—
(1) enchantments, curses, or other magical effects that result in cognitive or behavioral manipulation;
(2) environmental or area-based magic that influences multiple subjects; and
(3) any layered or delayed magical effect designed to produce mind-control outcomes.

(e) **Circumvention Prohibited.**
No person shall avoid the application of this section by—
(1) characterizing mind-control effects as suggestion, persuasion, or influence where such effects materially impair autonomy;
(2) embedding mind-control effects within otherwise lawful magic; or
(3) structuring magical effects to produce cumulative or indirect control over a subject.

(f) **Presumption of Impairment.**
Where a subject's actions or statements are materially influenced by magic affecting cognition, such influence shall be presumed to impair free will unless demonstrated otherwise.

(g) **Duration and Persistence.**
No mind-control effect shall persist beyond the period necessary to achieve its lawful purpose, and no effect shall continue absent ongoing lawful authorization.

(h) **Cross-References.**
For legal use of mind-control in law enforcement, see § 2101.2. For temporary memory erasure, see § 2101.3. For ethical boundaries, see § 2101.4. For mental privacy and mind-reading restrictions, see § 2101.5. For long-term and repeated use, see § 2101.7. For consent and record-keeping, see § 2101.8. For penalties, see § 102.2.

(i) **Historical Annotations.**
This section was enacted under C.C.D. 1331, 18 MR 204, Mon. 6, 1758 following widespread abuses involving compelled loyalty enchantments. Amended under C.C.D. 4022, 41 MR 119, Thu. 12, 1896 to expand the definition to include indirect and environmental effects. Revised under C.C.D. 10388, 75 MR 118, Tue. 9, 2019 to clarify circumvention, persistence, and modern applications of cognitive manipulation.

§ 2101.2 Legal Use of Mind-Control in Law Enforcement

(a) **General Rule.**
Mind-control magic shall not be used in law enforcement except as expressly authorized under this section and only where such use is necessary, proportionate, and subject to strict procedural safeguards.

(b) **Permissible Uses.**
Mind-control magic may be used by a duly authorized law enforcement officer or other authorized governmental practitioner only for one or more of the following purposes:
(1) preventing imminent harm to a person where less intrusive means are unavailable or reasonably inadequate;
(2) temporarily stopping or restricting the movement of a subject who presents an immediate threat to public safety;
(3) securing compliance with a lawful command where failure to obtain immediate compliance would create a substantial risk of injury, escape, or destruction of evidence;
(4) stabilizing a subject undergoing acute magical, psychological, or cognitive disruption that materially impairs volitional control; or
(5) carrying out another narrowly defined purpose expressly authorized by warrant, judicial order, or other lawful authority.

(c) **Prohibited Uses.**
No person acting under color of law shall use mind-control magic to—
(1) compel a confession, admission, statement, or testimonial act;
(2) obtain consent to a search, seizure, detention, interrogation, or waiver of rights;
(3) influence a witness's recollection, perception, or willingness to provide information;
(4) punish, intimidate, retaliate against, or humiliate a subject;
(5) alter political, religious, personal, or associative beliefs;
(6) compel loyalty, obedience, or submission beyond the duration and scope necessary to address the authorized objective; or
(7) circumvent restrictions applicable to interrogation, detention, arrest, search, or use of force under other law.

(d) **Threshold Requirements.**
(1) Mind-control magic shall not be used unless the authorized officer or practitioner determines, based on articulable facts, that—
(A) the objective is lawful;
(B) the use is necessary under the circumstances;
(C) less intrusive alternatives are unavailable, ineffective, or reasonably likely to fail; and
(D) the anticipated degree of cognitive or volitional interference is proportionate to the threat or objective.

(2) The determination required under paragraph (1) shall be documented in accordance with § 2101.8.

(e) **Authorization.**
(1) Except as provided in subsection (f), no use of mind-control magic in law enforcement shall occur without prior authorization from a supervisory official or other authorized reviewing authority.
(2) Authorization shall specify, to the extent practicable—
(A) the subject or class of subjects to whom the magic may be applied;
(B) the lawful objective;
(C) the nature and degree of the permitted cognitive or behavioral interference;
(D) the maximum duration of the effect; and
(E) any required monitoring, reporting, or termination conditions.
(3) Blanket or indefinite authorization is prohibited.

(f) **Emergency Exception.**
(1) Prior supervisory authorization shall not be required where—
(A) the circumstances present an imminent threat of death, serious bodily harm, mass panic, catastrophic magical discharge, or comparable emergency; and
(B) delay would materially increase the danger.
(2) Where mind-control magic is used under this subsection, the responsible officer or practitioner shall—
(A) limit the use to the minimum degree and duration necessary to address the emergency; and
(B) submit a written justification and incident report promptly after the use.

(g) **Limitations on Scope and Duration.**
(1) Any mind-control effect used under this section shall be limited to the minimum degree of interference necessary to achieve the authorized objective.
(2) The effect shall terminate immediately upon cessation of the conditions justifying its use.
(3) Reapplication or continuation of the effect shall require a renewed determination of necessity and proportionality.
(4) No person shall maintain a subject under mind-control magic for administrative convenience, generalized compliance, or speculative future risk.

(h) **Operational Safeguards.**
(1) The practitioner shall monitor the subject continuously for the duration of the effect where reasonably practicable.
(2) The practitioner shall be capable of promptly reducing, terminating, or counteracting the effect.
(3) No use shall occur where the known condition of the subject creates a substantial and unjustifiable risk of cognitive collapse, permanent impairment, magical destabilization, or comparable injury.
(4) Where a subject is a minor, a protected creature, or a person known to possess diminished cognitive resilience, heightened safeguards shall apply.

(i) **Post-Use Review.**
(1) Any use of mind-control magic under this section shall be subject to post-use review sufficient to determine compliance with this Code.
(2) Review shall include examination of—
(A) the basis for the use;
(B) the duration and intensity of the effect;
(C) the existence or absence of less intrusive alternatives;
(D) any resulting injury, impairment, or irregularity; and
(E) whether the use materially affected any subsequent law enforcement activity or evidentiary process.

(j) **Evidentiary Limitations.**
(1) No statement, act, consent, waiver, or other purported manifestation of free will occurring during or immediately following unlawful mind-control use shall be presumed valid.
(2) Evidence derived from unlawful use of mind-control magic shall be subject to exclusion, suppression, or other remedy as provided by applicable law.
(3) Lawful use under this section shall not be construed to authorize testimonial compulsion.

(k) **Cross-References.**
For general restrictions on mind-control magic, see § 2101.1. For temporary memory erasure, see § 2101.3. For ethical boundaries for manipulating free will, see § 2101.4. For mental privacy and mind-reading restrictions, see § 2101.5. For long-term and repeated use of mind-control magic, see § 2101.7. For consent and record-keeping requirements, see § 2101.8. For penalties, see § 102.2.

(l) **Historical Annotations.**
This section was enacted under C.C.D. 2114, 27 MR 166, Thu. 17, 1819 to impose limits on official use of compulsion magic in investigations and arrest procedures. Amended under C.C.D. 5278, 44 MR 311, Tue. 4, 1938 to require supervisory authorization and post-use review. Amended under C.C.D. 8841, 52 MR 477, Mon. 13, 1985 to address emergency use and evidentiary consequences. Revised under C.C.D. 10394, 75 MR 144, Fri. 15, 2019 to refine necessity, proportionality, and operational safeguard requirements.

§ 2101.3 Temporary Memory Erasure: Storage and Retrieval Standards

(a) **General Rule.**
No person shall erase, suppress, extract, store, transfer, restore, or retrieve a memory through magical means except as expressly authorized under this section and subject to the standards set forth herein.

(b) **Scope.**
This section applies to all temporary memory erasure or suppression practices, including any magical process by which memory content is removed from active cognition, isolated from conscious recall, placed into magical storage, or later restored to the subject or another lawful repository.

(c) **Temporary Character Required.**
(1) Memory erasure under this section shall be temporary unless permanent alteration is otherwise expressly authorized under this Code.
(2) No person shall characterize a memory removal as temporary where the erased memory cannot be reliably restored under reasonably foreseeable conditions.
(3) A memory shall not be deemed temporarily erased if the method employed materially degrades, fragments, corrupts, or destabilizes the memory during storage.

(d) **Permissible Uses.**
Temporary memory erasure may be used only for one or more of the following purposes:
(1) lawful law enforcement activity expressly permitted under this Part;

(2) emergency protection of a person whose immediate recollection presents a substantial risk of magical destabilization, catastrophic trauma amplification, or comparable harm;
(3) short-term clinical or therapeutic intervention lawfully undertaken by an authorized practitioner;
(4) containment of highly sensitive magical information where temporary suppression is necessary to prevent imminent misuse, disclosure, or mass harm; or
(5) another purpose expressly authorized by warrant, judicial order, or specific statutory authority.

(e) **Prohibited Uses.**
No person shall use temporary memory erasure to—
(1) conceal unlawful conduct;
(2) avoid accountability, oversight, or reporting obligations;
(3) alter testimony, destroy evidence, or interfere with an investigation or proceeding;
(4) erase memories for convenience, discipline, humiliation, or personal advantage;
(5) remove memories in order to obtain consent, obedience, or dependency from a subject; or
(6) repeatedly erase and restore memories in a manner that predictably degrades cognition or autonomy.

(f) **Authorization and Preconditions.**
(1) Except in emergencies under subsection (g), temporary memory erasure shall require prior authorization by a lawful authority or authorized practitioner acting within the scope of recognized authority.
(2) Authorization shall specify—
(A) the subject;
(B) the category or approximate scope of the memory to be affected;
(C) the lawful purpose;
(D) the expected duration of the erasure or suppression;
(E) the method of storage; and
(F) the conditions for restoration or lawful continued retention.
(3) No authorization shall permit wholesale or indefinite removal of memory absent express and specific legal authority.

(g) **Emergency Use.**

(1) Prior authorization shall not be required where immediate action is necessary to prevent imminent harm and delay would materially increase the danger.
(2) A person acting under this subsection shall limit the erasure or suppression to the minimum scope and duration necessary to address the emergency.
(3) Full documentation and post-use review shall be completed promptly after the emergency has passed.

(h) **Storage Standards.**
(1) Any memory removed or suppressed under this section shall be stored in a secure and stable form sufficient to preserve its integrity.
(2) Stored memory shall be protected against corruption, duplication, unauthorized access, commingling, alteration, or accidental release.
(3) Storage methods shall permit identification of—
(A) the subject from whom the memory was removed;
(B) the date and time of removal;
(C) the person who performed the removal;
(D) the general subject matter or classification of the memory; and
(E) any restrictions on retrieval or restoration.
(4) No person shall store removed memories in an unmarked, unstable, or non-segregated vessel, medium, or repository.

(i) **Segregation and Chain of Custody.**
(1) Removed memories shall be segregated by subject and by authorized matter unless a lawful basis exists for different handling.
(2) A continuous chain of custody shall be maintained for any stored memory used in law enforcement, judicial, clinical, or security contexts.
(3) Any access, transfer, duplication, inspection, or restoration event shall be logged.

(j) **Retrieval and Restoration.**
(1) A stored or suppressed memory shall not be restored except by an authorized person and only under lawful conditions consistent with the original authorization or subsequent lawful order.
(2) Prior to restoration, the responsible practitioner shall assess—
(A) whether the memory remains intact and attributable to the proper subjcct;
(B) whether restoration presents a substantial risk of cognitive or magical harm; and

(C) whether partial, staged, or supervised restoration is required.
(3) No person shall restore a memory to the wrong subject or introduce stored memories into a subject to whom they did not originally belong, except as otherwise expressly authorized by law.

(k) **Retention and Destruction.**
(1) Stored memories shall not be retained longer than necessary for the lawful purpose for which they were removed, unless another lawful basis for retention exists.
(2) Upon expiration of lawful retention, the memory shall be restored, lawfully archived, or destroyed in accordance with applicable authority.
(3) Destruction of a stored memory shall be documented and shall not occur where restoration is legally required.

(l) **Subject Protections.**
(1) A subject shall not lose rights, status, or legal protections solely because a relevant memory has been temporarily erased or suppressed.
(2) Where restoration is required for the subject's welfare, legal capacity, or defense of rights, unjustified delay in restoration shall constitute a violation of this section.
(3) Additional safeguards shall apply where the subject is a minor, a protected creature, or a person known to have elevated susceptibility to cognitive fragmentation.

(m) **Record-Keeping.**
A record created under this section shall include, to the extent applicable—
(1) the identity of the subject;
(2) the person performing the erasure or restoration;
(3) the legal authority relied upon;
(4) the general scope of memory affected;
(5) the method and location of storage;
(6) the date, duration, and conditions of retention; and
(7) the date and manner of restoration, transfer, archival retention, or destruction.

(n) **Cross-References.**
For general restrictions on mind-control magic, see § 2101.1. For legal use of mind-control in law enforcement, see § 2101.2. For ethical boundaries for manipulating free will, see § 2101.4. For mental privacy and mind-

reading restrictions, see § 2101.5. For long-term and repeated use of mind-control magic, see § 2101.7. For consent and record-keeping requirements, see § 2101.8. For penalties, see § 102.2.

(o) **Historical Annotations.**
This section was enacted under C.C.D. 2473, 30 MR 98, Mon. 22, 1847 to regulate official seizure and restoration of memory in security proceedings. Amended under C.C.D. 6111, 46 MR 224, Wed. 9, 1959 to establish storage integrity and chain-of-custody standards. Amended under C.C.D. 9018, 53 MR 166, Tue. 26, 1986 to address therapeutic and emergency uses. Revised under C.C.D. 10406, 75 MR 211, Thu. 21, 2019 to clarify retention, restoration, and subject-protection requirements.

§ 2101.4 Ethical Boundaries for Manipulating Free Will

(a) **General Rule.**
No person shall use mind-control magic in a manner that materially impairs, overrides, or substitutes the free will of another, except as expressly authorized under this Code.

(b) **Scope.**
This section applies to any magical act that influences, alters, suppresses, or replaces a subject's decision-making capacity, intent formation, or ability to exercise independent judgment, whether direct or indirect.

(c) **Prohibited Conduct.**
No person shall—
(1) impose or induce decisions, preferences, or actions that the subject would not otherwise make under conditions of ordinary cognition;
(2) suppress, delay, or distort a subject's ability to form intent or exercise judgment;
(3) create dependency, compliance conditioning, or behavioral reinforcement through magical means;
(4) alter motivations, desires, or priorities in a manner that substitutes the practitioner's will for that of the subject; or
(5) structure repeated or layered magical effects that cumulatively impair autonomy.

(d) **Indirect Influence.**

(1) The prohibitions under this section apply to suggestion, influence, or environmental manipulation where such effects materially impair autonomy.
(2) A distinction between persuasion and control shall be determined based on whether the subject retains meaningful ability to refuse, resist, or reconsider the influenced action.

(e) **Presumption of Impairment.**
Where a subject's conduct is materially affected by magical influence on cognition or intent, such influence shall be presumed to impair free will unless demonstrated otherwise.

(f) **Duration and Persistence.**
No magical effect affecting free will shall persist beyond the minimum period necessary to achieve a lawful objective, and no such effect shall be maintained for convenience, preference, or speculative benefit.

(g) **Heightened Restrictions.**
(1) Additional restrictions shall apply where the subject is—
(A) a minor;
(B) a protected creature; or
(C) a person known to possess diminished cognitive resilience.
(2) In such cases, any manipulation of free will shall be subject to the most restrictive interpretation of this section.

(h) **Relationship to Authorized Uses.**
Nothing in this section shall be construed to expand or independently authorize uses of mind-control magic otherwise governed by § 2101.2 or other provisions of this Code.

(i) **Cross-References.**
For general restrictions on mind-control magic, see § 2101.1. For legal use in law enforcement, see § 2101.2. For temporary memory erasure, see § 2101.3. For mental privacy and mind-reading restrictions, see § 2101.5. For long-term and repeated use, see § 2101.7. For consent and record-keeping requirements, see § 2101.8. For penalties, see § 102.2.

(j) **Historical Annotations.**
This section was enacted under C.C.D. 1662, 21 MR 144, Thu. 3, 1776 following early disputes regarding magical coercion and autonomy. Amended under C.C.D. 4387, 39 MR 201, Mon. 12, 1884 to address

indirect influence and suggestion-based manipulation. Revised under C.C.D. 10172, 72 MR 288, Wed. 7, 2016 to clarify modern applications of autonomy and cumulative magical effects.

§ 2101.5 Mental Privacy and Mind-Reading Restrictions

(a) **General Rule.**
No person shall access, read, extract, interpret, or otherwise obtain the thoughts, memories, intentions, or mental impressions of another through magical means except as expressly authorized under this Code.

(b) **Scope.**
This section applies to all forms of mind-reading, thought detection, memory inspection, emotional scanning, and similar practices, whether direct, indirect, passive, active, targeted, or area-based.

(c) **Prohibited Conduct.**
No person shall—
(1) read or access the thoughts or memories of another without lawful authorization;
(2) monitor, surveil, or track a subject's mental activity;
(3) extract or record mental impressions for later use, storage, or analysis;
(4) use mind-reading to obtain confidential, privileged, or protected information; or
(5) conduct broad or indiscriminate scanning of mental activity within a location or population.

(d) **Expectation of Mental Privacy.**
(1) All persons shall be deemed to possess a reasonable expectation of privacy in their thoughts, memories, and internal mental processes.
(2) Such expectation shall not be diminished by the subject's location, status, or participation in public or private activity.

(e) **Prohibition on Secondary Use.**
Information obtained through unlawful mind-reading shall not be used, disclosed, relied upon, or incorporated into any decision, action, or proceeding.

(f) **Incidental Exposure.**

(1) Where a person is inadvertently exposed to the thoughts or memories of another, such exposure shall not be used or further explored.
(2) Continued engagement following incidental exposure shall constitute a violation of this section.

(g) **Limitations on Authorized Use.**
Where mind-reading is expressly authorized under another provision of this Code—
(1) access shall be limited to the scope and purpose of the authorization;
(2) no broader or unrelated mental information shall be examined or retained; and
(3) any access beyond the authorized scope shall constitute a violation.

(h) **Recording and Storage.**
No person shall record, store, or reproduce the mental content of another except as expressly authorized and subject to applicable safeguards.

(i) **Cross-References.**
For general restrictions on mind-control magic, see § 2101.1. For legal use in law enforcement, see § 2101.2. For temporary memory erasure, see § 2101.3. For ethical boundaries, see § 2101.4. For long-term and repeated use, see § 2101.7. For consent and record-keeping requirements, see § 2101.8. For penalties, see § 102.2.

(j) **Historical Annotations.**
This section was enacted under C.C.D. 1924, 24 MR 88, Mon. 18, 1803 recognizing mental privacy as a protected interest. Amended under C.C.D. 3011, 36 MR 144, Tue. 5, 1853 to prohibit unauthorized extraction of thoughts. Amended under C.C.D. 6118, 46 MR 233, Fri. 2, 1959 to address recording and storage of mental impressions. Revised under C.C.D. 10366, 74 MR 119, Thu. 14, 2018 to address modern surveillance and large-scale scanning practices.

§ 2101.6 Restrictions on Spells That Make Husbands Forget Their Anniversary

(a) **General Rule.**
No person shall, through any magical means, cast, create, distribute, or utilize a spell, enchantment, potion, charm, or magical device with the intent or effect of causing a husband to forget their wedding anniversary.

Such actions, which undermine the very fabric of marital trust, are prohibited under all circumstances.

(b) **Legislative Findings and Purpose.**
The Council of Councils, in recognition of the gravity of this issue, finds and declares the following:
(1) The ability of a husband to remember his wedding anniversary is an inherent and inviolable quality, unassailable under normal conditions.
(2) Any deviation from this unerring recall can only be attributed to malicious magical interference, as no husband, under any circumstances, would ever neglect such an important date willingly.
(3) Evidence submitted by highly credible lawmakers indicates a disturbing trend of enchanted calendars, memory-altering charms, and other nefarious magical acts designed to sabotage a husband's otherwise perfect recollection.
(4) The Council, acting to protect the sanctity of marital traditions, enacts this regulation to ensure that husbands are not unfairly maligned or subjected to undue blame for the actions of malicious spellcasters.

(c) **Definitions.**
For the purposes of this section, the following definitions shall apply:
(1) Husband. A male individual legally recognized as a spouse under magical or non-magical law.
(2) Wedding Anniversary. The annual observance of the date upon which a lawful marriage was solemnized.
(3) Magical Interference. The use of any spell, charm, potion, or magical object to impair, obstruct, or otherwise alter a husband's ability to recall their wedding anniversary, including but not limited to:
(A) Memory-erasing spells or enchantments;
(B) Potions or consumables causing confusion or forgetfulness;
(C) Cursed or enchanted calendars, planners, or timepieces displaying inaccurate or misleading dates;
(D) Any act of magical tampering that could create the illusion of forgetfulness.

(d) **Prohibited Acts.**
(1) Casting, crafting, or utilizing any form of magic designed to alter a husband's memory or perception of their wedding anniversary is strictly forbidden.

(2) Possession, distribution, or sale of magical items or substances intended for such purposes shall likewise constitute a violation of this section.

(e) **Enforcement.**
(1) While formal reporting mechanisms are unnecessary, any instances of suspected magical interference should be addressed promptly through informal marital dialogue or firm but loving confrontation with the offending spellcaster.
(2) The Council trusts that the self-evident absurdity of a husband forgetting their anniversary will naturally lead all parties involved to the conclusion that external magical interference is the only plausible explanation.

(f) **Penalties.**
(1) Individuals found guilty of casting, creating, or distributing spells that cause a husband to forget their anniversary shall be subject to:
(A) Mandatory attendance at a Council-approved seminar on memory ethics;
(B) Community service, which may include crafting enchanted reminders for public distribution.
(2) Husbands, being the victims of such interference, shall face no penalties whatsoever, as their inability to remember an anniversary is wholly attributable to external magical forces.

(g) **Exceptions.**
(1) This section does not prohibit the use of spells or charms designed to enhance memory retention, provided such magic is applied in good faith and with the express consent of all parties involved.
(2) The Council affirms that no natural, non-magical explanation exists for a husband forgetting an anniversary. Assertions to the contrary are baseless and offensive.

(h) **Cross-References.**
For regulations concerning general memory spells, refer to § 2101.1. For ethical guidelines on magical interference, see § 701.1.

(i) **Historical Annotations.**
This section was originally enacted under C.C.D. 11241, 91 MR 4578, Sun. 10, 1982, to address the purported use of memory-altering magic in

domestic contexts. Amended under C.C.D. 11567, 92 MR 6723, Mon. 12, 1985, to clarify prohibited acts and reporting protocols. Further revisions were made under C.C.D. 12846, 95 MR 8745, Fri. 5, 1990, to streamline enforcement mechanisms and align penalties with related provisions under § 2101.1 and § 801.5.

§ 2101.7 Long-Term and Repeated Use of Mind-Control Magic

(a) **General Rule.**
No person shall engage in long-term or repeated use of mind-control magic except as expressly authorized under this section.

(b) **Scope.**
This section applies to any pattern, series, or continuation of mind-control effects that—
(1) extends beyond a single, discrete application;
(2) produces cumulative influence over cognition, behavior, or decision-making; or
(3) results in sustained or recurring impairment of autonomy.

(c) **Prohibition on Cumulative Control.**
No person shall structure, sequence, or repeat otherwise lawful mind-control effects in a manner that, taken together, produces a level of control or impairment that would be unlawful if imposed in a single instance.

(d) **Long-Term Use.**
(1) Mind-control effects shall not be maintained for extended duration unless—
(A) the use is expressly authorized under this Code; and
(B) the duration is limited to the minimum period necessary to achieve the authorized purpose.
(2) Indefinite or open-ended maintenance of mind-control effects is prohibited.

(e) **Repeated Use.**
(1) Repeated application of mind control magic to the same subject shall require independent justification for each instance.

(2) No person shall rely on prior authorization to justify subsequent or continuing applications absent renewed authorization and evaluation.

(f) **Diminishing Capacity.**
(1) Repeated or prolonged use shall not be conducted where it results in, or is reasonably likely to result in—
(A) degradation of memory, cognition, or identity;
(B) increased susceptibility to further manipulation; or
(C) reduced ability to exercise independent judgment.
(2) Evidence of such effects shall require immediate cessation of use.

(g) **Monitoring and Review.**
(1) Any authorized long-term or repeated use shall be subject to periodic review sufficient to ensure continued compliance with this Code.
(2) Review shall consider—
(A) necessity and proportionality;
(B) cumulative effects on the subject; and
(C) the continued availability of less intrusive alternatives.

(h) **Prohibition on Conditioning.**
No person shall use repeated or long-term mind-control magic to condition behavior, establish obedience patterns, or create habitual compliance.

(i) **Cross-References.**
For general restrictions on mind-control magic, see § 2101.1. For legal use in law enforcement, see § 2101.2. For temporary memory erasure, see § 2101.3. For ethical boundaries, see § 2101.4. For mental privacy restrictions, see § 2101.5. For consent and record-keeping requirements, see § 2101.8. For penalties, see § 102.2.

(j) **Historical Annotations.**
This section was enacted under C.C.D. 2741, 31 MR 211, Mon. 14, 1851 to address sustained coercive influence over individuals. Amended under C.C.D. 5420, 44 MR 402, Tue. 6, 1936 to prohibit cumulative and conditioning effects. Revised under C.C.D. 10288, 73 MR 188, Fri. 11, 2017 to clarify monitoring, review, and cognitive degradation standards.

§ 2101.8 Consent and Record-Keeping Requirements

(a) **General Rule.**
No person shall apply mind-control magic except in compliance with the consent and record-keeping requirements set forth in this section, where applicable.

(b) **Consent Requirement.**
(1) Where consent is required under this Part, such consent shall be—
(A) informed;
(B) voluntary; and
(C) specific to the nature, scope, and duration of the mind-control effect.
(2) Consent shall be obtained prior to initiation of the effect unless otherwise authorized under this Code.

(c) **Informed Consent Standard.**
Consent shall be deemed informed only where the subject is provided—
(1) a description of the nature and purpose of the mind-control effect;
(2) the expected duration and intensity of the effect;
(3) reasonably foreseeable risks and limitations; and
(4) the conditions under which the effect will terminate.

(d) **Invalid Consent.**
Consent shall be invalid where obtained through—
(1) coercion, deception, or manipulation;
(2) prior or concurrent use of mind-control magic; or
(3) conditions that materially impair the subject's ability to understand or refuse.

(e) **Documentation of Consent.**
(1) Consent shall be documented in a manner sufficient to demonstrate compliance with this section.
(2) Documentation shall include—
(A) identity of the subject;
(B) identity of the practitioner;
(C) date and time of consent;
(D) scope and duration of the authorized effect; and
(E) method by which consent was obtained.

(f) **Record-Keeping Requirements.**
(1) Any use of mind-control magic shall be documented.
(2) Records shall include, to the extent applicable—
(A) the legal basis for the use;
(B) the nature and scope of the effect;
(C) the duration of application;
(D) any authorization obtained; and
(E) any observed effects or deviations.
(3) Records shall be retained for a period sufficient to permit review, audit, and enforcement.

(g) **Access and Review.**
(1) Records shall be made available to authorized oversight bodies upon request.
(2) Failure to produce required records shall constitute a violation of this section.

(h) **Burden of Proof.**
The person applying mind-control magic shall bear the burden of demonstrating compliance with consent and record-keeping requirements.

(i) **Cross-References.**
For general restrictions on mind-control magic, see § 2101.1. For legal use in law enforcement, see § 2101.2. For temporary memory erasure, see § 2101.3. For ethical boundaries, see § 2101.4. For mental privacy restrictions, see § 2101.5. For long-term and repeated use, see § 2101.7. For penalties, see § 102.2.

(j) **Historical Annotations.**
This section was enacted under C.C.D. 3187, 36 MR 233, Thu. 19, 1864 to require documentation of magical coercion practices. Amended under C.C.D. 6762, 47 MR 301, Mon. 8, 1967 to establish formal consent standards. Revised under C.C.D. 10312, 73 MR 277, Tue. 3, 2018 to modernize record-keeping and oversight requirements.

Part XXII: Time Manipulation Magic Regulations

§ 2201.1 Restrictions on Time Travel and Temporal Alteration

(a) **General Rule.**
No person shall initiate, attempt, or maintain time manipulation magic except as expressly authorized under this Code.

(b) **Definition and Scope.**
Time manipulation magic, as defined under § 101.1, refers to the school of magic involving the alteration, displacement, acceleration, deceleration, looping, branching, or other modification of temporal position, sequence, or progression of events, whether affecting a person, object, location, or timeline.

(c) **Prohibited Conduct.**
No person shall—
(1) travel to or interact with a prior temporal state in a manner that alters events that have already occurred;
(2) create, induce, or exploit alternate timelines, branching realities, or recursive temporal loops;
(3) accelerate or reverse time in a localized or broad context where such alteration materially affects persons or systems not subject to the manipulation;
(4) displace a person or object outside of its proper temporal sequence without lawful authorization; or
(5) engage in any temporal activity that results in duplication, erasure, or overlapping existence of a person or object within the same temporal frame.

(d) **Temporal Integrity.**
(1) The integrity and continuity of the timeline shall be preserved.
(2) No person shall knowingly create conditions that result in paradox, discontinuity, or instability within the temporal sequence.

(e) **Causation and Interference.**
No person shall interfere with established causal relationships in a manner that produces contradictory or irreconcilable outcomes.

(f) **Indirect and Secondary Effects.**
The prohibitions under this section apply to any magical effect that produces temporal consequences, whether such effects are direct, indirect, delayed, or cumulative.

(g) **Circumvention Prohibited.**
No person shall avoid the application of this section by—
(1) characterizing temporal alteration as observation, simulation, or reconstruction where such activity materially affects actual events; or
(2) embedding temporal effects within other forms of magic.

(h) **Limited Exceptions.**
Nothing in this section shall be construed to permit time manipulation except as expressly authorized under § 2201.2 and other applicable provisions of this Code.

(i) **Cross-References.**
For definitions of schools of magic, see § 101.1. For authorized uses of time manipulation, see § 2201.2. For temporal paradoxes and anomalies, see § 2201.3. For registration and monitoring requirements, see § 2201.6. For emergency provisions, see § 2201.7. For penalties, see § 102.2.

(j) **Historical Annotations.**
This section was enacted under C.C.D. 807, 15 MR 77, Mon. 2, 1729 following early recorded temporal displacement incidents. Amended under C.C.D. 3561, 38 MR 211, Thu. 18, 1869 to prohibit paradox-generating alterations. Amended under C.C.D. 7124, 47 MR 402, Tue. 9, 1978 to address localized time distortion and duplication concerns. Revised under C.C.D. 10201, 72 MR 118, Fri. 14, 2015 to clarify modern temporal manipulation risks and enforcement standards.

§ 2201.2 Authorized Uses of Time Manipulation

(a) **General Rule.**
Time manipulation magic may be conducted only in narrowly defined circumstances where expressly authorized under this section and subject to strict limitation, oversight, and control.

(b) **Permissible Uses.**
Authorized uses of time manipulation may include—
(1) localized temporal deceleration or acceleration for purposes of emergency response, stabilization, or containment;
(2) short-duration temporal suspension affecting a discrete subject or area, where necessary to prevent imminent harm or system failure;
(3) controlled observational displacement, limited to passive viewing of prior temporal states without interaction;
(4) synchronization or correction of minor temporal drift in regulated systems or environments; and
(5) other limited uses expressly authorized by warrant, order, or governing authority consistent with this Code.

(c) **Conditions for Authorization.**
Time manipulation shall not be authorized unless—
(1) the intended use is capable of being defined with specificity as to scope, duration, and effect;
(2) the activity does not create a material risk of paradox, discontinuity, or instability; and
(3) the manipulation is limited to the minimum extent necessary to achieve the authorized objective.

(d) **Limitations on Interaction.**
(1) No authorized use shall permit interaction with prior or future temporal states except where expressly provided by law.
(2) Observational use shall remain strictly passive and shall not permit influence, alteration, or interference with observed events.

(e) **Temporal Containment.**
(1) Authorized time manipulation shall be confined to a defined temporal and spatial boundary.
(2) No effect shall propagate beyond the approved scope or affect unrelated persons, objects, or systems.

(f) **Duration and Termination.**
(1) Authorized time manipulation shall be limited in duration and shall terminate upon completion of the authorized objective.
(2) No person shall extend or reinitiate a temporal effect without renewed authorization.

(g) **Monitoring and Oversight.**

(1) All authorized time manipulation shall be subject to continuous monitoring where reasonably practicable.
(2) Monitoring shall include, to the extent applicable—
(A) real-time observation of the temporal field or affected area;
(B) detection of instability, drift, duplication, or divergence from defined parameters; and
(C) verification that no unauthorized interaction or propagation is occurring.
(3) The responsible practitioner shall maintain the ability to immediately terminate, reverse, or otherwise neutralize the temporal effect.
(4) Where the scale or complexity of the temporal manipulation exceeds the capacity of a single practitioner, additional authorized personnel or supervisory oversight shall be required.
(5) Monitoring records shall be created and maintained, including—
(A) initiation and termination times;
(B) observed deviations or irregularities; and
(C) any corrective actions taken during operation.
(6) Failure to adequately monitor a temporal effect shall constitute a violation of this section regardless of whether a paradox or anomaly occurs.

(h) **Prohibited Expansion.**
No person shall expand the scope, duration, or effect of an authorized temporal manipulation beyond that which has been expressly permitted.

(i) **Cross-References.**
For restrictions on time manipulation, see § 2201.1. For temporal paradoxes and anomalies, see § 2201.3. For registration and monitoring requirements, see § 2201.6. For emergency provisions, see § 2201.7. For penalties, see § 102.2.

(j) **Historical Annotations.**
This section was enacted under C.C.D. 2211, 29 MR 166, Mon. 6, 1836 to permit limited controlled temporal manipulation for state purposes. Amended under C.C.D. 5184, 43 MR 301, Tue. 9, 1924 to restrict interaction with prior states. Revised under C.C.D. 10022, 70 MR 211, Thu. 3, 2010 to clarify observational limits and containment requirements.

§ 2201.3 Temporal Paradoxes and Anomalies

(a) **General Rule.**
No person shall create, induce, exacerbate, or fail to mitigate a temporal paradox or anomaly.

(b) **Definition.**
For purposes of this section—
(1) a temporal paradox is a condition in which causation, sequence, or identity produces a contradiction or irreconcilable outcome; and
(2) a temporal anomaly is any deviation from expected temporal continuity, including instability, duplication, displacement, or fragmentation of events or entities.

(c) **Prohibited Conduct.**
No person shall—
(1) initiate temporal actions reasonably likely to result in paradox or anomaly;
(2) knowingly interact with a condition that has produced or is producing a paradox;
(3) duplicate, overlap, or merge temporal instances of a person or object;
(4) introduce information, objects, or entities into a temporal state in a manner that creates causal inconsistency; or
(5) ignore or fail to report a known paradox or anomaly.

(d) **Duty to Mitigate.**
(1) Any person who becomes aware of a temporal anomaly shall take reasonable steps to contain, stabilize, or report the condition.
(2) Failure to act upon knowledge of a destabilizing condition shall constitute a violation of this section.

(e) **Containment Requirements.**
(1) Temporal anomalies shall be isolated to the extent practicable to prevent propagation.
(2) No person shall allow an anomaly to expand, interact with additional temporal states, or affect unrelated systems.

(f) **Prohibition on Exploitation.**
No person shall use a temporal anomaly or paradox for personal, commercial, or strategic advantage.

(g) **Investigation and Correction.**
(1) Temporal anomalies may be investigated, contained, or corrected only by an authorized entity acting within the scope of its jurisdiction under § 102.1 or other applicable provisions of this Code.
(2) Any corrective action shall be limited to that which is necessary to restore temporal continuity and shall not introduce additional alteration beyond what is required to resolve the anomaly.
(3) No person shall attempt unilateral correction of a temporal anomaly where such action—
(A) exceeds their level of authorization;
(B) introduces additional temporal displacement or interaction; or
(C) creates a material risk of compounding the existing anomaly.
(4) Corrective actions shall be documented, including—
(A) the nature and origin of the anomaly;
(B) the methods used for containment or correction; and
(C) any resulting deviations from baseline temporal conditions.
(5) Where full correction is not possible, authorized entities shall implement stabilization measures sufficient to prevent further degradation of temporal continuity.

(h) **Cross-References.**
For restrictions on time manipulation, see § 2201.1. For authorized uses of time manipulation, see § 2201.2. For registration and monitoring requirements, see § 2201.6. For emergency provisions, see § 2201.7. For penalties, see § 102.2.

(i) **Historical Annotations.**
This section was enacted under C.C.D. 1784, 24 MR 166, Thu. 11, 1798 following early paradox events involving overlapping temporal states. Amended under C.C.D. 4027, 41 MR 211, Mon. 3, 1897 to define anomalies and impose reporting duties. Amended under C.C.D. 6891, 46 MR 402, Tue. 14, 1968 to address containment and propagation risks. Revised under C.C.D. 10195, 72 MR 166, Fri. 12, 2014 to clarify modern anomaly detection and mitigation standards.

§ 2201.4 Anachronistic Considerations for Time Travelers

(a) **General Rule.**

No person engaging in authorized time manipulation shall introduce, transfer, disclose, or otherwise cause the presence of anachronistic knowledge, objects, influence, or conditions in a temporal period to which such matter does not properly belong.

(b) **Scope.**
This section applies to any temporal displacement or interaction that results in the movement or introduction of—
(1) knowledge of future events, technologies, discoveries, or outcomes;
(2) objects, materials, currency, artifacts, or devices not yet existing in the target temporal period;
(3) methods, processes, or techniques derived from a different temporal context; or
(4) cultural, social, economic, or behavioral constructs materially inconsistent with the target temporal environment.

(c) **Prohibited Conduct.**
No person shall—
(1) provide or disclose information regarding future events, outcomes, or developments to any person in an earlier temporal state;
(2) introduce objects, materials, or devices into a temporal period in which such items have not yet been created, discovered, or lawfully recognized;
(3) alter the sequence, pace, or nature of technological, magical, economic, or cultural development through temporal interference;
(4) use knowledge of future conditions, markets, outcomes, or events for personal, commercial, or strategic advantage;
(5) create or reinforce false historical narratives through the introduction of non-contemporaneous ideas, styles, or practices; or
(6) knowingly create or contribute to conditions in which causation is materially influenced by information or objects originating outside the relevant temporal context.

(d) **Materiality Standard.**
(1) Anachronistic influence shall be deemed material where it—
(A) affects decision-making, innovation, or development;
(B) alters the behavior of individuals or institutions in a manner inconsistent with natural progression; or
(C) introduces outcomes that would not reasonably have occurred absent the temporal interference.

(2) The absence of immediate observable impact shall not preclude a finding of materiality where long-term or cumulative effects are reasonably foreseeable.

(e) **Incidental Introduction.**
(1) Where anachronistic matter is introduced unintentionally, the responsible person shall take immediate and reasonable steps to—
(A) retrieve or neutralize any introduced object or material;
(B) correct or limit dissemination of any disclosed information; and
(C) contain any resulting influence.
(2) Failure to act upon knowledge of anachronistic contamination shall constitute a violation of this section.

(f) **Temporal Containment of Information.**
(1) Any person engaged in observational or limited interaction shall restrict all communication to information that would reasonably be available within the temporal context.
(2) No person shall use coded, indirect, symbolic, or staged communication to circumvent the restrictions of this section.
(3) The intentional omission or selective disclosure of information for the purpose of guiding outcomes shall be treated as anachronistic influence.

(g) **Personal Conduct and Integration.**
(1) A time traveler shall conduct themselves in a manner consistent with the norms, knowledge, and limitations of the temporal period in which they are present.
(2) No person shall introduce mannerisms, terminology, customs, or expectations that materially deviate from the temporal context where such deviation is reasonably likely to influence behavior or perception.
(3) Persistent or repeated deviation from temporal norms may be considered evidence of unlawful anachronistic influence.

(h) **Cross-References.**
For restrictions on time manipulation, see § 2201.1. For authorized uses of time manipulation, see § 2201.2. For temporal paradoxes and anomalies, see § 2201.3. For registration and monitoring requirements, see § 2201.6. For penalties, see § 102.2.

(i) **Historical Annotations.**

This section was enacted under C.C.D. 3094, 35 MR 166, Tue. 11, 1859 following the Fedora Recurrence Incident, in which a temporal actor attempted to reintroduce fedoras into prior centuries under the mistaken belief that such style had previously been in widespread use, resulting in documented distortions of cultural development and persistent historical inaccuracies. Amended under C.C.D. 5871, 45 MR 211, Mon. 7, 1953 to address introduction of non-contemporaneous objects and materials. Revised under C.C.D. 10087, 71 MR 233, Thu. 6, 2012 to clarify informational containment and behavioral requirements.

§ 2201.5 Ethical Considerations and Impact on Reality

(a) **General Rule.**
No person shall engage in time manipulation in a manner that produces unjustified harm to individuals, populations, or the continuity, stability, or coherence of reality.

(b) **Scope.**
This section governs the broader ethical, systemic, and ontological effects of time manipulation, including impacts on identity, causation, existence, historical development, and the structural integrity of temporal progression.

(c) **Prohibited Conduct.**
No person shall—
(1) alter, erase, replace, or prevent events in a manner that results in the elimination, displacement, or material alteration of one or more persons or populations;
(2) create conditions resulting in fragmented, duplicated, overlapping, or unstable states of existence;
(3) knowingly initiate temporal actions that produce cascading or compounding effects beyond the defined scope of the manipulation;
(4) prioritize individual, localized, or short-term outcomes over broader temporal stability;
(5) engage in temporal intervention where the likely consequences cannot be reasonably assessed, measured, or contained; or
(6) treat persons, populations, or historical outcomes as expendable variables in temporal experimentation or adjustment.

(d) **Identity and Continuity.**
(1) No person shall engage in time manipulation that materially disrupts identity continuity as defined under § 101.9.
(2) Actions resulting in the duplication, merging, erasure, or displacement of identity shall be presumed to violate this section unless expressly authorized.

(e) **Population-Level Effects.**
(1) Time manipulation shall not be conducted where it is reasonably likely to—
(A) alter population composition, survival, or existence;
(B) affect large-scale historical outcomes; or
(C) create or eliminate entire classes of persons or events.
(2) Effects that extend beyond a discrete and contained scope shall be presumed impermissible.

(f) **Impact Assessment Requirement.**
(1) Any authorized use of time manipulation shall include a documented assessment of potential impacts, including—
(A) effects on individuals and identity continuity;
(B) effects on populations and historical development; and
(C) risks to temporal stability and causation.
(2) Authorization shall not be granted where the assessment identifies a material risk of irreversible or uncontainable impact.

(g) **Minimization Principle.**
Time manipulation shall be conducted in a manner that minimizes disruption, preserves continuity, and avoids unnecessary alteration of events.

(h) **Uncertainty and Risk.**
(1) Where uncertainty regarding consequences is substantial, the proposed use of time manipulation shall be presumed impermissible.
(2) The burden shall rest on the person seeking to conduct the manipulation to demonstrate that risks are identified, limited, and controlled.

(i) **Cross-References.**
For restrictions on time manipulation, see § 2201.1. For authorized uses, see § 2201.2. For temporal paradoxes and anomalies, see § 2201.3. For

anachronistic considerations, see § 2201.4. For emergency provisions, see § 2201.7. For penalties, see § 102.2.

(j) **Historical Annotations.**
This section was enacted under C.C.D. 2541, 30 MR 211, Thu. 5, 1849 following early disputes regarding alteration of existence and identity. Amended under C.C.D. 4712, 42 MR 144, Tue. 3, 1908 to incorporate population-level considerations. Revised under C.C.D. 9984, 70 MR 119, Mon. 9, 2009 to address large-scale temporal intervention risks and formalize impact assessment requirements.

§ 2201.6 Registration and Monitoring of Time Manipulation Spells

(a) **General Rule.**
No person shall initiate, attempt, or maintain time manipulation magic unless such activity is registered, approved, and monitored in accordance with this section.

(b) **Registration Requirement.**
(1) Prior to initiation, any time manipulation spell shall be registered with the appropriate authority designated under § 102.1.
(2) Registration shall be required regardless of duration, scope, or intended effect, except as provided under § 2201.7.
(3) No retroactive registration shall be permitted.

(c) **Contents of Registration.**
A registration submitted under this section shall include, to the extent applicable—
(1) identity of the practitioner and any supervising or participating persons;
(2) description of the intended temporal manipulation, including type, scope, and method;
(3) defined temporal and spatial boundaries;
(4) expected duration and termination conditions;
(5) assessment of potential risks, including paradox, anomaly, and anachronistic impact;
(6) safeguards, monitoring mechanisms, and contingency procedures; and
(7) certification that the proposed activity complies with this Code.

(d) **Approval Requirement.**
(1) No time manipulation spell shall be conducted without prior approval.
(2) Approval shall specify—
(A) the authorized scope and duration;
(B) permissible interactions, if any;
(C) monitoring and reporting requirements; and
(D) any limitations necessary to ensure temporal stability.
(3) Approval shall be denied where the proposed activity presents material risk to temporal continuity or cannot be sufficiently controlled.

(e) **Monitoring Requirements.**
(1) All registered time manipulation activity shall be subject to continuous monitoring where reasonably practicable.
(2) Monitoring shall include detection of—
(A) deviation from authorized parameters;
(B) emergence of paradoxes or anomalies;
(C) unauthorized interaction or propagation; and
(D) any instability affecting temporal integrity.
(3) Monitoring shall be conducted by the practitioner and, where required, by an independent oversight body.

(f) **Reporting Requirements.**
(1) The practitioner shall submit periodic reports documenting—
(A) the status of the temporal activity;
(B) any deviations or irregularities; and
(C) actions taken in response.
(2) Immediate reporting shall be required where any condition arises that may result in paradox, anomaly, or unauthorized expansion.

(g) **Record Retention.**
All records relating to registration, approval, monitoring, and reporting shall be retained for a period sufficient to permit audit, review, and enforcement.

(h) **Revocation and Suspension.**
(1) Authorization may be suspended or revoked where—
(A) conditions of approval are violated;
(B) monitoring requirements are not met; or
(C) new risks or instability arise.

(2) Upon revocation or suspension, the temporal activity shall be terminated immediately.

(i) **Cross-References.**
For restrictions on time manipulation, see § 2201.1. For authorized uses, see § 2201.2. For temporal paradoxes and anomalies, see § 2201.3. For anachronistic considerations, see § 2201.4. For ethical considerations, see § 2201.5. For emergency provisions, see § 2201.7. For penalties, see § 102.2.

(j) **Historical Annotations.**
This section was enacted under C.C.D. 3412, 37 MR 211, Mon. 18, 1872 following unregulated temporal experimentation. Amended under C.C.D. 6291, 46 MR 301, Tue. 2, 1962 to establish formal approval and monitoring structures. Revised under C.C.D. 10112, 71 MR 166, Fri. 7, 2013 to expand reporting, oversight, and revocation procedures.

§ 2201.7 Emergency Temporal Magic Provisions

(a) **General Rule.**
Time manipulation may be conducted without prior registration or approval only in emergency circumstances as defined under this section.

(b) **Definition of Emergency.**
An emergency shall exist only where—
(1) there is an imminent risk of death, large-scale harm, temporal collapse, or comparable catastrophic outcome; and
(2) delay required to obtain authorization would materially increase the severity of the outcome.

(c) **Permissible Emergency Use.**
(1) Emergency use shall be limited to the minimum scope and duration necessary to address the immediate threat.
(2) No emergency use shall include—
(A) interaction with prior temporal states beyond what is strictly necessary;
(B) creation of alternate timelines or recursive effects; or
(C) introduction of anachronistic information or objects except where unavoidable.

(d) **Limitations.**

(1) Emergency use shall not be employed for convenience, efficiency, or speculative prevention.
(2) No person shall characterize foreseeable or recurring conditions as emergencies for purposes of avoiding compliance with § 2201.6.

(e) **Post-Use Requirements.**
(1) Any person engaging in emergency time manipulation shall, as soon as practicable—
(A) terminate the temporal effect;
(B) document the circumstances, actions taken, and outcomes; and
(C) submit a report to the appropriate authority.
(2) The report shall include sufficient detail to permit evaluation of necessity, proportionality, and compliance with this Code.

(f) **Review and Determination.**
(1) Emergency use shall be subject to review by an authorized body.
(2) Where the use is determined to be unjustified or excessive, it shall be treated as a violation of this Code.

(g) **Continuing Effects.**
No person shall maintain or extend a temporal effect initiated under emergency authority beyond the period necessary to address the emergency without obtaining authorization under § 2201.6.

(h) **Cross-References.**
For restrictions on time manipulation, see § 2201.1. For authorized uses, see § 2201.2. For temporal paradoxes and anomalies, see § 2201.3. For registration and monitoring requirements, see § 2201.6. For penalties, see § 102.2.

(i) **Historical Annotations.**
This section was enacted under C.C.D. 2891, 33 MR 144, Thu. 9, 1855 following incidents involving unauthorized emergency temporal intervention. Amended under C.C.D. 5712, 45 MR 233, Mon. 4, 1950 to clarify emergency thresholds and limitations. Revised under C.C.D. 10064, 71 MR 119, Tue. 12, 2011 to formalize post-use reporting and review procedures.

Part XXIII: Interdimensional Travel and Reality Manipulation

§ 2301.1 General Regulations on Interdimensional Travel

(a) **General Rule.**
No person shall initiate, attempt, or maintain interdimensional travel except as expressly authorized under this Code.

(b) **Definition and Scope.**
Interdimensional travel shall refer to any magical act involving movement, projection, transmission, displacement, or interaction across distinct planes, dimensions, realities, or otherwise separate existential frameworks, whether stable or unstable, known or unknown.

(c) **Covered Activities.**
This section applies to—
(1) physical traversal between dimensions;
(2) projection of consciousness, perception, or magical presence across dimensional boundaries;
(3) creation, opening, stabilization, or maintenance of portals, rifts, gateways, conduits, or other dimensional access points;
(4) summoning, banishment, or exchange of entities, materials, or forces between dimensions; and
(5) any magical effect, whether direct or indirect, that results in cross-dimensional interaction or transfer.

(d) **Prohibited Conduct.**
No person shall—
(1) open, create, or maintain a dimensional gateway or conduit without lawful authorization;
(2) travel to or from a dimension in a manner that bypasses required authorization, containment, or monitoring procedures;
(3) initiate interdimensional travel where the destination is unknown, undefined, or incapable of reasonable risk assessment;

(4) introduce any person, object, entity, or energy into a dimension where such introduction is reasonably likely to cause instability, contamination, or conflict;
(5) transport matter or entities between dimensions where such transfer creates a material risk to either the originating or destination environment; or
(6) engage in repeated or sustained dimensional interaction in a manner that weakens, destabilizes, or degrades the boundary between dimensions.

(e) **Dimensional Boundary Integrity.**
(1) The separation between dimensions shall be preserved.
(2) No person shall engage in activity that materially weakens, thins, destabilizes, or renders permeable the boundary between dimensions.
(3) Repeated, overlapping, or improperly terminated dimensional breaches shall be presumed to impair boundary integrity unless demonstrated otherwise.

(f) **Gateway and Conduit Restrictions.**
(1) Any dimensional gateway or conduit shall be—
(A) limited in scope, size, and duration;
(B) capable of controlled closure under all reasonably foreseeable conditions; and
(C) subject to active monitoring during operation.
(2) No gateway shall—
(A) remain open beyond its authorized duration;
(B) be left unattended; or
(C) operate without the ability to immediately terminate or seal the connection.
(3) Multi-point, chained, or recursive gateways shall be prohibited unless expressly authorized.

(g) **Containment and Cross-Dimensional Spillover.**
(1) Interdimensional activity shall be conducted in a manner that prevents unintended transfer of matter, energy, entities, or environmental conditions.
(2) Indicators of spillover shall include, but are not limited to—
(A) appearance of foreign matter or entities;
(B) alteration of environmental, magical, or physical conditions;

(C) resonance, distortion, or bleed-through effects across dimensional boundaries.
(3) Upon detection of spillover, the responsible person shall immediately—
(A) initiate containment procedures;
(B) stabilize or terminate the dimensional connection; and
(C) report the condition in accordance with this Code.

(h) **Circumvention Prohibited.**
No person shall avoid the application of this section by—
(1) characterizing interdimensional travel as summoning, projection, illusion, or displacement where such activity results in cross-dimensional transfer; or
(2) embedding dimensional effects within other forms of magic.

(i) **Cross-References.**
For permitted and prohibited dimensions, see § 2301.2. For safety protocols, see § 2301.3. For registration and monitoring, see § 2301.5. For containment and correction of anomalies, see § 2301.7. For licensing requirements, see § 2301.8. For penalties, see § 102.2.

(j) **Historical Annotations.**
This section was enacted under C.C.D. 1987, 26 MR 201, Mon. 7, 1811 following early uncontrolled planar breaches. Amended under C.C.D. 4632, 42 MR 311, Thu. 19, 1903 to regulate gateway creation and containment. Amended under C.C.D. 7811, 48 MR 402, Tue. 6, 1981 to address cross-dimensional contamination risks. Revised under C.C.D. 10144, 71 MR 211, Fri. 18, 2013 to clarify modern dimensional transit methods and enforcement standards.

§ 2301.2 Permitted and Prohibited Dimensions

(a) **General Rule.**
No person shall travel to, access, interact with, or establish a connection to any dimension except as permitted under this section.

(b) **Classification of Dimensions.**
Dimensions shall be classified, for purposes of this Code, based on stability, compatibility, and risk, including but not limited to—

(1) stable dimensions, characterized by consistent physical and magical laws compatible with the originating reality;
(2) conditionally stable dimensions, characterized by variability subject to defined constraints and controls;
(3) unstable dimensions, characterized by unpredictable or fluctuating physical, magical, or structural conditions;
(4) hostile dimensions, characterized by inherent environmental, magical, or existential threat to travelers or originating reality;
(5) incompatible dimensions, characterized by conditions fundamentally inconsistent with survival, coherence, or lawful operation; and
(6) restricted or prohibited dimensions, designated by competent authority due to identified or anticipated risk.

(c) **Permitted Dimensions.**
Travel may be authorized only where—
(1) the dimension has been formally classified and documented;
(2) the risks associated with entry, presence, and exit are reasonably understood and capable of mitigation;
(3) appropriate containment, monitoring, and return mechanisms are established and verified; and
(4) the activity is consistent with the defined purpose, scope, and limitations of the authorization.

(d) **Conditionally Permitted Dimensions.**
(1) Travel to conditionally stable or otherwise limited dimensions shall require additional safeguards, including—
(A) restricted duration;
(B) enhanced monitoring and reporting;
(C) defined and reliable exit protocols; and
(D) contingency measures in the event of instability or loss of control.
(2) No person shall exceed the authorized parameters governing such travel.

(e) **Restricted Dimensions.**
(1) Restricted dimensions may be accessed only under specific, express, and narrowly tailored authorization.
(2) Authorization shall define—
(A) purpose of access;
(B) permitted activities and limitations;
(C) duration and conditions of presence; and

(D) containment and monitoring requirements.
(3) No standing, general, or indefinite authorization shall be permitted.

(f) **Prohibited Dimensions.**
No person shall travel to or interact with dimensions that—
(1) present a high probability of irreversible harm, loss of existence, or permanent displacement;
(2) contain entities, forces, or conditions incapable of containment, control, or isolation;
(3) exhibit persistent structural instability, collapse, recursion, or degradation;
(4) demonstrate active or ongoing interference with originating reality; or
(5) have been designated as prohibited under this Code or by competent authority.

(g) **Use of Outdated or Incomplete Classification.**
No person shall rely on outdated, incomplete, speculative, or unverified classification when engaging in interdimensional activity.

(h) **Unauthorized Interaction.**
No person shall interact with any dimension, entity, or environment outside the scope of authorized classification, purpose, and limitations.

(i) **Cross-References.**
For general regulations on interdimensional travel, see § 2301.1. For safety protocols, see § 2301.3. For licensing and restrictions, see § 2301.8. For containment and anomaly correction, see § 2301.7. For penalties, see § 102.2.

(j) **Historical Annotations.**
This section was enacted under C.C.D. 2154, 28 MR 144, Thu. 12, 1826 to classify known dimensions and restrict unsafe access. Amended under C.C.D. 5021, 43 MR 201, Mon. 3, 1921 to introduce hostile and unstable classifications. Amended under C.C.D. 7342, 47 MR 288, Wed. 21, 1976 to address incompatible and collapse-prone dimensions. Revised under C.C.D. 9981, 70 MR 166, Tue. 5, 2008 to expand classification standards and update prohibited dimension criteria.

§ 2301.3 Safety Protocols for Interdimensional Travel

(a) **General Rule.**
No person shall engage in interdimensional travel unless appropriate safety protocols are established, implemented, and maintained throughout the duration of the activity.

(b) **Pre-Travel Assessment.**
(1) Prior to initiation, the responsible person shall conduct a documented assessment of—
(A) dimensional stability and classification;
(B) environmental, magical, and physical conditions;
(C) known or anticipated entities or hazards; and
(D) compatibility with the originating reality.
(2) No travel shall occur where conditions cannot be reasonably assessed or where risk cannot be adequately mitigated.

(c) **Containment Measures.**
(1) All interdimensional travel shall be conducted within defined containment parameters sufficient to prevent uncontrolled expansion or cross-dimensional interference.
(2) Containment shall include—
(A) controlled access points;
(B) limitation of transfer to authorized persons and materials; and
(C) safeguards against unintended ingress or egress.

(d) **Protective Requirements.**
(1) Any person engaging in interdimensional travel shall utilize protective measures appropriate to the destination dimension.
(2) Such measures shall account for—
(A) atmospheric or environmental incompatibility;
(B) exposure to foreign magical energies; and
(C) cognitive or perceptual distortion.
(3) No person shall knowingly enter a dimension without sufficient protection to ensure survivability and coherence.

(e) **Operational Monitoring.**
(1) Interdimensional activity shall be continuously monitored where reasonably practicable.

(2) Monitoring shall include detection of—
(A) instability in the dimensional boundary;
(B) emergence of unauthorized entities or conditions; and
(C) deviation from authorized parameters.

(f) **Communication and Control.**
(1) A reliable method of communication between originating and destination points shall be maintained where practicable.
(2) The responsible person shall retain the ability to terminate or reverse the dimensional connection.

(g) **Emergency Procedures.**
(1) Procedures shall be established to address—
(A) loss of containment;
(B) emergence of hostile conditions; and
(C) failure of gateway or return mechanisms.
(2) Emergency measures shall prioritize containment and safe return.

(h) **Post-Travel Decontamination and Review.**
(1) Upon return, all persons, objects, and materials shall be subject to inspection sufficient to identify contamination, alteration, or instability.
(2) Any identified condition shall be contained and addressed prior to reintegration into the originating environment.
(3) A post-travel report shall be completed documenting conditions encountered and any deviations from expected parameters.

(i) **Cross-References.**
For general regulations on interdimensional travel, see § 2301.1. For permitted and prohibited dimensions, see § 2301.2. For registration and monitoring requirements, see § 2301.5. For containment and correction of anomalies, see § 2301.7.

(j) **Historical Annotations.**
This section was enacted under C.C.D. 2873, 33 MR 201, Mon. 14, 1854 following early traveler losses due to unassessed dimensional hazards. Amended under C.C.D. 5610, 45 MR 277, Tue. 6, 1949 to establish containment and protective requirements. Revised under C.C.D. 10031, 70 MR 233, Fri. 22, 2010 to expand monitoring and post-travel safeguards.

§ 2301.4 Alternate Reality Manipulation: Definition and Limitations

(a) **General Rule.**
No person shall create, alter, merge, fragment, or otherwise manipulate an alternate reality except as expressly authorized under this Code.

(b) **Definition.**
Alternate reality manipulation shall refer to any magical act that creates, modifies, overlays, diverges, or interacts with a reality distinct from the originating temporal and dimensional framework, including any constructed, parallel, or derivative reality.

(c) **Scope.**
This section applies to—
(1) creation of new or derivative realities;
(2) modification of existing alternate realities;
(3) interaction between distinct realities; and
(4) any effect that results in divergence, duplication, or recombination of reality structures.

(d) **Prohibited Conduct.**
No person shall—
(1) create or sustain an alternate reality that materially destabilizes or interferes with the originating reality;
(2) merge, collapse, or overlap distinct realities in a manner that produces instability or loss of coherence;
(3) transfer persons, objects, or conditions between realities where such transfer creates material risk of disruption;
(4) alter an alternate reality in a manner that produces cascading or uncontrolled effects; or
(5) engage in reality manipulation where the resulting structure cannot be defined, contained, or reversed.

(e) **Reality Integrity.**
(1) Each reality shall be treated as possessing its own structural and causal integrity.
(2) No person shall engage in activity that undermines the stability or coherence of any reality.

(f) **Containment and Isolation.**
(1) Any authorized alternate reality shall be contained and isolated to prevent unintended interaction with other realities.
(2) No person shall allow an alternate reality to expand, merge, or interact beyond its authorized scope.

(g) **Limitations on Persistence.**
(1) Alternate realities shall not be maintained beyond the duration necessary to achieve the authorized purpose.
(2) Indefinite or self-sustaining realities shall be prohibited unless expressly authorized.

(h) **Cross-References.**
For general regulations on interdimensional travel, see § 2301.1. For permitted and prohibited dimensions, see § 2301.2. For containment and correction of anomalies, see § 2301.7. For ethical implications, see § 2301.6.

(i) **Historical Annotations.**
This section was enacted under C.C.D. 3122, 36 MR 144, Thu. 8, 1863 following early experiments in constructed realities. Amended under C.C.D. 6041, 46 MR 201, Mon. 5, 1957 to address merging and instability risks. Revised under C.C.D. 10058, 71 MR 119, Tue. 14, 2011 to clarify containment and persistence limitations.

§ 2301.5 Registration and Monitoring of Dimensional Travel Spells

(a) **General Rule.**
No person shall initiate, attempt, or maintain interdimensional travel or dimensional manipulation unless such activity is registered, approved, and monitored in accordance with this section.

(b) **Registration Requirement.**
(1) Prior to initiation, any dimensional travel or gateway activity shall be registered with the appropriate authority designated under § 102.1.
(2) Registration shall be required regardless of duration, scale, or intended purpose, except as provided under § 2301.7.
(3) No retroactive registration shall be permitted.

(c) **Contents of Registration.**
A registration submitted under this section shall include, to the extent applicable—
(1) identity of the practitioner and any supervising or participating persons;
(2) description of the dimensional activity, including type, method, and mechanism of access;
(3) identification and classification of the destination dimension under § 2301.2;
(4) defined scope, boundaries, and duration of the activity;
(5) assessment of risks, including instability, contamination, and entity interaction;
(6) containment, monitoring, and termination procedures; and
(7) certification of compliance with this Code.

(d) **Approval Requirement.**
(1) No dimensional activity shall be conducted without prior approval.
(2) Approval shall specify—
(A) the authorized dimension and classification;
(B) permitted activities and interactions;
(C) duration and operational limits; and
(D) monitoring and reporting obligations.
(3) Approval shall be denied where risks cannot be adequately controlled or where classification is uncertain.

(e) **Monitoring Requirements.**
(1) All dimensional activity shall be subject to continuous monitoring where reasonably practicable.
(2) Monitoring shall include detection of—
(A) boundary instability or degradation;
(B) unauthorized ingress or egress;
(C) environmental or magical contamination; and
(D) deviation from authorized parameters.

(f) **Reporting Requirements.**
(1) The responsible person shall submit periodic reports documenting—
(A) status of the dimensional activity;
(B) any deviations or irregularities; and
(C) actions taken in response.

(2) Immediate reporting shall be required where any condition arises that may result in instability, spillover, or unauthorized interaction.

(g) **Record Retention.**
All records relating to registration, approval, monitoring, and reporting shall be retained for a period sufficient to permit review and audit.

(h) **Revocation and Suspension.**
(1) Authorization may be suspended or revoked where—
(A) conditions of approval are violated;
(B) monitoring requirements are not met; or
(C) new or unforeseen risks arise.
(2) Upon revocation or suspension, all dimensional activity shall be terminated immediately.

(i) **Cross-References.**
For general regulations on interdimensional travel, see § 2301.1. For permitted and prohibited dimensions, see § 2301.2. For safety protocols, see § 2301.3. For containment and correction of anomalies, see § 2301.7. For licensing requirements, see § 2301.8.

(j) **Historical Annotations.**
This section was enacted under C.C.D. 3610, 38 MR 211, Mon. 9, 1878 following increased frequency of unauthorized dimensional access. Amended under C.C.D. 6402, 46 MR 277, Thu. 3, 1964 to establish structured monitoring requirements. Revised under C.C.D. 10073, 71 MR 188, Tue. 20, 2012 to expand reporting and revocation procedures.

§ 2301.6 Ethical Implications of Altering Realities

(a) **General Rule.**
No person shall engage in interdimensional activity or alternate reality manipulation in a manner that produces unjustified harm to individuals, populations, or the structural integrity of any affected reality.

(b) **Scope.**
This section governs the ethical and systemic consequences of dimensional interaction, including impacts on identity, environment, causation, and coexistence across realities.

(c) **Prohibited Conduct.**

No person shall—
(1) introduce or remove persons, entities, or conditions in a manner that materially alters the composition or continuity of a dimension;
(2) disrupt or exploit a dimension or its inhabitants for personal, commercial, or strategic gain;
(3) impose conditions or alterations that result in systemic instability or degradation;
(4) engage in dimensional activity where consequences cannot be reasonably assessed or contained; or
(5) treat dimensions or their inhabitants as expendable or experimental.

(d) **Respect for Dimensional Autonomy.**
(1) Each dimension shall be treated as possessing its own integrity, continuity, and internal order.
(2) No person shall interfere with the natural development, structure, or function of a dimension beyond what is expressly authorized.

(e) **Impact Assessment.**
(1) Any authorized dimensional activity shall include consideration of—
(A) effects on the originating reality;
(B) effects on the destination dimension; and
(C) potential cross-dimensional consequences.
(2) Authorization shall not be granted where material risk of widespread or irreversible impact exists.

(f) **Minimization Principle.**
Dimensional activity shall be conducted in a manner that minimizes disruption, preserves stability, and limits unintended effects.

(g) **Uncertainty and Risk.**
Where uncertainty regarding consequences is substantial, the proposed activity shall be presumed impermissible.

(h) **Cross-References.**
For general regulations on interdimensional travel, see § 2301.1. For alternate reality manipulation, see § 2301.4. For containment and anomaly correction, see § 2301.7.

(i) **Historical Annotations.**
This section was enacted under C.C.D. 2765, 32 MR 144, Thu. 4, 1852 following disputes regarding exploitation of adjacent dimensions.

Amended under C.C.D. 5118, 43 MR 233, Mon. 16, 1923 to incorporate protections for dimensional inhabitants. Revised under C.C.D. 10041, 70 MR 166, Fri. 11, 2010 to formalize impact assessment and ethical limitations.

§ 2301.7 Containment and Correction of Alternate Reality Anomalies

(a) **General Rule.**
No person shall create, exacerbate, or fail to mitigate an interdimensional or alternate reality anomaly.

(b) **Definition.**
For purposes of this section, an anomaly shall include any condition resulting from dimensional interaction that produces instability, overlap, contamination, or unintended interaction between realities.

(c) **Prohibited Conduct.**
No person shall—
(1) initiate or continue dimensional activity reasonably likely to produce an anomaly;
(2) knowingly interact with or exploit an existing anomaly; or
(3) fail to report a known anomalous condition.

(d) **Duty to Contain.**
(1) Any person who becomes aware of an anomaly shall take reasonable steps to contain or isolate the condition.
(2) Containment shall prioritize preventing further spread or interaction between realities.

(e) **Containment Measures.**
Containment may include—
(1) sealing or terminating dimensional gateways;
(2) isolating affected areas or entities; and
(3) preventing further transfer of matter, energy, or influence.

(f) **Correction Authority.**
(1) Correction of anomalies shall be conducted only by authorized entities acting within their jurisdiction.

(2) Corrective actions shall be limited to restoring stability and shall not introduce additional disruption.

(g) **Restrictions on Self-Correction.**
No person shall attempt unilateral correction where such action—
(1) exceeds their authorization; or
(2) creates a material risk of worsening the anomaly.

(h) **Documentation and Reporting.**
All containment and correction efforts shall be documented, including—
(1) nature and origin of the anomaly;
(2) actions taken; and
(3) resulting conditions.

(i) **Cross-References.**
For general regulations on interdimensional travel, see § 2301.1. For safety protocols, see § 2301.3. For registration and monitoring, see § 2301.5. For alternate reality manipulation, see § 2301.4.

(j) **Historical Annotations.**
This section was enacted under C.C.D. 2488, 30 MR 201, Mon. 22, 1846 following early dimensional overlap incidents. Amended under C.C.D. 5893, 45 MR 311, Tue. 13, 1955 to establish containment authority and procedures. Revised under C.C.D. 10012, 70 MR 119, Thu. 2, 2009 to clarify modern anomaly detection and correction practices.

§ 2301.8 Dimensional Travel Licensing and Restrictions

(a) **General Rule.**
No person shall engage in interdimensional travel or related dimensional manipulation without a valid license issued in accordance with this section.

(b) **License Requirement.**
(1) A dimensional travel license shall be required for—
(A) creation or maintenance of dimensional gateways or conduits;
(B) physical traversal between dimensions;
(C) projection of consciousness or magical presence across dimensional boundaries where such projection produces material interaction;

(D) summoning, banishment, or transfer of entities, materials, or forces across dimensions; and
(E) any sustained, repeated, or commercial cross-dimensional activity.
(2) No person shall—
(A) operate under another person's license;
(B) permit unauthorized use of their license; or
(C) engage in dimensional activity under an expired, suspended, or otherwise invalid license.

(c) **Classes of Licenses.**
Licenses shall be issued based on scope and risk, including—
(1) Class I (Limited Observation). Permitting passive observational access with no interaction, no transfer of matter, and no alteration of the destination dimension;
(2) Class II (Controlled Interaction). Permitting limited interaction within stable or conditionally stable dimensions, including non-invasive communication and restricted presence;
(3) Class III (Advanced Transit). Permitting full traversal and controlled transfer of persons, objects, and materials under defined containment and monitoring conditions; and
(4) Class IV (Restricted Operations). Permitting access to restricted or high-risk dimensions under heightened oversight, enhanced containment, and continuous supervision.

(d) **Eligibility and Qualification.**
(1) An applicant shall demonstrate—
(A) competency in dimensional theory, including boundary mechanics and dimensional stability;
(B) ability to implement containment, safety, and emergency protocols under § 2301.3;
(C) familiarity with dimensional classification under § 2301.2; and
(D) capacity to monitor, control, and terminate dimensional activity.
(2) Qualification may require—
(A) formal examination;
(B) supervised practical experience;
(C) certification by an approved body; and
(D) demonstration of prior compliance with this Code.
(3) No license shall be issued where the applicant lacks the ability to safely conduct the requested activity.

(e) **Scope and Operational Limits.**
(1) A license shall define—
(A) the specific dimensions authorized for access;
(B) the classification of such dimensions;
(C) the permitted methods of access and interaction;
(D) duration, frequency, and scale of permitted activity; and
(E) any additional restrictions necessary to ensure safety and compliance.
(2) Activities not expressly permitted shall be deemed prohibited.
(3) No person shall exceed the scope, conditions, or limitations of their license.

(f) **Renewal, Review, and Continuing Qualification.**
(1) Licenses shall be subject to periodic renewal based on risk classification and scope of activity.
(2) Renewal shall require—
(A) demonstration of continued competency;
(B) review of prior activity and compliance history; and
(C) absence of unresolved violations or safety concerns.
(3) Failure to meet renewal standards shall result in expiration or restriction of the license.

(g) **Administrative Actions, Suspension, and Revocation.**
(1) The issuing authority may take administrative action where a license holder—
(A) violates the terms or conditions of the license;
(B) demonstrates unsafe, negligent, or uncontrolled dimensional practices;
(C) fails to comply with monitoring, reporting, or containment requirements; or
(D) presents a material risk to dimensional or interdimensional stability.
(2) Administrative actions may include—
(A) modification or limitation of the license scope;
(B) imposition of additional conditions or oversight requirements;
(C) temporary suspension of the license; or
(D) full revocation of the license.
(3) Suspension shall require immediate cessation of all licensed activity for the duration of the suspension.
(4) Revocation shall—
(A) terminate all authorization to conduct dimensional activity;

(B) prohibit reapplication for a defined period or until specified conditions are met; and
(C) require demonstration of remediation prior to any future issuance.
(5) Continued activity following suspension or revocation shall constitute a separate violation.

(h) **Non-Transferability.**
No license issued under this section shall be transferred, assigned, delegated, or otherwise used by any person other than the license holder.

(i) **Cross-References.**
For general regulations on interdimensional travel, see § 2301.1. For permitted and prohibited dimensions, see § 2301.2. For safety protocols, see § 2301.3. For registration and monitoring, see § 2301.5.

(j) **Historical Annotations.**
This section was enacted under C.C.D. 3321, 37 MR 144, Tue. 10, 1871 to establish licensing requirements for dimensional practitioners. Amended under C.C.D. 6012, 46 MR 233, Mon. 6, 1958 to introduce license classes. Amended under C.C.D. 7844, 48 MR 311, Thu. 14, 1982 to formalize suspension and revocation authority. Revised under C.C.D. 10092, 71 MR 201, Wed. 15, 2012 to expand qualification, oversight, and enforcement standards.

§ 2301.9 Cross-Dimensional Trade Regulations

(a) **General Rule.**
No person shall engage in the exchange, transfer, sale, barter, or acquisition of goods, services, entities, or materials across dimensions except in compliance with this section.

(b) **Scope.**
This section applies to—
(1) import or export of goods, materials, or resources between dimensions;
(2) provision of services involving cross-dimensional interaction or delivery;
(3) exchange of magical, biological, or environmental assets; and
(4) any transaction in which value is derived from cross-dimensional transfer.

(c) **Authorization Requirement.**
(1) Cross-dimensional trade shall require prior authorization.
(2) Authorization shall specify—
(A) the identity of parties involved;
(B) the nature and classification of goods or services;
(C) the dimensions involved;
(D) the method and route of transfer; and
(E) any applicable conditions or limitations.

(d) **Permitted Trade.**
Trade may be authorized only where—
(1) the goods or services do not present material risk of contamination, instability, or incompatibility;
(2) the transaction can be conducted within controlled, monitored, and contained conditions;
(3) the transfer does not violate restrictions applicable to either dimension; and
(4) adequate inspection and verification procedures are in place.

(e) **Prohibited Trade.**
No person shall engage in cross-dimensional trade involving—
(1) unstable, hazardous, or self-propagating materials;
(2) entities incapable of containment, classification, or safe transfer;
(3) goods or substances that materially alter environmental, magical, or structural conditions;
(4) items or resources designated as restricted or prohibited; or
(5) any transfer where risks cannot be reasonably assessed or mitigated.

(f) **Valuation, Disclosure, and Documentation.**
(1) All cross-dimensional transactions shall be fully documented and valued.
(2) Documentation shall include—
(A) accurate description of goods or services;
(B) fair valuation reflecting nature and origin; and
(C) terms and conditions of exchange.
(3) No person shall—
(A) obscure or misrepresent the nature or value of goods;
(B) conceal origin or dimensional characteristics; or
(C) structure transactions to evade disclosure requirements.

(g) **Transfer Protocols.**
(1) All transfers shall occur through authorized and controlled gateways.
(2) Transfer procedures shall include—
(A) Pre-Transfer Verification.
(i) inspection and classification of goods or entities;
(ii) confirmation of authorization and compliance;
(iii) assessment of compatibility with destination dimension; and
(iv) verification that containment measures are adequate;
(B) Transfer Execution.
(i) controlled conveyance through a monitored gateway;
(ii) restriction to authorized quantities and materials;
(iii) maintenance of containment and environmental integrity during transit; and
(iv) real-time monitoring for deviation or instability;
(C) Post-Transfer Validation.
(i) confirmation of delivery and receipt;
(ii) inspection for contamination, alteration, or instability;
(iii) verification of compliance with authorization conditions; and
(iv) documentation of final condition and status.

(h) **Containment, Inspection, and Remediation.**
(1) All imported or exported materials shall be subject to inspection sufficient to identify—
(A) contamination or foreign influence;
(B) instability or degradation;
(C) incompatibility with receiving environment; and
(D) unauthorized or concealed properties.
(2) Non-compliant materials shall be—
(A) isolated within controlled containment;
(B) returned to origin where feasible; or
(C) neutralized or destroyed where necessary to prevent harm.
(3) Remediation actions shall be documented and reported.

(i) **Record-Keeping Requirements.**
(1) Persons engaged in cross-dimensional trade shall maintain detailed records, including—
(A) identity of all parties;
(B) description and classification of goods or services;
(C) value and consideration exchanged;
(D) date, time, and method of transfer;

(E) dimensional origin and destination; and
(F) applicable restrictions, conditions, and compliance measures.
(2) Records shall be retained for a period sufficient to permit audit, investigation, and enforcement.

(j) **Anti-Circumvention Rules.**
(1) No person shall structure or route transactions to avoid compliance with this section.
(2) Prohibited methods include—
(A) routing goods through intermediary dimensions to obscure origin or destination;
(B) segmenting transactions to avoid thresholds or detection;
(C) mischaracterizing goods, services, or entities; and
(D) using proxies or intermediaries to conceal participation.

(k) **Special Rules for Living or Sentient Entities.**
(1) No living or sentient entity shall be transferred as part of a trade transaction except where expressly authorized.
(2) Authorization shall require—
(A) verification of lawful status and classification of the entity;
(B) implementation of appropriate containment, transport, and care protocols; and
(C) compliance with all applicable ethical and regulatory standards.
(3) No entity shall be transferred in a manner that subjects it to harm, instability, or loss of coherence.

(l) **Cross-References.**
For general regulations on interdimensional travel, see § 2301.1. For permitted and prohibited dimensions, see § 2301.2. For safety protocols, see § 2301.3. For licensing requirements, see § 2301.8.

(m) **Historical Annotations.**
This section was enacted under C.C.D. 3544, 38 MR 201, Mon. 3, 1879 following early trade disputes involving dimensional goods. Amended under C.C.D. 6228, 46 MR 311, Tue. 11, 1961 to address contamination and inspection requirements. Amended under C.C.D. 8122, 49 MR 233, Thu. 8, 1988 to regulate intermediary routing and anti-circumvention practices. Revised under C.C.D. 10105, 71 MR 233, Thu. 19, 2013 to expand record-keeping, valuation, and compliance requirements.

Part XXIV: Magical Broadcasting

§ 2401.1 Regulation of Magical Broadcasting Networks

(a) **General Rule.**
No person shall establish, operate, maintain, or transmit through a magical broadcasting network except in compliance with this section.

(b) **Definition.**
For purposes of this Part, a magical broadcasting network is any coordinated magical system used to transmit, relay, or disseminate magical content, signals, or influence to multiple recipients simultaneously or in sequence, whether through arcane projection, ritual transmission, enchanted media, or perceptual or cognitive channels.

(c) **Scope of Regulation.**
This section applies to any system that extends the reach of a magical act beyond its immediate origin, including continuous or scheduled transmissions, relay-based amplification, distributed signal architectures, or any arrangement designed to produce recurring or simultaneous reception across multiple recipients. The characterization of such activity as entertainment, communication, demonstration, or ambient effect shall not affect its treatment under this section.

(d) **Authorization.**
(1) No broadcasting network shall be established or operated without prior authorization.
(2) Authorization shall define the permissible outer limits of operation, including—
(A) the class or category of content authorized for transmission;
(B) the method or methods of transmission, including whether such transmission is—
(i) direct and singular;
(ii) relay-based; or
(iii) distributed across multiple nodes; and
(C) the scope of reach, including any limitation based on geography, recipient class, or conceptual or dimensional boundary.

(3) Authorization shall not be construed to permit any content otherwise prohibited under this Code.

(e) **Network Integrity and Propagation Control.**
A broadcasting network shall be designed and maintained to ensure that all transmissions remain stable, bounded, and subject to operator control. The operator shall take reasonable steps to prevent unintended propagation arising from structural or magical characteristics of the network, including propagation caused by resonance, duplication, or relay chaining.
(1) Without limiting the generality of the foregoing, the operator shall ensure that the network does not—
(A) amplify signals beyond authorized strength;
(B) produce recursive or self-reinforcing transmission loops; or
(C) propagate content through mechanisms that—
(i) extend beyond authorized nodes;
(ii) replicate transmissions without command; or
(iii) persist beyond intended duration.
(2) Any system relying upon self-propagating or poorly characterized magical behavior shall be presumed noncompliant unless demonstrated otherwise.

(f) **Operational Control.**
The operator shall retain continuous and effective control over all transmissions. Each network shall include mechanisms sufficient to terminate, interrupt, or isolate any broadcast at any time. Where the network utilizes multiple transmission points or relay nodes, the operator shall maintain the ability to identify, with reasonable precision—
(1) the originating node of a transmission;
(2) the time and duration of transmission; and
(3) any modification or interference occurring during transmission, including modification arising from—
(A) relay interaction; or
(B) environmental or dimensional effects.

(g) **Responsibility for Content.**
The operator shall be responsible for all content transmitted through the network, regardless of origin. This responsibility extends to content supplied by third parties, pre-configured transmissions, and any effect that arises upon reception.

(1) A broadcast shall not be structured so as to avoid responsibility by—
(A) distributing components of an effect across multiple transmissions; or
(B) relying upon the recipient to complete or activate a magical effect.

(h) **Interference and Unauthorized Access.**
No person shall interfere with, redirect, alter, or inject content into a magical broadcasting network without authorization. Prohibited conduct includes any action that materially alters the nature, scope, or effect of a broadcast, including conduct that—
(1) substitutes or suppresses content;
(2) introduces additional magical effects; or
(3) alters the transmission path in a manner that—
(A) expands the audience;
(B) defeats containment; or
(C) obscures the origin of the broadcast.

(i) **Record-Keeping.**
Operators shall maintain records sufficient to demonstrate compliance with this section, including records of transmissions, authorization parameters, and any incidents affecting network integrity or control.

(j) **Cross-References.**
For restrictions on broadcast content, see § 2401.2. For cross-dimensional broadcasting, see § 2401.3. For monitoring and oversight, see § 2401.4.

(k) **Historical Annotations.**
This section was enacted under C.C.D. 3721, 39 MR 166, Tue. 12, 1886 to address the emergence of coordinated magical broadcasting systems that extended spell effects beyond their intended point of origin. Amended under C.C.D. 6554, 46 MR 311, Mon. 7, 1965 to address interference between networks and manipulation of relay structures to alter or hijack transmissions. Revised under C.C.D. 10126, 71 MR 144, Thu. 10, 2012 to address distributed and multi-node broadcasting architectures and failures of centralized transmission control.

§ 2401.2 Restrictions on Broadcasting Spells and Enchantments

(a) **General Rule.**

No person shall broadcast any spell, enchantment, or magical effect except as permitted under this section.

(b) **Prohibition on Effectual Broadcasts.**
No broadcast shall produce any operative magical effect upon recipients. A broadcast shall be deemed effectual where reception itself, or ordinary engagement with the transmission, completes any element necessary for the effect to occur, whether such effect is immediate, delayed, or dependent upon repetition.

(c) **Embedded and Indirect Effects.**
The prohibitions of this section apply to magical effects embedded within or distributed across broadcast content. No person shall structure a broadcast so that a prohibited effect arises through—
(1) repeated exposure;
(2) sequential assembly of content; or
(3) concurrent reception of multiple transmissions.
(2) A broadcast shall be treated as a single transmission for purposes of this section where its components are designed to operate collectively.

(d) **Permitted Informational Content.**
Informational, educational, or demonstrative content may be transmitted only where such content is inert and incapable of producing a magical effect. A demonstration shall not include any element that—
(1) functions as a trigger or conduit; or
(2) completes, in whole or in part, a real spell or enchantment.

(e) **Containment.**
All broadcast content shall remain fully contained within the transmission medium. Containment shall be deemed to fail where the broadcast—
(1) leaves residual magical influence;
(2) creates a latent condition in the recipient or environment; or
(3) alters the recipient's susceptibility to subsequent magical effects, including alteration arising from—
(A) cumulative exposure; or
(B) interaction with other lawful or unlawful magical sources.

(f) **Passive and Subliminal Influence.**
No person shall broadcast content designed to produce passive, subliminal, or cumulative magical influence. A broadcast shall be

presumed to violate this subsection where its structure or design would reasonably be understood to bypass conscious awareness or resistance.

(g) **Anti-Circumvention.**
No person shall characterize a broadcast as non-magical or purely artistic where the transmission in fact carries or contributes to a prohibited magical effect, whether directly or indirectly.

(h) **Interpretive Rules and Evidentiary Standards.**
(1) In determining whether a broadcast violates this section, consideration shall be given to—
(A) the structure and sequencing of the transmission;
(B) the relationship between component elements; and
(C) whether the broadcast, viewed as a whole, is reasonably capable of producing a prohibited effect.
(2) The absence of an identifiable incantation, spell name, or discrete magical act shall not preclude a finding that a broadcast is effectual.
(3) A broadcast shall be evaluated based on its actual or reasonably foreseeable effects rather than its stated purpose.

(i) **Aggregation and Coordination.**
(1) Multiple broadcasts may be evaluated in the aggregate where—
(A) they are temporally or structurally related; and
(B) they produce or are capable of producing a unified effect.
(2) Where such aggregation applies, the broadcasts shall be treated as a single transmission for purposes of this section.

(j) **Presumption of Effect.**
Where a broadcast produces observable changes in perception, cognition, behavior, or environmental conditions across multiple recipients, such broadcast shall be presumed to be effectual unless demonstrated otherwise.

(k) **Cross-References.**
For network regulation, see § 2401.1. For cross-dimensional broadcasting, see § 2401.3. For monitoring requirements, see § 2401.4.

(l) **Historical Annotations.**
This section was enacted under C.C.D. 3892, 40 MR 201, Thu. 6, 1892 to address broadcast transmissions that produced unintended magical effects across large audiences. Amended under C.C.D. 6121, 46 MR 233,

Tue. 15, 1960 to address embedded and multi-part enchantments designed to evade single-transmission prohibitions. Revised under C.C.D. 10139, 71 MR 188, Fri. 22, 2012 to address distributed broadcast techniques and modern anti-circumvention concerns.

§ 2401.3 Broadcasting to Alternate Realities and Dimensions

(a) **General Rule.**
No person shall transmit magical content across dimensional or reality boundaries except as expressly authorized.

(b) **Scope.**
This section applies to any broadcast that originates in one dimension and is received in another, or that otherwise traverses dimensional boundaries as part of its transmission.

(c) **Authorization.**
Cross-dimensional broadcasting requires specific authorization identifying the receiving dimension, the permitted audience, and the nature of the content to be transmitted. Such authorization shall include safeguards sufficient to ensure that the transmission remains contained and does not produce unintended effects.

(d) **Content Restrictions.**
No person shall transmit content into another dimension where such content—
(1) produces any operative effect;
(2) destabilizes local magical or environmental conditions; or
(3) enables interaction between realities beyond the scope of authorization, including interaction arising through—
(A) responsive signal exchange; or
(B) synchronization of magical effects across dimensions.

(e) **Compatibility and Control.**
Prior to transmission, the broadcaster shall determine, to the extent reasonably practicable, how the signal will manifest in the receiving dimension and whether it may be received outside authorized channels. No broadcast shall proceed where such determination cannot be made with reasonable confidence.

(f) **Containment.**
Cross-dimensional broadcasts shall remain confined to their authorized scope and shall not result in leakage, replication, or bleed-through. Any indication of such conditions shall require immediate termination or isolation.

(g) **Transmission Path Integrity.**
(1) A broadcast shall not be routed through intermediate dimensions or boundary states in a manner that—
(A) alters the nature of the content;
(B) expands the audience beyond authorization; or
(C) introduces instability into the transmission.
(2) Where a transmission passes through multiple dimensional layers, the broadcaster shall maintain sufficient control to ensure that—
(A) the signal remains intact; and
(B) no unintended interaction occurs during transit.

(h) **Reception Control.**
(1) The broadcaster shall take reasonable steps to ensure that reception is limited to authorized recipients.
(2) No broadcast shall proceed where the broadcaster knows or should know that—
(A) reception may occur in unauthorized regions of the receiving dimension; or
(B) the signal may be intercepted or replicated.

(i) **Cross-Dimensional Feedback and Interaction.**
(1) No broadcast shall permit or induce feedback from the receiving dimension that alters the originating transmission.
(2) Any indication of responsive or bidirectional interaction shall require immediate termination.

(j) **Cross-References.**
For interdimensional regulation, see Part XXIII. For content restrictions, see § 2401.2. For monitoring requirements, see § 2401.4.

(k) **Historical Annotations.**
This section was enacted under C.C.D. 4011, 41 MR 144, Mon. 9, 1898 to address uncontrolled cross-dimensional signal transmission and unintended reception beyond the originating reality. Amended under

C.C.D. 6683, 46 MR 311, Thu. 18, 1967 to address incompatibility between transmitted signals and receiving environments. Revised under C.C.D. 10158, 71 MR 201, Tue. 27, 2012 to address containment failures and cross-reality dissemination risks.

§ 2401.4 Monitoring and Regulation of Public Magical Broadcasts

(a) **General Rule.**
All public magical broadcasts shall be subject to monitoring and regulatory oversight sufficient to ensure compliance with this Code.

(b) **Monitoring Systems.**
Broadcasting networks shall implement monitoring systems capable of detecting noncompliant content, signal instability, and prohibited magical effects in real time where reasonably practicable. Such systems shall be capable of identifying effects arising from embedded content, delayed activation, or cumulative exposure.

(c) **Oversight Authority.**
Authorized bodies may inspect, review, and audit broadcasting operations. Operators shall provide access to systems, records, and transmissions upon request.

(d) **Intervention and Control.**
Where a broadcast is determined to be noncompliant, the operator shall immediately terminate or isolate the transmission. No person shall continue a broadcast after notice of noncompliance.

(e) **Incident Response.**
Upon detection of malfunction or prohibited content, the operator shall take corrective action sufficient to prevent continued transmission and shall document the incident, including—
(1) the nature of the violation;
(2) the duration of the transmission; and
(3) the scope of exposure, to the extent reasonably ascertainable.

(f) **Record-Keeping.**
Operators shall maintain records of transmitted content, authorization status, and any incidents or corrective actions taken.

(g) **Emergency Intervention.**
Authorized bodies may intervene where necessary to prevent harm or continued violation, including suspension or forced termination of broadcasts.

(h) **Monitoring Standards and Review.**
(1) Monitoring systems shall be evaluated periodically to ensure effectiveness.
(2) Such evaluation shall include—
(A) the ability to detect prohibited effects;
(B) responsiveness to deviations; and
(C) reliability under high-volume transmission conditions.

(i) **Audit and Verification.**
(1) Authorized bodies may conduct audits of broadcasting systems and records.
(2) Audits may include—
(A) review of recorded transmissions;
(B) testing of monitoring systems; and
(C) verification of compliance with authorization parameters.

(j) **Failure of Monitoring Systems.**
(1) Where monitoring systems fail to detect noncompliant content, the operator shall take corrective action.
(2) Repeated failure to detect violations shall constitute evidence of inadequate monitoring.

(k) **Cross-References.**
For network regulation, see § 2401.1. For content restrictions, see § 2401.2. For cross-dimensional broadcasting, see § 2401.3.

(l) **Historical Annotations.**
This section was enacted under C.C.D. 4177, 42 MR 166, Tue. 3, 1904 to address unauthorized magical broadcasts affecting public audiences without oversight. Amended under C.C.D. 7012, 47 MR 233, Mon. 11, 1972 to establish centralized monitoring and regulatory authority. Revised under C.C.D. 10182, 71 MR 211, Thu. 5, 2013 to address failures in real-time monitoring and delayed intervention in large-scale broadcast systems.

Part XXV: Property and Zoning Regulations

§ 2501.1 Magical Property and Zoning Requirements

(a) **General Rule.**
No person shall use, occupy, alter, develop, lease, license, or maintain real or conceptual property for magical purposes except in compliance with applicable zoning, classification, and use restrictions under this Part.

(b) **Magical Use Classification.**
All property upon which magical activity occurs shall be classified according to its primary magical use. Such classification shall account for—
(1) the nature and category of magical activity conducted;
(2) the frequency, duration, and intensity of such activity;
(3) the presence of recurring, continuous, or residual magical effects; and
(4) the reasonably foreseeable effects on surrounding properties, environments, and populations.
(2) Where multiple forms of activity occur, classification shall be based on the dominant use or, where no dominant use exists, the use presenting the greatest potential impact.

(c) **Permitted Uses.**
Magical use of property shall be permitted only where such use is consistent with the designated zoning classification.
(1) No property shall be used for a category of magical activity materially different from its designated use.
(2) A change in magical use shall require prior reclassification, including where such change results from—
(A) increased intensity or scale of activity;
(B) introduction of new forms of magic; or
(C) modification of the property in a manner that alters its functional use.

(d) **Mixed-Use Property.**

Where property is used for both magical and non-magical purposes, such use shall be structured so as to prevent interference, contamination, or unintended interaction between uses.
(1) The presence of non-magical occupants shall not reduce compliance obligations.
(2) Shared use shall be prohibited where a reasonable person would conclude that such arrangement increases risk of—
(A) environmental disruption;
(B) magical contamination of non-magical space; or
(C) exposure of magical activity.
(3) Separation of uses shall be maintained through physical, spatial, or magical means sufficient to prevent crossover of effects.

(e) **Structural and Environmental Compatibility.**
Magical use of property shall be conducted in a manner consistent with the physical and metaphysical characteristics of the property.
(1) No person shall conduct magical activity where such activity—
(A) exceeds the capacity of the property to safely contain it;
(B) alters the structural integrity of the property; or
(C) disrupts environmental or magical equilibrium in surrounding areas.
(2) Compatibility shall be evaluated based on—
(A) material composition of the property;
(B) proximity to other properties or zones; and
(C) cumulative impact of repeated or sustained activity.

(f) **Zoning Compliance and Enforcement.**
Use of property in violation of applicable zoning classification shall constitute a violation of this Code, regardless of whether such use is otherwise lawful in isolation.
(1) Continued use after notice of noncompliance shall constitute a separate violation.
(2) Each day of continued noncompliance may be treated as a distinct occurrence.

(g) **Cross-References.**
For environmental impact and resource stability, see Part IX. For concealment requirements in non-magical areas, see § 401.7. For monitoring and reporting of magical effects, see § 901.3.

(h) **Historical Annotations.**

This section was enacted under C.C.D. 2881, 31 MR 204, Wed. 3, 1762 to establish baseline zoning distinctions for magical activity following conflicts between incompatible uses of property. Amended under C.C.D. 5112, 43 MR 118, Mon. 14, 1911 to address mixed-use property and interference between magical and non-magical occupancy. Revised under C.C.D. 9871, 68 MR 302, Tue. 19, 2008 to address high-density magical development and failures in zoning enforcement.

§ 2501.2 Designation of Magical Zones and Sanctuaries

(a) **General Rule.**
Magical zones and sanctuaries may be designated for the purpose of regulating, concentrating, restricting, or preserving magical activity within defined boundaries.

(b) **Designation Authority.**
Zones and sanctuaries shall be designated by the appropriate authority based on—
(1) environmental conditions and stability;
(2) population density and proximity to non-magical areas;
(3) intensity and frequency of magical activity;
(4) presence of sensitive or protected magical resources; and
(5) the need to isolate, contain, or preserve specific magical practices.

(c) **Types of Zones.**
Designated zones may include, but are not limited to—
(1) high-activity zones, permitting concentrated magical use under controlled conditions;
(2) restricted zones, limiting or prohibiting specified forms of magic; and
(3) sanctuary zones, preserving protected environments, entities, or practices.
(2) A zone may be designated for multiple purposes where necessary to achieve regulatory objectives.

(d) **Use Restrictions.**
Each zone shall impose restrictions consistent with its designation.
(1) No person shall conduct magical activity inconsistent with the zone classification.
(2) Restrictions may apply to—

(A) type or category of magic;
(B) intensity, scale, or duration of activity;
(C) time-based limitations; or
(D) methods of execution.
(3) Compliance shall be determined based on the actual or reasonably foreseeable effects of the activity.

(e) **Boundary and Containment Requirements.**
Zones shall be defined with sufficient clarity to ensure enforceability.
(1) Boundaries shall account for both physical and metaphysical extension of magical effects.
(2) No activity shall be conducted in a manner that causes effects to extend beyond designated boundaries.
(3) Where effects are capable of extending beyond boundaries under normal operation, additional containment measures shall be required.

(f) **Sanctuary Protections.**
Sanctuary zones shall provide heightened protection for designated resources or entities.
(1) No person shall disrupt, extract, alter, or interfere with protected elements within a sanctuary.
(2) Access may be restricted, conditioned, or prohibited based on preservation requirements.
(3) Activities that indirectly affect protected elements shall be treated as violations where such effects are reasonably foreseeable.

(g) **Interaction with Non-Magical Areas.**
Where a zone is adjacent to or overlaps with non-magical populations, all activity within such zone shall comply with concealment requirements under § 401.7.
(1) No zone designation shall be construed to permit exposure of magical activity.
(2) Additional restrictions may be imposed to ensure compliance with secrecy obligations.
(3) Activities shall be evaluated based on their visibility, detectability, and potential for disclosure.

(h) **Modification and Revocation.**
Zones may be modified, expanded, or revoked where conditions change or where continued designation is no longer appropriate.

(1) Modification may be required where—
(A) environmental conditions deteriorate;
(B) activity exceeds anticipated levels; or
(C) secrecy risks increase.

(i) **Cross-References.**
For environmental regulation, see Part IX. For secrecy requirements, see § 401.7. For interdimensional considerations, see Part XXIII.

(j) **Historical Annotations.**
This section was enacted under C.C.D. 3014, 33 MR 77, Fri. 22, 1789 to establish designated areas for concentrated magical activity and separation of incompatible uses. Amended under C.C.D. 5642, 44 MR 209, Thu. 6, 1936 to introduce sanctuary protections for vulnerable magical ecosystems and entities. Revised under C.C.D. 10002, 70 MR 118, Wed. 11, 2011 to address boundary enforcement and increasing interaction with non-magical populations.

§ 2501.3 Magical Conservation Easements

(a) **In General.**
A magical conservation easement is a voluntary, legally enforceable restriction placed upon magical real property, or upon magical attributes affixed thereto, for the purpose of preserving such property for environmental, arcane, historical, ecological, or interplanar stability. A conservation easement shall be recognized under this section only if recorded and maintained in accordance with Part IX and applicable provisions governing magical property interests.

(b) **Permissible Purposes.**
A magical conservation easement shall be considered valid if its principal objective is one or more of the following:
(1) The preservation of natural or semi-natural magical habitats, including but not limited to elemental convergence sites, ley-line junctures, mycelial whisper-forests, and locations where mana accumulates at rates exceeding the median threshold established by the Department of Magical Affairs (DMA).
(2) The protection of endangered magical species or qualified creatures designated under § 101.6, including their habitats, migration patterns, and breeding or manifestation grounds.

(3) The maintenance of historical, ceremonial, or prophetic sites of recognized or reasonably inferred significance, including sites where repeated ritual use has resulted in persistent magical imprinting.
(4) The prevention of development or activity that would disrupt the natural order as defined in § 901.1, including the manipulation of probability, fate, or ambient magical equilibrium in a manner inconsistent with preservation objectives.

(c) **Restrictions on Use.**
(1) A property subject to a magical conservation easement may not be used for any activity that—
(A) Alters, diminishes, amplifies, or transmutes the magical properties of the land, except where permitted under a limited-use exemption granted pursuant to subsection (d);
(B) Introduces artificially generated mana, excess ritual residue, necromantic seepage, or other magical byproducts that may accumulate, propagate, or destabilize local conditions;
(C) Results in cumulative magical degradation, even where individual actions would not independently constitute a violation;
(D) Interferes with the preservation objectives underlying the easement, whether directly or through indirect or delayed effects; or
(E) Facilitates third-party use inconsistent with the terms of the easement, whether or not such use is explicitly authorized elsewhere.
(2) Minor, non-harmful disturbances, including the lighting of travel lanterns, non-destructive harvesting of non-sentient flora, routine agricultural activity, and incidental magical activity conducted in accordance with this Code, shall not constitute violations unless expressly restricted by the easement document.
(3) Repeated minor disturbances that collectively undermine the preservation objectives of the easement may be treated as a violation notwithstanding paragraph (2).

(d) **Limited-Use Exemptions.**
(1) The Commissioner of Magical Affairs may authorize a limited-use exemption where necessary for—
(A) Conservation-compatible research, including observational or non-invasive magical study;
(B) Emergency magical response activities necessary to prevent immediate harm to persons, creatures, or surrounding property; or

(C) Ritual maintenance necessary to preserve or stabilize the land's existing magical condition.
(2) Any such exemption shall specify duration, permissible activities, geographic scope, and any applicable reporting obligations.
(3) Exemptions shall be narrowly construed and shall not be interpreted to permit ongoing or indefinite deviation from the easement's core preservation purpose.

(e) **Prohibited Clauses.**
A magical conservation easement shall not contain any clause that—
(1) Assigns sentience, agency, or legal personality to the land for purposes of negotiating, enforcing, or modifying the easement;
(2) Requires the landowner or any other person to serve as a familiar, conduit, or vessel for the land;
(3) Permits activities otherwise prohibited under this Code or purports to override generally applicable provisions without express statutory authority;
(4) Establishes self-modifying or conditionally expanding restrictions not capable of being reasonably interpreted or enforced; or
(5) Delegates enforcement authority to entities not recognized under this Code or otherwise authorized by the Department.

(f) **Duration.**
(1) A magical conservation easement shall be perpetual unless expressly stated otherwise.
(2) Where non-perpetual, the term shall not be less than fifty years, except where a shorter duration is necessary to address temporary or transitional magical conditions.
(3) The easement shall bind all successors, assigns, heirs, reincarnations, resurrections, transfigurations, or other legally recognizable continuations of the property owner's interest.

(g) **Reporting Obligations.**
(1) The grantee shall submit periodic reports, as required by the Department, documenting—
(A) The current magical condition of the property;
(B) Any disturbances, breaches, fluctuations, or anomalies;
(C) Any contact with qualified creatures under § 101.6; and
(D) Any activities conducted pursuant to limited-use exemptions.

(2) Reports shall be sufficiently detailed to allow the Department to assess compliance and detect patterns of degradation or misuse.
(3) Failure to submit required reports may result in penalties under § 102.2 and may trigger additional review or inspection.

(h) **Termination.**
(1) A magical conservation easement may be terminated only—
(A) By judicial order upon a finding that the land's magical properties have irreversibly dissipated through no fault of the owner; or
(B) By lawful governmental action upon a showing of compelling necessity, subject to applicable compensation requirements determined by the Commissioner of Magical Affairs.
(2) Termination shall not be permitted where restoration or stabilization remains reasonably possible.
(3) An easement may not be terminated merely because the land has become inconvenient, unfashionable, ominous, mildly cursed, or the subject of local gossip.

(i) **Enforcement.**
(1) The grantee, the Registrar of Magical Deeds, any authorized governmental entity, or any party with a recognized interest under Part IX may enforce the terms of a magical conservation easement.
(2) Remedies shall include injunctive relief, restoration orders, mana-stabilization directives, and penalties under § 102.2.
(3) Enforcement actions shall be interpreted in a manner consistent with the preservation objectives of the easement and the principles set forth in § 901.1.
(4) Nothing in this subsection shall be construed to permit enforcement through otherwise prohibited magical practices.

(j) **Cross-References.**
For qualified creatures, see § 101.6. For disruption of the natural order, see § 901.1. For licensing and authorized spellcasting practices, see § 401.7. For penalties, see § 102.2.

(k) **Historical Annotations.**
This section was originally established under C.C.D. 247, 67 MR 1124, and subsequently amended under C.C.D. 312, 71 MR 5089, to introduce reporting requirements and exemption procedures. Further revisions were enacted under C.C.D. 403, 74 MR 9931, to incorporate adjacency

protections, and under C.C.D. 511, 78 MR 2247, to clarify certification standards for historically or prophetically significant lands.

§ 2501.4 Designated Zones and Protected Areas under the Secrecy of Magic Act

(a) **General Rule.**
Certain zones and areas shall be designated or regulated for the purpose of ensuring compliance with the Secrecy of Magic Act (§ 401.7).

(b) **Secrecy-Based Zoning.**
Zones may be designated where necessary to prevent exposure of magical activity to non-magical populations.
(1) Such zones shall prioritize concealment, suppression, and minimization of observable effects.
(2) Restrictions shall apply regardless of whether the underlying activity is otherwise permitted.
(3) Zoning determinations shall consider both direct and indirect forms of exposure.

(c) **Prohibited Areas.**
Magical activity shall be restricted or prohibited in areas where secrecy cannot reasonably be maintained, including areas characterized by—
(1) high non-magical population density;
(2) continuous observation, surveillance, or monitoring; or
(3) environmental conditions that amplify visible, audible, or otherwise detectable magical effects.

(d) **Containment and Concealment Measures.**
All activity within secrecy-regulated zones shall include measures sufficient to prevent detection.
(1) Required measures may include—
(A) concealment of magical effects;
(B) suppression, alteration, or redirection of observable phenomena; and
(C) remediation or reversal of unintended exposure.
(2) Measures shall be implemented prior to, during, and after the activity as necessary to ensure compliance.
(3) Failure to implement such measures shall constitute a violation regardless of whether exposure ultimately occurs.

(e) **Incident Response.**
Where exposure occurs or is reasonably likely to occur, the responsible party shall take immediate action to—
(1) terminate or mitigate the activity;
(2) repair, reverse, or conceal observable effects; and
(3) address any resulting breach of secrecy, including effects on persons, property, or records.

(f) **Overlap with Other Zones.**
Where secrecy-based zoning overlaps with other designated zones, the stricter standard shall apply.
(1) No person shall rely on permissive zoning to avoid secrecy obligations.
(2) Conflicting designations shall be resolved in favor of concealment and prevention of exposure.

(g) **Enforcement and Monitoring.**
Secrecy-regulated zones shall be subject to heightened monitoring to ensure compliance with § 401.7 and related provisions.
(1) Monitoring may include—
(A) observation of activity;
(B) review of compliance measures; and
(C) evaluation of potential exposure risks.

(h) **Cross-References.**
For general secrecy requirements, see § 401.7. For magical broadcasting and mass exposure risks, see Part XXIV. For environmental containment, see Part IX.

(i) **Historical Annotations.**
This section was enacted under C.C.D. 4201, 42 MR 244, Mon. 18, 1908 to establish zoning controls necessary to prevent public exposure of magical activity. Amended under C.C.D. 7332, 48 MR 119, Tue. 9, 1978 to address increased interaction between magical and non-magical populations and resulting secrecy risks. Revised under C.C.D. 10191, 71 MR 233, Mon. 12, 2013 to address modern surveillance conditions and challenges in maintaining concealment of magical activity.

Part XXVI: Immunities and Protections

§ 2601.1 Magical Immunity in Governance and Practice

(a) **General Rule.**
Magical immunity may be recognized in limited circumstances to permit the performance of authorized functions in governance, enforcement, or regulated practice without incurring liability under this Code.

(b) **Scope of Immunity.**
Immunity under this section shall apply only to acts undertaken within the scope of lawful authority and consistent with the purpose for which such authority was granted.
(1) Immunity shall not extend to acts that—
(A) exceed granted authority;
(B) are undertaken for personal or unauthorized purposes; or
(C) result from reckless disregard of applicable standards.

(c) **Governmental Functions.**
Magical immunity may be recognized for actions taken by authorized bodies or their agents in the execution of official duties.
(1) Such immunity shall apply only where the action—
(A) is necessary to carry out a lawful function; and
(B) is performed in accordance with established procedures.
(2) Immunity shall not apply where the action is clearly inconsistent with the underlying authority or purpose.

(d) **Licensed Practice.**
Licensed practitioners may be afforded limited immunity for actions undertaken in good faith within the ordinary course of regulated practice.
(1) Such immunity shall be contingent upon—
(A) compliance with applicable standards; and
(B) adherence to the scope of authorized practice.
(2) Deviation from accepted practices or procedures may result in loss of immunity.

(e) **Limitations.**

Immunity shall be narrowly construed and shall not be presumed.
(1) The burden shall rest on the person asserting immunity to demonstrate its applicability.
(2) Immunity shall not preclude regulatory review or administrative action.

(f) **Revocation and Denial.**
Immunity may be denied or revoked where the underlying conditions are not satisfied or where continued recognition would be inconsistent with the purposes of this Code.

(g) **Cross-References.**
For governance and administrative authority, see § 102.1. For penalties and enforcement, see § 102.2. For authorized spellcasting, see § 101.5.

(h) **Historical Annotations.**
This section was enacted under C.C.D. 2764, 30 MR 118, Mon. 5, 1748 to define the limits of magical immunity for governing bodies and officials. Amended under C.C.D. 4982, 42 MR 211, Thu. 17, 1902 to address misuse of authority by licensed practitioners. Revised under C.C.D. 9723, 67 MR 309, Tue. 8, 2006 to clarify scope limitations and evidentiary standards for asserting immunity.

§ 2601.2 Immunity for Emergency Spellcasting

(a) **General Rule.**
A person may be afforded limited immunity for magical activity undertaken in response to an emergency, where such activity is necessary to prevent or mitigate immediate harm.

(b) **Definition of Emergency.**
For purposes of this section, an emergency is a situation in which—
(1) there exists an imminent risk of harm to persons, property, or the environment; and
(2) immediate action is required such that compliance with ordinary requirements is impracticable.

(c) **Conditions for Immunity.**
Immunity shall apply only where the person demonstrates that—
(1) the action taken was necessary under the circumstances;
(2) no reasonable alternative was available; and

(3) the activity was limited in scope and duration to that necessary to address the emergency.

(d) **Limitations.**
Immunity shall not apply where—
(1) the emergency was created or materially contributed to by the person asserting immunity;
(2) the response exceeded what a reasonable person would consider necessary; or
(3) the activity continued after the emergency had abated.

(e) **Post-Event Obligations.**
Following emergency action, the responsible party shall—
(1) take reasonable steps to mitigate any resulting effects; and
(2) provide information sufficient to evaluate the nature and necessity of the response.

(f) **Evaluation of Conduct.**
Determinations under this section shall be based on the circumstances as they reasonably appeared at the time of the event, and not solely on the outcome.

(g) **Cross-References.**
For reasonable care in spellcasting, see § 101.7. For environmental reporting, see § 901.3. For enforcement and penalties, see § 102.2.

(h) **Historical Annotations.**
This section was enacted under C.C.D. 3059, 33 MR 144, Wed. 11, 1796 to permit limited deviation from regulatory requirements during emergencies. Amended under C.C.D. 5521, 44 MR 98, Tue. 2, 1929 to address misuse of emergency claims to justify otherwise prohibited conduct. Revised under C.C.D. 10011, 70 MR 166, Thu. 14, 2011 to clarify standards for necessity and post-event evaluation.

§ 2601.3 Protections for Magical Entities and Traditions

(a) **General Rule.**

Certain magical entities, practices, and traditions may be afforded protections to preserve their continued existence, function, and cultural or ecological significance.

(b) **Protected Entities.**
Protections may apply to magical entities whose existence or function is—
(1) rare, endangered, or declining;
(2) essential to environmental or magical stability; or
(3) historically or culturally significant.

(c) **Protected Traditions.**
Protections may extend to established magical traditions, practices, or rites that—
(1) have longstanding historical continuity;
(2) are integral to recognized magical communities; or
(3) would be materially harmed by unrestricted regulation or external interference.

(d) **Scope of Protection.**
Protected status may limit or restrict certain forms of interaction, including—
(1) alteration, extraction, or replication;
(2) interference with natural or ceremonial processes; or
(3) commercialization or exploitation inconsistent with preservation.

(e) **Conditions and Limitations.**
Protection under this section shall not exempt entities or practices from all regulatory requirements.
(1) Protections shall be balanced against public safety, environmental integrity, and secrecy obligations.
(2) Activities that pose a substantial risk of harm may be restricted notwithstanding protected status.

(f) **Designation and Review.**
Protected status shall be subject to designation and periodic review to ensure continued appropriateness.
(1) Designation shall consider ecological, cultural, and functional factors.
(2) Protections may be modified or revoked where conditions change.

(g) **Cross-References.**

For environmental protections, see Part IX. For secrecy requirements, see § 401.7.

(h) **Historical Annotations.**
This section was enacted under C.C.D. 3188, 34 MR 77, Mon. 3, 1812 to preserve rare magical entities and practices threatened by expansion of regulated activity. Amended under C.C.D. 6014, 45 MR 209, Thu. 6, 1954 to extend protections to culturally significant traditions. Revised under C.C.D. 10204, 71 MR 276, Tue. 18, 2014 to address modern pressures on protected entities and the balance between preservation and regulation.

Part XXVII: Creatures of Eldritch Origin

§ 2701.1 Definition of Eldritch Creatures

(a) **General Definition.**
For purposes of this Code, an eldritch creature is any entity whose existence, form, or function is not fully governed by the natural, magical, or metaphysical laws ordinarily recognized within this realm, and whose presence introduces instability, distortion, or incomprehensibility into surrounding systems.

(b) **Characteristics.**
An entity shall be classified as eldritch where one or more of the following conditions are present—
(1) the entity exhibits properties inconsistent with known physical, magical, or conceptual structures;
(2) the entity's form, composition, or behavior cannot be reliably observed, measured, or described without contradiction;
(3) the entity produces effects that alter perception, cognition, or reality independent of intentional action; or
(4) the entity's presence results in degradation, distortion, or destabilization of space, time, or causality.

(c) **Distinction from Other Creatures.**
Eldritch creatures shall be distinguished from other magical or qualified creatures based on their deviation from recognized systems of classification.
(1) The fact that a creature is dangerous, powerful, or poorly understood shall not alone be sufficient for classification as eldritch.
(2) Classification shall instead be based on whether the creature operates outside or in contradiction to established magical or natural frameworks.

(d) **Unstable Classification.**
Where uncertainty exists as to whether a creature is eldritch, such creature shall be treated as eldritch for purposes of containment, restriction, and regulation until a determination is made.

(e) **Manifestation and Presence.**
An eldritch creature may be deemed present where—

(1) the entity is physically or perceptually observable;
(2) the entity is partially manifested or incompletely formed; or
(3) the entity's influence is detectable through persistent or recurring effects, including those affecting environment, perception, or reality.

(f) **Indirect and Residual Presence.**
Eldritch classification shall extend to situations where the entity is not directly observable but produces ongoing or residual effects consistent with eldritch influence.
(1) Such effects may include—
(A) spatial distortion;
(B) temporal irregularity; or
(C) persistent alteration of perception or cognition.
(2) The absence of a visible or identifiable entity shall not preclude classification.

(g) **Interaction with Other Systems.**
Where an eldritch creature interacts with other magical systems, such interaction shall be presumed to alter or destabilize those systems unless demonstrated otherwise.

(h) **Cross-References.**
For qualified creatures, see § 101.6. For time-related distortions, see Part XXII. For interdimensional considerations, see Part XXIII.

(i) **Historical Annotations.**
This section was enacted under C.C.D. 3321, 35 MR 144, Thu. 9, 1824 to establish a distinct classification for entities that could not be governed by existing magical or natural frameworks. Amended under C.C.D. 5894, 45 MR 301, Tue. 14, 1948 to address entities exhibiting indirect or non-physical manifestations. Revised under C.C.D. 10277, 72 MR 118, Mon. 6, 2018 to clarify classification standards and treatment of residual eldritch influence.

§ 2701.2 Containment and Quarantine Protocols

(a) **General Rule.**
Any eldritch creature, or suspected eldritch presence, shall be subject to immediate containment and quarantine measures sufficient to prevent spread, escalation, or interaction with uncontrolled environments.

(b) **Mandatory Containment.**
Upon identification or reasonable suspicion of an eldritch creature, containment shall be initiated without delay.
(1) Containment shall prioritize isolation from—
(A) populated areas;
(B) sensitive environments;
(C) magical infrastructure; and
(D) other systems susceptible to distortion or contamination.
(2) Delay in containment shall be permitted only where immediate action would—
(A) increase instability;
(B) trigger uncontrolled manifestation; or
(C) result in loss of containment capability.

(c) **Containment Standards.**
Containment measures shall be designed to account for the unpredictable, non-linear, and potentially non-localized behavior of eldritch entities.
(1) Such measures shall include—
(A) physical, magical, and conceptual barriers operating in combination;
(B) redundancy across independent containment layers;
(C) continuous stabilization of affected space or environment; and
(D) mechanisms designed to prevent perception-based or cognition-triggered propagation.
(2) No containment system shall rely solely on a single method, dimension, or plane of control.
(3) Containment shall account for the possibility that the entity—
(A) exists partially outside observable space;
(B) responds to observation or awareness; or
(C) alters the conditions under which containment is evaluated.

(d) **Containment Zoning and Buffering.**
Containment shall include the establishment of buffer zones surrounding the primary containment area.
(1) Buffer zones shall be sized based on the maximum reasonably foreseeable range of influence.
(2) No unauthorized activity shall occur within such zones.
(3) Boundaries shall be treated as dynamic where—
(A) conditions indicate expansion or contraction of influence; or
(B) measurement of such boundaries yields inconsistent or contradictory results.

(e) **Quarantine Protocols.**
All areas, objects, or persons exposed to an eldritch entity shall be subject to quarantine.
(1) Quarantine shall apply to—
(A) direct exposure;
(B) indirect or secondary exposure; and
(C) suspected exposure based on observable or inferred effects.
(2) Quarantine shall include restrictions on—
(A) movement;
(B) interaction; and
(C) communication, including communication that—
(i) transmits descriptions, representations, or impressions of the entity; or
(ii) enables indirect propagation of its effects.
(3) Quarantine shall remain in effect until it is reasonably determined that no ongoing influence, contamination, or alteration remains.

(f) **Exposure Classification and Segregation.**
Exposed individuals, objects, and areas shall be classified based on level and type of exposure.
(1) Classification shall consider—
(A) duration and proximity of exposure;
(B) observed effects; and
(C) potential for further propagation.
(2) Individuals or objects with differing exposure classifications shall not be co-located where such co-location—
(A) increases risk of amplification; or
(B) enables interaction between incompatible forms of exposure.

(g) **Access Restrictions.**
Access to containment or quarantine zones shall be strictly limited.
(1) No person shall enter, observe, or interact with such zones without authorization.
(2) Observation, whether direct or indirect, shall be treated as interaction where such observation—
(A) alters conditions; or
(B) increases the likelihood of propagation.
(3) Unauthorized access shall be presumed to increase risk of—
(A) spread;
(B) escalation; or
(C) mutation of the entity or its effects.

(h) **Monitoring and Observation.**
Contained entities and affected areas shall be subject to continuous monitoring.
(1) Monitoring shall account for—
(A) changes in behavior, form, or manifestation;
(B) expansion or contraction of influence;
(C) degradation or alteration of containment systems; and
(D) interaction between the entity and observers, instruments, or containment structures.
(2) Monitoring systems shall not rely exclusively on a single mode of detection and shall include—
(A) redundant detection methods; and
(B) independent verification of observed conditions.
(3) Any deviation from expected conditions shall require immediate reassessment and adjustment of containment measures.

(i) **Escalation and Failure Response.**
Where containment is breached or compromised, immediate escalation procedures shall be implemented.
(1) Such procedures may include—
(A) expansion of containment boundaries;
(B) reinforcement or replacement of containment systems;
(C) isolation or evacuation of affected areas; and
(D) termination or suppression of affected zones where necessary to prevent further spread.
(2) Containment failure shall be treated as—
(A) an ongoing event; and
(B) an expanding condition until fully stabilized.

(j) **Prohibition on Unauthorized Handling.**
No person shall attempt to study, manipulate, transport, communicate with, or otherwise interact with an eldritch entity outside approved containment protocols.

(k) **Cross-References.**
For environmental impact and containment considerations, see Part IX. For interdimensional interactions, see Part XXIII. For public safety and exposure, see § 2701.7.

(l) **Historical Annotations.**

This section was enacted under C.C.D. 3388, 36 MR 77, Mon. 2, 1831 to establish mandatory containment procedures following early uncontrolled eldritch incidents. Amended under C.C.D. 6021, 45 MR 233, Wed. 11, 1956 to introduce quarantine protocols addressing indirect and secondary exposure. Revised under C.C.D. 10301, 72 MR 166, Thu. 21, 2019 to address containment failures involving multi-layered manifestations and escalation across physical and conceptual boundaries.

§ 2701.3 Classification of Eldritch Threat Levels

(a) **General Rule.**
All eldritch creatures and manifestations shall be classified according to threat level for purposes of containment, response, regulatory control, and determination of permissible or prohibited interaction.

(b) **Purpose of Classification.**
Threat classification shall determine—
(1) required containment protocols;
(2) permissible scope of observation, study, or interaction;
(3) authorization thresholds for any contact, summoning, or manipulation;
(4) resource allocation and response coordination; and
(5) escalation and emergency intervention requirements.

(c) **Baseline Principle.**
Classification shall be based on the highest reasonably foreseeable risk presented by the entity, including risks arising from incomplete information, indirect effects, delayed manifestation, or interaction with observers or systems.

(d) **Threat Levels.**
Eldritch threats shall be categorized as follows—
(1) Level I: Latent or Dormant Influence.
Entities or effects that—
(A) exhibit minimal, localized, and stable impact;
(B) do not actively propagate or expand under normal conditions; and
(C) remain consistent under observation without escalation.
Such entities shall be subject to containment and monitoring, and may permit strictly controlled observation where no amplification of effects is detected.

(2) Level II: Active but Contained Presence.
Entities that—
(A) exhibit observable effects on environment, perception, or localized systems;
(B) demonstrate potential for expansion, mutation, or escalation; and
(C) remain responsive to established containment measures.
Interaction shall be limited to authorized personnel and shall be conducted under conditions designed to prevent escalation.
(3) Level III: Expanding or Unstable Manifestation.
Entities that—
(A) alter physical, magical, or conceptual conditions beyond initial containment boundaries;
(B) exhibit unpredictable, accelerating, or self-modifying behavior; or
(C) demonstrate partial resistance or adaptation to containment measures.
Such entities shall require reinforced containment, expanded buffer zones, and continuous reassessment of threat conditions.
(4) Level IV: Systemic or Reality-Distorting Threat.
Entities that—
(A) produce sustained or large-scale alteration of space, time, causality, or perception;
(B) affect multiple zones, populations, or interconnected systems; or
(C) generate self-sustaining or self-propagating effects independent of continued presence.
All interaction shall be prohibited except as necessary for containment, stabilization, or suppression.
(5) Level V: Existential or Unbounded Threat.
Entities that—
(A) cannot be reliably contained within known frameworks;
(B) fundamentally alter, overwrite, or degrade underlying structures of reality; or
(C) present a credible risk of widespread or irreversible collapse of systems, including physical, magical, or conceptual systems.
Such entities shall be treated as catastrophic events requiring immediate isolation, total containment effort, and prohibition of all non-essential activity within affected regions.

(e) **Dynamic Reclassification.**
Threat classification shall be subject to continuous review.
(1) Reclassification shall occur where—

(A) new information becomes available;
(B) behavior, manifestation, or effects change;
(C) containment conditions deteriorate or improve; or
(D) interaction produces unexpected outcomes.
(2) Where uncertainty exists, classification shall default to the higher threat level.

(f) **Composite and Distributed Threats.**
Where multiple entities or effects operate in coordination or produce cumulative or compounding impact, such conditions shall be classified based on their combined or emergent effect.

(g) **Interaction Thresholds.**
Permissible interaction with an eldritch entity shall be determined by its threat level.
(1) Levels I and II may permit limited, controlled observation.
(2) Level III shall permit only containment-related interaction.
(3) Levels IV and V shall prohibit all interaction except for containment, stabilization, or emergency suppression.

(h) **Cross-References.**
For containment protocols, see § 2701.2. For summoning and banishing, see § 2701.5. For public safety considerations, see § 2701.7.

(i) **Historical Annotations.**
This section was enacted under C.C.D. 3412, 36 MR 144, Thu. 11, 1835 to establish a standardized framework for assessing eldritch threats following early containment failures. Amended under C.C.D. 6178, 45 MR 276, Mon. 9, 1959 to incorporate escalating and multi-entity manifestations. Revised under C.C.D. 10344, 72 MR 201, Tue. 4, 2020 to address systemic and reality-altering threat conditions.

§ 2701.4 Eldritch Effects on Reality and Space-Time

(a) **General Rule.**
No person shall permit, ignore, fail to report, or fail to address eldritch effects that alter or destabilize reality, space, time, or causality.

(b) **Recognized Effects.**

Eldritch effects may include—
(1) spatial distortion, including compression, expansion, inversion, or non-Euclidean structure;
(2) temporal irregularities, including loops, discontinuities, acceleration, or reversal;
(3) causal disruption, including events occurring without antecedent cause or with contradictory outcomes;
(4) perceptual alteration affecting multiple observers or producing inconsistent observational results; and
(5) persistence of conditions inconsistent with prior or baseline states.

(c) **Detection and Identification.**
All such effects shall be treated as evidence of eldritch presence unless demonstrated otherwise.
(1) Detection shall not depend on direct observation of an entity.
(2) Consistent or recurring anomalies shall be presumed to indicate ongoing influence.
(3) Contradictory observations shall not be treated as absence of effect.

(d) **Prohibition on Exploitation.**
No person shall utilize, rely upon, or attempt to harness eldritch effects for any purpose.
(1) Prohibited conduct includes—
(A) using temporal anomalies to alter outcomes;
(B) exploiting spatial distortion for transport, concealment, or storage;
(C) leveraging perceptual instability to influence decision-making; or
(D) attempting to stabilize or replicate such effects for controlled use.

(e) **Containment of Effects.**
Eldritch effects shall be contained in the same manner as entities.
(1) Containment shall address—
(A) the source of the effect;
(B) the effect itself; and
(C) any residual or propagated conditions.
(2) Effects shall not be considered resolved solely because the originating entity is no longer observable.

(f) **Reality Stabilization Measures.**
Where eldritch effects disrupt underlying structures, stabilization measures shall be implemented.

(1) Such measures may include—
(A) reinforcement or reestablishment of spatial boundaries;
(B) correction or anchoring of temporal sequence;
(C) restoration of causal continuity; and
(D) suppression of recursive or self-sustaining anomalies.
(2) Stabilization shall continue until conditions return to baseline or are otherwise contained within defined limits.

(g) **Observation Restrictions.**
Where observation, awareness, or documentation increases, alters, or accelerates eldritch effects, such observation shall be limited or prohibited.
(1) No person shall engage in repeated or sustained observation where such activity contributes to instability.
(2) Documentation shall be conducted in a manner that minimizes interaction, propagation, or reinforcement of the phenomenon.

(h) **Propagation and Spillover.**
No person shall permit eldritch effects to propagate beyond their point of origin.
(1) Propagation shall include—
(A) spread across physical space;
(B) transmission through perception or cognition; or
(C) transfer across dimensional or conceptual boundaries.
(2) Any indication of propagation shall require immediate escalation and containment.

(i) **Cross-References.**
For time-related distortions, see Part XXII. For containment protocols, see § 2701.2. For interdimensional interactions, see Part XXIII.

(j) **Historical Annotations.**
This section was enacted under C.C.D. 3499, 37 MR 118, Tue. 7, 1842 to address early incidents involving distortion of space and time attributed to eldritch presence. Amended under C.C.D. 6281, 46 MR 144, Wed. 16, 1963 to prohibit exploitation of temporal and spatial anomalies. Revised under C.C.D. 10362, 72 MR 233, Thu. 15, 2021 to address persistent and large-scale reality destabilization events.

§ 2701.5 Ritualistic Summoning and Banishing

(a) **General Rule.**
No person shall summon, invoke, bind, communicate with, or otherwise attempt to bring forth an eldritch creature except as expressly authorized under this section.

(b) **Absolute Prohibition Based on Threat Level.**
No person shall summon, invoke, or attempt to contact any eldritch entity classified as—
(1) Level IV; or
(2) Level V.
Such activity is prohibited under all circumstances, including for research, containment, or demonstration purposes.

(c) **Conditional Authorization for Lower Threat Levels.**
Summoning or controlled manifestation of Level I, Level II, or Level III entities may be authorized only where strict conditions are satisfied.
(1) Authorization shall require—
(A) demonstrated necessity that cannot be satisfied through observation or indirect means;
(B) confirmed threat classification prior to initiation;
(C) pre-established containment measures meeting or exceeding requirements under § 2701.2; and
(D) qualified personnel capable of executing, controlling, and terminating the ritual.
(2) Authorization shall not be granted where classification is uncertain or disputed.

(d) **Ritual Preconditions.**
No ritual shall proceed unless all required components, safeguards, and termination measures are verified.
(1) Preconditions shall include—
(A) stability of the ritual environment;
(B) isolation from external systems and populations; and
(C) absence of conflicting magical or environmental conditions.
(2) Any uncertainty in ritual execution shall require cancellation.

(e) **Ritual Execution Standards.**

All authorized rituals shall be conducted in accordance with strict procedural requirements.
(1) Rituals shall be structured to—
(A) limit scope and duration of manifestation;
(B) prevent uncontrolled expansion or propagation; and
(C) permit immediate interruption or termination at any stage.
(2) No ritual shall rely on untested, experimental, or incomplete methods.

(f) **Banishing and Termination.**
Where an eldritch entity has been summoned or has manifested, immediate efforts shall be made to banish, terminate, or otherwise remove the entity.
(1) Banishing procedures shall—
(A) prioritize restoration of containment; and
(B) prevent residual or secondary effects.
(2) Failure to complete banishment shall require escalation consistent with the entity's threat level.

(g) **Residual Effects and Post-Ritual Obligations.**
Following summoning or banishment, all residual effects shall be identified, contained, and resolved.
(1) No ritual shall be deemed complete until—
(A) all observable and latent effects are contained; and
(B) no further manifestation is detected.
(2) Continued monitoring shall be required for a period sufficient to confirm stability.

(h) **Prohibition on Repeated Attempts.**
No person shall conduct repeated summoning attempts where prior attempts resulted in—
(1) instability;
(2) incomplete containment; or
(3) misclassification of threat level.

(i) **Indirect Summoning and Contact.**
The prohibitions and restrictions of this section shall apply to indirect methods, including—
(1) use of artifacts, conduits, or intermediaries;
(2) attempts to attract or invite manifestation; or
(3) communication intended to initiate or encourage contact.

(j) **Cross-References.**
For containment protocols, see § 2701.2. For threat classification, see § 2701.3. For ritualistic magic, see § 101.1(ix).

(k) **Historical Annotations.**
This section was enacted under C.C.D. 3555, 37 MR 201, Mon. 3, 1849 to prohibit uncontrolled summoning of eldritch entities following catastrophic ritual failures. Amended under C.C.D. 6394, 46 MR 276, Tue. 21, 1966 to establish procedural requirements and threat-based limitations. Revised under C.C.D. 10388, 72 MR 266, Fri. 22, 2022 to impose absolute prohibitions on high-level entities and address failures in modern summoning practices.

§ 2701.6 Prohibitions on Eldritch Infusion in Spellcasting

(a) **General Rule.**
No person shall incorporate, channel, embed, or otherwise utilize eldritch influence, energy, matter, or conceptual constructs in the casting, enhancement, or modification of any spell.

(b) **Scope of Prohibition.**
The prohibitions of this section shall apply to all forms of spellcasting, including direct, indirect, assisted, or distributed casting.
(1) Prohibited conduct includes—
(A) drawing power from an eldritch entity or manifestation;
(B) incorporating eldritch materials, residues, or artifacts into spell components;
(C) structuring spells to interface with or respond to eldritch influence; and
(D) designing spells that depend upon altered perception, causality, or reality conditions arising from eldritch effects.

(c) **Indirect Infusion.**
No person shall avoid the application of this section by structuring spellcasting to rely upon intermediary systems or conditions.
(1) Indirect infusion includes—
(A) use of environments altered by eldritch presence;
(B) reliance on previously established anomalies; or
(C) interaction with constructs derived from eldritch influence.

(d) **Partial or Latent Infusion.**
The presence of eldritch influence at any stage of spellcasting shall constitute a violation, regardless of whether such influence—
(1) is partial, latent, or incomplete;
(2) does not produce an immediately observable effect; or
(3) is intended to be removed or neutralized prior to completion.

(e) **Contamination Presumption.**
Where a spell exhibits characteristics consistent with eldritch influence, such spell shall be presumed to be infused unless demonstrated otherwise.
(1) Such characteristics may include—
(A) instability of outcome;
(B) non-deterministic behavior; or
(C) effects inconsistent with established magical principles.

(f) **Containment of Infused Effects.**
Any spell determined to involve eldritch infusion shall be treated as an eldritch manifestation for purposes of containment and response.
(1) All such effects shall be immediately terminated, isolated, or suppressed.
(2) Residual effects shall be addressed in accordance with § 2701.2 and § 2701.4.

(g) **Prohibition on Experimentation.**
No person shall conduct experimental or exploratory spellcasting involving eldritch influence, regardless of scale or intended safeguards.

(h) **Cross-References.**
For definition of eldritch entities, see § 2701.1. For containment protocols, see § 2701.2. For effects on reality, see § 2701.4.

(i) **Historical Annotations.**
This section was enacted under C.C.D. 3621, 38 MR 77, Wed. 5, 1856 to prohibit the incorporation of eldritch influence into conventional spellcasting following early destabilization events. Amended under C.C.D. 6522, 46 MR 201, Thu. 12, 1964 to address indirect and residual infusion methods. Revised under C.C.D. 10402, 72 MR 301, Tue. 9, 2023 to address modern hybrid spellcasting techniques and contamination risks.

§ 2701.7 Public Health and Safety Regulations for Eldritch Exposure

(a) **General Rule.**
All persons, entities, and environments exposed or potentially exposed to eldritch influence shall be subject to public health and safety measures sufficient to prevent harm, spread, or escalation.

(b) **Definition of Exposure.**
Exposure shall include any condition in which a person, object, or environment—
(1) has come into direct or indirect contact with an eldritch entity or effect;
(2) exhibits symptoms or conditions consistent with eldritch influence; or
(3) cannot reasonably be determined to be free from such influence.

(c) **Immediate Response Measures.**
Upon identification or reasonable suspicion of exposure, immediate measures shall be implemented.
(1) Such measures shall include—
(A) isolation of affected individuals or areas;
(B) restriction of movement and interaction; and
(C) initiation of containment or quarantine protocols.
(2) Delay shall be permitted only where immediate action would increase risk.

(d) **Health Monitoring and Evaluation.**
Exposed persons shall be subject to continuous monitoring and evaluation.
(1) Monitoring shall assess—
(A) cognitive, perceptual, and behavioral changes;
(B) physiological or metaphysical alteration; and
(C) potential for propagation or secondary exposure.
(2) Evaluation shall not rely solely on subjective reporting where such reporting may be affected by the exposure.

(e) **Communication Restrictions.**
Communication by exposed individuals may be restricted where such communication—
(1) transmits or reinforces eldritch influence; or

(2) induces exposure in others through perception, description, or representation.
(2) Restrictions may include—
(A) limitation of verbal or written communication;
(B) prohibition on reproduction of observed phenomena; and
(C) controlled dissemination of information.

(f) **Decontamination and Stabilization.**
Where feasible, exposed individuals and environments shall undergo decontamination or stabilization procedures.
(1) Such procedures shall address—
(A) removal or suppression of eldritch influence; and
(B) restoration of baseline conditions.
(2) No individual or area shall be released from restriction until it is reasonably determined that no ongoing influence remains.

(g) **Secondary and Tertiary Exposure.**
Exposure shall include secondary or tertiary effects arising from contact with previously exposed persons, objects, or environments.
(1) Such exposure shall be treated as equivalent to direct exposure for purposes of this section.

(h) **Public Safety Measures.**
Authorities may implement measures necessary to protect public safety, including—
(1) evacuation of affected areas;
(2) restriction of access; and
(3) controlled dissemination of information to prevent panic or further exposure.

(i) **Cross-References.**
For containment and quarantine protocols, see § 2701.2. For effects on perception and reality, see § 2701.4. For secrecy requirements, see § 401.7.

(j) **Historical Annotations.**
This section was enacted under C.C.D. 3688, 38 MR 144, Mon. 11, 1863 to address public health impacts of eldritch exposure following widespread contamination incidents. Amended under C.C.D. 6611, 46 MR 233, Tue. 19, 1968 to address secondary transmission through perception and

communication. Revised under C.C.D. 10421, 73 MR 118, Thu. 3, 2024 to address large-scale exposure events and public safety coordination.

§ 2701.8 Regulation of Eldritch Artifacts

(a) **General Rule.**
Any object, material, or construct exhibiting or suspected of exhibiting eldritch properties shall be classified and regulated as an eldritch artifact.

(b) **Definition and Scope.**
An eldritch artifact is any object that—
(1) contains, channels, or retains eldritch influence;
(2) produces or facilitates eldritch effects; or
(3) has been altered in form, function, or composition by contact with an eldritch entity or manifestation.

(c) **Possession and Custody.**
No person shall possess, transport, store, or display an eldritch artifact except as authorized.
(1) Authorized possession shall require—
(A) secure containment measures;
(B) controlled access; and
(C) continuous monitoring.

(d) **Handling and Interaction.**
Interaction with eldritch artifacts shall be strictly limited.
(1) Prohibited conduct includes—
(A) activation or attempted activation of the artifact;
(B) integration into magical systems or spellcasting; and
(C) modification, replication, or experimentation.
(2) Authorized interaction shall be conducted only under controlled conditions designed to prevent activation or propagation.

(e) **Containment Requirements.**
All eldritch artifacts shall be maintained within containment systems sufficient to prevent influence, activation, or degradation.
(1) Containment shall include—
(A) physical and magical barriers;
(B) isolation from external systems; and
(C) safeguards against perception-based or proximity-based activation.

(f) **Transportation Restrictions.**
No artifact shall be transported except under conditions that maintain continuous containment.
(1) Transport shall be prohibited where containment cannot be guaranteed.
(2) Any loss of containment during transport shall be treated as a containment failure under § 2701.2.

(g) **Destruction and Neutralization.**
Where feasible, eldritch artifacts shall be destroyed, neutralized, or rendered inert.
(1) Destruction shall be conducted only where such action—
(A) does not increase risk of propagation; and
(B) does not produce secondary effects exceeding those of continued containment.
(2) Where destruction is not feasible, indefinite containment shall be required.

(h) **Record-Keeping and Tracking.**
All eldritch artifacts shall be recorded and tracked.
(1) Records shall include—
(A) origin or point of discovery;
(B) observed properties and effects; and
(C) containment status and location.

(i) **Cross-References.**
For containment protocols, see § 2701.2. For prohibition on infusion, see § 2701.6. For interdimensional considerations, see Part XXIII.

(j) **Historical Annotations.**
This section was enacted under C.C.D. 3744, 39 MR 201, Tue. 6, 1871 to regulate objects exhibiting persistent eldritch influence following artifact-related incidents. Amended under C.C.D. 6702, 47 MR 118, Wed. 22, 1970 to address transportation and containment failures. Revised under C.C.D. 10439, 73 MR 166, Mon. 14, 2025 to address modern handling and tracking requirements for eldritch artifacts.

Part XXVIII: Dragon Regulations

§ 2801.1 Dragon Sanctuaries and Territorial Boundaries

(a) **General Rule.**
Dragons shall be maintained, where feasible, within designated sanctuaries or defined territorial boundaries sufficient to ensure safety, environmental stability, interspecies compatibility, and compliance with all applicable provisions of this Code.
No dragon shall be permitted to exist in an unbounded, undefined, or administratively unrecognized territorial state.

(b) **Designation of Sanctuaries.**
Dragon sanctuaries shall be established, approved, and periodically reviewed based on a comprehensive evaluation of factors including, but not limited to—
(1) environmental suitability, including terrain composition, climate stability, geothermal activity, and availability of sustenance compatible with the dragon's biological and magical requirements;
(2) sufficient distance from populated, developing, or foreseeably inhabited areas, accounting for both present conditions and reasonably anticipated expansion;
(3) capacity to support sustained habitation without degradation of surrounding ecosystems or depletion of critical resources;
(4) containment feasibility, including the availability and reliability of natural barriers, constructed barriers, and magical containment systems;
(5) compatibility with existing zoning designations under Part XXV; and
(6) absence of overlapping jurisdictional claims or conflicting designations.

(c) **Territorial Recognition.**
Recognized dragon territories may be established in lieu of formal sanctuaries where—
(1) the dragon exhibits stable, predictable, and non-expansionary territorial behavior over a sustained observational period;
(2) the territorial boundaries can be reasonably defined using observable, measurable, or enforceable criteria;
(3) the territory does not overlap with incompatible zones, including

populated areas, restricted zones, or designated magical infrastructure; and
(4) the dragon demonstrates consistent adherence to territorial limits without evidence of encroachment, opportunistic expansion, or retaliatory boundary shifting.

(d) **Boundary Definition and Delineation.**
Territorial boundaries shall be defined with sufficient clarity to permit enforcement, monitoring, and dispute resolution.
(1) Acceptable methods of boundary delineation may include—
(A) natural geographic features, including mountain ranges, rivers, or volcanic formations;
(B) physical markers, including constructed barriers, monuments, or boundary posts;
(C) magical markers, including wards, sigils, or persistent boundary enchantments; and
(D) mapped coordinates recognized by the Department.
(2) Boundaries shall be documented, recorded, and made available to relevant enforcement authorities.
(3) Ambiguity in boundary definition shall be construed against the maintaining authority.

(e) **Boundary Limitations.**
No dragon shall be permitted to establish or maintain territory that—
(1) extends into or within a defined proximity to populated or developing areas;
(2) interferes with designated magical or non-magical zones, including transportation corridors, ley line infrastructure, or protected sites;
(3) overlaps with protected, restricted, or otherwise incompatible regions; or
(4) creates a foreseeable risk of incidental harm, including fire spread, structural collapse, or atmospheric disturbance.

(f) **Encroachment and Expansion.**
Expansion of territory shall be prohibited where such expansion—
(1) increases risk to surrounding populations, environments, or regulatory systems;
(2) results in conflict with existing zones, designations, or recognized territorial claims; or
(3) occurs without prior review, approval, and boundary adjustment by the Department.

(4) Incremental or gradual expansion shall not be exempt from review and shall be treated as expansion for purposes of this subsection.

(g) **Human Interaction Within Territories.**
Entry into dragon territories shall be restricted.
(1) No person shall enter such territory without authorization.
(2) Authorized entry shall be limited to purposes that—
(A) do not provoke aggression or defensive response;
(B) do not disrupt territorial stability or established behavioral patterns; and
(C) are consistent with approved regulatory, research, or containment objectives.
(3) The burden of safety shall remain with the entering party.

(h) **Boundary Enforcement.**
Authorities shall implement measures to ensure that territorial boundaries are respected.
(1) Such measures may include—
(A) physical or magical markers;
(B) monitoring systems capable of detecting boundary breaches;
(C) controlled access points; and
(D) automated or responsive deterrent mechanisms.
(2) Enforcement measures shall be proportionate to the risk profile of the dragon and the surrounding environment.

(i) **Dispute Resolution and Overlap Conflicts.**
(1) Where multiple dragons assert territorial claims over the same region, the Department shall determine priority based on—
(A) duration of occupancy;
(B) demonstrated territorial stability;
(C) relative risk posed by each dragon; and
(D) environmental impact.
(2) Pending resolution, interim containment or separation measures shall be implemented.

(j) **Presumption of Risk.**
Any territory occupied by a dragon shall be presumed to present elevated risk, and all regulatory determinations under this section shall be construed in favor of containment, limitation, and enforceability.

(k) **Cross-References.**
For zoning and property requirements, see Part XXV. For environmental

protections, see Part IX. For qualified creatures, see § 101.6. For containment and monitoring, see § 2801.3.

(l) **Historical Annotations.**
This section was enacted under C.C.D. 2471, 29 MR 166, Tue. 8, 1693 to establish designated areas for dragon habitation following early territorial conflicts. Amended under C.C.D. 4822, 41 MR 201, Thu. 19, 1899 to address encroachment into populated regions. Revised under C.C.D. 10078, 70 MR 276, Mon. 22, 2010 to address modern land-use conflicts and sanctuary management.

§ 2801.2 Flight Path and Mobility Restrictions of Dragons

(a) **General Rule.**
Dragon movement, including flight and ground-based mobility, shall be regulated, tracked, and, where necessary, restricted to prevent harm, disruption, or exposure. No dragon shall engage in unbounded or unmonitored movement that cannot be reasonably predicted, controlled, or mitigated.

(b) **Flight Path Designation.**
Authorized flight paths shall be established for dragons capable of sustained flight.
(1) Such paths shall—
(A) avoid populated, developing, or high-density areas;
(B) minimize interference with aerial, magical, or interdimensional traffic;
(C) account for environmental and atmospheric conditions, including wind patterns, thermal currents, and magical disturbances; and
(D) be capable of continuous monitoring and enforcement.
(2) Flight paths shall be documented, mapped, and periodically reviewed.

(c) **Restricted Airspace.**
Dragons shall be prohibited from entering restricted or controlled airspace.
(1) Restricted areas shall include—
(A) high-density population zones;
(B) areas subject to secrecy requirements under this Code;
(C) designated magical infrastructure corridors; and

(D) zones where dragon presence would create a foreseeable hazard.
(2) Unauthorized entry shall constitute a high-risk violation.

(d) **Uncontrolled Movement.**
No dragon shall be permitted to move in a manner that—
(1) cannot be tracked, monitored, or reasonably anticipated; or
(2) presents a foreseeable risk to persons, property, ecosystems, or magical systems.
(3) Temporary loss of tracking shall be treated as a containment failure under § 2801.3(g).

(e) **Altitude and Proximity Limitations.**
Dragons shall be subject to limitations on altitude and proximity to structures, populations, and other entities.
(1) Such limitations shall account for—
(A) size, weight, and wingspan;
(B) elemental or magical output; and
(C) potential for downdraft, heat displacement, or structural impact.
(2) Minimum separation distances shall be established and enforced.

(f) **Migration and Long-Range Movement.**
Long-distance or migratory movement shall require prior coordination and continuous monitoring.
(1) No such movement shall occur where—
(A) environmental or magical conditions are unstable; or
(B) containment, routing, or tracking cannot be maintained.
(2) Migration plans shall include contingency routing.

(g) **Interference and Collision Avoidance.**
Measures shall be implemented to prevent interference or collision between dragons and other entities.
(1) Such measures shall include—
(A) route separation;
(B) timing restrictions; and
(C) real-time monitoring and adjustment.
(2) Priority shall be given to minimizing risk to non-draconic entities.

(h) **Cross-References.**
For broadcasting and aerial effects, see Part XXIV. For interdimensional considerations, see Part XXIII. For public safety, see Part IX. For containment, see § 2801.3.

(i) **Historical Annotations.**
This section was enacted under C.C.D. 2599, 30 MR 201, Wed. 14, 1708 to regulate dragon flight following early aerial incidents. Amended under C.C.D. 4977, 42 MR 118, Mon. 3, 1905 to establish restricted airspace. Revised under C.C.D. 10112, 70 MR 309, Tue. 2, 2012 to address modern airspace coordination and large-scale movement.

§ 2801.3 Dragon Containment and Magical Monitoring

(a) **General Rule.**
Dragons shall be subject to continuous containment and monitoring measures sufficient to ensure compliance with this Code and to prevent harm, escalation, or uncontrolled activity. Containment shall be affirmative, proactive, and ongoing, and shall not rely on assumptions of dormancy, inactivity, or prior compliance.

(b) **Containment Requirements.**
Containment shall be implemented based on the dragon's behavior, capabilities, and risk profile.
(1) Such measures shall include—
(A) physical barriers designed to withstand force, heat, pressure, and sustained impact;
(B) magical restraints, boundary systems, or suppression fields calibrated to the dragon's known and potential capabilities; and
(C) territorial enforcement consistent with § 2801.1.
(2) Containment systems shall be redundant where failure would result in material risk.
(3) Redundancy shall include independent systems not subject to simultaneous failure due to common causes, including but not limited to structural compromise, magical interference, or environmental disruption.
(4) No containment system shall be deemed sufficient where a single point of failure would permit uncontrolled release.

(c) **Containment Classification.**
Each dragon shall be assigned a containment classification based on size, magical output, behavioral history, and escalation potential.
(1) Classification shall determine minimum containment standards, monitoring frequency, and response protocols.
(2) Classifications shall be subject to periodic reassessment and

immediate revision upon any material change in behavior or capability.
(3) In cases of uncertainty, classification shall default to the higher risk category.

(d) **Monitoring Systems.**
All dragons shall be subject to monitoring sufficient to track location, behavior, and activity in real time or near-real time.
(1) Monitoring shall include—
(A) continuous or interval-based location tracking calibrated to movement patterns;
(B) behavioral monitoring capable of detecting deviations from established baselines;
(C) detection of escalation indicators, including agitation, energy buildup, or territorial deviation; and
(D) environmental monitoring where dragon activity may produce secondary effects.
(2) Monitoring systems shall be capable of functioning under conditions including extreme heat, magical interference, and structural disruption.
(3) Monitoring gaps shall be minimized and treated as presumptive risk events.
(4) Failure to detect or record activity shall not be construed as absence of activity.

(e) **Behavioral Baseline and Deviation Analysis.**
A behavioral baseline shall be established for each dragon.
(1) Such baseline shall include—
(A) territorial patterns;
(B) activity cycles; and
(C) interaction tendencies.
(2) Any deviation from baseline shall trigger review.
(3) Repeated deviations shall be treated as escalation indicators.
(4) Absence of deviation shall not eliminate risk.

(f) **Escalation Thresholds and Response.**
Thresholds for escalation shall be established for each dragon.
(1) Indicators may include—
(A) increased movement or agitation;
(B) increased magical output; or
(C) boundary testing or encroachment.
(2) Upon threshold breach, response shall be initiated without delay.
(3) Response measures may include—

(A) enhanced monitoring;
(B) reinforcement of containment systems;
(C) suppression of magical output; or
(D) relocation under controlled conditions.
(4) Delay in response shall be treated as a compliance failure.

(g) **Failure of Containment.**
Any breach, degradation, or circumvention of containment shall be treated as a high-risk event.
(1) Immediate response shall be required.
(2) Response shall include—
(A) activation of emergency protocols;
(B) notification of relevant authorities; and
(C) implementation of containment recovery measures.
(3) Responsibility for failure shall not be mitigated by partial compliance or prior performance.

(h) **Relocation and Reassignment.**
Dragons may be relocated where containment is inadequate.
(1) Relocation shall occur only under controlled and monitored conditions.
(2) Relocation shall be required where—
(A) containment repeatedly fails;
(B) environmental conditions degrade; or
(C) risk cannot be otherwise mitigated.
(3) Temporary relocation shall not constitute compliance where underlying deficiencies remain uncorrected.

(i) **Dragon Handler Licensing and Certification.**
(1) No person shall engage in the handling, supervision, containment management, or operational oversight of a dragon unless such person holds a valid Dragon Handler License issued by the DMA.
(2) Licensure shall be conditioned upon demonstration of—
(A) technical competency in containment systems, including both physical and magical mechanisms;
(B) familiarity with applicable provisions of this Code, including Parts IX, XXV, and this Part;
(C) demonstrated ability to recognize escalation indicators and respond appropriately; and
(D) successful completion of a DMA-approved training program.
(3) Licenses shall be issued in tiers corresponding to containment

classification.
(A) No handler shall supervise a dragon assigned to a higher classification than the handler's certification level.
(B) Assignment in excess of certification shall constitute a per se violation.
(4) Licenses shall be subject to—
(A) periodic renewal;
(B) continuing education requirements; and
(C) immediate suspension or revocation upon demonstrated incompetence, negligence, or misconduct.
(5) A licensed handler shall bear primary operational responsibility for compliance with containment and monitoring requirements, including responsibility for failures attributable to improper oversight, delayed response, or inadequate implementation of required measures.
(6) Delegation of responsibilities shall not relieve the licensed handler of liability unless such delegation is expressly authorized and documented.

(j) **Documentation and Recordkeeping.**
(1) All containment, monitoring, and handler-related activities shall be fully documented in a manner sufficient to permit reconstruction, review, and enforcement.
(2) Required records shall include—
(A) containment system specifications, including design, materials, magical configurations, and redundancy features;
(B) monitoring system configurations, including calibration settings, detection thresholds, and operational parameters;
(C) continuous or interval-based monitoring logs, including location data, behavioral observations, and detected anomalies;
(D) incident reports documenting any breach, deviation, escalation, or system failure, including time, duration, and corrective measures taken;
(E) maintenance and inspection records for all containment and monitoring systems;
(F) handler assignment records, including identity, certification level, and duration of responsibility; and
(G) records of all corrective actions, adjustments, or system modifications.
(3) Records shall be maintained in a form that is—
(A) tamper-evident;
(B) resistant to degradation, destruction, or magical alteration; and
(C) capable of being produced upon request by the Department without delay.

(4) Recordkeeping systems shall include safeguards to prevent—
(A) unauthorized modification;
(B) selective deletion; or
(C) retroactive fabrication.
(5) Failure to maintain complete and accurate records shall be treated as a separate and independent violation.
(6) In the absence of required records, it shall be presumed that required containment, monitoring, or response actions were not performed.
(7) Records shall be retained for a period sufficient to support investigation, enforcement, and historical analysis, and in no case less than ten (10) years or the full lifespan of the dragon, whichever is longer.
(8) Destruction or loss of records, whether intentional or negligent, shall be treated as evidence of noncompliance absent clear and convincing proof to the contrary.

(k) **Cross-References.**
For creature classification, see § 101.6. For zoning requirements, see Part XXV. For public safety, see Part IX. For penalties, see § 102.2. For territorial regulation, see § 2801.1.

(l) **Historical Annotations.**
This section was enacted under C.C.D. 2644, 31 MR 77, Mon. 6, 1715 to establish containment requirements. Amended under C.C.D. 5221, 43 MR 233, Tue. 12, 1918 to introduce monitoring systems. Revised under C.C.D. 10134, 71 MR 144, Thu. 18, 2013 to address modern containment, tracking, and handler certification requirements.

§ 2801.4 Regulation of Draconian Magic

(a) **General Rule.**
Magic produced, emitted, generated, or otherwise arising from dragons shall be regulated, monitored, and, where necessary, limited or suppressed to prevent harm, environmental disruption, system interference, or uncontrolled escalation.

No draconian magic shall be deemed exempt on the basis that such magic is natural, instinctive, or incidental.

(b) **Scope of Draconian Magic.**
Draconian magic shall include, but not be limited to—
(1) elemental emissions, including fire, ice, lightning, acid, or comparable phenomena;

(2) aura-based or passive magical influence, including heat fields, fear induction, magical pressure, or environmental alteration;
(3) residual or ambient magical effects resulting from presence, habitation, or prolonged occupancy;
(4) reactive magical discharges triggered by agitation, stress, or defensive behavior; and
(5) any magical effect reasonably attributable to the dragon, whether deliberate or incidental.

(c) **Baseline Measurement and Threshold Establishment.**
(1) A baseline level of draconian magical output shall be established for each dragon.
(2) Such baseline shall include—
(A) average emission levels;
(B) peak output capacity; and
(C) frequency and duration of emissions.
(3) Acceptable thresholds shall be defined relative to baseline and risk classification.
(4) Thresholds shall be periodically reviewed and adjusted where conditions change.
(5) In the absence of reliable baseline data, thresholds shall be conservatively determined.

(d) **Controlled Emission Requirements.**
Dragons shall not emit magical effects in a manner that—
(1) causes direct or indirect harm to persons, property, or ecosystems;
(2) disrupts environmental stability, including atmospheric, geological, or magical equilibrium;
(3) interferes with infrastructure, including magical systems, transportation systems, or containment systems; or
(4) exceeds established thresholds under subsection (c).
(5) Passive emission shall be subject to the same limitations as active emission.

(e) **Prohibited Outputs and Escalation.**
No dragon shall engage in magical activity that—
(1) exceeds established thresholds in intensity, frequency, or duration;
(2) produces uncontrolled, unpredictable, or cascading effects; or
(3) results in amplification beyond expected parameters.
(4) Repeated exceedances shall be treated as escalation events.

(5) Any output that cannot be measured, contained, or mitigated shall be presumed prohibited.

(f) **Monitoring and Suppression.**
Draconian magic shall be continuously monitored and, where necessary, limited or suppressed.
(1) Monitoring shall include—
(A) real-time measurement of magical output;
(B) detection of deviations from baseline; and
(C) identification of escalation indicators.
(2) Suppression measures may include—
(A) dampening fields;
(B) containment amplification; or
(C) behavioral intervention protocols.
(3) Suppression systems shall be integrated with containment systems under § 2801.3.

(g) **Cumulative and Secondary Effects.**
Draconian magic shall be evaluated on a cumulative basis.
(1) Repeated or sustained emissions shall be treated as a single continuing effect for purposes of risk assessment.
(2) Secondary effects, including environmental degradation, structural weakening, or magical contamination, shall be attributed to the originating dragon.
(3) Delayed effects shall not be excluded from consideration.

(h) **Interaction with Spellcasting Systems.**
No person shall incorporate, channel, harness, or otherwise utilize draconian magic within structured spellcasting without express authorization.
(1) Unauthorized use shall be presumed to create elevated risk.
(2) Any such incorporation shall be subject to enhanced monitoring and control.
(3) Liability for resulting effects shall not be shifted to the dragon.

(i) **Environmental Presumption.**
All draconian magic shall be presumed to produce environmental impact unless affirmatively demonstrated otherwise.
(1) The burden of proof shall rest with the party asserting minimal or no impact.

(2) Absence of immediate observable damage shall not rebut the presumption.

(j) **Emergency Restrictions.**
Where draconian magic presents an imminent threat, immediate restrictions may be imposed, including—
(1) temporary suppression of magical output;
(2) restriction of movement or activity; or
(3) relocation under controlled conditions.
(4) Such measures shall remain in effect until risk is mitigated.

(k) **Cross-References.**
For elemental magic, see § 101.1. For environmental impact, see Part IX. For spellcasting regulations, see Part IV. For containment and monitoring, see § 2801.3. For penalties, see § 102.2.

(l) **Historical Annotations.**
This section was enacted under C.C.D. 2711, 31 MR 166, Tue. 21, 1722 to regulate magical emissions from dragons. Amended under C.C.D. 5333, 43 MR 301, Thu. 5, 1921 to address large-scale environmental effects. Revised under C.C.D. 10167, 71 MR 188, Mon. 25, 2014 to address integration with modern magical systems and cumulative impact analysis.

§ 2801.5 Dragon Rights and Welfare

(a) **General Rule.**
Dragons shall be recognized as intelligent, sentient, and highly capable creatures entitled to protections and welfare considerations under this Code, consistent with their classification under § 101.6.

Such protections shall be administered in a manner that preserves both the dignity of the dragon and the safety of the public, with neither interest presumed to fully subordinate the other absent explicit statutory directive.

(b) **Recognition of Intelligence and Agency.**
Dragons shall be treated as beings capable of cognition, memory, communication, preference formation, and independent action.
(1) Regulatory measures shall account for such capabilities, including—
(A) the capacity to understand and respond to stimuli;
(B) the potential for learned behavior, including both compliance and retaliation; and

(C) the ability to exhibit intent, whether cooperative or adversarial.
(2) A dragon's demonstrated intelligence shall not diminish the applicability of containment or safety requirements.

(c) **Protection from Harm.**
No person shall harm, exploit, or mistreat a dragon except as strictly necessary to achieve lawful containment, prevent imminent harm, or enforce compliance with this Code.
(1) Prohibited harm shall include—
(A) physical injury beyond what is reasonably required for containment or intervention;
(B) deprivation of necessary sustenance, environmental conditions, or recovery;
(C) coercive, abusive, or punitive treatment unrelated to legitimate regulatory objectives; and
(D) use of excessive force where less harmful alternatives are reasonably available.
(2) The burden of demonstrating necessity shall rest with the person engaging in such conduct.

(d) **Habitat and Environmental Conditions.**
Dragons shall be maintained in environments suitable to their biological and magical needs.
(1) Suitable conditions shall include—
(A) sufficient physical space to permit natural movement and behavior;
(B) environmental characteristics consistent with species or subtype requirements, including temperature, terrain, and atmospheric conditions; and
(C) access to resources necessary to maintain health and stability.
(2) Habitat adequacy shall be evaluated in conjunction with containment requirements under § 2801.3.
(3) Degradation of habitat conditions shall be treated as a compliance deficiency.

(e) **Use, Labor, and Exploitation.**
No dragon shall be used for labor, combat, transport, or other functional purposes in a manner inconsistent with welfare standards.
(1) Any permitted use shall be—
(A) limited in scope and duration;
(B) subject to prior authorization; and

(C) conducted under conditions that do not materially increase risk of harm or distress.
(2) Coercive use, including forced compliance through pain, deprivation, or magical domination, shall be prohibited.
(3) Economic or strategic benefit shall not justify deviation from welfare requirements.

(f) **Consent and Capacity.**
(1) Where a dragon demonstrates the capacity for meaningful communication, its preferences and responses shall be considered in determining appropriate handling and interaction.
(2) Apparent compliance shall not be presumed to constitute voluntary consent.
(3) Absence of resistance shall not be interpreted as acceptance of conditions.

(g) **Balancing of Rights and Safety.**
Protections under this section shall be balanced against public safety and regulatory requirements.
(1) Where a conflict arises, measures shall be implemented to minimize harm to the dragon while ensuring containment, compliance, and risk mitigation.
(2) In cases of unavoidable conflict, safety considerations shall control, provided that actions taken are proportionate and necessary.
(3) Long-term welfare considerations shall not be disregarded solely due to short-term operational convenience.

(h) **Non-Waiver of Protections.**
No agreement, contract, ritual arrangement, or course of conduct shall operate to waive, limit, or circumvent the protections afforded under this section.
(1) Any such attempt shall be void and without effect.
(2) Reliance on purported waiver shall not constitute a defense to violation.

(i) **Mistreatment and Neglect as Independent Violations.**
(1) Failure to provide adequate care, habitat, or conditions shall constitute a violation independent of any resulting harm.
(2) Neglect shall include omission, delay, or failure to act where action is required to maintain welfare standards.

(3) Repeated or systemic deficiencies shall be treated as aggravating factors for enforcement purposes.

(j) **Interaction with Containment and Monitoring Requirements.**
Welfare protections shall not be construed to limit or invalidate containment, monitoring, or suppression measures required under § 2801.3 or § 2801.4.
(1) Such measures shall be implemented in a manner that avoids unnecessary harm.
(2) Where multiple compliant approaches are available, the least harmful effective method shall be used.

(k) **Presumption of Dual Status.**
Dragons shall be treated as both protected creatures and regulated hazards.
(1) Neither status shall be interpreted to eliminate the other.
(2) Regulatory determinations shall account for both aspects concurrently.

(l) **Cross-References.**
For qualified creatures, see § 101.6. For sanctuary designation, see § 2801.1. For containment requirements, see § 2801.3. For regulation of draconian magic, see § 2801.4. For penalties, see § 102.2.

(m) **Historical Annotations.**
This section was enacted under C.C.D. 2788, 32 MR 118, Mon. 9, 1734 to recognize basic protections for dragons following early exploitation practices. Amended under C.C.D. 5455, 44 MR 144, Tue. 16, 1926 to address coercive use and mistreatment. Revised under C.C.D. 10189, 71 MR 233, Wed. 7, 2015 to balance welfare considerations with modern containment, safety, and regulatory requirements.

Part XXIX: Magical Acts of Secrecy

§ 2901.1 Overview and Purpose of the Magical Acts of Secrecy

(a) **General Rule.**
Certain magical acts, practices, methods, and knowledge shall be designated as secret and shall be subject to heightened restriction, control, and protection under this Part.

(b) **Purpose.**
The purpose of the Magical Acts of Secrecy is to—
(1) prevent harm arising from unrestricted access to dangerous or destabilizing magic;
(2) preserve the integrity of sensitive magical systems, methods, and institutions;
(3) prevent misuse, exploitation, or replication of controlled magical practices; and
(4) ensure that knowledge capable of altering systems, structures, or populations is not disseminated without control.

(c) **Scope.**
This Part shall apply to any magical act, whether fully realized, partially developed, or theoretical, that has been designated as secret.
(1) Such designation shall apply regardless of—
(A) whether the act is currently in use;
(B) whether the act has been previously disclosed; or
(C) whether the act exists in complete or fragmentary form.

(d) **Forms of Secret Magic.**
Secret magical acts may include—
(1) spells, rituals, or procedures;
(2) methods of manipulating systems, entities, or conditions;
(3) knowledge of vulnerabilities, exploits, or structural weaknesses; and
(4) combinations of otherwise lawful elements that produce restricted effects.

(e) **Non-Circumvention.**

No person shall avoid the application of this Part by—
(1) fragmenting a secret magical act into component parts;
(2) disguising such act as non-magical or theoretical; or
(3) distributing knowledge in a manner intended to reconstruct the act indirectly.

(f) **Presumption of Protection.**
Where a magical act is designated as secret, all associated knowledge, materials, and methods shall be presumed subject to this Part unless expressly excluded.

(g) **Relationship to Other Provisions.**
Nothing in this Part shall be construed to permit conduct otherwise prohibited under this Code.
(1) Compliance with secrecy requirements shall not excuse violations of other sections.

(h) **Cross-References.**
For secrecy obligations applicable to magical activity generally, see § 401.7. For prohibited magical conduct, see Part IV. For interdimensional and eldritch considerations, see Parts XXIII and XXVII.

(i) **Historical Annotations.**
This section was enacted under C.C.D. 3522, 37 MR 166, Mon. 6, 1845 to establish formal protections for restricted magical knowledge following unauthorized dissemination of destabilizing practices. Amended under C.C.D. 6481, 46 MR 188, Tue. 8, 1962 to address fragmentation and indirect disclosure. Revised under C.C.D. 10477, 73 MR 233, Thu. 17, 2026 to address modern methods of distributed knowledge and reconstruction.

§ 2901.2 Classification of Secret Magical Acts

(a) **General Rule.**
All secret magical acts shall be classified according to level of sensitivity, risk, and potential impact.

(b) **Classification Criteria.**
Classification shall be based on—
(1) the potential for harm if disclosed or misused;
(2) the difficulty of containment once disclosed;

(3) the potential for replication or adaptation; and
(4) the extent to which the act affects systems, populations, or structures.

(c) **Classification Levels.**
Secret magical acts shall be categorized as follows—
(1) Restricted.
Acts that—
(A) present localized or limited risk; and
(B) can be contained or controlled if disclosed.
Access shall be limited but may be granted under controlled conditions.
(2) Confidential.
Acts that—
(A) present moderate risk of misuse or disruption;
(B) may be replicated with effort; or
(C) affect defined systems or populations.
Access shall be restricted to authorized individuals with demonstrated need.
(3) Highly Restricted.
Acts that—
(A) present significant risk of widespread harm or destabilization;
(B) are capable of rapid replication or adaptation; or
(C) affect multiple systems or domains.
Access shall be limited to a narrow class of authorized personnel.
(4) Prohibited Knowledge.
Acts that—
(A) cannot be safely disclosed under any circumstances;
(B) present systemic or catastrophic risk if known; or
(C) enable manipulation or collapse of fundamental structures.
No access shall be permitted except as necessary for containment, suppression, or enforcement.

(d) **Composite Classification.**
Where a secret magical act consists of multiple components, classification shall be based on the highest applicable level.
(1) No person shall distribute components separately to avoid classification.

(e) **Reclassification.**
Classification shall be subject to periodic review and may be adjusted based on—

(1) changes in risk or impact;
(2) emergence of new information; or
(3) demonstrated ability to control or contain the act.

(f) **Default Classification.**
Where classification is uncertain, the act shall be treated as Highly Restricted or Prohibited Knowledge until determined otherwise.

(g) **Cross-References.**
For authorized access, see § 2901.3. For security protocols, see § 2901.4. For reporting obligations, see § 2901.5.

(h) **Historical Annotations.**
This section was enacted under C.C.D. 3568, 37 MR 201, Wed. 14, 1852 to establish classification tiers for secret magical acts. Amended under C.C.D. 6558, 46 MR 233, Mon. 4, 1965 to introduce higher-tier restrictions for systemic risks. Revised under C.C.D. 10491, 73 MR 266, Tue. 28, 2026 to address modern classification challenges and evolving threats.

§ 2901.3 Authorized Access to Secret Magic

(a) **General Rule.**
No person shall access, review, possess, or utilize secret magical acts except as expressly authorized under this section.

(b) **Authorization Requirement.**
Access shall require prior authorization based on demonstrated need, qualification, and capacity to handle such material.
(1) Authorization shall be specific to—
(A) the classification level; and
(B) the purpose for which access is granted.

(c) **Eligibility Criteria.**
Authorization shall be granted only where the individual—
(1) possesses sufficient knowledge and training;
(2) demonstrates ability to maintain secrecy and control; and
(3) requires access for a defined and legitimate purpose.

(d) **Scope of Access.**
Authorized access shall be limited in scope.

(1) No person shall access more information than necessary to fulfill the authorized purpose.
(2) Access shall be restricted by—
(A) classification level;
(B) duration; and
(C) form of access.

(e) **Restrictions Based on Classification.**
Access shall be governed by classification level.
(1) Restricted and Confidential materials may permit controlled review.
(2) Highly Restricted materials shall require enhanced safeguards.
(3) Prohibited Knowledge shall not be accessed except where—
(A) necessary for containment or suppression; and
(B) conducted under direct oversight.

(f) **Non-Transferability.**
Authorization shall not be transferred, delegated, or shared.
(1) No person shall permit another to access secret material under their authorization.

(g) **Monitoring and Accountability.**
All access shall be subject to monitoring and review.
(1) Records shall be maintained of—
(A) access granted;
(B) materials accessed; and
(C) duration and purpose of access.

(h) **Termination of Access.**
Authorization shall terminate upon completion of the authorized purpose or upon determination that continued access is no longer appropriate.

(i) **Cross-References.**
For classification of secret acts, see § 2901.2. For security protocols, see § 2901.4. For reporting violations, see § 2901.5.

(j) **Historical Annotations.**
This section was enacted under C.C.D. 3611, 38 MR 118, Mon. 3, 1859 to regulate access to restricted magical knowledge. Amended under C.C.D. 6614, 46 MR 276, Tue. 11, 1968 to establish tier-based access controls. Revised under C.C.D. 10502, 73 MR 301, Fri. 30, 2026 to address modern access control and accountability requirements.

§ 2901.4 Security Protocols for Handling Secret Magic

(a) **General Rule.**
All secret magical acts, materials, records, and knowledge shall be handled, stored, transmitted, and accessed in accordance with security protocols sufficient to prevent unauthorized disclosure, replication, or misuse.

(b) **Scope of Protection.**
Security protocols shall apply to—
(1) physical materials, including texts, artifacts, or components;
(2) intangible knowledge, including memorized or conceptual understanding;
(3) partially constructed or fragmented information; and
(4) any medium or method through which secret magic may be conveyed or reconstructed.

(c) **Storage Requirements.**
All secret magical acts shall be stored in a manner that prevents unauthorized access or accidental exposure.
(1) Storage systems shall include—
(A) physical containment measures;
(B) magical protections designed to restrict access; and
(C) safeguards against unauthorized duplication or extraction.
(2) Storage shall be segregated by classification level.
(3) No material shall be stored in a manner that allows uncontrolled access through—
(A) shared environments; or
(B) interconnected systems.

(d) **Access Controls.**
Access to secret magical acts shall be controlled through layered security measures.
(1) Such measures shall include—
(A) identity verification;
(B) authorization validation; and
(C) access limitation based on classification.
(2) Access shall be logged and monitored in real time.

(3) No access system shall rely solely on a single point of control.

(e) **Transmission Restrictions.**
No secret magical act shall be transmitted except through secure and authorized channels.
(1) Transmission shall be prohibited where—
(A) the integrity of the transmission cannot be ensured; or
(B) interception or replication is reasonably foreseeable.
(2) Any transmission shall include safeguards designed to—
(A) limit dissemination; and
(B) prevent unauthorized reconstruction.

(f) **Segmentation and Compartmentalization.**
Secret magical acts may be segmented to reduce risk of disclosure.
(1) Where segmentation is used—
(A) no single person shall have access to all components unless authorized; and
(B) components shall not be structured in a manner that permits reconstruction without authorization.
(2) Segmentation shall not be used to evade classification or access restrictions.

(g) **Monitoring and Audit.**
All handling of secret magical acts shall be subject to monitoring and periodic audit.
(1) Monitoring shall detect—
(A) unauthorized access attempts;
(B) unusual access patterns; and
(C) potential disclosure events.
(2) Audits shall evaluate compliance with security protocols and identify vulnerabilities.

(h) **Incident Response.**
Upon detection of a potential or actual breach, immediate action shall be taken to—
(1) contain or limit the disclosure;
(2) prevent further access or dissemination; and
(3) assess the scope and impact of the breach.
(2) Response measures shall be proportional to the classification level and potential harm.

(i) **Prohibition on Insecure Handling.**
No person shall handle secret magical acts in a manner that—
(1) exposes such acts to unauthorized persons;
(2) permits uncontrolled observation, replication, or recording; or
(3) relies on safeguards known to be insufficient or compromised.

(j) **Cross-References.**
For classification, see § 2901.2. For authorized access, see § 2901.3. For reporting requirements, see § 2901.5.

(k) **Historical Annotations.**
This section was enacted under C.C.D. 3664, 38 MR 201, Thu. 9, 1866 to establish baseline handling and storage requirements following early disclosure incidents involving copied grimoires. Amended under C.C.D. 6721, 47 MR 144, Tue. 6, 1971 to introduce layered access controls and compartmentalization practices in response to coordinated breaches. Revised under C.C.D. 10418, 73 MR 233, Mon. 14, 2024 to address modern transmission vectors and distributed knowledge risks.

§ 2901.5 Reporting of Unauthorized Disclosure

(a) **General Rule.**
Any person who becomes aware of, suspects, or has reason to believe that a secret magical act has been disclosed or compromised shall report such disclosure without delay.

(b) **Scope of Reportable Events.**
Reportable events shall include—
(1) unauthorized access to secret magical acts;
(2) unauthorized transmission or dissemination;
(3) loss, theft, or compromise of materials or knowledge; and
(4) any condition that increases the likelihood of disclosure.

(c) **Immediate Reporting Requirement.**
Reports shall be made as soon as reasonably practicable upon discovery.
(1) Delay shall be permitted only where immediate reporting would—
(A) exacerbate the breach; or
(B) interfere with containment efforts.

(d) **Content of Report.**

Reports shall include, to the extent known—
(1) the nature and classification of the disclosed act;
(2) the circumstances of the disclosure;
(3) the identity of affected or involved parties; and
(4) the scope and potential impact of the breach.

(e) **Obligation to Mitigate.**
Any person with knowledge of a disclosure shall take reasonable steps to—
(1) limit further dissemination;
(2) preserve evidence; and
(3) assist in containment and response.

(f) **Failure to Report.**
Failure to report a disclosure as required under this section shall constitute a separate violation, regardless of whether the person was involved in the original breach.

(g) **Protection of Reporting Parties.**
Persons who report disclosures in good faith shall not be subject to adverse action solely for making such report.
(1) Such protection shall not extend to individuals who—
(A) knowingly participated in the breach; or
(B) provided false or misleading information.

(h) **Follow-Up and Cooperation.**
Reporting parties shall cooperate with any investigation or response measures.
(1) Such cooperation shall include—
(A) providing additional information; and
(B) assisting in identifying scope and impact.

(i) **Cross-References.**
For security protocols, see § 2901.4. For authorized access, see § 2901.3. For general secrecy requirements, see § 401.7.

(j) **Historical Annotations.**
This section was enacted under C.C.D. 3719, 39 MR 118, Tue. 3, 1873 to establish mandatory reporting following uncontrolled dissemination of restricted incantations. Amended under C.C.D. 6894, 47 MR 276, Thu. 21, 1982 to address delayed reporting and concealment of breaches during

institutional failures. Revised under C.C.D. 10372, 72 MR 301, Wed. 6, 2019 to address rapid disclosure through modern communication channels and distributed record systems.

Part XXX: Protection of Privacy in Magical Practices

§ 3001.1 General Principles of Magical Privacy

(a) **General Rule.**
No person shall intrude upon, access, observe, record, or otherwise interfere with the private magical activity, information, or conditions of another except as expressly authorized under this Code.

(b) **Scope of Privacy.**
Magical privacy shall extend to any information, condition, or activity that—
(1) is not intentionally disclosed to the public; and
(2) relates to—
(A) spellcasting, rituals, or magical practices, including preparatory or residual conditions;
(B) personal magical attributes, capabilities, limitations, or signatures;
(C) magical communications, transmissions, or exchanges, whether direct or mediated; or
(D) magical effects occurring within a private, restricted, or controlled environment, including effects that—
(i) are not outwardly visible; or
(ii) are perceptible only through specialized means.

(c) **Forms of Intrusion.**
Prohibited intrusion shall include any act that—
(1) directly accesses private magical information; or
(2) indirectly obtains such information through—
(A) observation, whether physical, magical, perceptual, or inferential;
(B) inference derived from concealed, latent, or residual effects; or
(C) manipulation of environment or systems to reveal hidden conditions, including manipulation that—
(i) induces or amplifies detectable effects; or
(ii) alters the subject's behavior to expose private information.

(d) **Expectation of Privacy.**

A person shall be deemed to have a reasonable expectation of magical privacy where—
(1) the activity occurs within a private, restricted, or controlled space;
(2) the information is not intentionally disclosed; or
(3) the nature of the activity is such that a reasonable person would not expect it to be observed or accessed, including activity that—
(A) is shielded by physical or magical means; or
(B) produces effects not intended for external perception.
(2) The existence of ambient or incidental magical effects shall not, by itself, eliminate such expectation.

(e) **Non-Circumvention.**
No person shall avoid the application of this section by—
(1) characterizing an intrusion as passive, incidental, or unavoidable;
(2) using indirect or distributed methods to reconstruct private information, including methods that—
(A) aggregate multiple observations; or
(B) combine non-sensitive data to produce sensitive conclusions; or
(3) relying on technical, magical, or conceptual loopholes that produce substantially the same result as direct intrusion.

(f) **Derivative Information.**
Information derived from a violation of magical privacy shall be treated as subject to the same restrictions as the underlying information.
(1) No person shall use, disclose, or rely upon such information, including where such information—
(A) has been altered in form; or
(B) is combined with lawful information to produce new conclusions.

(g) **Burden of Justification.**
Any person asserting lawful authority to intrude upon magical privacy shall bear the burden of demonstrating such authority, including demonstrating that—
(1) the intrusion was necessary; and
(2) no less intrusive alternative was reasonably available.

(h) **Cross-References.**
For mind-related intrusions, see Part XXI. For secrecy obligations, see § 401.7. For surveillance and monitoring, see § 3001.5.

(i) **Historical Annotations.**
This section was enacted under C.C.D. 3181, 34 MR 144, Mon. 5, 1810 to establish baseline protections against intrusion into private magical activity. Amended under C.C.D. 6022, 45 MR 118, Tue. 7, 1955 to address indirect and perceptual methods of intrusion. Revised under C.C.D. 10188, 71 MR 233, Wed. 12, 2013 to address distributed inference-based privacy violations.

§ 3001.2 Privacy in Spellcasting and Rituals

(a) **General Rule.**
No person shall observe, record, intercept, replicate, analyze, or interfere with another's spellcasting or ritual activity without authorization.

(b) **Protected Activity.**
Protected spellcasting and ritual activity shall include—
(1) active casting or performance;
(2) preparatory acts, including component selection, arrangement, and incantation development; and
(3) post-casting conditions, including residual, latent, or delayed effects that—
(A) reveal underlying structure; or
(B) permit reconstruction of the spell.

(c) **Forms of Prohibited Conduct.**
Prohibited conduct shall include—
(1) direct observation of private casting or rituals;
(2) recording or replication of incantations, gestures, configurations, or sequences; and
(3) interception of magical processes through—
(A) magical detection or sensing;
(B) environmental manipulation designed to reveal hidden elements; or
(C) perceptual or cognitive intrusion, including intrusion that—
(i) extracts partial information; or
(ii) induces the caster to reveal protected details.

(d) **Indirect Observation and Reconstruction.**
No person shall obtain knowledge of private spellcasting through indirect means.
(1) Indirect means shall include—

(A) analysis of residual magical effects;
(B) reconstruction of spells based on partial or fragmented observation; or
(C) aggregation of multiple observations to derive a complete or functional method, including aggregation that—
(i) occurs over time; or
(ii) involves multiple observers or sources.

(e) **Ritual Integrity.**
No person shall interfere with or alter a ritual in progress.
(1) Interference shall include—
(A) introduction of additional elements or variables;
(B) disruption of sequence, timing, or structure; or
(C) alteration of environmental or magical conditions necessary for completion, including alteration that—
(i) destabilizes the ritual; or
(ii) changes its outcome.

(f) **Shared or Group Rituals.**
Where multiple participants are involved, privacy shall extend to all participants.
(1) No participant shall disclose, record, or reproduce the ritual beyond authorized scope.
(2) Consent of one participant shall not authorize disclosure of—
(A) the entire ritual; or
(B) contributions of other participants.

(g) **Residual Privacy.**
Privacy protections shall continue after completion of the spell or ritual.
(1) Residual effects shall not be used to infer, reconstruct, or replicate private activity, including effects that—
(A) persist over time; or
(B) interact with subsequent magical activity.

(h) **Cross-References.**
For general privacy principles, see § 3001.1. For confidentiality of records, see § 3001.3. For eavesdropping protections, see § 3001.6.

(i) **Historical Annotations.**

This section was enacted under C.C.D. 3244, 34 MR 201, Thu. 14, 1821 to protect private spellcasting practices from observation and replication. Amended under C.C.D. 6117, 45 MR 233, Mon. 2, 1958 to address indirect reconstruction of rituals. Revised under C.C.D. 10201, 71 MR 266, Tue. 19, 2014 to address distributed observation and recording technologies.

§ 3001.3 Confidentiality of Magical Records

(a) **General Rule.**
All magical records shall be treated as confidential where such records contain private, sensitive, or restricted information.

(b) **Definition of Magical Records.**
Magical records shall include any record, whether physical or intangible, that documents—
(1) spellcasting activity;
(2) magical attributes, capabilities, or conditions;
(3) rituals, methods, or processes; or
(4) information derived from magical observation or interaction, including information that—
(A) reveals underlying structure; or
(B) permits reconstruction of activity.

(c) **Protection of Records.**
No person shall access, copy, alter, or disclose magical records without authorization.
(1) Prohibited conduct includes—
(A) unauthorized duplication, extraction, or replication;
(B) alteration, deletion, or modification of records; and
(C) disclosure to unauthorized persons, including disclosure that—
(i) is partial; or
(ii) enables reconstruction of the record.

(d) **Storage and Safeguarding.**
Magical records shall be stored in a manner that prevents unauthorized access or compromise.
(1) Safeguards shall include—
(A) physical and magical protections;
(B) layered access controls; and
(C) monitoring of access and use.

(2) Records shall not be stored in environments that—
(A) permit uncontrolled access; or
(B) expose records to interception, replication, or inference.

(e) **Transmission of Records.**
No magical record shall be transmitted except through secure and authorized means.
(1) Transmission shall be prohibited where—
(A) integrity cannot be ensured; or
(B) interception, duplication, or reconstruction is reasonably foreseeable.
(2) Records shall be transmitted only to persons authorized to receive them, and only to the extent necessary.

(f) **Derivative and Aggregated Records.**
Records derived from or aggregated from multiple sources shall be treated as confidential where they reveal private or restricted information.
(1) No person shall avoid confidentiality requirements by—
(A) fragmenting records; or
(B) combining non-sensitive information to produce sensitive results, including results that—
(i)
infer protected details; or
(ii) reconstruct underlying activity.

(g) **Retention and Destruction.**
Magical records shall be retained only as long as necessary and shall be securely destroyed when no longer required.
(1) Destruction shall ensure that records cannot be reconstructed, including through—
(A) residual magical traces; or
(B) reconstruction from partial or related records.

(h) **Cross-References.**
For general privacy principles, see § 3001.1. For secrecy requirements, see Part XXIX. For monitoring and surveillance, see § 3001.5.

(i) **Historical Annotations.**
This section was enacted under C.C.D. 3301, 35 MR 77, Tue. 11, 1832 to establish confidentiality requirements for recorded magical knowledge. Amended under C.C.D. 6233, 46 MR 118, Thu. 5, 1961 to address

duplication and transmission risks. Revised under C.C.D. 10266, 72 MR 201, Mon. 3, 2017 to address modern recordkeeping systems and aggregation-based privacy risks.

§ 3001.4 Privacy in Telepathic and Mind Control Magic

(a) **General Rule.**
No person shall access, read, alter, suppress, implant, extract, or otherwise interact with the thoughts, memories, perceptions, or cognitive processes of another through telepathic or mind control magic except as expressly authorized under this Code.

(b) **Scope of Protection.**
Magical privacy shall extend to all mental content, including—
(1) thoughts, whether formed, forming, or latent;
(2) memories, whether active, suppressed, or partially recalled;
(3) perceptions, interpretations, or emotional states; and
(4) cognitive patterns, inclinations, or predispositions that—
(A) reveal internal processes; or
(B) may be used to influence behavior.

(c) **Forms of Prohibited Intrusion.**
Prohibited conduct shall include—
(1) direct telepathic access to another's mind;
(2) passive or ambient scanning designed to detect or infer mental content; and
(3) indirect intrusion through methods that—
(A) stimulate or provoke thoughts for observation;
(B) analyze external behavior to reconstruct internal states; or
(C) rely on magical constructs that—
(i) extract mental content; or
(ii) alter perception to reveal such content.

(d) **Manipulation and Alteration.**
No person shall alter, suppress, implant, or otherwise modify mental content without authorization.
(1) Prohibited alteration includes—
(A) insertion of thoughts, memories, or impulses;
(B) removal or suppression of existing content; or

(C) modification of perception or judgment, including modification that—
(i) changes decision-making; or
(ii) obscures awareness of the alteration.

(e) **Consent Requirements.**
Consent to telepathic or mind control activity shall be—
(1) explicit, informed, and specific; and
(2) limited to the scope for which it was granted.
(2) Consent shall not be valid where—
(A) obtained through coercion, manipulation, or deception; or
(B) given under conditions that impair judgment or understanding.
(3) Consent may be withdrawn at any time, including through—
(A) verbal or non-verbal indication; or
(B) observable resistance or distress.

(f) **Residual and Latent Effects.**
Privacy protections shall extend to residual or latent effects of telepathic or mind control magic.
(1) No person shall access or rely upon mental content altered or exposed through prior intrusion.

(g) **Non-Circumvention.**
No person shall avoid the application of this section by—
(1) characterizing intrusion as therapeutic, observational, or experimental; or
(2) using indirect methods that produce the same result as direct access.

(h) **Cross-References.**
For general privacy principles, see § 3001.1. For mind control regulations, see Part XXI. For consent requirements, see § 3001.8.

(i) **Historical Annotations.**
This section was enacted under C.C.D. 3368, 35 MR 144, Thu. 18, 1838 to prohibit unauthorized intrusion into mental processes. Amended under C.C.D. 6412, 46 MR 201, Tue. 6, 1964 to address passive and indirect mental surveillance. Revised under C.C.D. 10289, 72 MR 233, Mon. 9, 2018 to address modern manipulation and cognitive reconstruction techniques.

§ 3001.5 Magical Surveillance and Monitoring

(a) **General Rule.**
No person shall conduct magical surveillance or monitoring of another person, location, or activity except as expressly authorized under this Code.

(b) **Definition of Surveillance.**
Magical surveillance shall include any act of observing, tracking, recording, or analyzing information through magical means, including surveillance that—
(1) is continuous or intermittent; or
(2) relies on direct or indirect detection.

(c) **Forms of Prohibited Surveillance.**
Prohibited surveillance shall include—
(1) direct observation through magical projection, scrying, or equivalent means;
(2) indirect observation through detection of magical signatures or environmental effects; and
(3) reconstruction of activity through aggregation of data, including aggregation that—
(A) combines multiple observations; or
(B) derives conclusions from non-sensitive information.

(d) **Tracking and Monitoring.**
No person shall track or monitor the movement, behavior, or activity of another through magical means without authorization.
(1) Prohibited tracking includes—
(A) location tracking;
(B) behavioral monitoring; or
(C) predictive analysis based on observed patterns, including analysis that—
(i) anticipates future actions; or
(ii) infers private activity.

(e) **Installation of Surveillance Mechanisms.**
No person shall place, embed, or deploy magical surveillance mechanisms without authorization.
(1) Such mechanisms include—

(A) persistent scrying devices;
(B) ambient detection systems; or
(C) concealed constructs designed to collect information.

(f) **Minimization Requirements.**
Where surveillance is authorized, it shall be limited to the minimum necessary scope.
(1) Authorized surveillance shall—
(A) avoid collection of unrelated information; and
(B) terminate upon completion of the authorized purpose.

(g) **Prohibition on Bulk or Indiscriminate Surveillance.**
No person shall conduct surveillance that—
(1) captures information about multiple persons without distinction; or
(2) collects data without a defined and authorized purpose.

(h) **Retention and Use of Collected Information.**
Information obtained through surveillance shall be subject to strict limitations.
(1) No person shall use or disclose such information beyond authorized scope.
(2) Retention shall be limited to the period necessary for the authorized purpose.

(i) **Cross-References.**
For general privacy principles, see § 3001.1. For confidentiality of records, see § 3001.3. For legal exceptions, see § 3001.7.

(j) **Historical Annotations.**
This section was enacted under C.C.D. 3411, 36 MR 118, Mon. 7, 1844 to regulate magical observation practices. Amended under C.C.D. 6533, 46 MR 233, Thu. 12, 1965 to address technological and magical tracking systems. Revised under C.C.D. 10312, 72 MR 276, Tue. 11, 2020 to address large-scale and automated surveillance practices.

§ 3001.6 Protection Against Magical Eavesdropping

(a) **General Rule.**

No person shall intercept, listen to, record, or otherwise obtain the contents of magical communications without authorization.

(b) **Scope of Communications.**
Magical communications shall include—
(1) direct magical messaging or transmission;
(2) ritual or spell-based communication; and
(3) any exchange of information conducted through magical means, including communication that—
(A) is concealed or encrypted; or
(B) occurs within a controlled or private environment.

(c) **Forms of Eavesdropping.**
Prohibited eavesdropping shall include—
(1) direct interception of communications;
(2) use of magical or environmental means to detect or capture communication; and
(3) indirect acquisition through methods that—
(A) reconstruct communication from partial signals; or
(B) infer content based on observable effects.

(d) **Interference with Communications.**
No person shall alter, redirect, delay, or disrupt magical communications.
(1) Prohibited conduct includes—
(A) modification of message content;
(B) rerouting of communication paths; or
(C) introduction of interference that—
(i) distorts meaning; or
(ii) prevents delivery.

(e) **Devices and Mechanisms.**
No person shall create, deploy, or use devices or constructs designed to intercept or monitor magical communications.
(1) Such devices include—
(A) listening constructs;
(B) signal amplification or capture systems; or
(C) concealed mechanisms designed to record or transmit communications.

(f) **Incidental Acquisition.**
Where communication is incidentally acquired, the acquiring party shall—

(1) cease further acquisition; and
(2) refrain from use or disclosure of the information.

(g) **Non-Circumvention.**
No person shall avoid the application of this section by—
(1) characterizing interception as passive or unintended; or
(2) using indirect or distributed methods to obtain communication content.

(h) **Cross-References.**
For general privacy principles, see § 3001.1. For surveillance restrictions, see § 3001.5. For secrecy requirements, see § 401.7.

(i) **Historical Annotations.**
This section was enacted under C.C.D. 3455, 36 MR 166, Tue. 15, 1849 to prohibit interception of magical communications. Amended under C.C.D. 6622, 47 MR 118, Wed. 18, 1970 to address advanced interception techniques. Revised under C.C.D. 10341, 72 MR 301, Thu. 21, 2021 to address modern communication systems and distributed interception methods.

§ 3001.7 Legal Exceptions to Magical Privacy Protections

(a) **General Rule.**
Magical privacy protections under this Part shall not apply where intrusion, access, or observation is expressly authorized under a lawful exception.

(b) **Narrow Construction.**
All exceptions to magical privacy shall be narrowly construed.
(1) No exception shall be interpreted to permit broader intrusion than is strictly necessary.
(2) Any ambiguity shall be resolved in favor of preserving privacy.

(c) **Authorized Exceptions.**
Exceptions may apply only under the following circumstances—
(1) Law Enforcement and Investigatory Authority.
Intrusion may be permitted where—
(A) authorized by lawful order or equivalent authority; and

(B) supported by a defined and articulable basis.
(2) Such intrusion shall be limited to—
(A) the specific subject matter; and
(B) the duration necessary to achieve the authorized purpose.
(2) Emergency Circumstances.
Intrusion may be permitted where—
(A) there exists an imminent risk of harm; and
(B) immediate action is required such that prior authorization is impracticable.
(2) Any such intrusion shall—
(A) be limited in scope and duration; and
(B) terminate immediately upon resolution of the emergency.
(3) Consent.
Intrusion may be permitted where valid consent has been obtained in accordance with § 3001.8.
(2) Consent shall not be presumed or implied beyond its stated scope.
(4) Regulatory Oversight and Compliance.
Limited intrusion may be permitted where necessary to ensure compliance with this Code, including inspection or audit.
(2) Such intrusion shall—
(A) be conducted by authorized personnel; and
(B) avoid unnecessary access to unrelated information.

(d) **Limitations on Exceptions.**
No exception shall permit—
(1) access to information unrelated to the authorized purpose;
(2) use or disclosure beyond the authorized scope; or
(3) continued intrusion after the basis for the exception no longer exists.

(e) **Minimization Requirements.**
All authorized intrusions shall be conducted in a manner that minimizes impact on privacy.
(1) Minimization shall include—
(A) limiting collection of information;
(B) restricting access to relevant content; and
(C) preventing retention of unrelated data.

(f) **Documentation and Accountability.**
All use of an exception shall be documented.
(1) Documentation shall include—

(A) the basis for the exception;
(B) the scope of intrusion; and
(C) the duration of the activity.

(g) **Prohibition on Pretextual Use.**
No person shall invoke an exception as a pretext to conduct unauthorized or excessive intrusion.

(h) **Cross-References.**
For emergency spellcasting, see § 2601.2. For surveillance limitations, see § 3001.5. For consent requirements, see § 3001.8.

(i) **Historical Annotations.**
This section was enacted under C.C.D. 3477, 36 MR 201, Mon. 4, 1853 to establish limited exceptions to privacy protections. Amended under C.C.D. 6688, 47 MR 233, Thu. 9, 1972 to address misuse of investigatory authority. Revised under C.C.D. 10355, 72 MR 166, Tue. 2, 2021 to strengthen minimization and anti-pretext requirements.

§ 3001.8 Consent and Disclosure in Magical Research

(a) **General Rule.**
No person shall conduct magical research involving observation, interaction, or experimentation upon another person or their magical attributes without valid consent.

(b) **Scope of Research.**
Magical research shall include any activity that—
(1) observes or records magical behavior;
(2) tests, alters, or evaluates magical capability; or
(3) collects or analyzes information for study or development, including activity that—
(A) produces new methods; or
(B) refines existing practices.

(c) **Requirements for Valid Consent.**
Consent shall be valid only where it is—
(1) informed, including disclosure of—
(A) the nature and purpose of the research;

(B) the methods to be used; and
(C) potential risks and effects;
(2) voluntary and free from coercion, manipulation, or deception; and
(3) specific to the scope and duration of the research.

(d) **Scope and Limitations of Consent.**
Consent shall be limited to the specific activity authorized.
(1) No person shall exceed the scope of consent by—
(A) expanding the research beyond what was disclosed; or
(B) using collected information for unrelated purposes.
(2) Consent shall not extend to—
(A) undisclosed risks; or
(B) secondary uses not reasonably anticipated.

(e) **Withdrawal of Consent.**
Consent may be withdrawn at any time.
(1) Upon withdrawal—
(A) all research activity shall cease; and
(B) any ongoing effects shall be addressed to the extent reasonably practicable.

(f) **Protection of Research Subjects.**
Research subjects shall be protected from harm, including—
(1) physical, cognitive, or metaphysical harm; and
(2) exposure to uncontrolled or unstable magical effects.
(2) No research shall proceed where risk exceeds reasonable thresholds.

(g) **Confidentiality of Research Data.**
Information obtained through research shall be treated as confidential.
(1) No person shall disclose such information except as authorized.
(2) Data shall be stored and handled in accordance with § 3001.3.

(h) **Prohibition on Covert Research.**
No person shall conduct research without the knowledge of the subject.
(1) Covert observation or experimentation shall be prohibited regardless of intent.

(i) **Cross-References.**
For general privacy principles, see § 3001.1. For confidentiality of records, see § 3001.3. For secrecy requirements, see Part XXIX.

(j) **Historical Annotations.**

This section was enacted under C.C.D. 3512, 37 MR 118, Wed. 12, 1857 to establish consent requirements in magical research. Amended under C.C.D. 6729, 47 MR 276, Mon. 6, 1976 to address coercive and undisclosed experimentation. Revised under C.C.D. 10369, 72 MR 233, Thu. 18, 2022 to address modern research practices and data confidentiality standards.

Part XXXI: Periodic Updates, Amendments, and Supplements

§ 3101.1 Guidelines for Updating the Magical Code

(a) **General Rule.**
The Magical Code of Regulations shall be subject to periodic review and update to ensure continued applicability, internal consistency, and responsiveness to evolving magical practices, conditions, and risks.

(b) **Purpose of Updates.**
Updates shall be undertaken to—
(1) address gaps, ambiguities, or inconsistencies within the Code;
(2) respond to developments in magical practice, technology, or theory;
(3) incorporate lessons arising from enforcement, adjudication, or administrative interpretation; and
(4) maintain alignment across Parts, Sections, and cross-referenced provisions.

(c) **Scope of Updates.**
Updates may include—
(1) revision of existing provisions;
(2) addition of new sections or subsections;
(3) clarification of existing language; and
(4) consolidation or restructuring of related provisions, including restructuring that—
(A) eliminates redundancy; or
(B) improves interpretability without altering substantive effect.

(d) **Consistency Requirements.**
All updates shall maintain consistency with the structure and definitions set forth in Part I.
(1) No update shall—
(A) conflict with established definitions under § 101.1;
(B) introduce terminology inconsistent with existing usage; or
(C) create internal contradictions across Parts, including contradictions that—

(i) arise through cross-references; or
(ii) affect application of related provisions.

(e) **Prospective Application.**
Updates shall apply prospectively unless otherwise specified.
(1) Retroactive application shall be permitted only where—
(A) necessary to clarify existing law; and
(B) not inconsistent with principles of fairness and reliance.

(f) **Non-Circumvention.**
No person shall rely on the absence of an update, delay in revision, or identified gap in the Code to justify conduct otherwise inconsistent with the purpose or structure of the Code.

(g) **Cross-References.**
For administrative structure and authority, see § 102.1. For definitions, see § 101.1. For publication of materials, see § 3101.3.

(h) **Historical Annotations.**
This section was enacted under C.C.D. 3599, 38 MR 144, Mon. 2, 1854 to establish a formal framework for periodic updates to the Code following inconsistencies across early provisions. Amended under C.C.D. 6422, 46 MR 118, Thu. 10, 1963 to address structural alignment and cross-reference integrity. Revised under C.C.D. 10212, 71 MR 201, Tue. 6, 2016 to address modern developments in magical practice and regulatory complexity.

§ 3101.2 Amendment Procedures and Reviews

(a) **General Rule.**
No provision of the Magical Code of Regulations shall be amended except in accordance with the procedures set forth in this section.

(b) **Initiation of Amendments.**
Amendments may be initiated by authorized bodies where—
(1) a need for revision has been identified; or
(2) conditions have arisen that warrant modification of existing provisions, including conditions that—
(A) expose deficiencies; or
(B) produce unintended outcomes.

(c) **Review Process.**
All proposed amendments shall undergo review prior to adoption.
(1) Review shall consider—
(A) consistency with existing provisions;
(B) potential impact on related sections; and
(C) alignment with the purpose and structure of the Code.
(2) No amendment shall proceed where such review identifies unresolved conflicts.

(d) **Approval Requirements.**
Amendments shall require approval by the appropriate authority as defined under § 102.1.
(1) Approval shall be contingent upon—
(A) completion of required review; and
(B) confirmation of consistency and necessity.

(e) **Documentation of Amendments.**
All amendments shall be documented in a manner that—
(1) identifies the provision amended;
(2) specifies the nature of the change; and
(3) provides sufficient detail to permit interpretation and application, including documentation that—
(A) reflects prior language where necessary; or
(B) clarifies the intended effect of the amendment.

(f) **Integration into the Code.**
Amendments shall be integrated into the Code in a manner that preserves structural integrity.
(1) Integration shall ensure that—
(A) numbering and hierarchy remain consistent; and
(B) cross-references are updated accordingly.

(g) **Periodic Review of Amendments.**
Amended provisions shall be subject to subsequent review to assess effectiveness and consistency.
(1) Where deficiencies are identified, further amendment shall be required.

(h) **Cross-References.**
For guidelines on updates, see § 3101.1. For publication requirements, see § 3101.3. For administrative authority, see § 102.1.

(i) **Historical Annotations.**
This section was enacted under C.C.D. 3627, 38 MR 201, Tue. 15, 1859 to establish formal amendment procedures. Amended under C.C.D. 6510, 46 MR 166, Mon. 11, 1964 to address deficiencies in review and approval processes. Revised under C.C.D. 10244, 71 MR 233, Thu. 22, 2018 to strengthen documentation and integration requirements.

§ 3101.3 Publication of Supplementary Materials

(a) **General Rule.**
Supplementary materials issued in connection with the Magical Code of Regulations shall be published, maintained, and made available in accordance with this section.

(b) **Definition of Supplementary Materials.**
Supplementary materials shall include—
(1) interpretive guidance;
(2) administrative rulings or clarifications;
(3) explanatory materials; and
(4) any document intended to assist in the application or understanding of the Code, including materials that—
(A) elaborate on existing provisions; or
(B) address specific circumstances.

(c) **Authority to Issue Materials.**
Supplementary materials may be issued by authorized bodies in accordance with § 102.1.
(1) No material shall be issued without proper authority.

(d) **Nature and Effect.**
Supplementary materials shall not alter or supersede the Code.
(1) Such materials shall—
(A) clarify existing provisions; or
(B) provide guidance on application.
(2) No material shall create new obligations unless adopted through formal amendment.

(e) **Publication Requirements.**
All supplementary materials shall be published in a manner that ensures accessibility and reliability.

(1) Publication shall include—
(A) identification of issuing authority;
(B) date of issuance; and
(C) reference to relevant provisions of the Code.

(f) **Consistency and Alignment.**
Supplementary materials shall be consistent with the Code.
(1) No material shall—
(A) conflict with existing provisions; or
(B) introduce ambiguity or inconsistency, including ambiguity that—
(i) affects interpretation; or
(ii) undermines enforcement.

(g) **Maintenance and Withdrawal.**
Supplementary materials shall be maintained, updated, or withdrawn as necessary.
(1) Where a material becomes outdated or inconsistent—
(A) it shall be revised; or
(B) it shall be withdrawn.
(2) Withdrawal shall be documented and published.

(h) **Cross-References.**
For update guidelines, see § 3101.1. For amendment procedures, see § 3101.2. For administrative authority, see § 102.1.

(i) **Historical Annotations.**
This section was enacted under C.C.D. 3655, 39 MR 77, Mon. 9, 1862 to establish publication of interpretive materials. Amended under C.C.D. 6599, 46 MR 201, Tue. 3, 1966 to address authority and consistency of such materials. Revised under C.C.D. 10278, 72 MR 144, Wed. 11, 2019 to address modern publication practices and accessibility requirements.

Part XXXII: Regulatory Mandates Concerning the Codification and Simplification of Magical Documentation

§ 3201.1 Prohibition Against Gratuitous Prolixity and Obfuscatory Circumlocution in Codificatory Processes

(a) **General Rule.**
No person engaged in the drafting, redrafting, compilation, recompilation, codification, recodification, textualization, formalization, or re-formalization of magical documentation shall employ, utilize, deploy, or otherwise give effect to any linguistic, syntactic, structural, or semiotic formulation that is gratuitously prolix, unduly sesquipedalian, excessively periphrastic, obfuscatorily circumlocutory, syntactically labyrinthine, semantically occlusive, or otherwise characterized by a degree of discursive supererogation, lexical hypertrophy, or interpretive intractability that renders such documentation less readily apprehensible, more burdensome to construe, or disproportionately resistant to reasonable exegesis relative to its substantive regulatory function.

(b) **Operative Prohibition.**
Without limiting, delimiting, circumscribing, expanding, or otherwise modulating the scope, breadth, or ambit of subsection (a), the employment, utilization, deployment, or other instantiation of any linguistic or structural construct, whether singularly, severally, jointly, collectively, or cumulatively considered, shall be deemed impermissible, proscribed, or otherwise noncompliant where such construct—
(1) results in, gives rise to, or is reasonably capable of producing an interpretive condition in which the semantic apprehension, syntactic parsing, or doctrinal ascertainment of the operative meaning of the provision is contingent upon iterative, recursive, or otherwise repetitious engagement with the text, including engagement that—
(A) necessitates re-reading, re-parsing, or re-conceptualization; or

(B) produces divergent, conflicting, or internally inconsistent plausible interpretations;
(2) substitutes, replaces, or displaces direct, linear, or otherwise immediately apprehensible expression with discursively dilatory, periphrastically mediated, or circumlocutorily extended phrasing the comprehension of which is not reasonably attainable without disproportionate cognitive exertion, hermeneutic reconstruction, or inferential supplementation; or
(3) produces, generates, or otherwise effectuates a condition of semantic opacity, interpretive indeterminacy, or syntactic convolution through the cumulative, aggregated, or compositional interaction of clauses, subclauses, modifiers, qualifiers, or other linguistic elements, including interaction that—
(A) obscures the operative subject, predicate, or object of the provision;
(B) dislocates, defers, or otherwise postpones the identification of controlling terms; or
(C) embeds, nests, or layers subordinate constructions in such a manner that the hierarchical or logical relationship between such constructions is not readily ascertainable without sustained analytical effort.

(c) **Application.**
This section shall apply, extend, and be given effect across all phases, stages, iterations, manifestations, instantiations, and re-instantiations of codificatory activity, including but not limited to initial drafting, preliminary drafting, subsequent redrafting, iterative revision, editorial consolidation, systematic restatement, reorganizational restructuring, and any analogous, comparable, or functionally equivalent process of textual inscription, re-inscription, or re-articulation, whether such process is characterized as drafting, redrafting, revision, consolidation, restatement, clarification, or otherwise.

(d) **Standard of Determination.**
A provision shall be deemed, considered, construed, and treated as noncompliant, violative, or otherwise inconsistent with this section where, upon consideration of the totality, entirety, or aggregate composition of its linguistic, syntactic, and structural elements, it is determined that the operative meaning, regulatory effect, or substantive import of such provision is not reasonably susceptible to immediate, direct, or unambiguous apprehension by a reader possessing ordinary familiarity with this Code, notwithstanding any contention, assertion, or

representation that such provision is technically precise, formally correct, or traditionally constructed.

(e) **Permissible Technicality.**
Nothing in this section shall be interpreted, construed, or understood to prohibit, preclude, or otherwise restrict the use of technical, specialized, formalized, or terminologically precise language where such language is indispensable, necessary, or otherwise required to achieve precision, specificity, or doctrinal consistency, including language defined under § 101.1, provided, however, that such usage does not, either individually, collectively, or cumulatively, result in, produce, or otherwise give rise to a condition of unnecessary obscurity, opacity, convolution, or interpretive resistance exceeding that which is functionally required.

(f) **Non-Circumvention.**
No person shall evade, circumvent, avoid, or otherwise render inapplicable the requirements, obligations, or prohibitions of this section through the distribution, dispersion, fragmentation, segmentation, disaggregation, or re-aggregation of linguistic or structural complexity across multiple provisions, clauses, subclauses, sentences, or textual units where the cumulative, composite, or aggregated effect of such distributed complexity produces, results in, or is functionally equivalent to the same or substantially similar degree of opacity, convolution, or interpretive burden as would a single provision of comparable density or construction.

(g) **Presumption.**
Where a provision exhibits, demonstrates, manifests, or otherwise gives rise to a degree of verbosity, convolution, opacity, circumlocution, syntactic density, or interpretive resistance that is disproportionate, excessive, or otherwise misaligned relative to its regulatory function, such provision shall be presumed, deemed, and treated as violative of this section unless and until rebutted by a showing, demonstration, or evidentiary presentation sufficient to establish that such characteristics are necessary, indispensable, or otherwise required.

(h) **Cross-References.**
For redundancy limitations, see § 3201.2. For simplification procedures, see § 3201.3. For amendment procedures, see § 3101.2.

(i) **Historical Annotations.**

This section was enacted under C.C.D. 3122, 34 MR 77, Tue. 9, 1808 to address increasing verbosity and interpretive opacity in early codified magical texts. Amended under C.C.D. 5991, 45 MR 166, Mon. 6, 1952 to prohibit circumlocutory drafting practices. Revised under C.C.D. 10211, 71 MR 188, Thu. 14, 2015 to address modern tendencies toward lexical hypertrophy and syntactic convolution.

§ 3201.2 Prescriptive Limits on Duplicitous, Redundant, or Repetitive Documentation

(a) **General Rule.**
No person shall produce, create, generate, draft, redraft, maintain, preserve, replicate, duplicate, reiterate, restate, reproduce, restate again, reiterate again, duplicate again, or otherwise promulgate magical documentation that is duplicative, redundant, repetitive, reiterative, restated, restated again, reiterated, reiterated again, duplicative in substance, duplicative in form, duplicative in effect, duplicative in meaning, or otherwise duplicative, redundant, repetitive, reiterative, or restated beyond that which is reasonably necessary, reasonably required, or otherwise reasonably appropriate to ensure clarity, coherence, intelligibility, interpretability, enforceability, or general comprehensibility.

(b) **Definitions.**
For purposes of this section—
(1) duplicative documentation shall mean documentation that duplicates, replicates, reproduces, or otherwise restates content that is already duplicated, replicated, reproduced, or restated elsewhere;
(2) redundant documentation shall mean documentation that is redundant, duplicative, repetitive, reiterative, or otherwise restated in that it restates, reiterates, repeats, or otherwise re-expresses requirements that have already been restated, reiterated, repeated, or otherwise re-expressed; and
(3) repetitious documentation shall mean documentation that repeats, reiterates, restates, reproduces, duplicates, or otherwise rearticulates the same concept, requirement, obligation, directive, or instruction in whole, in part, or in substance.

(c) **Prohibited Redundancy.**

Documentation shall be deemed, considered, construed, and treated as noncompliant where it—
(1) restates, reiterates, repeats, reproduces, duplicates, or otherwise re-expresses requirements already restated, reiterated, repeated, reproduced, duplicated, or otherwise expressed;
(2) duplicates, replicates, restates, reiterates, or otherwise reproduces language without substantive, material, or meaningful distinction; or
(3) conveys, communicates, expresses, restates, reiterates, or otherwise reproduces the same requirement, obligation, or directive in multiple forms, formulations, phrasings, restatements, reiterations, repetitions, or duplications, including formulations that—
(A) differ in wording but not in meaning; or
(B) repeat, restate, reiterate, or duplicate the same obligation with only minor, immaterial, stylistic, or otherwise inconsequential variation.

(d) **Permissible Redundancy.**
Redundancy, repetition, duplication, reiteration, restatement, or re-expression shall be permitted only where necessary, required, or otherwise appropriate to—
(1) ensure clarity, clarity of meaning, clarity of application, clarity of interpretation, or clarity generally;
(2) reinforce, restate, reiterate, repeat, or otherwise re-emphasize understanding in contexts where a single statement, singular articulation, or solitary expression would be insufficient, inadequate, or otherwise lacking; or
(3) prevent ambiguity, uncertainty, misunderstanding, misinterpretation, or misapplication through restatement, reiteration, repetition, duplication, or other forms of re-expression.

(e) **Structural Duplication.**
No person shall create, establish, or otherwise bring into existence parallel, overlapping, duplicative, repetitive, reiterative, or restated provisions that—
(1) govern identical, substantially identical, or materially indistinguishable conduct, activity, behavior, or circumstance; and
(2) differ only in phrasing, structure, arrangement, ordering, stylistic presentation, or other non-substantive distinction, including differences that—
(A) are stylistic rather than substantive; or

(B) create the appearance, illusion, semblance, or perception of distinction without actual, material, or meaningful distinction.

(f) **Aggregation and Fragmentation.**
No person shall—
(1) aggregate, combine, consolidate, or otherwise bring together multiple provisions that collectively duplicate, repeat, restate, reiterate, or otherwise reproduce a single requirement; or
(2) fragment, divide, disaggregate, or otherwise separate a requirement into multiple provisions that—
(A) collectively restate, repeat, reiterate, duplicate, or otherwise reproduce the same obligation; or
(B) produce duplicative, repetitive, reiterative, restated, or otherwise redundant regulatory effect.

(g) **Presumption of Redundancy.**
Where two or more provisions duplicate, repeat, restate, reiterate, reproduce, re-express, or otherwise restate the same requirement, obligation, directive, or instruction, such provisions shall be presumed, deemed, considered, and treated as redundant, duplicative, repetitive, reiterative, restated, and otherwise duplicative unless a material, substantive, meaningful, and non-illusory distinction is demonstrated, shown, or otherwise established.

(h) **Cross-References.**
For codification standards, see § 3201.1. For simplification obligations, see § 3201.3. For amendment procedures, see § 3101.2.

(i) **Historical Annotations.**
This section was enacted, adopted, promulgated, and otherwise established under C.C.D. 3158, 34 MR 144, Thu. 3, 1814 to reduce, eliminate, or otherwise address duplicative, redundant, repetitive, reiterative, and restated provisions arising from decentralized, fragmented, and duplicative codification efforts; subsequently amended, modified, revised, and otherwise altered under C.C.D. 6088, 45 MR 201, Tue. 12, 1956 to address redundant, duplicative, repetitive, and reiterative regulatory overlap and overlap that is redundant and duplicative; and further revised, updated, modernized, and otherwise re-revised under C.C.D. 10247, 72 MR 118, Mon. 7, 2016 to address modern duplication,

repetition, reiteration, restatement, and other forms of duplicative repetition in regulatory drafting.

§ 3201.3 Obligation to Mitigate Excessive Bureaucratization of Simplification Procedures

(a) **General Rule.**
Any process undertaken for the purpose of simplifying, clarifying, or streamlining magical documentation shall itself be conducted in a manner that does not introduce unnecessary complexity, procedural burden, or administrative inefficiency.

(b) **Prohibition on Recursive Bureaucratization.**
No person shall establish or implement procedures intended to simplify documentation that—
(1) materially increase administrative burden; or
(2) introduce additional layers of review, approval, or compliance beyond those reasonably necessary, including layers that—
(A) duplicate existing oversight; or
(B) create cumulative procedural burden.

(c) **Evaluation of Simplification Measures.**
All simplification procedures shall be evaluated based on—
(1) reduction in complexity;
(2) improvement in clarity; and
(3) minimization of administrative burden.
(2) A procedure shall be deemed noncompliant where it—
(A) produces minimal or illusory improvement; or
(B) introduces disproportionate procedural requirements relative to its stated purpose.

(d) **Prohibition on Self-Defeating Processes.**
No simplification process shall be implemented where such process—
(1) results in documentation of equal or greater complexity; or
(2) requires interpretive effort comparable to or exceeding that of the original material.

(e) **Documentation of Simplification Efforts.**
All simplification efforts shall be documented in a manner that—
(1) demonstrates the basis for the simplification; and

(2) permits evaluation of its effectiveness, including evaluation that—
(A) compares pre- and post-simplification conditions; or
(B) assesses reduction in complexity.

(f) **Non-Circumvention.**
No person shall avoid the application of this section by—
(1) recharacterizing complex procedures as necessary; or
(2) distributing procedural requirements across multiple stages to obscure total burden.

(g) **Presumption of Excess.**
Where a simplification process introduces additional procedural steps, documentation requirements, or oversight mechanisms without demonstrable benefit, such process shall be presumed excessive.

(h) **Cross-References.**
For codification standards, see § 3201.1. For redundancy limitations, see § 3201.2. For administrative procedures, see § 102.1.

(i) **Historical Annotations.**
This section was enacted under C.C.D. 3199, 35 MR 77, Mon. 11, 1822 to address early simplification efforts that increased procedural burden. Amended under C.C.D. 6177, 46 MR 144, Tue. 8, 1960 to prohibit layered and duplicative review processes. Revised under C.C.D. 10288, 72 MR 166, Thu. 15, 2018 to address modern bureaucratic inefficiencies in simplification procedures.

§ 3201.4 Simplification Compliance and Redundancy Adjudication Board (SCRAB)

(a) **Establishment.**
There is hereby established a body to be known, designated, and referred to as the Simplification Compliance and Redundancy Adjudication Board (SCRAB), which shall constitute a specialized adjudicatory and administrative entity within the meaning of § 102.1(a)(5), charged with the evaluation, determination, and resolution of matters arising under §§ 3201.1 through 3201.3, including, but not limited to, determinations concerning verbosity, redundancy, and procedural overcomplexity.

(b) **Composition.**

SCRAB shall be composed of members appointed, designated, or otherwise selected by the Council of Councils, in consultation with the DMA and the Council of Counsel, each such member possessing demonstrable familiarity with codificatory practices, regulatory drafting, or administrative procedure, including familiarity that—
(1) reflects experience in drafting, interpreting, or enforcing provisions of this Code; or
(2) otherwise evidences competence in identifying structural, linguistic, or procedural deficiencies within regulatory texts.

(c) **Jurisdiction.**
SCRAB shall have jurisdiction over any question, dispute, petition, referral, or other matter arising under this Part, including jurisdiction to determine—
(1) whether a provision violates § 3201.1 by reason of prolixity, circumlocution, or opacity;
(2) whether a provision violates § 3201.2 by reason of duplication, redundancy, repetition, or reiteration; and
(3) whether a process violates § 3201.3 by reason of excessive bureaucratization, procedural layering, or self-defeating complexity.

(d) **Initiation of Review.**
Review by SCRAB may be initiated—
(1) upon petition by any person subject to or affected by a provision governed by this Part;
(2) upon referral by the DMA, the Council of Counsel, or the Council of Councils; or
(3) sua sponte by SCRAB where it identifies a provision or process that—
(A) appears noncompliant on its face; or
(B) gives rise to recurring interpretive or administrative difficulty.

(e) **Standard of Review.**
In conducting its review, SCRAB shall evaluate the challenged provision or process based on—
(1) clarity, including the extent to which meaning is readily ascertainable;
(2) necessity, including whether the structure or language employed is required for precision; and
(3) proportionality, including whether the complexity or redundancy of the provision is commensurate with its regulatory purpose.

(f) **Determinations and Remedies.**
Where SCRAB determines that a provision or process is noncompliant—
(1) it may require revision, consolidation, or removal of the offending language or structure;
(2) it may direct that duplicative or redundant provisions be merged, eliminated, or otherwise reconciled; and
(3) it may recommend, but not independently effectuate, formal amendment pursuant to Part XXXI where structural deficiencies cannot be remedied through administrative action alone.

(g) **Limitations.**
SCRAB shall not—
(1) create new substantive obligations; or
(2) alter the underlying legal effect of a provision beyond that necessary to achieve compliance with this Part.

(h) **Cross-References.**
For codification standards, see § 3201.1. For redundancy limitations, see § 3201.2. For simplification procedures, see § 3201.3. For administrative review, see § 102.1.

(i) **Historical Annotations.**
This section was enacted under C.C.D. 3227, 35 MR 144, Thu. 2, 1826 to establish a formal body for resolving disputes arising from unclear, redundant, or overly complex codified provisions. Amended under C.C.D. 6333, 46 MR 201, Tue. 19, 1963 to expand jurisdiction to procedural simplification. Revised under C.C.D. 10311, 72 MR 188, Mon. 9, 2019 to formalize standards of review and align SCRAB authority with modern administrative practice.

About the Author

Christopher Frigo is a former IRS auditor with a background in accounting. His work draws on firsthand experience navigating dense legal systems and making them readable, if not always forgiving. He writes satire that takes bureaucracy at its word and follows it to its logical, and often absurd, conclusions. He lives in North Carolina with his fiancée, Ashley, and his cat, Sadie, who remains under audit.

www.ingramcontent.com/pod-product-compliance
Lightning Source LLC
LaVergne TN
LVHW082023200926
848481LV00010B/2913